The Recording Industry

Geoffrey P. Hull
Middle Tennessee State University

D1301518

Allyn and Bacon
Boston • London • Toronto • Sydney • Tokyo • Singapore

Vice President, Editor in Chief: Paul Smith
Series Editor: Karon Bowers
Editorial Assistant: Leila Scott
Marketing Manager: Kris Farnsworth
Editorial Production Service: Chestnut Hill Enterprises, Inc.
Manufacturing Buyer: Megan Cochran
Cover Administrator: Jennifer Hart

Library of Congress Cataloging-in-Publication Data
Hull, Geoffrey P.
    The recording industry / Geoffrey P. Hull
      p. cm.
    Includes bibliographical references and index.
    ISBN 0-205-19689-6
    1. Sound recording industry--United States. 2. Sound recordings--
Industry and trade. 3. Music trade--United States. I. Title.
ML3790.H84   1997
338.4'778149'0973--dc21   97-27580
                                          CIP
                                          MN

Printed in the United States of Amerca

10 9 8 7 6 5 4 3 2 1   02 01 00 99 98 97

Contents

Preface   xi

Acknowledgments   xiii

PART 1   *The Scope and Impact of the Recording Industry in America*   *1*

1   **Overview: America's Favorite Music**   **3**
Rapid Growth of a Major Media Player   *3*
    Sales by Configuration: Past Five Years   5
Diverse Musical Tastes   *6*
    Sales by Genre of Popular Music   7
    Sales by Place of Purchase   8
Who Buys Recordings?   *9*
Ways of Understanding the Recording Industry   *12*
    A Systems Approach   12
    Technology and the Recording Industry System   17
    The Recording Industry as a Mass Medium   18
    The Three Income Streams Model   19

2   **Recordings: The Main Stream**   **27**
Basic Functions   *27*
Oligopoly   *27*
    Oligopoly from Birth to the Fifties   28

Mom and Pop and Rock 'n' Roll   29
Back to Oligopoly   29
The 1990s and Beyond   30
The Big Six   *30*
Warner Music Group   30
Sony Music   31
PolyGram   32
BMG   32
EMI   32
MCA   33
The Structure of Record Companies   *35*
Corporate Structure   35
Structure at the Label Level   36
Label President   36
Business Affairs   36
Accounting   37
International Division   37
Marketing   38
Sales   38
Promotion   38
Advertising   38
Publicity   39
Artist Relations   39
A&R   39
A&R Administration   40
Producers   40
Profitability in the Recording Industry   *40*
The "Indies"   *41*
Size of the Indie Labels   42
Indie Labels and Indie Distribution   42
Diversity in Spite of Itself   *43*
Summary   *43*

3   **Music Publishing: The Second Stream**   **46**
The Music Business Three Income Stream Model—Revisited   *46*
Music Publishing: Then and Now   *47*
Overall Structure   *48*
Music Publishing Functions   *52*
Basic Functions   52
Publishing Company Structure   52
Copyright Acquisition   *53*
The Traditional Way   53

The "Modern" Model   54
Songwriter Agreements   56
Other Copyright Acquisition Methods   60
Sharing the Publishing   60
Exploiting Copyrights   61
Income Sources   61
Performance Licensing   61
Comparing ASCAP, BMI, and SESAC   65
Mechanical Licensing   66
Print Publishing   68
Synchronization Rights   69
Songwriting   69

4   Live Entertainment: The Third Stream   73
The Major Players   75
Personal Managers   76
Structure of the Personal Management Business   76
What *Does* a Personal Manager Do?   76
Management Agreements   78
Talent Agents   79
The Agent's Role   79
Agency Structure   80
Agency Licensing   81
Agency Agreements   82
Promoters   82
The Role of the Concert Promoter   82
The Structure of the Promotion Business   83
Promoter-Artist Agreements   85
The Venue   86
Venue Agreements   86
In-House Promotion   87
Ticket Selling   88
The Labels in the Concert Business   89
Sponsored Tours   90
The Unions   90
The AFM   90
AGVA   91
IATSE   91
The Management Team   92
Conflicts of Interest   92
Summary   93

5   **Relationships to Other Media   95**
Recordings in Radio   96
    Overview: A Love/Hate Relationship   96
    The Historical Context: 1920s–1955   97
    Radio Turns to Records   98
    Diversity in Radio Brings Diversity in Music   99
    Less Diversity in Ownership and More Diversity
        in Programming?   101
    The View from the Charts   102
    Radio Music Listenership   103
Music and Recordings in Television   106
    Before Music Video   106
    Music Television   107
    Selling Music Video   109
Recordings and Film   110
Recordings and the Print Media   112
    Sizing Up Print   113
    Trade Publications   113
    Consumer Publications   115
Summary   116

PART 2   *Recording Industry Core Functions   121*

6   **Production and the A&R Function   123**
Finding and Recording New Talent   124
    New or Used?   124
    Who Has "Good Ears"?   125
    Money Matters   126
Artists' Recording Contracts   127
    Bargaining Position   127
    Commitment—A Two-Way Street   127
    Royalty Rates and Deductions   129
    Advances   130
    A Gold Record and a Bounced Check   130
    Publishing Rights and Controlled Compositions   131
    Video Rights   133
    Union Agreements: AFM and AFTRA   134
Record Production   135
    Producer Functions   135
    Kinds of Producers   136
    Producer Pay   137
    Stages of Production   137
    Production Budgeting   138

Creative Controls   139
Master Delivery Requirements   139
Acquisition through Licensing   139
Studios and Recording Engineers   140
Studios Then and Now   140
Audio Engineers   141
The Industrial Model   141
Kinds of Studios   142
Studio Business Survival   143
Profile of a Typical Recording Studio   143
Recording Engineers   144
Organizations   145
Going to School   145
Summary   146

7   **The Marketing Function   149**
The Four Ps of Marketing   149
Product   150
Style of Music   151
Specialty Markets   151
Repackaging   153
Configuration   153
Price   158
Price and Demand   158
Price and Profit   160
Minimum Advertised Prices   161
Promotion   162
Radio   162
Samplers   163
Listening Stations   163
Place   164
Distribution   164
Product Availability   167
Product Placement   168
Place in Time   168
The Season to Be Jolly   168
Entering the Information Age   170
Universal Product Code   170
SoundScan   170
Broadcast Data Systems   172
Market Research   173
Summary   174

8   Retailing: Software on Hard Copies   177
Overview   177
Record Retail: 1890 to 1950   178
    The Early Years   178
    The End of Monopolies   178
    Depression and Recovery   178
Rack Jobbers   179
    Shipped Out Platinum Came Back Gold   180
    The Handleman Company   181
The Chain Gang   181
    Chain Retail Record Stores   181
    The Weakest Link   183
    Overall Growth of Record Sales   183
    Overextended Chains   183
    Price Competition Problems   184
Internationalization of Record Retailing   186
    U.S. Chains Abroad   186
    Foreign Chains in the United States   187
Indies: The "Mom and Pop" Stores   187
    Creating a Niche   187
Retail Management Considerations   188
    Multiple Configurations   189
    Packaging   189
    Shrinkage   190
    Breadth of Inventory   190
Used CDs   191
    Sharing the "Blame" for the Used CD Market   192
    Pressure Points   193
Record Clubs   194
Future of Record Retailing   196
    The End of Record Stores?   196

**PART 3   *Legal Environment of the
                Recording Industry   201***

9   Copyright Basics in the Recording Industry   203
Duration of Copyright   204
    P.D. or Not P.D.?   205
Formalities: Notice and Registration   205
    Notice   206
    The Case of "Boogie Chillen"   206

Registration   207
Registration Tips for Unsigned Bands and Songwriters   208
The "Fair Use" Limitation and Parody   209
The Fair Use Factors   209
The Case of "Oh, Pretty Woman"   210
Joint Authorship/Joint Works   211
Works Made for Hire   212
The Case of the Homeless Statue   213
Termination Rights   213
Termination Problems   214
The "Manufacturing Clause" and Parallel Imports   215
Domestic Problems   215
Foreign Problems   216
Poor Man's Copyright   217
Summary   217

10 Copyright in Sound Recordings and Songs   220
Sound Recordings   220
Pre-1972—A Recording Is Not a Song   220
Enter—The Pirates   222
1972-1977—A Sound Recording Is Still Not a Song   223
1978–Present—A Sound Recording Is *Still* Not a Song   224
Record Rental   225
Home Recording   226
Digital Audio Performance Rights   228
Musical Compositions   229
Initial Copyright Ownership—A Song Is a Song   229
Copyright in Musical Arrangements   229
Compulsory Mechanical License   230
Performing Rights and Music   232
Infringement and Remedies   234
Sampling—"Thou Shalt Not Steal"   234
The Case of "Alone Again, Naturally"   234
Sample Once—Infringe Twice   235
Infringement and Remedies—"You Stole My Song!"—
Every Songwriter's Nightmare   235
The Case of "How Deep is Your Love"   236
The Case of "My Sweet Lord"   236
New Directions for Copyright   237
Everyone Is a Manufacturer and Distributor   238
Everyone Is an Author   239
Where Is the Editor?   240

Highway Robbery on the Information Superhighway   240

11 Piracy and Other Legal Problems   245
Piracy of Phonorecords   245
     Counterfeiting   246
     Bootlegging   247
     Remedies for Piracy   247
     International Dimensions of Piracy   248
     Pirates in Cyberspace?   249
Payola   249
     Independent Promotion and the Isgro Trial   251
     Organized Crime   252
Antitrust Problems   252
Perspective   253

Appendix: The Recording Industry on the Internet   255

Glossary   265

Bibliography   285

Index   299

Preface

It is to no one's surprise that the recording industry has changed substantially in the little more than one hundred years it has been in existence. Edison's "talking machine" was invented in 1877 and first sold to the public in 1889. The Victor Talking Machine Company introduced the world to disc recordings in 1901. In the early days, the record companies made recordings primarily so that people would have a reason to buy the playback machines. As the popularity of the machines and recordings grew during the 1920s, the player manufacturers and others began to sell the recordings as commercial products in and of themselves. The Depression of the 1930s brought about the near collapse of the industry. After World War II those firms that had survived began to experience a new prosperity. Entertainment media in general began to flourish. The marriage of necessity between radio and records of the 1930s became a marriage of convenience in the 1940s and 1950s.

The rock and roll explosion of the mid 1950s energized the industry. Markets expanded. More artists, recordings, and labels appeared overnight. Retail began to grow with distribution through mass merchants at first taking the lead, then retail chains grew with the growth of shopping malls and the movement towards a service economy in general. FM stereo broadcasting meant more radio stations needed recordings to play and those recordings being played sounded better than on their AM competitors. The compact disc gave the sound recorded another quantum leap in quality. Sales of recordings continued to reach new heights. Retail stores grew in size and number. More recordings were accessible to more people in more places.

The growth of the industry influenced its structure. Large entertainment conglomerates, operating on an international scale, began to control the bulk of the industry. They acquired different branches of the entertainment industry, including film, television, recordings, consumer electronics, music publishing, and record labels, and in some instances even record retail chains. Broadcasting also began a consolidation as first the Federal Communications Commission, then Congress, relaxed ownership rules allowing more stations to be owned by one entity. In what was generally known as the music business, the influence of recordings became dominant. The sale and marketing of hit and non-hit recordings dominated the music publishing and live entertainment businesses. Sheet music sales dwindled to about fifteen percent of publishing revenues, and royalties from the sale of recordings and airplay of those recordings made up the bulk of music publishing earnings. Large tours of major recording artists contributed the bulk of the live entertainment earnings.

Technology has always played a central role in the development of the industry. Developments since the invention of recording have enlarged and enhanced the market for recordings, making higher quality recordings more accessible to more people. Technological advances on the production end of the process meant that recordings could sound "better." Diffusion of recording technology of high quality and low cost into the "semi professional" market meant that musicians could create recordings and market them without having to access the capital and facilities of a major record company. More artists could create and market more recordings. With the advent of the Internet, it is now possible for those musicians to market those recordings on a worldwide basis without access to the distribution systems of the major labels. The impact of that remains to be seen. Diffusion of high quality, low cost, portable playback equipment meant people could enjoy more music in more places.

In all, it is time to take another look at the recording industry as it enters a post industrial phase. What this book does is to examine what the recording industry had become in the mid 1990s. That examination is from an economic perspective, since the most significant changes have been what would be generally described as economic. There is no particular Marxist or other critique of the industry. With due respect to those who prefer a cultural or social perspective, there are other publications which do that and such a perspective is not particularly helpful in understanding how and why the industry functions the way it does. Economics is the key to the importance of the recording industry as an entertainment medium of mass communication. Economics is the key to understanding how the three income streams in the industry (the sale of recordings, music publishing, and live appearances) have become dominated by the recording interests and how those streams are interrelated. Therefore, the primary perspective here is economic. The three parts of the book examine 1) the industry overall, its relation to other media and its three primary parts, or income streams; 2) the production and marketing functions in detail, including record retailing; 3) the legal structures of copyright law that are so critical to the recording industry, as well as several related laws of significance.

In summary, there are several themes that wind their way through the pages that follow:

- The recording industry is now the dominant force in the music business.
- Technological advances have enhanced the industry's ability to make profits from recordings and songs and made those recordings and songs more accessible to more people.
- Although highly concentrated in six large multinational firms, the industry continues to serve the public through the development and dissemination of more recordings by more artists than ever before. The public is the beneficiary of this diversity.
- The industry continues to change, being driven by largely economic considerations on a global scale.

A final point: the recording industry would be of paltry significance, indeed, were it not for the ability of music through recordings to speak to and excite people. The creative people who combine words and music into songs, create recorded performances, and perform those songs live speak to us in many ways. Our pleasurable task is to listen to, watch, appreciate, and enjoy their creations.

ACKNOWLEDGMENTS

A number of people, places, and organizations have provided valuable support in the preparation of this book. Industry organizations providing a wealth of information include the National Association of Recording Merchandisers (NARM), The Recording Industry Association of America (RIAA), The National Music Publishers' Association (NMPA), The American Federation of Musicians (AFM) Local 257, and The National Association of Music Merchandisers (NAMM). NARM charts and data are reprinted with permission of the National Association of Recording Merchandisers. The greatest industry source is *Billboard*. Thanks for reporting nearly 100 years of recording and entertainment industry news and events. (Yes, *Billboard* is more than 100 years old, but its first six years included very little entertainment industry news.) *Billboard* charts and information reprinted with permission of BPI Communications. One must also include more recent publications such as *Pollstar* "The Concert Hotwire," *Performance, R&R,* and *Gavin* as important sources of information.

I found a great deal of research support and resources on the campus of Middle Tennessee State University. Probably the greatest resource was the Center for Popular Music. Thanks especially to director Paul Wells, and Bruce Nemerov, as well as the rest of the staff of the Center. How else could I have found a copy of "Payola Blues" or hundreds of other publications about the recording industry without the Center's collection? I don't want to think about it. The Todd Library's *Billboard* and *Variety* collection and its on-line databases, especially Infotrac, proved most helpful. MTSU's commitment to fiber optics and computers made surfing the World

Wide Web a breeze and brought a wealth of information right to my desktop. Administrative thanks to my department chair, Rich Barnet, for letting me "do my thing," and to the dean of the College of Mass Communication, Deryl Leaming, for moral support as well as the time for research and writing. Thanks to all my colleagues in the Recording Industry Department for being, well, collegial. Students John Hall and Renée Edde helped find and verify most of the Web sites listed in the Internet Appendix. Renée, my student assistant for four years, provided research help, photocopying, a cheerful disposition, and she relieved me of some tedious duties so I could focus more on writing. Thanks to Jim Progris, now at the University of Miami, Coral Gables, for deciding that I just might make a college teacher and hiring me as an adjunct faculty member for the Commercial Music/Recording program at Georgia State University back in 1974. Thanks to Ed Kimbrell at MTSU for deciding I just might be able to build a recording industry program at Middle Tennessee State back in 1977.

Just as most recording artists would not be successful without record companies, most authors would not be successful without publishers. Al Greco of Fordham University, the series editor for the Allyn & Bacon Series in Mass Communication, of which this book is a part, took a chance on asking a not-very-well-known writer to tackle the recording industry book. Thanks for the opportunity and for your mentoring. I hope you are not disappointed. Allyn & Bacon folks who deserve a "thanks" are Joe Opiela and his assistant, Kate Tolini, Paul Smith, and Karon Bowers and her assistant, Leila Scott. Thanks to the following reviewers for helping me to hone the manuscript and to define what this book is, and is not, about: Donald Cusic, Belmont University; Steve Jones, University of Tulsa; William Moylan, University of Massachusetts at Lowell; David Sanjek, BMI Archives; Lyn Schenbeck, Georgia State University; and Paul Wells, Middle Tennessee State University.

In the miscellaneous category, thanks to Ben Keith of Cayenne Pepper Music for permission to use the quote from "Payola Blues" and Bill Lowery of Lowery Music for his quote about great songs.

Is it "sappy" to thank one's wife? No. Not when she is the one who has had to put up with the frustration, stress, and long hours of her partner's writing a book, and who has been there to help me through it all in so many different ways. "Thanks, Patty."

Part 1

The Scope and Impact of the Recording Industry in America

Recordings are one of the most important mass media in the United States. Americans spend more money on prerecorded music purchases than on consumer magazines or theatrical exhibitions of motion pictures, and nearly as much as they spend on newspapers. They spend more time listening to recordings than they do consuming any other media except broadcast and cable television. The first of the three major divisions of this book locates the recording industry's economic and social place in the United States. To do so, Chapter 1 explores the nature of the recording industry in the mid-1990s, including its products and markets, its relation to the external environment, and its place as a medium of mass communication. Analytically, it is proposed that the industry can best be understood by considering that it is composed of three primary income streams: the sale of recordings, the sale and use of songs (primarily the music publishing industry), and live entertainment. Chapter 2 explains the main revenue-generating stream, the sale of recordings, and its oligopolistic (but competitive) market structure. The music publishing business owes over three-fourths of its revenues to recordings and is so dominated by the recording industry that it is a part of that industry. Chapter 3 examines how that came to be. The artists whose popular recordings drive the sales of CDs and cassettes also dominate the sales of tickets to live performances. Chapter 4 details the operations of that income stream and its interrelationships with recordings and recording artists. Chapter 5 then examines the impact of the recording industry on other media, particularly broadcasting, and the relationships of those media to the recording industry.

1

Overview:
America's Favorite Music

"Research shows these people [the baby boomers] to be very music oriented."[1]

In February 1996 a new king of solo album sales was crowned in the United States. With certified album sales of 58 million units, Garth Brooks edged by his nearest competitor, Billy Joel, who had certified sales of 57 million units. Rounding out the top five all time best selling solo artists were Elton John (51 million units), Michael Jackson (48 million units), and Elvis Presley (41 million units).[2] The composition of this top five elite is testament to the growth of the recording industry in the early 1990s, the eclectic musical tastes of American consumers, and the impact of the recording industry on groups and cultures representing a variety of tastes. That a country music artist should occupy the top spot is evidence that something is different in the industry and, perhaps, in society.

RAPID GROWTH OF A MAJOR MEDIA PLAYER

The recording industry experienced dramatic change through the 1980s and 1990s. Significant changes in technology, markets, and organizations made the industry substantially different from its former self of the 1960s and 1970s. These changes necessitate a reexamination of both its internal and external structure and function. This chapter and those that follow gather the evidence of the changes, explore the reasons for them, and examine their impact on the recording industry.

The recording industry primarily serves the market for prerecorded musical performances through the sale of compact discs (CDs) and tapes. However, it is also a significant force in the broadcasting industry, because the majority of the programming content of commercial radio is playback of those same musical sound recordings. Music videos and performances by popular recording acts provide significant content for cable and broadcast television. Hit motion pictures are often enhanced or even propelled by the presence of music by hit recording artists. Even in the consumer magazine industry the presence of the recording industry is felt through popular publications like *Rolling Stone* and *Spin,* which focus on popular music artists and recordings. The music performed by artists made popular through the sales of their recordings is largely responsible for the concert and live music industry. And these are only some of the direct effects. The desire of people to make popular music and become part of the recording industry is the driving force behind the sales of millions of dollars musical instruments every year. The National Association of Music Merchants (NAMM) reports musical products sales for 1995 of $5.47 billion, out of which only $560 million was the school musical instrument market.[3] A Gallup survey conducted for NAMM found that there are about 62 million amateur musicians in the United States (age five or over) and that eighty-one percent of survey respondents felt that music participation was an important part of life.[4] Without the recordings produced by the recording industry consumers certainly would not have purchased an estimated $408,171,000,000 worth of audio playback hardware in 1994.[5]

Even considering just the sale of prerecorded tapes and discs, the recording industry is a major player in the entertainment and media industries. From 1984 to 1994 recorded music moved from fifth to fourth place in consumer media expenditures, surpassing consumer magazines, closing rapidly on daily newspapers, and extending the margin over theatrical motion pictures to nearly two to one. Americans spend an estimated 12.14 percent of their media dollars on recorded music, up from 11.18 percent in the previous decade.

Adjusting for increases in the consumer price index for entertainment,[6] as indicated in Table 1-1, the data is still impressive. Americans have been on an entertainment spending binge, and the recording industry, more than any other consumer medium except home video, is reaping the rewards.

More significant, for its cultural impact, is the fact that Americans are now spending more time listening to recorded music. Not counting the time spent listening to radio (which is primarily the same recorded music), out of the estimated almost 3,300 hours per year that the average person spends consuming media, 257 hours (7.8 percent) were spent listening to recordings, more time than on any other media except network television (28.1 percent) and basic cable (11.2 percent).[7]

TABLE 1-1   Consumer Spending for Media 1984–1994
Per Person Expenditures

Media	1984 Expenditures	1994 Expenditures[2]	1994 in 1984 Dollars[3]	Percent Increase 1994 $	Percent Increase 1984 $
Cable (basic and pay)	40.36	88.94	59.25	120.4	46.8
Recorded Music	22.51	50.11	33.38	122.6	48.3
Daily Newspapers	40.52	58.20	38.77	43.6	−4.3
Consumer Magazines	24.32	35.47	23.63	45.8	−2.8
Consumer Books	40.17	80.63	53.72	100.7	33.7
Home Video[1]	12.87	73.86	49.21	473.9	282.4
Movies in Theaters	20.76	25.64	17.08	23.5	−17.7
Total	201.51	412.85	275.05	104.9	

Source: *Statistical Abstract of the United States 1995*: 568.

[1]Pre-recorded tapes only
[2]1994 sales are projected
[3]1984 = 100   1994 = 150.1

Sales by Configuration: Past Five Years

For the first half of the nineties the recording industry saw rapid sales growth in terms of number of units shipped and dollar volume of those units. Although the number of units shipped leveled off in 1995, the dollar volume of those shipments continued to climb, thanks mainly to the continued increase in shipments of the higher priced compact disc albums and singles relative to the declining shipments of lower priced cassette albums and singles (see Tables 1-2 and 1-3). The flat sales in total units for 1995 caused Recording Industry Association of America (RIAA) chairman, Jay Berman, to comment, "It's safe to say that, with rare exceptions,

TABLE 1-2   Sales of Recordings by Configuration, 1991–1995
(Unit shipments in millions of units, net after returns)

	1991	1992	1993	1994	1995
Cassette	360.1	366.4	339.5	345.4	272.6
CD	333.3	407.5	495.4	662.1	727.6
LP	4.8	2.3	1.2	1.9	2.2
Cassette Single	69	84.6	85.6	81.1	70.7
Vinyl Single	22	19.8	15.1	11.7	10.2
CD Single	5.7	7.3	7.8	9.3	17.2
Video	6.1	7.6	11	11.2	12.6
Total	801	895.5	955.6	1122.7	1113.1

Source: Recording Industry Association of America.

TABLE 1-3 Dollar Volume of Sales by Configuration (Based on Manufacturers Suggested List Prices, in $ Millions)

	1991	1992	1993	1994	1995
Cassette	$3,019.6	$3,116.3	$2,916.8	$2,976.4	$2,303.6
CD	4,337.7	5,326.5	6,511.4	8,464.5	9,401.7
LP	29.4	13.5	10.6	17.8	25.1
Cassette Single	230.4	298.8	298.5	274.9	236.3
Vinyl Single	63.9	68.4	51.2	47.2	46.7
CD Single	35.1	45.1	45.8	56.1	88.6
Video	118.1	157.4	213.3	231.1	220.3
Total	$7,834.2	$9,024.0	$10,046.6	$12,068.0	$12,322.3

Source: Recording Industry Association of America.

we've pretty much exhausted the catalog-replacement business. What's selling now is what's being released now."[8] If Berman is correct, then the depth of catalog product in CD configuration stocked in many larger record stores is going to strain retailers' abilities to purchase new product and ultimately end up in the distributors' warehouses as returns. Or, it may be that sales of catalog product for replacement of vinyl or cassette albums with compact discs are still active at retail, it is just that the retailers have all finally got their catalog stocks up to an appropriate level, thus causing manufacturers' shipments of catalog to drop, relative to new releases. The RIAA does represent the distributors and manufacturers, and not the retailers.

DIVERSE MUSICAL TASTES

Annual sales popularity charts reveal that Americans have a real mix of musical tastes. For example, the top five albums for 1995 included a new pop/rock band, the best selling solo artist of all time (a country act), a mellow R&B group whose a capella vocals and harmonies were often reminiscent of the 1960s, a reunion tour album by a megastar group of the 1970s, and an urban/dance female vocal group

TABLE 1-4 Billboard's Top Albums, 1995

1. *Cracked Rear View Mirror*—Hootie and the Blowfish
2. *The Hits*—Garth Brooks
3. *II*—Boyz II Men
4. *Hell Freezes Over*—The Eagles
5. *CrazySexyCool*—TLC

Source: *Billboard*, "The Year in Music," 23 December 1995: YE–22.

TABLE 1-5   Billboard's Top Female Album Artists, 1995

1. Mariah Carey (3 charted albums)
2. Alanis Morissette (1 album)
3. Sheryl Crow (1 album)
4. Selena (6 albums)
5. Melissa Ethridge (1 album)

Source: *Billboard*, "The Year in Music," 23 December 1995: YE–26.

with plenty of sex appeal. Because the *Billboard* album charts are computed based on retail sales, they are a good barometer of purchasing activity by consumers.

A glance at the top male and female solo album artists reveals a similar mixture of styles and consumer tastes. In the women's group there were two "alternative" artists, a Tejano singer, a rock artist, and the leader is a pop/R&B artist.

The growing influence and strength of country music is apparent in the top male album artists of 1995. Three of the top five artists were country performers. Kenny G is an instrumental, jazz/pop musician. Tom Petty is a rock performer with a recording history going back to 1976!

Sales by Genre of Popular Music

The eclectic nature of the public's taste was also reflected in the overall trends in genre of music purchased. No longer was rock music dominating the sales of recordings with nearly fifty percent of all shipments as it was in the mid 1980s. In 1995 the share of rock had dropped to under 34 percent of shipments while shares of urban/rap and country had risen to over 16 percent each. The share of "pop" had been steadily declining since the mid 1980s.

The 1995 top twenty-three selling albums all sold over three million units each during the year. A look at these artists, too, reveals a wide mix of musical genres and the wide spectrum of Americans' musical tastes. In some instances these recordings sold strongly in select markets. In others they "crossed over" into the general mainstream market and were purchased by a truly diverse lot of people. Whether appeal-

TABLE 1-6   Billboard's Top Male Album Artists, 1995

1. Garth Brooks (4 charted albums)
2. Kenny G (2 albums)
3. Tim McGraw (2 albums)
4. John Michael Montgomery (2 albums)
5. Tom Petty (1 album)

Source: *Billboard*, "The Year in Music," 23 December 1995: YE–26.

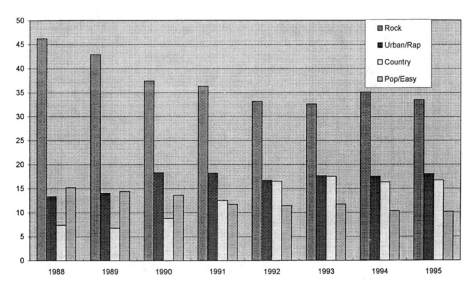

FIGURE 1-1   Sales by Genre (Percent of Dollar Volume)
Source: Recording Industry Association of America.

ing strongly to a particular taste unit, such as Green Day's *Dookie,* or to a much wider audience such as Hootie and the Blowfish's *Cracked Rear View Mirror,* they were all part of what can be defined as popular music. The list even includes two "Christmas" albums and two "children's movie" soundtracks. Now that's diversity. (See Table 1-7 on page 10.)

It should be noted that these top twenty-three albums alone accounted for over 107 million units sold. That is 10.7 percent of all album-format recordings sold in 1995. If one tallies up the platinum (1,000,000 unit sales) and multiplatinum (each additional 1,000,000 units sold) certifications by the RIAA in 1995, there were 191 platinum and 294 multiplatinum albums. The total of 485 albums accounts for over 846 million units (including the top twenty-three in multiplatinum for this purpose). This statistic upholds the often spoken remark that a small number of albums account for the lion's share of the sales—in this case 84.6 percent of the sales are accounted for by only 485 albums, out of the thousands released in 1995.

Sales by Place of Purchase

Americans have also become more eclectic in where they purchase their recordings. In the mid 1980s the record store was by far the dominant place where recordings were purchased. By 1995 alternative "places" of purchasing recordings accounted for nearly as many sales as record stores. The "other" category in Figure 1-2 includes department stores, mass merchant discount stores, such as Wal–Mart and K–Mart, as well as audio specialty stores, such as Circuit City. The share of sales through such locations grew nearly 50 percent in a six-year period. Even more dra-

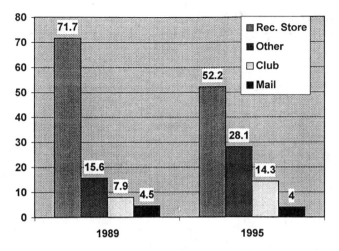

FIGURE 1-2   Sales by Location (Percent of Dollar Volume)
Source: Recording Industry Association of America.

matic was the nearly 100 percent growth in the share of recordings purchased through record clubs.

Record retailing changed. The big chains did not wipe out the independents as predicted. In the mid 1970s as much as two-thirds of all record sales were through rack locations. The typical rack location would handle 500 to 1,000 titles. No wonder the majority of sales were accounted for by only 200 titles. The rapid growth of record store chains in the late 1970s and 1980s meant more recordings could be available to more consumers. The typical store of the times stocked 8,000 to 10,000 titles. In the 1990s the chains discovered they were overbuilt and some major chains, including Wherehouse and Camelot, went into bankruptcy proceedings. The trend had shifted to even larger "megastores" with Tower, HMV, Virgin, and Media Play opening locations with five to ten times the space and inventory of the typical mall retail chain location. The additional space meant that a wider variety of recordings could be carried. Even the rack jobbers began to put in larger locations. A greater diversity of recordings was available to more people in more places.

WHO BUYS RECORDINGS?

> *"A popular music fan is generally wedded to a specific*
> *style current in the idiom in . . . adolescence."*
> —R. SERGE DENISOFF, 1975[9]

A 1977 prediction, based on Denisoff's observation and other research at the time, was that the popular music of the year 2000 would most likely resemble what could

TABLE 1-7   Best Selling Albums, 1995

Units Sold (RIAA Certified, Millions)	Artist	Title
11 million	Hootie and the Blowfish	*Cracked Rear View Mirror*
8 million	Garth Brooks	*The Hits*
7 million	TLC	*CrazySexyCool*
6 million	Boyz II Men	*II*
5 million	Mariah Carey	*Daydream*
	Eagles	*Hell Freezes Over*
	Kenny G	*Miracles: The Holiday Album*
	Pearl Jam	*Vitalogy*
	Live	*Throwing Copper*
	Green Day	*Dookie*
	Michael Jackson	*HIStory: Past, Present and Future, Book 1*
4 million	Alanis Morissette	*Jagged Little Pill*
	Shania Twain	*The Woman in Me*
	The Cranberries	*No Need to Argue*
	Beatles	*Live at the BBC*
3 million	Aerosmith	*Big Ones*
	Mary J. Blige	*My Life*
	Garth Brooks	*The Garth Brooks Collection*
	Mannheim Steamroller	*Christmas in the Aire*
	Nirvana	*MTV Unplugged in New York*
	Tom Petty	*Wildflowers*
	Soundtrack	*The Lion King*
	Soundtrack	*Pocahontas*

Source: RIAA (Based on Platinum Sales Certifications, 1995).

generally be included under the rubric of Pop–Contemporary music in 1977.[10] That music included all categories of rock, but not middle of the road (MOR), country, or Rhythm and Blues (R&B). In 1976, 23 percent of "adult buyers" (age 25–45) preferred country music,[11] which at that time sounded much less like other pop and rock music than it did by 1995. The baby boomers entered the over fifty group in significant numbers in 1996. That group probably grew up liking rock or some music with a similar feel. We should remember that rock blends elements of country and R&B to various degrees. What the statistics of Figure 1-3 indicate had occurred by the mid 1990s should, therefore, be no surprise.

Consumers of American popular music and recordings are getting older as a group, and they are still consuming. Figure 1-3 illustrates the dramatic shift in the percentage of recordings purchased by consumers of various age brackets over the years from 1989 to 1995. In 1989 over half of the consumers were under age twenty-five and only 18 percent over the age of forty. By 1995 the under twenty-five group had dropped to 40 percent and the forty and over group had grown to 24.4 percent. The data in Table 1-8 show that this increase, especially in the forty-five and over

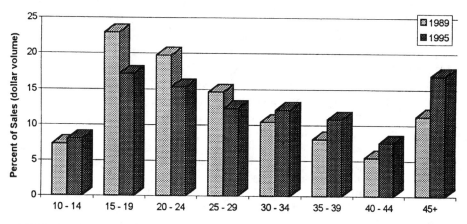

FIGURE 1-3   Age of Record Buyers, 1989, 1995
Source: Recording Industry Association of America.

group, had been consistent for some time. Fortunately for the recording industry, the dire predictions made in 1977 that the baby boomers would quit buying music as they aged, proved to be incorrect. As a result, the industry was no longer a "youth" or teen dominated market. In order to be effective the recording companies had to appeal to a wider age range of taste groups.

The increased share of recording sales accounted for by older buyers is even more dramatic when compared to the slight increase in population share of that same group. While the share of the population of the United States of the forty-five and over group increased from 31 percent to 32.3 percent from 1989 to 1994 (a 7.4 percent increase in population share), the share of recordings purchased by that age group grew from 11.2 percent to 16.9 percent—an increase of 50.9 percent in market

TABLE 1-8   Sales by Age of Consumers (Percent of Dollar Volume)

AGE	1989	1990	1991	1992	1993	1994	1995
10–14	7.3	7.6	8.2	8.6	8.6	7.9	8.0
15–19	22.9	18.3	18.1	18.2	16.7	16.8	17.1
20–24	19.7	16.5	17.9	16.1	15.1	15.4	15.3
25–29	14.6	14.6	14.5	13.8	13.2	12.6	12.3
30–34	10.4	13.2	12.5	12.2	11.9	11.8	12.1
35–39	8.0	10.2	9.8	10.9	11.1	11.5	10.8
40–44	5.4	7.8	6.7	7.4	8.5	7.9	7.5
45+	11.2	11.6	12.5	12.9	14.8	16.1	16.9

Source: Recording Industry Association of America.*

*There is an inexplicable conflict in the RIAA reported data in consumer profiles 1993 and earlier and 1994 and later. The data in the table are the figures reported in 1994 and 1995, except for 1989, which is from the 1993 report.

share! That increase in share, coupled with the increase in overall recording sales during the same period, represents an increase in recordings purchased by the forty-five and over age group of 109.8 percent, going from $90.4 million in 1989 to $189.7 million in 1994. The "boomers" were *still* buying recordings.

Is the recording industry alive and well as we near the turn of the century? You bet! Americans are buying more music, from a wider variety of genres, listening to it more, and continuing to buy as they get older. That's a marketing picture that should make any label executive smile.

WAYS OF UNDERSTANDING THE RECORDING INDUSTRY

There are several useful models for examining the recording industry. Systems theory is useful for exploring the industry on a macro scale, its relations to the business environment, and overall processes. Cultural theory is of some use in examining the relationship of the outputs of the industry, recordings and popular music, to society. Economics, and the three income stream model used below, is most useful in examining the inner workings of the industry and its components.

A Systems Approach

Systems theory is a business management tool used to develop an understanding of how an enterprise must function. Systems theory stresses that there are five components of any business system: inputs, some transformation process, outputs (the products that are the results of the transformation process), a feedback process that will influence the selection of inputs into the next round of processing, and an external environment within which the organization carries out its processes.[12] Viewing the recording industry in this manner, one would conclude that the inputs are songs, musicians, engineers, producers, studios, plastic, paper, performances, and technology. The transformation processes are the recording of masters, duplicating of the masters into CDs and tapes, and marketing. Outputs of the recording industry are CDs and tapes as products and as cultural artifacts, profits and losses for the owners, and employee (including the artists and writers) satisfaction. Feedback occurs primarily through purchases by consumers of recordings and live performances, and listening to or viewing the broadcast media. The external environment contains the social, political, legal, and economic forces that exist outside of the organization (see Figure 1-4). Another key concept in systems analysis is the difference between *closed* and *open* systems. A closed system does not need to interact with the environment to survive, an open system must. From that perspective, the recording industry is an open system because of its dependence on popular tastes and culture for its market. A final systems concept, *entropy,* refers to the tendency of any organized system to eventually decay into disorganization. If a business does not receive new

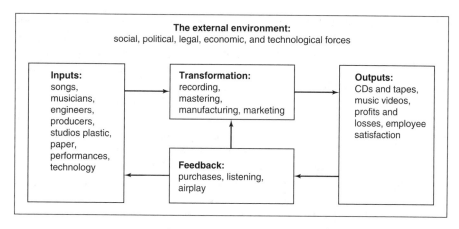

FIGURE 1-4   The Recording Industry as System

energy from its environment and inputs it will cease to exist. The recording industry must constantly seek new creative inputs from the artists and song writers or it will stagnate. The entropy concept has been found to explain that more product diversity is associated with more entropy in the music industry.[13]

The External Environment

Society.   The external environment is extremely important to the recording industry. Its products are largely consumed on the basis of taste preferences. As the tastes and desires of the consumers change the record company must be aware and alter its products. The history of the industry is full of examples that show how a particular label or even the entire industry failed to keep in touch with consumer tastes. Probably the most famous example is the birth and growth of the popularity of rock and roll when the major labels of the day either did not even know it existed, or chose to ignore it. Keeping up with consumer tastes and new trends in music is one job of the artist and repertoire (A&R) department of a label. The A&R department is also charged with finding new creative inputs in terms of songs and performers. If the A&R department has too many failures, the label will be in serious danger of dying. Chapter 6 discusses the A&R function in detail.

Popular music, the mainstay of the recording industry, clearly interfaces with society. It both influences society and is influenced by it. The depth of that influence is highly debatable. Certainly it influences dress fashions when recording artists appear on stage or in videos in certain attire, such as when pre- and early teen girls imitated Madonna's style of dress.[14] Social themes are often mirrored in the music, either because that makes the music more acceptable to people or because the recording artist wants to convey a viewpoint on those themes. Did Ozzy Osbourne's recording "Suicide Solution" *cause* some teens to commit suicide or did it *reflect* the despair that some teens felt that drove them to commit suicide?[15] Most researchers have concluded that the relationships between popular music, its performers, and consumers, are complex and not easily reduced to simple statements.[16] For instance, was Madonna in the mid and late 1980s suggesting that girls should become "Boy Toys" or was she instilling a new sense of liberation for young women?[17] Popular music researcher Simon Frith concludes, "The political meaning of *all* popular music . . . is a matter of negotiation."[18]

Prerecorded music has become a significant component of nearly everyone's life. Half or more of the adult population purchases recorded music every year. That is a much higher percentage than those who vote in elections. Americans spend more time listening to recordings than they do consuming any other medium except television (broadcast and cable). Recorded music provides opportunities and frameworks for social interchange and expression through dance and karaoke. On a scale of one to ten respondents in one national survey rated the importance of music in their lives as 6.96 on a ten point scale. Music buyers rated it a 7.89 and classical music buyers a 10.00.[19] Recording artists attempt to engage in social dialog with consumers through their songs and recordings, and sometimes cause social controversies.

International trade agreements, such as the North American Free Trade Agreement (NAFTA) and General Agreement on Tariffs and Trade (GATT), take into consideration the free exchange of cultural products such as recordings and movies. They cause nations to discuss and debate the impact of "outside" cultural products on the local culture. They provide protection for the copyrights embodied in these cultural products on a global basis so that the very same nations who complain of cultural imperialism cannot steal the work of artists, writers, and producers and sell it as pirate merchandise around the world.

Political Environment.   Usually the political environment is not as important to the recording industry as the other external factors. However, every now and then it becomes extremely important. The political/social reactions against rock and roll in the late 1950s brought about the payola law and caused serious economic losses to a number of industry figures at the time, most notably Dick Clark. Many elements of the peace movement during the late 1960s found expression in popular music. The political establishment reacted by attacking popular music that had "drug-related" lyrics. In the late 1980s the feminists reacted against rap lyrics that they perceived to be misogynist and caused a number of labels and radio stations to quit programming certain artists. During that same time period there was a political reaction to violence and profanity in lyrics and music videos. This lead to the formation of the Parents Music Resource Center backed by Tipper Gore (then *Senator* Al Gore, Jr.'s wife).[20] Congressional hearings ultimately led the industry to self-regulation and the identification of some recordings with a warning label that said "Parental Advisory Explicit Content." Prior to the labeling program some states passed laws forbidding the sale of material "harmful to persons under eighteen" and some sales clerks in retail stores were even arrested.[21] Later some states sought to prohibit the sale of recordings with "Parental Advisory" labels to minors. Some stores stopped carrying recordings by artists such as the rap act "2 Live Crew" and others. One retailer said, "We're not trying to play God, promote censorship, or anything like that. We're just looking out for our image."[22] As late as 1996 the National Association of Recording Merchandisers (NARM) and the RIAA were still promoting parental awareness of the parental advisory labeling program.[23] At the same time these two organizations successfully lobbied against passage of some state obscenity laws that would pro-hibit sale of "parental advisory" albums to minors.[24] Similar concerns were raised about "Death Metal" acts such as "Judas Priest." They successfully fought a lawsuit claiming that a subliminal message of "do it, do it" in one of their songs caused two men (eighteen and twenty years old) to commit suicide after listening to the album.[25] The overall significance of these attacks on popular music is debatable. Communi-cation researchers DeFleur and Dennis conclude, "a number of popular music forms have been charged with being the cause of moral collapse when they came on the scene, yet our society has somehow held together. Undoubtedly it will survive what-ever is in store."[26]

Legal Environment.   The legal environment of the recording industry is simi-lar to that of most businesses in terms of labor laws, environmental regulations, and tax laws. Copyright law, however, is a special legal environment that conveys sig-nificant benefits for the industry. It enables the industry to protect its main outputs, songs and recordings, from unauthorized duplication, thereby helping insure profit-ability. Copyright (or at least a related right) enables performers to protect their live performances from unauthorized recording, distribution, or unauthorized broadcast. Payola laws limit the extent of control that the labels have over a very important avenue of promotion, radio airplay. Antitrust laws and regulations limit the industry's attempts to control prices and may limit consolidation. International trade treaties protect audio and video recordings throughout the world. Chapters 9, 10, and 11 discuss the legal environment of the recording industry in detail.

Economic Environment.   The overall economy is also important to the re-cording industry. It is a leisure time industry, relying on the use of discretionary income from consumers for the purchases of recordings and live performance tick-ets. In times of serious economic downturn, when people have less discretionary income, the sale of recordings declines. The National Music Publishers' Association (NMPA) observed the importance of the overall economy to the recording industry internationally. In the NMPA's first International Survey of Music Publishing Rev-enues, a statistical analysis of the data indicated that music publishing revenues were probably more sensitive to per capita GNP than to age or population.[27] During the depression in the 1930s in the United States the record industry survived, barely, on performance revenues from radio airplay and on the sale of recordings to juke-boxes.

The world economy is moving in many areas from international to *trans-national*. There is not just a market in France and a market in Brazil and a market in China. There is a global market and individual submarkets. Management guru and futurist Peter Drucker tells us, "[T]he goal of management in a transnational enterprise that operates in one world market is *maximization of market share*, not the traditional short-term 'profit maximization' of the old-style corporation."[28] What we used to call the "majors," those record labels that owned their own distribution system, have realized this. Six international entertainment powerhouses are rapidly dividing up the world recording market. They are buying out independent labels in countries all over the world. They are creating partnerships in manufacturing and distribution all over the world. Media economist Harold Vogel attributes this need for large distribution systems to high wastage (many products will not succeed) and short life cycles of the "hit" recordings (usually less than a year). He says, "[B]ecause efficiency in this area requires that retailers located over a wide geographic swath have their inventories quickly replenished, most records are distributed by large organizations with sufficient capital to stock and ship hundreds of thousands of units at a moment's notice."[29] They are selling recordings from their own labels and from local labels all over the world. They are integrating horizontally and vertically, controlling more music publishing, film production, television production, audio and video hardware manufacturing, and radio, television, and cable broadcasting. They have learned that there is money to be made in many small successes, not just blockbuster hits. There is good reason to own a label that sells gospel music or new age music even though those recordings may sell no more than a couple of hundred thousand units, because they can be profitable sales. They are willing to let people who know the markets for that kind of music make the creative and production decisions and they, the big six, supply the distribution.

Even from a micro perspective, examining only recording industry organizations and structures, one cannot help but be struck by the fact that there are major influences on how the industry functions from other industries as well as from society. The most notable interface with another industry is with broadcasting, particularly radio, and to a lesser extent, television. These are the two primary means that the recording industry uses to promote its products to potential consumers.

Radio has changed. No longer does Top 40 airplay dominate the promotion and sale of all recordings. From 1986 to 1995 the number of radio stations reporting predominantly music formats increased by over 2,000 and the number of different formats reported nearly doubled, going from twelve to twenty-three.[30] The two major radio tip sheets, *Radio & Records (R&R)* and *Gavin*, more than doubled the number of airplay charts reported in each publication over that same period. *Gavin* went from five charts in 1986 to thirteen in 1996, and *R&R* went from six in 1986 to fifteen in 1996. Even as concentration of radio station ownership increased in 1990s at a mind-numbing rate, after the deregulation of ownership rules with the Communications Act of 1996, broadcasting executives were predicting further diversity in radio formats. (Chapter 5 examines the relationship of the recording and broadcast industries in detail.) The net result of all these changes was a greater diversity of music available to be heard by more people.

Technology and the Recording Industry System

The recording industry owes its existence to technology. Refinements and advances in technology have affected all parts of the system. On the input side it is easier for more musicians and writers to make high quality recordings and the quality that can be made is higher. In the transformation process sophisticated control over recording and advances in reproduction have made more product available at lower production costs, and enabled more sophisticated and lower cost distribution of that product. More methods of exposure are available thanks to cable television and video cassettes. On the output side the availability of high quality and lower cost playback systems has stimulated demand. The feedback loop has improved with more accurate and faster data gathering mechanisms.

What Thomas Edison did not know in 1877 was that his "talking machine" invention would lay the groundwork for a "music machine." Emile Berliner's disc recording system made this even more likely because the original recordings were easier to replicate into copies, thereby opening up much greater possibility for a mass-produced item for the general population. Advances in player and recording technology through the 1940s made the music reproduced even more lifelike. Stereo proved that consumers wanted their music to sound even better and more like a real performance. Cassette tapes made the medium more portable so that it could go with Americans in their ubiquitous automobiles, even without playing it on the radio. Smaller amplifiers and players soon meant that prerecorded music could go to the beach, for a jog, for a walk in the park, or to the gymnasium for a workout. The compact disc and digital recording propelled the quality of sound available and the ease of use and durability to higher levels. Digital transmission may make new delivery systems possible so that people can have an even greater diversity of recordings to choose from. Reductions in the costs of manufacturing recordings and in the playback systems led to further market penetration for the players and the recordings. High quality, inexpensive recordings and playback systems were within the reach of nearly everybody. The subsequent greater demand for recordings infused more revenues into the industry and made an even greater diversity of product available. Large labels could afford to take more chances on a wider variety of artists. Small labels could find new artists with niche or emerging markets, make smaller investments, and still earn a profit on a relatively small sales base.

The electronic revolution also had a significant impact on the creative inputs for the industry. As the sophistication of "home" recording equipment improved it became possible for creative musicians and writers to have more control over the process of recording. Digital quality recordings could be made in small studios.

Musical Instrument Digital Interface (MIDI) and synthesis gave musicians and writers nearly total control over the creation of complex musical arrangements and works. Lower production costs meant that more people could make music and market it. With the prospect of digital delivery it may be that any musician capable of making a recording can at least get that recording out for people to hear if they want to.

Electronic data gathering mechanisms improved market research for record companies, broadcasters, music publishers, record distributors, and retailers. The Universal Product Code led to better inventory management systems for retail and distribution. Ultimately, the SoundScan system of gathering sales information on a national basis allowed the development of sophisticated marketing plans and test marketing. Broadcast Data Systems' electronic monitoring of radio and television stations led to more accurate airplay information for labels and performing rights organizations.

The Recording Industry as a Mass Medium

Popular music, the primary content of the recording media, can be partially understood as communication and the recording industry as a mass medium. The main activity of the recording industry is the production and distribution of symbolic content to widely dispersed heterogeneous audiences. It uses several technologies to do this, including digital recording and reproduction, analog recording and reproduction, and video recording and reproduction. Media theorist Dennis McQuail has said that the recording industry as a medium has several unique characteristics:

- Multiple technologies of recording and dissemination;
- Low degree of regulation;
- High degree of internationalization;
- Younger audience;
- Subversive potential;
- Organizational fragmentation; and
- Diversity of reception possibilities.[31]

This would appear to be a fair characterization except that the nature of the audience appears to be growing older, as noted earlier.

Popular music communicates in many ways, some intended by the artist and songwriter, some not. Consumers form social groups based on their likes and dislikes of certain genres or artists. Some music is consumed privately to soothe ravaged psyches or to excite them. Music may be used for social activities such as dancing. Music communicates through physical activities, cognitive activities, and emotion. Popular culture analyst James Lull writes, "Music promotes experiences of the extreme for its makers and listeners, turning the perilous emotional edges, vulnerabilities, triumphs, celebrations, and antagonisms of life into hypnotic, reflective tempos that can be experienced privately or shared with others."[32]

It is clear that music and recordings fit a model of communication that allows for different meanings to be constructed by the message sender(s) and receiver(s). They also fit a model that includes gatekeepers, individuals through whom the intended message must pass on its way to the receiver. The gatekeeper "determines what information is passed and how faithfully it is reproduced."[33] An early application of this model focused on radio programmers as gatekeepers.[34] Gatekeepers are considered by some as only those that mediate between the industry and its consumers. From a broader perspective of the earlier definition above, if the sender is the artist and the receiver is the listener or consumer, then there are other gatekeepers as well. If the artist is not also the songwriter, then the writer must get through the music publisher's gate. The publisher must get through the producer's gate. The producer must get through the label A&R department's gate. The recording must get through the radio and video gates, unless those gates can be held open with payola or through agreements that the programmer will play certain cuts. The retailer keeps gates as well as shop, deciding what recordings to stock, how many to stock, and whether to feature a particular recording. The rack jobber keeps a relatively small gate, only letting through the hits that could sell in large quantity through fairly small record departments in mass merchandise chains.

Gatekeeper theory is useful in explaining the desire of the various players to use any device they can to keep the gates open so their communication can pass. The problem with this approach is that it tends to assume that the gatekeepers care which recordings pass through the gates. A given label does not care which of its recordings become hits, unless they have invested substantial amounts in some superstar artist. It takes *some* hits to sustain a large label but not usually any particular hit. A small label that has a small roster of artists who make recordings on small budgets may not need hits so much as it needs consistent sales in order to survive. Dedication to the music and sufficient sales may be enough.[35] Radio stations program recordings they think their listeners will like, or at least not dislike, but that is usually without regard to the artist or label. Retailers care that they sell recordings, but as long as the profit on any two given albums is equal it does not really matter which one a customer purchases. If one considers the artist or songwriter as communicator, then they are so far removed from the gatekeeper that they have little contact or influence.

The Three Income Streams Model

While all of these viewpoints shed some light on the functions of the recording industry, it can best be understood in terms of an economic model. At the heart of that economic model are three streams of income: one generated through the utilization of a song, one from the utilization of a particular recorded performance of that song, and one generated from live performances of that song (see Figure 1-5). At the head of each income stream is a creative act: a song is written, a recording is produced, a live performance given. These creative acts give rise to legal rights associated with the acts. The songwriter's creative act results in a copyright in a musical composition. The record label, producer, and recording artist's creative acts result in copyright in the sound recording. Performers have a right to keep others from recording or broadcasting their performances. Three distinct legal rights, three distinct creative acts, and three distinct treatments of a song produce three distinct income streams.

This particular three income-stream model is superior to those that focus on songs. While one might argue that "the song is the thing" because it is included in all three streams, it is really the recording that provides most of the drive for the cash flows in all three streams. Utilizing these three streams is more inclusive than following three streams of royalties, one from the sale of recordings, one from the sale of music, and one from the performance of music, because it also includes the live performance of the artist. That live performance is a revenue generating act for the artist aside from whether it generates any royalties for the music publisher.[36]

Including live performance as an income stream also brings it under the general rubric of the recording industry, which is certainly correct because the existence of popular recording artists and their performances accounts for most of the revenues generated in that stream. Finally, including the live performance stream accounts for more points of interconnection between the various streams and leads to the development of a more complete model. It is the presence of the cash flow that drives the major players in the industry to seek to gain control over and participate in all three income streams, not a conscious or unconscious desire to foist any particular kind or quality of music on the consuming public.

Who's Who in the Recording Industry

Before launching into the construction of a model, one is always advised by the instructions to check the parts list to be sure that all the parts are included, to be sure that one knows what a component is before attempting its assembly into the finished product. For that reason the basic function of all of the players in each of the three streams is defined below. The order is that in which they appear in the income stream in Figure 1-5. The simplicity of some of the definitions belies the complex relationships often set up by some individuals wearing more than one functional "hat" in the industry.

The Recordings Stream

- *Recording artists:* Sometimes referred to as "royalty artists," these are the people who perform for recordings by playing instruments and/or singing a particular performance that is recorded. The recording artist may or may not be a live performing artist, and may or may not be a songwriter. Most recording artists make money from the income stream by getting a royalty payment based on the sales of copies of the recordings that they make.
- *Record labels:* These organizations "hire" artists to make recordings that they plan on marketing in some way to the public. They usually sign the artist to a recording contract promising to pay the artist a royalty for recordings sold in

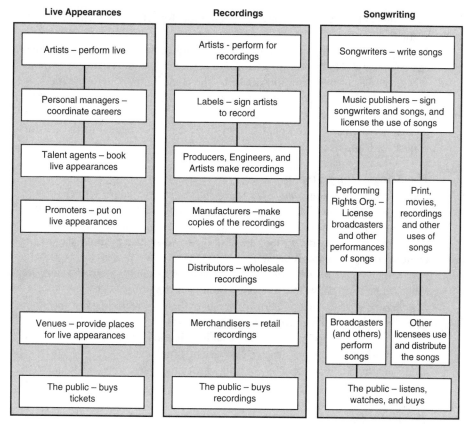

FIGURE 1-5 The Recording Industry: Three Income Stream Model

return for the artist's promise to record exclusively for that particular label.

- *Record producers:* These individuals are in charge of the process of creating the recording. They assist the artists by helping select material, studios, and assistants and by helping the artists give their best performance. They assist the labels by taking care of the business aspects of the recording process and by delivering a marketable product.

- *Side musicians/vocalists:* These people usually work on a per-job basis for the artist or producer to help create the desired recording. They are to be distinguished from the recording artists because side musicians do not generally receive royalties from the sale of recordings.

- *Recording engineers:* They assist the producer and artist by running the equipment necessary first to capture the performance on tape (or some other medium) and then to shape the final sound that the artist and producer ultimately want on the recording.

- *Record manufacturers:* They are often (but not necessarily) the same as the label, and make copies of the recordings suitable for sale in some manner to the ultimate consumers.

- *Distributors:* These businesses handle the copies of the recordings so that they can be conveyed to the consumer for purchase. For the most part, they whole-sale the copies of the recordings made by the manufacturers to the retailers.
- *Merchandisers:* Retailers sell copies of the recordings to the consuming public.
- *The public:* In this income stream this is the record buying public. This may be a different segment of the public from those who buy tickets to live perfor-mances or listen to broadcasts.

The Songwriting Stream

- *Songwriters (including composers and lyricists):* These people write songs.
- *Music publishers:* Publishers acquire rights to songs from songwriters and then license the uses of those songs. Most music publishers sign songwriters to con-tracts agreeing to pay the writer a share of the royalties that the publisher makes from licensing the uses of the song.
- *Performing rights organizations:* Such organizations license broadcasters and others to perform songs, either live or from recordings.
- *Broadcasters:* These media perform songs by playing recordings of the songs or by broadcasting live performances of the songs.
- *The public:* People listen and watch, usually with no charge other than serving as an audience for the broadcaster's advertising messages.
- *Other media:* They create movies, print sheet music and songbooks, make re-cordings, and utilize the songs in other ways that create royalties for the pub-lisher and songwriter.
- *The public:* People watch and buy these other uses of the songs.

The Live Appearances Stream

- *The musicians and singers:* The artists perform live for appearances primarily in concerts, in nightclubs, on television, and on radio. Not all live performers are recording artists, though most aspire to be, and not all recording artists are live performers, though most need to be.
- *Personal managers:* These people assist artists in the development and coordi-nation of their careers as performing artists and as recording artists. They are located in this income stream because most of their day-to-day functions re-volve not around recordings, but around live appearances.
- *Talent agents (a.k.a. booking agents):* Agents book live appearances for per-formers.
- *Promoters:* They put on live appearances by performers by arranging for the performer, the venue, the date, the production, and the marketing for the perfor-mance.
- *Venues:* These are places for live appearances by artists, including clubs, con-cert halls, arenas, and stadiums.

- *The public:* People purchase tickets to or otherwise attend live artist performances.

The existence of the music publishing and live performance streams is important to the recording industry because the labels often have an economic stake in these other two streams. All of the major record industry conglomerates, and many individual labels, producers, and artists have publishing interests. Live performance is the crucible in which many new acts are formed. It may be an important medium to expose the public to the artists and their sound in order to promote the sale of recordings. Live performance may keep an artist's catalog of recordings selling long after the artist's recording career has peaked.

Perhaps most significantly, it is from the public participation in each stream that the income is generated. Unless the public buys concert tickets or attends clubs and

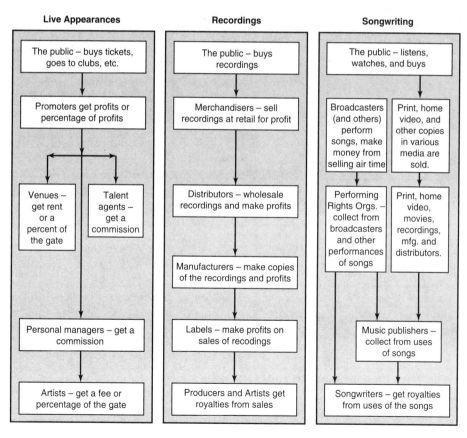

FIGURE 1-6   The Cash Flow in the Three Income Stream Model

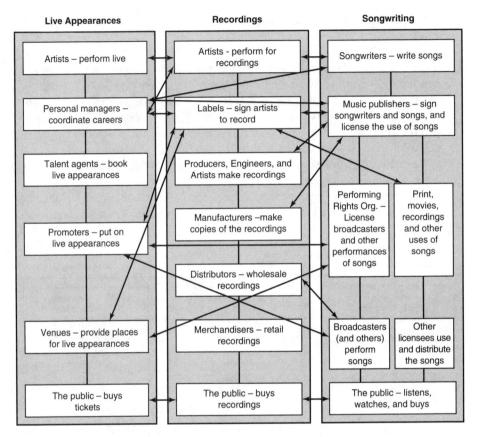

FIGURE 1-7   Three Income Streams—The Hard Way

purchases food and drink, there is no source of revenue for the live appearance stream. Unless the public buys copies of recordings there is little revenue generated in the recordings stream. Unless the public either consumes the actual products such as sheet music or recordings, or attends movies, or provides an audience for the advertisers on radio or television, there is little or no money in the songwriting stream. It is also the public that is the target in a communications model discussed later. Figure 1-6 indicates the income flow in each stream.

Three Income Streams the Hard Way

In order for a player in any stream to maximize security and profitability, participation in the other two streams is necessary. Figure 1-7 illustrates some of the many additional monetary and legal connections that exist between the various streams. These relationships between the three streams are examined in detail in each of the next three chapters.

NOTES

[1]Recording Industry Association of America, *Rewind/Fast Forward: 45 Years and Beyond @ the Recording Industry Association of America* (1996): 28.

[2]Chris Morris, "Garth Takes Solo Sales Record," *Billboard,* 16 March 1996: 13.

[3]National Association of Music Merchants, *1966 Music USA* (1996): 4, 14.

[4]Ibid., 48–49.

[5]"73rd Annual Statistical Surveys and Report," *Dealerscope Merchandising*, July 1995: 35.

[6]U.S. Dept. of Labor, Bureau of Labor Statistics, *Monthly Labor Review,* Nov. 1995.

[7]*Statistical Abstract of the United States,* U.S. Department of Commerce, Bureau of the Census, 1995: 568.

[8]Paul Verna, "RIAA Report Shows Stagnant '95 Shipments for Music, Video," *Billboard*, 2 March 1996: 3.

[9]R. Serge Denisoff, *Solid Gold.* New Brunswick, NJ: Transaction Books (1975): 33.

[10]Geoffrey Hull, "The Aging of America: The Recording and Broadcasting Industries Awareness of Shifting Demographic Patterns," *NARAS Institute Journal*, Vol. 1, No. 1 (1977): 3.

[11]NARM, *Consumer Research Study: The Growing Adult Market*, March 1976.

[12]See, for example, Richard L. Daft, *Management.* New York: Dryden Press (1988): 53–55; R. Wayne Mondy and Shane R. Premeaux, *Management Concepts Practices and Skills.* Boston: Allyn & Bacon (1993): 36–38.

[13]Peter J. Alexander, "Entropy and Popular Culture: Product Diversity in the Popular Music Recording Industry," 61 *American Sociological Review* (1996): 171.

[14]For this and other examples, see, Lisa A. Lewis, *Gender Politics and MTV* (Philadelphia: Temple University Press, 1990).

[15]For one perspective see, Tipper Gore, *Raising PG Children in an X-Rated Society* (Nashville, TN: Abingdon: 1987): Chapter 5.

[16]See, for example, Cathy Schwichtenberg, "Music Video, the Popular Pleasures of Visual Music," in James Lull, *Popular Music and Communication* (2nd ed., 1992): 116; Deanna Campbell Robinson, and others, *Music at the Margins* (1991): 1–31; R. Serge Denisoff, *Tarnished Gold* (1986): 1–35.

[17]Lisa A. Lewis, *Gender Politics and MTV* (1990).

[18]Simon Frith, "Critical Response," in Deanna Campbell Robinson, and others, *Music at the Margins* (1991): 287 (emphasis in original).

[19]Recording Industry Association of America, "Recording Industry Releases 1995 Consumer Profile," press release 5 April 1996: 2.

[20]Tipper Gore, *Raising PG Kids in an X-Rated Society* (1987).

[21]Chris Morris, "Fla. Clerk Faces Obscenity Charge for Cassette Sale," *Billboard,* 2 May 1987: 1.

[22]Camelot Music executive Jim Bonk quoted in Geoff Mayfield, "Camelot Pulls Live Crew," *Billboard*, 2 May 1987: 87.

[23]"Industry to Enhance Awareness of Parental Advisory Logo," *NARM Sounding Board*, Nov. 1995 (on-line version); National Association of Recording Merchandisers, "Parental Advisory Program Bolstered," press release on NARM's Internet site, 12 Sept. 1996.

[24]"Censorship Is Back . . . But So Are We!" *NARM Sounding Board*, August 1995, on-line version.

[25]"Band Is Held Not Liable in Suicides of Two Fans," *New York Times*, The Arts section, 25 August 1990.

[26]Melvin L. DeFleur and Everette E. Dennis, *Understanding Mass Communication* (4th ed., 1991): 475.

[27]National Music Publishers' Association, *International Survey of Music Publishing Revenues* (1991): 11. The NMPA points out that their first survey had a limited database of only eighteen nations and that the relationship was only significant at a "reduced" level of statistical significance. Based on the available information, the author estimates that reduced level to be 90 percent. The statistical analysis was not included in later editions of the report.

[28]Peter F. Drucker, *Managing for the Future* (1992): 8.

[29]Harold L. Vogel, *Entertainment Industry Economics* (1986): 149.

[30]*Broadcasting & Cable Yearbook*, 1986 and 1996.

[31]Dennis McQuail, *Mass Communication Theory* (1994): 20.

[32]James Lull, "Popular Music and Communication," in *Popular Music and Communication* (2nd ed., 1992): 1.

[33]Werner J. Severin and James W. Tankard, Jr., *Communication Theories: Origins, Methods and Used in the Mass Media* (3rd ed., 1988): 43.

[34]Paul Hirsch, *The Structure of the Popular Music Industry* (monograph from Institute for Social Research, University of Michigan), (Ann Arbor, Michigan, 1969).

[35]The story of Theresa Records, small jazz label, is eloquently told in Herman Gray, *Producing Jazz* (1988).

[36]Don Cusic, *Music in the Market* (1996): 25; Harold L. Vogel, *Entertainment Industry Economics* (1986): 137.

2

Recordings: The Main Stream

BASIC FUNCTIONS

In order to produce income in this stream, a record company, usually referred to as a "label," gains control over a master recording of a performance by an artist and then sells copies to consumers. Usually this takes the form of getting the artist to sign an exclusive recording agreement with the label, producing a recording, then manufacturing and marketing copies of that recording for purchase by consumers. The label therefore has two basic functions that it must perform: acquire masters and market those masters. The acquisition of masters is discussed in detail in Chapter 6 on the production and A&R function. Marketing is discussed in detail in Chapter 7. This chapter examines the overall market structure of the recordings stream and the structure of a typical individual label within that stream.

OLIGOPOLY

From almost every perspective the recording industry is either already in an oligopolistic state or heading towards oligopoly. *Oligopoly* is usually defined as a "few" sellers occupying the market, with "few" being everything between one firm (monopoly) to many firms (pure competition). A more useful definition, which takes into account the concentration of the market in the number of sellers, defines three levels of oligopoly. In a *dominant firm* oligopoly, one firm holds 50 to 90 percent of the market. In a *tight oligopoly*, a concentration of four firms holds more than 60 percent of the market. If it takes more than four firms to reach 60 percent of the market, but less than "many," that is still an oligopoly but would be deemed "*effective competition.*"[1]

It should be noted that oligopoly is not a "four-letter word," either literally or figuratively. There is nothing inherently bad about an oligopoly existing in any given market. Oligopoly is simply a word that describes a market in which there are certain kinds of conditions. Generally, markets are described by four significant factors: the number of firms, the seller concentration, the product differentiation, and the barriers to entry.[2] The number of firms involved in the distribution of recordings is relatively small, as discussed below, but the number of individual labels is large. Looking at market share of the individual labels (Table 2-1), one can see a market that is fairly well spread. If one considers label ownership, on the theory that the individual labels do not operate autonomously within their corporate organizations, then there is a much higher concentration of sellers. Although all labels sell the same basic products, recordings, there is usually very high differentiation among those recordings. That is why some recordings find favor with consumers and are "hits" and others are not. That is why some recordings are the toast of the critics and others are panned. That is why consumers have favorite artists and favorite recordings. On the label side, the barriers to entry are not as great as they once used to be. There are many acts wanting to record, costs of recording are lower than they used to be, and the label does not have to manufacture its own recordings (most of these factors are discussed in more detail in Chapter 6). From the perspective of the distribution of recordings, there are high barriers to entry. Setting up a nationwide distribution system for recordings entails warehouses, inventory, and personnel, all creating high barriers to entry. On the other hand, if recordings are distributed through cyberspace on the Internet, then barriers to entry are very low.

Oligopoly from Birth to the Fifties

For most of its existence the recording industry has been in a state of "tight oligopoly." Thomas Edison's monopoly lasted only nine years from the invention of the "talking machine" in 1877. The founding of his Edison Speaking Phonograph Company in 1878 led Alexander Graham Bell to create a better cylinder and player and form the American Graphophone Company in 1887. Edison first started offering cylinders for sale to the public in 1889. Shortly thereafter Columbia was formed and started offering cylinders for sale for coin-operated players. By 1901 the Victor Talking Machine Company was formed and began offering Emile Berliner's (the German who invented disk recording) disk players and recordings. Columbia began to market both cylinders and disks under patent licenses. By 1909 the three companies with patent monopolies (or licenses) controlled the market: Edison, Columbia, and Victor. A three-firm tight oligopoly continued until the 1950s, although the firms comprising the top three changed over time. Edison folded in the market crash of 1929, but Decca emerged in the 1930s.[3] By 1950 RCA Victor and Decca claimed 67 percent of *Billboard*'s Top Pop Records chart. Mercury and Capitol were emerging as significant labels with a 10 percent share each and Columbia had dropped to a less than 4 percent share.[4] The popularity charts of *Billboard* magazine are a convenient and reasonably accurate way to measure a record's or label's success. Although the methodologies used in compiling the charts have changed somewhat over time, they have always included a significant sales component.

During the early 1950s, more labels and artists began to emerge but the tight oligopoly remained. Phonograph players became more plentiful in the home market. Jukeboxes became more plentiful. As late as 1953 the top four firms, Columbia (reenergized by Broadway cast albums, MOR hits, and Mitch Miller recordings), Capitol, Mercury, and RCA Victor, controlled 78 percent of the charted records.[5] Only seven labels had any chart action at all. As R&B, country, and folk became more popular more labels appeared in the year-end chart summary. In 1954 fourteen labels reported Top 30 chart activity but there was still a tight oligopoly with RCA Victor, Capitol, Mercury, and Columbia controlling 62 percent of chart activity.[6]

Mom and Pop and Rock 'n' Roll

The birth of rock 'n' roll in 1955 ended the tight oligopoly and brought effective competition with the emergence of many independent labels, especially R&B, into the top charts. In 1955 it took the top six labels to garner a 60 percent share. In 1956 the top six labels controlled only 53 percent of the top chart share. *Billboard* reported twenty-five R&B hits on the charts and twenty rock hits (many of them cover versions of R&B songs by pop artists such as Perry Como).[7] The public's demand for the new music drove sales of recordings up with a 44 percent increase in sales volume from 1955 to 1956. The new artists came from everywhere, on dozens of new labels, and the chart share of the independents skyrocketed to 76 percent in 1958.[8] Even as albums began to replace singles as the dominant selling product in the early 1960s, it was clear that the oligopoly was broken. The 1962 *Billboard* album chart summary showed forty-two labels with at least one charted album and the top six firms controlled less than 50 percent of those records.[9]

Back to Oligopoly

Over the next twenty years the major corporations began to assert more control through branch distribution (see Chapter 7) and mergers. By 1972 the top five labels only controlled 31.4 percent of the album charts, but the top five *corporations* controlled 58.2 percent of those charts. The industry was returning to a tight oligopoly (four firms controlling more than 60 percent) with the top four corporations controlling 52.6 percent of the album chart (WEA 26.2 percent, CBS 13.1 percent, A&M, 7.7 percent, Capitol and RCA tied at 5.6 percent).[10] As the 1970s wore on into the 1980s the oligopoly became more pronounced. The most significant independent labels joined the branch distribution system. In 1979 A&M joined RCA distribution followed by Arista and Ariola in 1983. United Artists merged with Capitol in 1979. In 1983 Chrysalis went to CBS distribution and Motown went to MCA. In the flurry of consolidation and merger of the late 1980s and early 1990s, *ownership* became the key factor. Large labels bought out smaller labels. The identity of the smaller label may have been retained but ownership was usually in the hands of a large entertainment conglomerate.

The 1990s and Beyond

By the 1990s the structure of the industry had returned to a tight oligopoly. The top four distributing firms controlled about 62 percent of the market in the United States for the first half of the 1990s. WEA averaged about 21.5 percent, Sony about 15.5 percent, and PolyGram (PGD) and BMG about 12.8 percent each. Independent labels had been increasing their share of the market, from 14.6 percent in 1993 to 21.2 percent in 1996.[11] (Chapter 7, Figure 7-6 shows details.) The likelihood is that the tight oligopoly will continue. Even if the share of independent labels increased to 20 percent, the remaining 80 percent would still be divided among six companies. If the big six divided up their 80 percent evenly (one-sixth of 80 is 13.3), and there is no indication that would happen, four of them would control over 53 percent of the market. As indicated above, once an independent label begins to show significant market share and profitability, it is subject to being purchased by one of the big six. Unlike the situation in the late 1950s, the large companies do not ignore new musical genres or trends.

THE BIG SIX[12]

Six large international conglomerates own and control the bulk of the recording industry in the world, not just the United States. In case there is any doubt that the recording industry operates on an international level, one only has to look at the ownership of the six largest record companies: Warner Music Group is owned by a U.S. company, Time Warner; Sony Music is owned by the Japanese Sony Corporation; PolyGram is owned by PolyGram N.V. of the Netherlands; BMG is owned by Bertlesman A.G. in Germany; EMI Ltd. is a U.K. firm; MCA is owned by the Canadian Seagram's Ltd. Not every one of the large entertainment conglomerates breaks out the earnings or sales of their music divisions. Where that information is available it is given in the discussion of the "big six" that follows.

Warner Music Group

Time Warner Entertainment Company is the world's largest entertainment company. It got even larger in 1996 with the merger of Turner Broadcasting System. Warner Brothers records began as the music division of Warner Brothers film company to control music interests for its film productions in the 1920s. In the depression of the 1930s, Warner sold off its music publishing interests. In 1958 it reformed its music publishing and record labels, primarily to promote and sell its film and television related music. Warner Brothers had early 1960s success with the Everly

Brothers and Bill Cosby comedy recordings and bought Frank Sinatra's MOR label, Reprise, in 1963–1965 (they purchased the label in halves). In 1967 Warner Brothers purchased Atlantic Records and was in turn purchased by 7 Arts. In 1969 the Kinney Corporation (not the shoe company, but a building services, construction, and parking company) purchased 7 Arts and changed its name to Warner Communications, Inc. With the addition of the Elektra Records label purchased in 1970, Warner/Elektra/Atlantic Distribution (later just WEA Distribution) was formed. Time Warner was formed by the merger of print publishing giant Time, Inc., and "electronic" publishing giant Warner Communications, Inc. The music division of this giant is Warner Music Group, which consists of the labels and Warner/Chappel Music Publishing. In addition, it owns WEA Inc., which consists of WEA Corporation, the branch distribution system, WEA Manufacturing, which owns CD, CD–ROM, and videocassette manufacturing facilities, and Ivy Hill, a printing and packaging arm.[13] The Time Warner parent corporation also owns twenty-four magazines, book publishing, film and television production and distribution, a TV network, cable systems and cable programming, and theme parks. Time Warner reported 1994 operating revenues as $7.4 billion, with total assets of $16.7 billion. Warner Music Group labels are: Warner Brothers, Atlantic, Atco, Elektra/Asylum, Reprise.

Sony Music

Sony Corporation, the Japanese electronics manufacturing company, saw the importance of developing software industries to complement its hardware manufacturing when it entered into an agreement with CBS Records to create the Digital Audio Disc Corporation, the first manufacturer of compact discs in the United States. The cornerstones of Sony Music are Sony Music Publishing and the venerable label Columbia Records. Columbia, originally the Columbia Graphophone Company of pre-1900, existed as a separate entity until the depression saw the merger of Columbia Graphophone, Gramophone Company, and Parlophone to create Electric and Musical Industries, Ltd. (EMI) in England. EMI sold its American stock to the American Record Corporation (ARC). Columbia Broadcasting System (CBS) purchased ARC in 1938 and revitalized the Columbia label. Columbia seceded from EMI in England in 1952. Sony built its music interests primarily through the acquisition of CBS Records group for $2 billion in 1988 from CBS, Inc. Sony's music group revenues amounted to about $5.6 billion in 1995, that is about 64 percent of Sony's entertainment business revenues of $8.75 billion, and about 12 percent of Sony's total revenues for that year.[14] Sony also owns film production and distribution interests in Columbia Pictures and Tri-Star Pictures, as well as home video production and distribution, television production companies, and a large consumer electronics division. Sony Music labels are: Columbia, Epic, and Epic Associated Labels. Sony Music also owns half of the Columbia House record club; Warner owns the other half. Sony also owns a branch distribution system (Sony Distribution) and CD and tape manufacturing facilities in the United States.

PolyGram

PolyGram N.V. is a Dutch (Netherlands) entertainment holding company that in turn is 75 percent owned by Philips Electronics N.V. PolyGram built its recording interests piecemeal. Philips originally purchased Polydor (a German label) in the early 1950s, and then Mercury Records in 1961. MGM Records was acquired in 1972. PolyGram was formed in 1972 when parent company Philips merged Polydor with Phonogram International. In 1989 PolyGram acquired the Island Records Group, in 1990 A&M Records, and then R&B powerhouse Motown in 1993 for $300 million. In 1994 PolyGram acquired a 50 percent interest in Def Jam Records. PolyGram labels include: Mercury, Polydor, London, Vertigo, Verve, Wing, A&M, Island, Motown, Decca, Deutche Grammophon, and Philips Classics. 1994 total assets were about $4.6 billion, with revenues of $5.5 billion. The parent also owns television and film production and distribution, music publishing, manufacturing, and the PGD (PolyGram Distribution) branch distribution system.

BMG

BMG is part of the German corporation, Bertlesman, A.G. BMG used to stand for "Bertlesman Music Group" but that was shortened to BMG. BMG's record business took off in the United States when it acquired Arista Records from its founder Clive Davis in 1979. In 1986 BMG purchased all the RCA Victor interests from General Electric (which had earlier that year acquired RCA Corporation's recording interests for $6.4 billion). BMG labels include: Ariola, RCA, LaFace/Arista, Zoo Entertainment, Private, Windham Hill, Disques Vogue, Jive/Silvertone, Wired, Mushroom, Deconstruction, American Recordings, Absorbing, Gun, Red Rooster, Goldrush, K&P, Chodwig, MSM, Expressive, Coconut, Nahsa, MCI, Sing Sing, Jupiter, and Lawine. BMG's labels operate under BMG Entertainment. Under that same group are BMG Music Publishing and BMG Music, the distribution and manufacturing operations, and the record club, BMG Music Service. The parent company also owns television and radio stations (outside of the United States), film production and distribution, magazine publishing, book publishing, and newspapers. Bertlesman owns in whole or part over two hundred entertainment and publishing entities throughout the world and continued to expand in the mid 1990s, acquiring 73 percent of Ricordi (the largest Italian independent record company) and 50 percent of the New Age label Private Music in 1994.[15] Net revenues in 1994 were DM 18.4 billion (about $13,301 million) with total assets of DM 9.9 billion (about $7.2 billion).

EMI

EMI began with the merger of three labels in the United Kingdom in 1930. Columbia Graphophone, Gramophone Company (the "His Masters Voice" folks), and Parlophone joined to create Electric and Musical Industries, Ltd. (later just EMI,

Ltd.). EMI remained a primarily European operation until 1956 when it acquired Capitol Records in the United States. Capitol had been formed in the United States in 1942 by Johnny Mercer, Buddy DeSylva, and Glenn Wallichs. In the United States Capitol–EMI Industries grew into a major label with a branch distribution system. In 1974 EMI acquired the rights to the substantial Decca U.K. catalog. (There were two Decca record companies until 1974. Decca U.K. was formed in 1929 and U.S. Decca in 1934.) Thorn EMI, PLC was formed in 1979 when electrical/electronics company Thorn merged with EMI. The new company began expansion with the acquisition of Chrysalis Records in 1989, SBK Entertainment World in 1990, Filmtrax and Thames Television in 1990, the Virgin Music Group in 1992, Sparrow Corporation (a gospel label) in 1992, and Toshiba–EMI Music Publishing and Star Song publishing in 1994. In 1996 Thorn and EMI demerged. The resulting EMI Group contained two divisions: EMI Music Group operated the sixty-five labels and twenty-three music publishing companies, including Capitol, EMI Records, EMI Music Publishing, Virgin Records Ltd., and Capitol–EMI Music. The Music Group also includes EMD (EMI Music Distribution, formerly Cema Distribution) distribution, and manufacturing facilities. The HMV group operated a retail division consisting of 240 record stores, 144 of which were outside of the United Kingdom. Profits of the EMI music division were estimated at $547.8 million the year of the demerger with profits of the HMV Group estimated at $29.9 million.[16] The demerger fueled speculation that EMI would be purchased by some other conglomerate, at a speculated price of $9+ billion.[17] At the end of 1996 that remained speculation with no particular buyers being mentioned.

MCA

The early history of MCA is particularly interesting. It began in New York 1924 as a talent agency and moved to California in 1937 to add film talent to its operations. Television talent booking was added in 1949. The company moved into the production business in 1959 with the purchase of Universal Studios film facilities. MCA added recordings in 1962 when it purchased U.S. Decca and shortly thereafter the Coral and Kapp labels. The ABC–Dunhill labels were added in 1979. MCA purchased about 20 percent ownership of Motown Records in 1988 but later sold that interest for $60 million in 1993 when Motown was purchased entirely by PolyGram. Ownership of MCA moved to Japan in 1990 when the electronics giant, Matsushita Electric Industrial Company, purchased it for $6.13 billion. MCA added Geffen Records to the label roster in 1991 and the company changed the name of its branch distribution system to Uni Distribution. A recent acquisition of note is 50 percent of the rock and rap label Interscope for a reported $200 million in 1996.[18] The Seagram Company, Ltd. of Canada (the beverage company) purchased 80 percent of Matsushita's ownership of MCA in 1995 for $5.7 billion. The new parent, Seagram, earns about 63 percent of its revenues from the sales of beverages, spirits and wines, and 37 percent from its holdings in MCA. MCA revenues were $5.6 billion in 1995 and Seagram had total assets of nearly $13 billion in 1995. MCA labels include

MCA, Geffen, DGC, and GRP. MCA continues to own film and television production and distribution as well as the record labels, the record and video distribution
system, and music publishing interests.

The success of the big six at producing the hits is illustrated in Tables 2-1 and 2-
2. The success of the various individual labels tends to vary from year to year as
shown in Table 2-1. The only independent labels appearing in that table are East
West, Jive, and Disney. All others are owned by the big six. The relative success of
the major labels is illustrated in Table 2-2. For each of the years 1993–1995 there is
a Sony label (Columbia or Epic), a WEA label (Warner Bros. or Atlantic), a BMG
label (Arista), and MCA.

An important point about these two tables is that they show significant diversity
and lack of concentration when looking at the individual labels (Table 2-1) and
much more concentration when looking at the distributing labels (Table 2-2). The
top five distributing labels had 80 to 89 percent of the albums in the top 200 in 1993–
1995. That represents significant concentration. However if the individual labels
function autonomously in terms of A&R and marketing in finding, developing, and
promoting new talent, then there is much less concentration of label power and there
should be much more diversity of music to be heard, regardless of who the corporate
owner of any individual label might be.

**TABLE 2-1   Top Album Labels of the Mid-1990s (by Number of Albums
and Position in *Billboard*'s Top 200 Albums Chart)**

1993		1994		1995	
Label	Albums	Label	Albums	Label	Albums
Arista	20	Columbia	37	Atlantic	34
Columbia	48	MCA	39	Arista	23
Epic	40	Arista	24	Columbia	40
MCA	32	Atlantic	38	Epic	31
Liberty	16	Epic	30	Warner Bros.	28
Atlantic	39	A & M	18	A & M	18
Warner Bros.	28	Virgin	16	Geffen	13
Reprise	32	DGC	11	MCA	25
Mercury	19	Capitol	20	Reprise	12
Virgin	12	Reprise	30	Capitol	9
A & M	20	Geffen	17	Disney	10
Capitol	23	Warner Bros.	26	Motown	5
Geffen	13	Interscope	13	Island	8
East West	17	Elektra	24	Interscope	16
Elektra	17	Jive	16		

Source: *Billboard*, Year End Supplements, 25 Dec. 1993: YE-18; 24 Dec. 1994: YE-24; 23 Dec.
1995: YE-26.

TABLE 2-2   Top 200 Albums by Distributing Labels (by Number of Albums and Position in *Billboard*'s Top 200 Albums Chart)

1993		1994		1995	
Label	Albums	Label	Albums	Label	Albums
Warner Bros.	93	Atlantic	68	Warner Bros.	76
Columbia	64	Warner Bros.	83	Atlantic	56
Arista	25	Columbia	50	Arista	36
Epic	54	MCA	56	MCA	43
MCA	50	Arista	32	Epic	51

Source: *Billboard*, Year End Supplements, 25 Dec. 1993: YE-18; 24 Dec. 1994: YE-24; 23 Dec. 1995: YE-26.

THE STRUCTURE OF RECORD COMPANIES

Corporate Structure

The upper level structure of the big six recording companies is basically the same. As shown in Figure 2-1, each corporate owner usually holds several different businesses in addition to its recording companies. These other business range from other entertainment enterprises such as film, television, and magazine publishing, to consumer electronics, to alcoholic beverages. The music group usually includes at least music publishing and record companies, but may also include record retail operations. The record group then usually includes various labels, which tend to operate as free-standing units for purposes of A&R and marketing, the record distribution system, which distributes all labels owned by the company plus others under a variety of agreements, and a manufacturing division, which makes all of the owned labels' CDs and tapes and usually also special orders from outside labels.

The conglomerates have significant vertical integration. That means they seek to own and control all aspects in the production of their products from the raw ingredients to retail sale to consumers. Most of these corporations own labels that control the creative inputs from recording artists. They own music publishing companies, controlling the creative inputs from songwriters. They own manufacturing facilities to make the tapes and CDs that will be sold to the public. They own distribution companies to get the recordings to the retailers. At least one (EMI) owns retail stores where the final sale is made, and three (BMG, Time Warner, and Sony) have ownership interests in record clubs, another form of retail selling. They also seek horizontal integration when they buy up competing labels in order to insure a larger total share of the recording market.

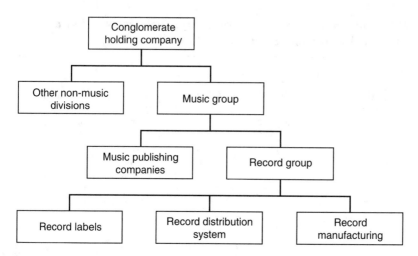

FIGURE 2-1   Typical "Big Six" Conglomerate Structure

Structure at the Label Level

Although the two basic functions of any label are A&R and marketing, any given label may perform those functions in depth, spread across a number of departments and personnel, or simply either not do them or hire an outside organization to provide the service (outsourcing). Figure 2-2 illustrates the divisions likely to be present at a large label. While there is not a great deal of commonality in what a given label may call a particular department, the divisions are typical.

The basic responsibilities of each department are as follows:

Label President

This person is usually someone who has experience in A&R, though not necessarily. Sometimes the presidents come from the business affairs departments and are attorneys, less often they are from the marketing departments. The president oversees all operations, but depending on the depth of his or her personal involvement in A&R, either as a producer or "talent scout," the other divisions may have additional independence. (Note that the business affairs and accounting divisions are "staff" divisions not directly involved in the production and marketing of the recordings.)

Business Affairs

This is usually the legal department of the label. It is in charge of negotiating artist and producer agreements and other licensing arrangements, including sampling and film use. Distribution deals with other labels, soundtrack album deals, and foreign licensing deals are typically finalized by this department. An advantage of this split

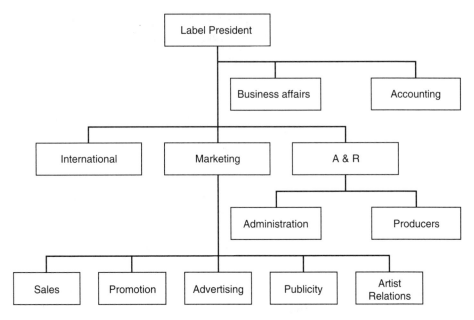

FIGURE 2-2　Typical Individual Label Organization

of the negotiating function from the president or A&R people is that it enables the creative people and the marketing people to be at peace with the artist, while any hard-nosed bargaining goes on with individuals who are not as likely to have to deal with the artist in later production or marketing of the recordings.

Accounting

Accounting is critical to the profitability of the company in any business that depends on so many sales of so many different individual units and there are so many people with an interest in each unit. The counting of sales, returns, free goods, and promotional albums and the payment of royalties to at least three (artist, producer, and music publisher) but as many as a dozen or more interests (multiple artists, multiple producers, a different publisher for each song) per recording is a complex task. The accounting departments can rest assured that artists, producers, publishers, and the Harry Fox Agency are all likely to audit the account books for any given album or artist once every year or two.

International Division

This unit works out international distribution deals and coordinates marketing plans around the world. It may be responsible for A&R in foreign territories. Some smaller labels either hire other labels outside of the United States or hire a major U.S. label to take care of international marketing and distribution for them.

Marketing

This is usually the largest division of a label. However, a small independent label may rely on a deal with a major label to supply all of these services while the small label only provides an A&R function. The term "marketing" (see Chapter 7) is significantly more broad than most record companies use the term in their internal structure. Although actual distribution is through a separate distributing company, the responsibility of the marketing department is to get the recordings to the consumer through retail and rack sales, and to promote consumer awareness of the records through radio and TV airplay, print publicity, and advertising in any and all media.

Sales

The sales department is responsible for getting orders for records from rack jobbers, major retail chains, and one-stops. There may be merchandising specialists working in sales whose job it is to visit stores and help set up displays. Sales people may be organized on a national, regional, or local basis, or may be set up by account size or type, then regionalized or localized.

Promotion

The primary job of promotion is to get exposure through radio and video airplay. Some labels separate the radio and video promotion arms. Most large labels have their own promotion staffs and hire independent promotion people as well. Promotion people work with radio and TV broadcast outlets, and work with the artist when the artist is on a tour, whether it be a paying tour with concerts, or a promotional tour with showcases for local media people to hear the act. The promotion staff sees to it that the "right" people from the media and record retail get the opportunity to hear their artists whenever their artist is playing in a given locale. Promotion people may even have to take the artists around to visit local radio and television stations or record stores while the artist is on tour.

Advertising

Advertising personnel create the media plans to go with a given album or single. Because the advertising plan must be careful to promote a unified and consistent image of the artist and album, many labels create the actual advertisements that go to retailers or local radio or television stations. The advertising department will also make national media buys or dispense co-op advertising money to retailers and distributors who come up with advertising plans for label recordings. Co-op advertising money in the recording industry most often means that the label will pay 100 percent of the advertising costs for certain kinds of ads. Sometimes a label will go for a true cooperative advertising plan in which the expense is shared by the label and the retailer.

Publicity

Publicity consists of nonpaid exposure other than radio or music video airplay. This department contains people who write press releases, create press kits including artist bios (biographies) and photos, and try to get the artist appearances as talk show guests or performers on radio or TV. Publicity is probably one of the easiest functions for a label to farm out to independent publicists. In fact, an artist's manager will often have an independent publicity firm working alongside of the label public relations people. The publicity people try to see to it that while an artist is touring there is publicity material flowing to the media in towns where the artist will be performing, but ahead of the artist's actual appearance date. Publicity people will work with promotion people to set up press conferences or "meet and greet" opportunities for local media. The publicity department is also in charge of trying to get album reviews in local and national media.

Artist Relations

This department may go by a number of other names, including product development and career development. Whatever it is called, it has the primary task of coordinating the work of the other departments to be sure that there is a unified marketing plan for every album. People in this department often work with the personal manager of the artist to insure that a uniform image is projected. They may work with the artist or producer during the recording of an album to get a better idea of what the album is about and to develop a marketing plan that the artist will support. They will make sure that copies of the recordings for sales and promotion, as well as advertising and publicity, follow the artist whenever the artist is on tour. Artist relations is a function that labels began to add during the late 1970s as they became aware that marketing plans had to be more sophisticated in order to succeed.

A&R

The A&R (Artist and Repertoire) department is in charge of finding and recording artists. It may also look for songs for artists who do not write their own. Because the A&R department is in charge of delivery of a completed product, ready to be marketed, it also has to perform administrative duties associated with the finished master.

A&R Administration

This is where the coordination takes place for getting mechanical licenses and clearances for sampling. The administrative people must make sure that all people who played on an album get proper credits. They may help the producers screen material for an artist if asked. They coordinate delivery of the recording, artwork, and liner notes to make sure that all materials necessary to complete production of the tapes and discs are delivered to the manufacturing plants. They make sure that all musicians, artists, and producers get paid when they are supposed to for the initial production of the album.

Producers

These people are in charge of the recording process. They may find the talent and record it, record it after others have found it, or screen talent being pitched to the label. They may be "staff" producers who work for a salary and royalty or entirely independent of the label and just work for a royalty and advances. (See Chapter 6 for an in-depth discussion of producers.)

PROFITABILITY IN THE RECORDING INDUSTRY

In a given year it is likely that less than one percent of records will sell over 250,000 units (see discussion below). The large record labels are fond of saying that less than 20 percent of the recordings they release ever recoup their costs. The high profit margins on compact discs must make one a little suspicious of that calculation. As explained in Chapter 6, recording costs and some marketing costs are generally recouped (recovered) out of artist royalties. Table 2-3 illustrates a typical (and somewhat simplified) situation for pre- and post-recoupment profits. Using these figures, the label does not pay the artists their royalties of two dollars per copy until that royalty adds up to the total recoupable amounts. Suppose a major label spends $200,000 in recoupable production and marketing costs. Suppose total production and marketing costs are $300,000. It will take sales of 100,000 units for artist royalties to equal the "recoupable" amounts. By that time the label's gross profits, after deducting the actual costs of publisher royalties and manufacturing, are $630,000—over $300,000 of actual profits. Even allowing for the label paying for its overhead, that is a substantial figure for a relatively "low selling" album. To reach the *economic* break-even point, where the total fixed costs (production and marketing) are equal to gross profits, only takes sales of 47,620 units (rounded up). That is calculated by dividing the $300,000 production and marketing costs as "fixed" by the $6.30 gross margin per disc sold. Consider the situation of an artist who has a lower royalty rate of only about one dollar per disc. It would take sales of 300,000 units to recoup artist advances. By that time the label would have gross profits of $1,890,000. Even after deducting the $300,000 in fixed costs for production and

TABLE 2-3   Pre- and Post-Recoupment Profitability

	Pre-Recoupment	Post-Recoupment
Wholesale price	$10.50	$10.50
Less: Manufacturing costs	$ 2.00	$ 2.00
Artist and producer royalties	$ 0.00	$ 2.00
Mechanical royalties	$ 0.70	$ 0.70
Distributor charges	$ 1.50	$ 1.50
Gross margin	$ 6.30	$ 4.30

marketing the label then has a net profit of $1,590,000 on that recording. So, for a lot of artists who never see any royalties on the sale of their albums the record companies *are* making money.[19] Thus, the labels can afford to try to release more albums, even if sales are relatively low. In effect, they are being subsidized by the artists because recoupment of advances at the artist royalty rate is a lot slower than actual recovery of total fixed costs at the label's gross margin per CD rate. This high profitability, particularly on CD sales, also fuels the independent labels.

THE "INDIES"

Independent record companies are usually thought of as those not owned by one of the major labels or conglomerates. Such a definition is rather broad, covering everything from a small label in a large city with a couple of artists, which just markets recordings on a local or regional level, to Disney, which is part of a major entertainment company (just not one of the big six), to a label with a significant artist roster and national distribution through independent distributors, such as Rounder or Alligator, or a label that has its recordings distributed by one of the big six but is not owned by them. Some people would argue that the latter is not a true indie because it is not distributed through true independent distributors, but in a time of consolidation and vertical integration any label that is not *owned* by a major label is deserving of the title of "indie."

The indies play an important role in the recording industry. They are a development area for record labels. Several of what might now be called major labels began life as indies, Warner Brothers, Arista, and MCA, for example. The indies provide consumers with diversity and specialty music that the larger labels often ignore because the small volume of sales, in the 3,000 to 30,000 units range, is not enough for a large label to consider. They also provide the larger labels with a source of new talent and new directions in music. The rock and roll explosion began on independent labels. New Age music began as an independent phenomenon and many of the labels were then bought out by the large corporations as it proved to be commercially successful. Rap began on small inner-city independents, then entered the mainstream, then was bought into by the large labels.

Size of the Indie Labels

SoundScan and RIAA data indicate that the independent labels account for about 21 percent of the sales, yet they release about 66 percent of the titles. Of over 17,000 titles released in 1995, 11,000 were by independent labels—almost a two-to-one ratio of independent releases to major label releases. The vast majority (90.5 percent) of current releases (not just new, but catalog as well) sell less than 5,000 copies per year. The number of recordings selling over 250,000 per year was just 148 in 1995, but those recordings accounted for over half of the total sales volume. Most of those were released by the major labels.[20]

How do the independent labels survive? The growth of the megastores carrying tens of thousands of titles has provided a place for the independent labels to sell their products to a larger audience. They have also relied on specialty independent stores in larger cities. They keep production and marketing costs low. Coupled with the high profit margins in CDs, low-cost albums can turn a profit with minimal sales. As Table 7-1 in the marketing chapter indicates, a low-cost CD generates a margin of over six dollars per copy. If that recording can sell 3,000 units it will earn over $18,000 in profits. If recording and marketing costs are kept low, $10,000 or less, then there is substantial profit. There is even profitability in having more low-budget, low-selling albums than having fewer. Because these recordings are not so costly to make or market, more titles can be released aimed at a very small market. That is the same as it was even back in the 1940s. A *Billboard* article describes indie labels in 1949 as having break-even points on singles of 5,000 units, compared to the majors' break-even points of 15,000 units.[21] The National Association of Independent Record Distributors (NAIRD) represents over 700 small labels, mostly in the specialty music areas of bluegrass, reggae, dance, jazz, classical, and others. That figure of 700 does not even count the thousands of custom albums that do not go through independent distribution but are sold by the artists only in their own locales or at their performances.

Indie Labels and Indie Distribution

Although some independent labels are distributed by the majors, most indie records find their way to the marketplace through independent distributors. Most independent distributors operate on a regional basis and some even on a national basis. A trend of the 1990s was the growth in size of independent distributors and the consolidation of independent distribution into fewer firms. For example, in 1995 Passport Music Distribution was formed out of Encore Distribution and Sound Solutions (USA), (an import and budget distributor). Passport, in turn, was part of the largest independent distributor, Alliance Entertainment, which also owns Independent National Distributors and the labels Castle Communications, Concord Jazz, and Red Ant Entertainment.[22]

DIVERSITY IN SPITE OF ITSELF

A particularly popular criticism of the recording industry is that it is run by huge conglomerates that for one reason or another are bent upon shoving much "bad" music down the throats of consumers while "good" music and artists languish without access to the system.[23] To be sure, there is much in popular music at any given time that may not measure up well on some critical scale. The labels are large bureaucratic organizations that tend to be conservative in their releases and follow the patterns of previous successes. At the same time a large label must be aware that, because the majority of releases are not likely to produce much profit, the only way to stabilize revenues is to have a large number of releases so that enough of them will make enough profits to support the superstructure. The big six conglomerates must behave like the investor for a retirement fund. Wall Street analysts know that the best way to minimize risk in the stock market is through a diversity of holdings. That way the main risk is only that inherent in stocks as a kind of investment instead of a particular company. So the large label will release artists that essentially compete with each other as well as those from other labels instead of risking large sums on a single artist who might not catch the public's fancy.[24] Large numbers of releases make it likely that more consumers will find recordings that they like and will buy. The worst problem for the industry would be a market diminished overall because there were fewer releases.[25] The trend, then, should be towards diversity of music being offered rather than towards homogeneity. That trend has been noticed by some observers as not what would have been predicted by the presence of larger and larger conglomerates controlling more and more of the market.[26] In fact one observer predicts that levels of high product diversity are most associated with moderately concentrated markets and that less diversity is associated with low and high levels of concentration.[27] The question is whether the recording industry is at such a high level of concentration (about as high as it could get and still meet the "effective competition" definition earlier) that diversity will begin to suffer.

SUMMARY

In any discussion of the basic structure of the recording industry it is important to remember that there at least three perspectives from which to discuss the labels. First, one can look at the individual names on individual labels. For some purposes that may be the best way because individual labels, even if owned by the same corporate conglomerate, tend to compete with each other for artists and for the consumers' dollars. Labels can also be viewed based on ownership at the corporate level.

From that perspective, the six conglomerates control about 80 percent of the industry. Finally, one could look at labels from the perspective of distribution. The number of distribution firms is smaller than the number of individual labels, or the number of label firms, due to the high costs associated with distribution. The concentration of distribution in the six multinationals is about the same as the concentration of market share by corporate ownership, but there are significantly fewer competing independent distributors and they too appeared to be going through a phase of concentration of ownership in the mid 1990s. The individual label perspective focuses on the A&R function. The distribution perspective focuses on the marketing function. The ownership perspective focuses on the profitability of the "bottom line." All three perspectives can provide valuable insight into the workings of the recording industry. Each is used at different times throughout this book

NOTES

[1]Richard Caves, *American Industry: Structure, Conduct and Performance* (6th ed. 1987): 10.
[2]See for example, Caves, supra note 1; Paul Keat and Philip K. Y. Young, *Managerial Economics: Economic Tools for Today's Decision Makers* (1992): 402.
[3]Russell Sanjek and David Sanjek, *American Popular Music Business in the 20th Century* (1991).
[4]"Top Pop Records, 1949" *Billboard*, 12 January 1950: 14.
[5]Nev Gehman, "Poll Clocks 35 Also-Rans for Every Solid-Selling Disk Hit," *Billboard*, 3 January 1953: 1.
[6]Nev Gehman, "The Year's Music Roundup," *Billboard*, 2 January 1954: 11.
[7]Gary Kramer, "Record Firm Rule of Thumb Slips from Fickle Public Pulse," *Billboard*, 22 December 1956: 1.
[8]Bob Rolontz, "72 Labels Landed on Charts in '58—a Feverish Year," *Billboard*, 5 Jan. 1959: 3.
[9]"LP Crown to Columbia, Victor Tops in Singles," *Billboard*, 5 Jan. 1963: 4.
[10]"Columbia and WEA Top Charts for 3rd Straight Year," *Billboard*, 17 Feb. 1993: 1.
[11]Ed Christman, "WEA Remains Top U.S. Music Distributor in '95," *Billboard*, 20 Jan. 1996: 55; Ed Christman, "WEA's '94 Market Share Dips Slightly, But Still Top U.S. Distributor with 21.1%," *Billboard*, 21 Jan. 1995: 54; "SoundScan Releases 1996 Music Industry Figures," Reuters Financial Service, 6 Jan. 1996 (LEXIS).
[12]Unless specifically noted, the information for this section comes from several sources, including: Standard and Poor's *Stock Reports* and *Industry Surveys;* Guy A. Marco, *Encyclopedia of Recorded Sound in the United States* (1993); Russell Sanjek and David Sanjek, *American Popular Music Business in the 20th Century* (1991).
[13]"Warner Cos. Restructured as WEA Inc.," *Billboard*, 11 Nov. 1995: 60.
[14]*Sony Corporation and Consolidated Subsidiaries Annual Report 1995*, on-line edition (http://www.sony.co.jp/Corporate Cruise/).
[15]Mark Dezzani, "BMG Buys Europe's Last 'Major' Indie," *Billboard* 20 Aug. 1994: 38; Don Jeffrey, "Acquired by BMG, Private Music Begins a New Age," *Billboard*, 5 Feb 1994: 6.

[16]Jeff Clark–Meads, et al., "Thorn EMI Demerger Proceeding Smoothly," *Billboard*, 31 Aug. 1996: 1.

[17]Eric Boehm, "For Those with Cash EMI Has the Flash," *Variety*, 12 Aug. 1996: 7.

[18]Chris Morris, "MCA Purchases 50% of Interscope," *Billboard*, 2 March 1996: 13.

[19]See also, Don Cusic, *Music in the Market* (1996): 179.

[20]Tom Silverman, "Preserving Diversity in the Music Biz," *Billboard*, 18 May 1996: 6.

[21]"Indies' Surprise Survival," *Billboard*, 3 Dec. 1949:1.

[22]Ed Christman, "Alliance to Acquire Red Ant Entertainment," *Billboard*, 24 Aug. 1996: 3; Jim Bessman, "Indie Distributor Changes More Than Name," *Billboard*, 20 May 1995: 47; Ed Christman, "Alliance Shifts Distrib Gears: Trans World Fills No. 2 Slot," *Billboard*, 5 Feb. 1994: 64.

[23]See, for example, Reebee Garofalo, "How Autonomous Is Relative: Popular Music, the Social Formation and Cultural Struggle," *Popular Music*, Jan. 1987: 77.

[24]A structure observed by Richard A. Peterson and David G. Berger, "Measuring Industry Concentration, Diversity, and Innovation in Popular Music," 61 *American Sociological Review* (1996): 175.

[25]An argument made in Jon Stratton "Capitalism and Romantic Ideology in the Record Business," *Popular Music*, 3 (1993): 183.

[26]Robert Burnett, "The Implications of Ownership Changes on Concentration and Diversity in the Phonogram Industry," *Communication Research*, Dec. 1992: 749.

[27]Peter J. Alexander, "Entropy and Popular Culture: Product Diversity in the Popular Music Recording Industry," 61 *American Sociological Review* (1996): 171.

3

Music Publishing:
The Second Stream

This income stream is referred to as the music publishing stream and not the songwriting stream because very few people have ever made any money from writing a song. The money was made from the publication (uses) of that song. Even when songwriters "own their own" songs, the songs are almost always actually owned, in the copyright sense, by a music publisher, even if it is the songwriter's music publishing company. Therefore the primary focus of this chapter is music publishing instead of songwriting. However, there are so many aspiring songwriters in bands and as "just plain" songwriters that the development of writers deserves some mention here. The same has been done for aspiring recording artists throughout the book.

THE MUSIC BUSINESS THREE INCOME STREAM MODEL—REVISITED

The three income streams in the music business discussed in Chapter One, recordings, music publishing, and live performances, are interrelated. The common element in the relationship is recordings. There would be very little music publishing revenue without popular recordings. The sale of the recordings provides mechanical royalties for the publishers of the songs on those recordings—about 34 percent of music publishing income (see Figure 3-1). Another 15 percent of publishing revenues are derived from radio airplay of recordings (Table 3-1). The majority of print music sales are of piano–vocal editions and "folios" of popular singles and albums. A substantial portion of television music performances, although there is no available estimate of the percentage, are either songs made popular by recordings or of recordings included in soundtracks of television programs. The same holds true for synchronization royalties from motion pictures. Finally, the vast majority of live and recorded performances (12 percent of publishing revenues) are of songs made popular by recordings. Even if only a third of the television performance and film synchronization royalties are the result of songs being made popular by recordings, that would account for another 6.5 percent of publishing revenues. Totaling these up, *an estimated 77 percent of music publishing royalties are the result of popular recordings.*

MUSIC PUBLISHING: THEN AND NOW

"Copyrights Don't Talk Back."[1]

The music publishing business is not what it used to be. In the 1890s music publishers sold millions of copies of sheet music. In 1893 *After the Ball* became the first song to sell one million copies of sheet music. Hit songs sold as many as two million copies in print by 1909. Even though sound recordings were catching on in 1920 and accounted for about three million dollars of publishing revenue, sheet music sales still accounted for over 16 million dollars, about 88 percent, of publishing income. Sheet music sales plummeted during the Depression to a low of about two million dollars in 1933. During that same time performance revenues, largely from radio, grew and sustained the music publishing industry through World War II.[2] Print sales failed to make a significant recovery after the war. *Billboard* reported in 1955 that publishers faced finding new income because sales of even the most popular songs

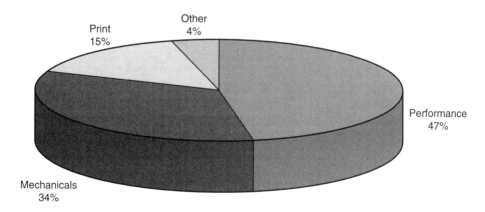

FIGURE 3-1   U.S. Music Publishing Income Sources: 1994
Source: National Music Publishers' Association.

TABLE 3-1   Music Publishing Income Sources: U.S. Details 1992–1994 (Millions U.S. Dollars)

Source	1992	1993	1994
Radio Performance	$ 147	$ 156	$ 184
TV/Cable/Satellite	$ 258	$ 209	$ 242
Live & Recorded	$ 97	$ 127	$ 150
Phono/Mechanical	$ 305	$ 365	$ 427
Synchronization	$ 51	$ 51	$ 52
Print	$ 172	$ 177	$ 187
TOTAL	$1,048	$1,102	$1,242

Source: National Music Publishers' Association, Inc.

in sheet music were usually less than 300,000 units. The "reliable" source of income was performance royalties.[3] That, however, was before rock and roll jolted record sales into ever higher gears and pushed mechanical royalties into a close second place behind performance royalties. Even though revenue from print music recovered and accounted for about 38 percent of the publishers' estimated $283 million share of revenues by 1978, the music business had been forever changed.[4] By the 1990s the recording industry dwarfed music publishing. In 1994 domestic revenue from the sale of recordings was $12 billion—nearly ten times the $1.24 billion reported by the National Music Publishers' Association for that same year.[5] Revenues from the sale of recordings and from performances accounted for 83 percent of music publishing income while distribution of print music now is reduced to a share of about 15 percent (see Figure 3-1). A century of technological innovation and evolution and the concomitant change in copyright laws (see Chapters 9 and 10) has turned an industry that once created and marketed products into a copyright industry that primarily licenses others to utilize its properties.

OVERALL STRUCTURE

Music publishing is now an integral part of the recording industry. Every major label owns publishing interests. Many smaller labels, independent producers, and recording artists own publishing interests. Despite the existence of literally thousands of small music publishers, most of the rights are administered through a handful of publishing giants. The small songwriter, artist, and producer-owned publishing companies simply do not have the expertise or personnel to deal with the complexities of music publishing. They enter into agreements with some of the giants to copublish or to administer their catalogs.

The large publishing companies are getting larger by acquisition of smaller companies or by entering administration or copublishing agreements that allow the "Goliaths" to share in the revenues generated by the "Davids." The willingness of the larger companies to use this approach makes it possible for smaller companies to exist and be profitable. It also removes one of the mediators between the songwriters and their audiences. No longer is the publisher trying to second-guess what an artist or producer will want to record and therefore accepting only "safe" songs. "Safe" songs in the 1990s are songs that are written by songwriter/artists who are already under contract or who have good possibilities of obtaining recording contracts.

The two largest music publishers in the world, EMI Music and Warner/ Chappell Music, are owned by two of the largest recording conglomerates in the world. In the late 1980s and 1990s record conglomerates actively built their music publishing interests. All of them have engaged in major publishing acquisitions. Sony Music had no publishing when it started in 1989 with the acquisition of the CBS record labels. CBS had earlier divested itself of its music publishing with the sale of CBS Songs to SBK Entertainment in 1986. At that time CBS Songs was one of the five largest music publishers in the world. By 1993 Sony Music had emerged as a top ten music publisher in the U.S. through acquisitions such as the Tree catalog (Tree was the most successful country music publisher at that time) in 1989. In 1994 Sony Music entered a "co-venture" deal with Michael Jackson, who owns many Beatles tunes in his ATV Music catalog. Sony reportedly paid Jackson $100 million for that deal and continues to expand.[6] PolyGram International Music Publishing went from a major player to minor league when it sold Chappell Music to Warner Brothers in 1984 for about $200 million. PolyGram immediately reentered the publishing fray with the acquisition of Dick James Music (early Elton John/Bernie Taupin catalog) in early 1985, Cedarwood (a Nashville firm), and others.[7] BMG Music Publishing began in 1987 and went on a rebuilding spree after the acquisition of RCA's labels and music interests, buying seventy-three catalogs in a five-year period from 1988 to 1993. BMG acquired foreign licensing from Famous Music (Viacom's music publishing division of Paramount) in 1995 when Famous's previous deal with Warner/Chappell expired.[8] BMG competes with PolyGram for the number three spot among the music publishers of the world. MCA Music Publishing also announced its intention to compete globally through catalog acquisition. MCA mentioned no specific catalogs except to say a seven-figure deal was pending for a Nashville company.[9]

The competitiveness of the conglomerate-owned publishing companies is evident in their success at having their songs on hit recordings. As Tables 3-2 through 3-4 indicate, the top two popular music publishers in terms of chart share across all three most popular genres, pop, R&B, and country, are EMI and Warner/Chappell. Sony would be fairly clearly third with Zomba and PolyGram about tied for fourth, and MCA and Almo are roughly tied for sixth. Zomba (owned by Clive Calder of the UK) and Almo (owned by Rondor Music International) are independent.

Why the sudden attention to music publishing by the recording conglomerates? For one thing, the mechanical royalties paid by record companies to music publishers for the right to make recordings of songs are expenses to the labels. If labels owned publishing in the songs their artists recorded, they could take their mechanical royalty expenses out of their record company pockets and put them as revenues

**TABLE 3-2   Top Pop Publishers, 1992–1995
(by Number of Singles in Top 100)**

Publisher	Average Rank	Years in Top 5	Average Number of Singles
EMI Music	1	4	188
Warner/Chappell	2	4	102
Sony Music	3.3	3	41.7
Zomba	4.5	2	45
PolyGram Music	4	2	24
MCA Music	3	1	50.5
Almo	5	2	18.5
Velvet Apple	5	1	2

Source: *Billboard*, Year End Issues, 1992–1995.

into their publishing company pockets. Most recording artists in the 1990s were entirely self contained—they wrote and performed their own compositions. It was no longer necessary to obtain songs from a music publisher who had songwriters creating songs for other people to record. The record companies marketed the recordings that created the hit songs. Why, reasoned the labels, should some other party get all the benefit from the label's promotion of the recordings? Finally, the income stream from music publishing is more stable and longer term than the income stream from the hit recording that produced the hit song. A label will probably get only three or four shots at earning income on a hit record: the original recording, a greatest hits collection, perhaps a boxed set if the artist really has a long career, and later reissues as historical or collector's items. Every one of these also makes money for the publisher. In addition, the publisher gets royalties every time the original record gets played on the radio as an "oldie," whenever the artist performs it on

**TABLE 3-3   Top R & B Publishers, 1992–1995
(by Number of Singles in Top 100)**

Publisher	Average Rank	Years in Top 5	Average Number of Singles
EMI Music	1	4	206
Warner/Chappell	2	4	107
Zomba	3.7	3	63.3
MCA Music	3.3	3	58.7
Sony Music	4	3	30.7
PolyGram Music	5	1	38
Willesden	4	1	22
Flyte Tyme	5	1	12

Source: *Billboard*, Year End Issues, 1992–1995.

**TABLE 3-4   Top Country Publishers, 1992–1995
(by Number of Singles in Top 100)**

Publisher	Average Rank	Years in Top 5	Average Number of Singles
Sony Music	1.25	4	62.5
Warner/Chappell	2.25	4	59.75
EMI Music	3	4	58
PolyGram Music	4	4	36.75
Almo	4	2	25
MCA Music	5	1	35
BMG Music	5	1	34

Source: *Billboard*, Year End Issues, 1992–1995.

television, when it is turned into background music for use in hotels, restaurants, and other businesses or organizations (sometimes referred to as in a tongue-in-cheek manner as "elevator music"), when sheet music is sold, and most importantly, when someone else records it. The potential to earn royalties even without recordings is limited but clearly illustrated by the song "Happy Birthday." Very few recordings are made of "Happy Birthday" any more, but the asking price for the copyright that song, which is *not* public domain, was $12 million in 1988. "Happy Birthday" reportedly earns one million dollars a year in royalties.[10]

Cover versions, recordings made by an artist different from the one who originally recorded a song, can generate publishing profits for years. For example, the song "Who's Sorry Now," originally written in 1923 and a Number 2 hit for Connie Francis in 1958, has been recorded over four hundred times by artists all over the world, ranging from the Glenn Miller Orchestra, to Willie Nelson, to Nat "King" Cole by 1985.[11] That is what publishers call an "evergreen," a song that keeps on earning royalties long after the popularity of the original recording has faded. Country songwriter/artist Dolly Parton wrote her song, "I Will Always Love You," for her 1974 *Jolene* album. It was a number one country single that year. Then in 1982 it was included in the film version of *The Best Little Whorehouse in Texas* and again hit the top of the country charts. But the greatest success came from the smash hit performance by R&B/Pop artist Whitney Houston in the soundtrack for the movie *The Bodyguard* over a decade later.[12] Even songs written and originally recorded by rock artists may turn into hits by other artists years later. In 1977 the rock group Aerosmith had a number two hit with "Walk This Way." Nine years later, Run-D.M.C. had a number one hit with a version of it in a genre, Rap, that did not even exist when Aerosmith's first version was recorded.[13]

Copyrights generally last for the life of the songwriter plus fifty years (or for seventy-five years for works first published between 1906 and 1978; see Chapter 9 for details), long after most people have lost any interest in purchasing the original recording of a song. The value of the copyrights in the master recording is likely to have a much shorter life. The record company can therefore extend the earning potential of the hit recording they originally created by having an interest in the song that the recording made popular as well as in the original recording.

MUSIC PUBLISHING FUNCTIONS

Basic Functions

Music publishers perform much the same functions with songs that labels perform with recordings. The primary difference is that the publisher deals with an intangible property right, the copyright, and the label, although it will acquire copyrights in the sound recordings (masters), is much more concerned about selling physical copies of those masters in the forms of CDs and tapes. The primary functions of a music publisher are then, the acquisition of copyrights and the exploitation, in a positive business sense, of those copyrights.

Publishing Company Structure

Music publishing company internal structure and functioning very much mirrors the two primary functions of acquisition and exploitation of copyrights. Those functions are usually split between creative and administrative divisions. The creative division is in charge of signing songs and songwriters to contracts with the company, promoting the company's catalog of songs to prospective users ("song plugging"), and possibly developing potential songwriter/artists in a role not unlike that of A&R people at record labels. Usually the people undertaking these roles are known as "professional managers." (Do not confuse professional managers at music publishing companies with personal managers for artists, discussed in Chapter 4.) The professional manager is frequently a song doctor, working with songwriters to help them create the most marketable songs. Professional managers must know producers, artists, A&R people, movie producers, and as many other potential users of their songs as they can to fulfill the role of song plugger. Because they become familiar with what makes the best recording for a song and often produce the demos used to promote the song to producers and the like, it is not uncommon for professional managers to become record producers as well.[14]

The administrative side of the music publishing company is the paperwork side of the business. It will usually include copyright administration, licensing, accounting, and perhaps business/legal affairs units. The copyright administration unit takes care of registration of the publisher's songs with the Copyright Office, recordation of other information with the Copyright Office, such as notices of death or transfers of ownership, and renewal of copyrights for songs published prior to 1978. The licensing unit works with the Harry Fox Agency (or other mechanical licensing agency) and the publisher's performing rights organization affiliate for the clearance of new compositions and recordings, and directly issues other licenses, including print licensing, advertising uses, and others. Because the music publishing business is one of pennies earned from royalties from the various uses of the songs, the accounting unit is very important. With thousands of uses for thousands of songs by hundreds of different songwriters it is a major task to insure that everyone receives their proper payments for their songs. If there is a separate business/legal affairs department it will be in charge of contract negotiation with songwriters, complex license negotiations, and catalog acquisitions.

COPYRIGHT ACQUISITION

The Traditional Way

The classic model for copyright acquisition goes like this. Songwriters, either on their own or under contract to music publishers, are moved to write songs about something. Melody and lyrics are created and woven together. The songs are presented in some manner ("pitched"), perhaps by a live performance, perhaps by a demonstration recording ("demo"), to publishers. The publisher tries to assess the potential that the song has for being recorded by other people. If the publisher believes a song is likely to be recorded the publisher signs a contract with the songwriter in which the songwriter assigns the copyright to the publisher in exchange for roughly half of any royalties that may be generated by the exploitation of the song. The publisher and songwriter enter into a kind of partnership, with the songwriter creating a product that the publisher will then attempt to market. The publisher will probably have a high quality demo made of the song to present it to people likely to record it. The publisher will then "pitch" the song to recording artists, producers, and A&R people at record labels with the hope of attracting someone to record it. Once it is recorded and released the publisher will then (perhaps) help promote it to radio stations. If the song is successful enough, the publisher might have sheet music printed and sold. The publisher will also try to get other artists to cover the song. The publisher may try to get it used in motion pictures. Meanwhile, the publisher will sit back and collect royalties from the sale of copies of the recording, and from the performances of the song on radio and television. Generally speaking, half of the money is kept by the publisher and half is paid to the songwriter.

For a long time, beginning before the invention of phonograph recordings, that is the way it worked. In the late 1800s and early 1900s songwriters wrote tunes, publishers' employees called "song pluggers" pitched them to minstrel show performers and vaudeville performers. The song pluggers got their name from the fact that a performance before an audience was called a "plug" for the song. People would not buy sheet music for the songs until they had heard the song in performance. The more plugs a song got, the more exposure it got. The more exposure it got, the more sheet music it sold. In those days it was more common for a songwriter to receive a flat fee for a song than a royalty. Songwriters wrote tunes that went into their own or others' theatrical productions. With the advent and increasing popularity of recordings in the early 1900s, the song pluggers pitched tunes to recording artists and A&R people at record companies to get them recorded. In the 1920s, 1930s, and 1940s song pluggers pitched tunes to band leaders to get them performed on network or local radio. For many of these plugs the publisher would often pay a "gratuity" to the performer. This widespread practice later turned into "payola" in the record industry (see Chapter 11).

The "Modern" Model

*"There are fewer and fewer artists who are
just singers. I mean, Bing Crosby's gone."*[15]

The emergence of rock and roll transformed the music publishing business just as it transformed radio and the recording industry in general. In rock it was much more common for the songwriter who wrote the song and the artist who recorded the song to be the same person. Some say it was this "genuineness" of message from songwriters interpreting their own compositions that created much of the appeal of rock music. For performers who understood the business, it may have been an attempt to gain some economic rewards from their performance of a song, in addition to its sales in recordings. Because there was no performance right in a recording, the only way to share in the income generated by radio and television performances was to be a songwriter or copyright owner of the musical composition.[16] While there were great pop songwriters who did not record their own material in the 1960s and 1970s (Bert Bacharach, Carole King and Gerry Goffin, Brian Holland, Lamont Dozier, and Eddie Holland [the Holland–Dozier–Holland team who wrote many of Motown's great hits] to name just a few), the trend was, and still is, towards the artist/writer dominating the popular music field, particularly rock. Even in country music, the last bastion of the "traditional" songwriter–publisher relationships, the artist/writer has become the dominant model (Table 3-5). (The 1994 and 1995 numbers in country in Table 3-5 are a bit of an aberration.) Many of the songwriters whose names appear in *Billboard's* top ten songwriters lists defy categorization. Kenneth Edmonds (a.k.a. "Babyface") is one of the most successful songwriters of the 1990s. He is a recording artist with hit records of his own, he has produced other artist's hits, plus he has his songs recorded by artists whom he does not produce. A significant number of the songwriter/artists in the Top 10 list not only write for themselves, but for other artists as well. It is extremely rare to find a songwriter in the pop Top 10 list who is a songwriter only. One of the most successful of such songwriters is Diane Warren. The other trend of the 1990s is cowriting. Two-thirds of the songwriters in the Top 10 lists for 1991–1995 wrote songs with other songwriters, producers, or artists.

TABLE 3-5   Top Songwriter Trends

	1991	1992	1993	1994	1995
Pop					
Artist	7	5	6	7	8
Producer	2	3	3	2	0
Writer	1	2	1	1	2
R&B					
Artist	4	7	6	4	5
Producer	3	1	2	2	3
Writer	3	2	2	4	2
Country					
Artist	6	6	7	2	2
Producer	0	1	0	1	2
Writer	4	3	3	7	6

Source: Compiled from *Billboard's* Music Publishing Spotlights, 1 June 1996, 3 June 1995, 7 May 1994, 8 May 1993, 16 May 1992.

How does a publisher proceed to acquire copyrights under the new model? Many publishers have taken on an A&R function. They actively seek songwriters who are, or have the potential to become, recording artists as well. They attempt to sign these songwriters to publishing deals before they are signed to record companies. The publisher may pay the songwriter/artists an advance in a form that allows them to develop their writing, arranging, and performing talents without having to keep a "day job." The publisher also helps the songwriter/artist seek recording and management contracts, even going so far as to use the publishing company's studios to create a master that can be released on an independent label in the hopes of selling 20,000 to 30,000 copies. Songwriters/producers are also a target for this kind of development by publishers, particularly in the R&B and urban field. In exchange for that developmental advance and the possibility of future royalties, the songwriter/artists pledge their output of songs for several years to the publisher.[17] Perhaps the most successful example of this tactic is Alanis Morissette, whose *Jagged Little Pills* album became the best selling debut album by a female artist when it passed the eight million copies mark in 1996.[18] She had been signed to a publishing deal with MCA Music Publishing in Canada for seven years before her 1995 album debut.[19] Even in such developmental deals, the publishers often have to content themselves with a smaller share of the total publishing income by entering copublishing deals with the songwriter/artist's publishing company.[20]

Publishers also bid for the publishing rights to the songs of new songwriter/artists who have just signed with labels. If the songwriter/artist does not sign with the label's affiliated publishing company at the same time they sign a recording agreement, then the publishing is particularly attractive because there is a high probability that the songs will be earning royalties as soon as the songwriter/artist and label complete and market their first album.

Finally, publishers still sign individual songwriters to agreements even when the songwriter is not likely to develop into a recording artist. In such instances the song material has to be particularly strong because the publisher will have to find a market for it instead of having a ready-made market with a songwriter/artist's own recordings. It is also still possible for songwriters to have individual songs accepted by a music publisher even though the songwriter is not under any long-term agreement with the publisher. This is, however, becoming much less common in all genres.

Songwriter Agreements

Single Song Contracts

The most basic agreement between a publisher and songwriter is the single song agreement. It is signed whenever a publisher acquires the copyrights to a song, whether it is from an unknown songwriter for one song only, or from a songwriter under a long-term exclusive songwriter agreement (see below). Most of the terms in a single song agreement, like most of those in an exclusive agreement, are negotiable. What appears below are the terms likely to be in a typical agreement.[21] If the songwriters are of sufficient stature, have their own publishing companies already set up, or already have a recording agreement, then they may increase their share of the publishing revenues by negotiating a different kind of deal, such as copublishing or administration. One observer commented, "Fading into distant memory is the era when, by and large, a publisher took a song and held 100% of the publishing."[22]

Typical single song agreement terms:

- Grant of rights: The songwriter assigns (sells) all of the copyrights in the song to the publisher for the life of the copyrights, throughout the world. International rights are somewhat negotiable, especially if the publisher is not large enough to have the ability to market the song on a worldwide basis.

- Reversion: Any grant of copyright is subject to the Copyright Act's termination right. The songwriter has the statutory authority to end a transfer of ownership or nonexclusive license after a period of thirty-five to forty years (see Chapter 9 for details). A songwriter with some leverage may also be able to negotiate a contractual right to have the publisher transfer the copyrights back to the songwriter if the publisher fails to have the songs recorded or "published" within some set period of time, usually one to two years.

- Advances: Advances are prepayments of royalties that the publisher will seek to recoup out of royalties earned. In a single song agreement the advance is usually a small lump sum ranging from nothing to several hundred dollars. Several hundred dollars is typical. Publishers usually will not pay advances unless the songwriter has some track record of success or the near assurance that the song will be recorded by some popular artist or by the songwriter/artists themselves. Major advances occur only in exclusive songwriter agreements.

- Royalties:

    1. Mechanical royalties are usually divided 50/50 after any collection fee from the Harry Fox Agency or other mechanical collection organization is deducted.
    2. Performance royalties are usually split by the collecting performing rights organization (ASCAP, BMI, SESAC, and a few smaller agencies) and paid separately to the publisher and songwriter. Therefore, the songwriter does not usually get any percentage of what the publisher collects. *If* the performance income were paid 100 percent to the publisher then the songwriter would expect to get 50 percent of the publisher's net.
    3. Print royalties may simply be split 50/50 out of the publisher's net receipts. More often, the publisher pays a percentage royalty based on the wholesale or retail price of the music being sold, or even a "penny" rate (a flat rate of so many cents per copy sold). If a percentage of a price is used, the songwriter typically gets 10 percent to 15 percent of wholesale for folios (songbooks), 10 percent of wholesale for other print (not including sheet music). For sheet music (also known as piano–vocal editions) publishers often pay a penny rate of seven to ten cents per copy. This approach to sheet music does not come close to a 50/50 split because the publisher is paid a percentage of the retail price approximating 70 to 80 cents per copy. The per copy sheet music rate is not often negotiable. One songwriter refers to it as a "sacred cow."[23]
    4. "Other" royalties and fees covering a wide range of uses and unspecified uses are usually split 50/50 of the publisher's net receipts.

- Cross-collateralization: The publisher will usually ask that any advances be recouped out of any royalties due to the songwriter under "this or any other agreement" between the two parties. For example, royalties earned in one year can be used to recoup advances paid in an earlier year. Royalties earned from one song can be used to recoup advances paid for a different song. The worst scenario is that publishing advances can be recouped from any recording royalties or advances, although it would be more common for recording advances to be recouped out of publishing advances if the songwriter/artist had signed recording and publishing agreements with the same company. A songwriter can usually at least limit the cross-collateralization in a publishing agreement to publishing royalties. On the other hand, a publisher would have no right to cross-collateralize against a songwriter/artist's income earned from a concert performance, because that agreement would not be between the songwriter/artist and the publisher, but rather between the songwriter/artist and a concert promoter.

- Demo costs: Publishers try to recoup demo costs by deeming them to be "advances" in their agreements with the songwriters. A new songwriter could expect 50 percent of demo costs to be recoupable, with as little as none recoupable for a songwriter with a good track record. Other publisher expenses are generally not recoupable at all.

Exclusive Songwriter Agreements

Under these contracts the songwriter agrees to deliver all of the songs written for a certain period of time to the publisher in exchange for a usually substantial advance against royalties. Previously written songs may also be covered if their copyrights have not already been transferred to some other publisher.

Typical exclusive songwriter agreement terms:

- Royalties: The base rates and splits are typically structured as in the single song agreement above.
- Exclusivity: These contracts are "exclusive"; that is, the songwriter agrees that no other publisher can have claim to the songs written during the agreement. To put it another way, the publisher says, "Thou shalt have no other publisher before me."
- Duration: The term of the agreement is usually for one year with up to four one-year options to extend the agreement for another year. These options are the publisher's. If the publisher wants to keep the songwriter under the contract, and keep paying the advances, then the publisher may elect to do so after the end of each year. If not, the contract simply ends. Of course, the publisher usually is able to keep the all copyrights in all songs written during the term of the agreement. The obligation to pay royalties on those songs would also continue after the end of the agreement, because each individual song is transferred for the life of the copyright under a single song agreement as outlined above.
- Advances: The primary reason for a songwriter to enter an exclusive agreement is the promise of the publisher to pay a substantial advance against royalties. These advances (sometimes known as a "draw") usually range from several hundred dollars a week for a new songwriter to thousands of dollars a week for an established songwriter, or a songwriter/artist who is successful. Even songwriter/artists without a recording agreement may get substantial advances if the publisher believes enough in the material and the ability of the songwriter/artist to get a recording contract. Publishing advances may even go so far as to purchase substantial amounts of recording equipment for songwriter/artists to perfect their craft.
- Output requirements: The publisher may require the songwriter to complete a certain minimum number of songs per year, typically twelve to twenty. The songs will usually have to be "accepted" by the publisher. The minimum may even be stated in terms of commercially recorded songs, especially if the songwriter is also an artist.

• Collaboration: Writing with other songwriters is especially important to a songwriter's creative processes and to getting material recorded. Some songwriters take half-finished songs to recording artists and suggest that they finish them together. The result is that the songwriter now is a half-writer of the song with the artist. Half a loaf is better than none, but it is important to make sure that the half loaf counts towards the minimum number of songs commitment if there is one. It is also important to the songwriter that other "collaborators," such as producers or artists who did not really create any of the composition, cannot be added as songwriters without the original songwriter's permission.

Songwriter Royalty Example

Assume an artist has a number one hit. How much money would the songwriter of that song make? As with many such questions in the recording industry, the answer is, "It depends." Several assumptions have to be made before one can even begin to calculate.

• First, it is likely that this song is licensed for mechanical royalties at 3/4 of the statutory mechanical royalty rate, even if the songwriter is not the artist, because of restrictions on total mechanical royalties in many artist agreements (see Chapter 6 for details). At the 1995 statutory mechanical rate of 6.95 cents per copy that would equal 5.2125 cents per copy. Also assume that the mechanicals are collected through the Harry Fox Agency. It is not uncommon for a hit single to sell "gold" (500,000 units) so let's assume that is the case. Let's also assume that the album containing the song has also sold 500,000 units and is also licensed at a 3/4 rate.
• Assume that performance royalties are collected and divided by the PRO and paid 50 percent to the publisher and 50 percent to the songwriter separately. Performance royalties for one year vary greatly depending on the genre of the music, how long it is a hit, and whether it receives television airplay. One report had performance royalties for a country hit varying by as much as $80,000 or more depending on how much airplay even a "number one" song receives and on what stations. An "average" figure that is close for all three PROs would be about $140,000 for one year for either the publisher or songwriter share.[24] Another estimate placed royalties for an "major across-the-board chart song" at as much as $650,000 for a pop song with significant television airplay.[25]
• Assume a ten cent per copy rate for sheet music and that the song has sold 80,000 pieces. This assumption may be a bit rash because many singles do not have sheet music printed.
• Finally, assume the songwriter is under an exclusive agreement and has been receiving an advance for the past year of $300 per week, a total of $15,600.

Susie Songwriter Royalties

Mechanical Royalties:	
Single sales: 500,000 units @ 5.2125 cents	26,062.50
Album sales: 500,000 units @ 5.2125 cents	26,062.50
Total:	52,125.00
Less: HFA collection fee 3.5%	1,824.38
Net Mechanicals collections	50,300.62
Writer's share @ 50%	$ 25,150.31
Print sales: 80,000 copies @ 0.10 per copy	8,000.00
Gross earnings from publisher	$ 33,150.31
Less: recoupable advance 52 weeks @ $300	$ 15,600.00
Net due from publisher	$ 17,550.31
Performance royalties (writer's share paid directly to songwriter)	$140,000.00
Writer's earnings	$157,550.31
Plus advance	15,600.00
Writer's net earnings	$173,150.31

The advance is added back in to show that it is money that the songwriter actually had received during the year and probably used to live on. That looks like a respectable sum, but most songs are not number one hits. In fact estimates are that only about two to five percent of songwriters make $10,000 per year.[26] Also, if the song was cowritten with just one other person, Susie Songwriter would only receive half of the above amount from the various royalties.

Other Copyright Acquisition Methods

Because so many songwriters, producers, and recording artists have their own publishing companies, there are lots of small "catalogs" of songs (all the songs owned by a publisher are its "catalog") available for possible purchase. These small publishers' catalogs are often bought by larger publishers. Larger catalogs of independent publishers are also purchased, typically by the major publishers. In a catalog purchase the buying publisher usually obtains copyrights to all of the songs in the catalog as well as demos of those songs. The amount paid for the catalog varies greatly and depends on the number and value of the songs included.

Sharing the Publishing

A successful songwriter or songwriter/artist may be able to keep part of the publishing in their own publishing company and agree to split the ownership of the copyrights with a larger publisher. This is called copublishing. The songwriter still gets a 50 percent share, and the two publishers split the remaining 50 percent in a negotiated share, often 50/50. The net result of such a deal is that the songwriter gets 50 percent of the revenues, the songwriter's publishing company gets another 25 percent of the revenues (half of the publisher share), and the copublisher gets the other 25 percent of the revenues.[27] At a minimum, the copublisher then takes care of administrative duties associated with the songs, such as collection of royalties, licensing, and copyright administration. In addition, the copublisher may actively engage in plugging the song.

Instead of owning a share of the copyright the larger publisher may be content to make a deal just for a percentage share of the revenues earned in exchange for providing the administrative support for the catalog. These copyright administration deals usually involve catalogs from successful artists and producers and smaller independent publishing companies. Administration fees charged by the administrative publisher are typically 10 percent to 25 percent of gross publishing revenues. Gross publishing revenues would include the share of songwriter income that flows through the publisher, as well as the publisher share. Administrative deals usually do not last for the duration of the copyrights, but rather for a period of three to five years, including renewals.

EXPLOITING COPYRIGHTS

Income Sources

Most publishers make all of their revenue from licensing (permitting others to use) their copyrights. Unlike record companies, which make most of their money from the sale of copies of their masters, music publishers (with a few notable exceptions) do not directly sell copies of anything. They license other people to do that. Understanding the various income sources for music publishers is then understanding the various licensing arrangements that lead to these income sources. As Figure 3-1 indicated, music publishers earn most of their revenues from three sources: public performances, sale of recordings, and sheet music sales. Another significant source of revenue for some publishers is synchronization fees—licensing songs for their use in motion pictures, television, and home video. So, how does one get permission to use a song in any of these fashions? As any publisher would probably say, "No problem, just bring money."

Performance Licensing

Copyrights in songs include the right of public performance. Note that this is not limited to "for profit" performances because many nonprofit performances are not exempt by the copyright act (see Chapter 10 for more details).

There are tens of thousands of nightclubs, retail stores, radio stations, television stations, and other places where music is performed publicly. The practical difficulties inherent in any single publisher attempting to license all of these outlets has led to the creation of performing rights organizations (PROs), which act as clearing houses for the publishers to license large numbers of performance places and for the performance places to access the thousands of songs of thousands of publishers. There are three major PROs in the United States: ASCAP (The American Society of

Composers, Authors and Publishers), BMI (Broadcast Music, Inc.), and SESAC (SESAC is no longer an abbreviation of anything in particular).[28] Although these three organizations compete to sign songwriters and publishers, and aggressively pursued licensing previously unlicensed users in the early 1990s, the share of publishing income from performance licensing did not increase as steadily during that period as mechanical royalties (see Figure 3-2). A comparison of the three organizations on various points follows the description of basic performance licensing.

How Performance Licensing Works

The three PROs function in very similar manners. They all acquire nonexclusive rights to license public performances from the songwriters and music publishers that belong to their organizations. The rights are nonexclusive because the publishers retain the right to license the works directly themselves. The PROs obtain only *nondramatic* performance rights. Dramatic performances, those which involve the performance of more than one composition from an opera or musical theatrical production or the use of the composition to tell a story in some dramatic manner (as on stage or screen),[29] are licensed directly by the publisher or by a theatrical licensing agency that represents the publisher. Dramatic performance rights are known as "grand rights" and nondramatic performing rights are known as "small rights." Both the publisher and the songwriter of the composition must belong to the same performing rights organization. Most music publishers of any size operate at least two separate companies, affiliated with different PROs, so that any songwriter that the publisher may sign can be accommodated, whichever PRO the songwriter prefers.

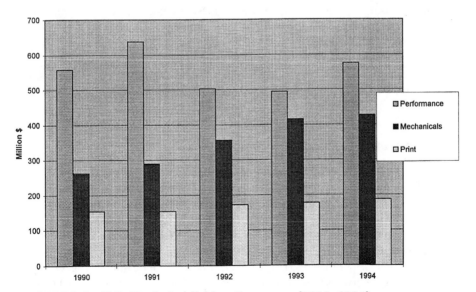

FIGURE 3-2   U.S. Music Publishing Revenues (1990–1994)
Source: National Music Publishers' Association, Inc.

The PROs then issue licenses to anyone and anywhere their music might be performed publicly. (See Chapter 10 for a definition of public performance under the Copyright Act.) Figure 3-3 indicates the flow of the licenses from the initial copyright owners to the licensees, and of the royalties/license fees collected from the licensees back to the songwriters and publishers. For most places where music is performed the most economical way to obtain permission to use a vast number of songs is to obtain a "blanket license." The blanket license from a performing rights organization allows the licensee to perform, or have performed under its roof, any of the compositions that the PRO represents, as many times as desired. Such a license is particularly valuable to radio stations and nightclubs where thousands of different songs may be performed, some of them hundreds of times. Keeping track of individual performances would be a real nightmare. The Supreme Court of the United States has even recognized the value of the blanket license. In an antitrust suit brought against BMI by Columbia Broadcasting System, the Court upheld the validity of the blanket license, saying,

> [T]he blanket license developed . . . out of the practical situation in the marketplace: thousands of users, thousands of copyright owners, and millions of compositions. Most users want unplanned, rapid, and indemnified access to any and all of the repertory of the compositions, and the owners want a reliable method of collecting for the use of their copyrights. Individual sales transactions in this industry are quite expensive, as would be individual monitoring and enforcement, especially in light of the resources of single composers. . . . A middleman with a blanket license was an obvious necessity if the thousands of individual negotiations, a virtual impossibility, were to be avoided.[30]

The PROs must also offer a per-use or per-program license to those users who wish to take advantage of it. Per-use or per-program licenses are more costly on a per-song basis, but may be less expensive overall than a blanket license if a broadcaster, particularly a television broadcaster, only needs access to a very limited number of clearly identified compositions on a regular basis.

Who Obtains the License?
Although technically speaking the actual musician performing a song live in a club would be liable for the public performance, it is the operator of the venue who is obtaining the benefit of the performances who must obtain the license. Therefore, owners of nightclubs, owners of radio and television stations, owners of retail outlets where background music is being played, and owners of concert venues (or the concert promoter if the venue does not have much music performed during a typical year), all must have performance licenses to cover the compositions performed in their establishments. There is an exception to the public performance right for a place publicly receiving a regular broadcast transmission on simple home-type receiving apparatus. (See Chapter 10 for more detail.)

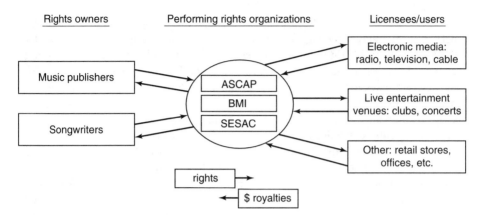

FIGURE 3-3   Performing Rights Licensing

How Much Is the License?

The cost of the license depends on a number of factors. Background music licenses cost less than live entertainment licenses. Live entertainment licenses cost less than broadcast performance licenses. The bigger the operation in terms of physical size, number of seats, amount of music being performed, power of transmitter, and other factors, the more the license costs. A small store might obtain background licenses for a few hundred dollars per year. A major night spot, such as a casino in Las Vegas, spends tens of thousands of dollars per year. A television network spends millions of dollars per year for broadcast performance licenses. ASCAP and BMI deduct their operating expenses from the available pot of money. SESAC does that as well as taking a profit for their owners.

Who Gets the Money?

The PRO collects the license fees from all of the various users, then attempts to determine how much money each song in the PRO's repertoire is entitled to receive. This daunting task is accomplished somewhat differently by the different PROs (see below). Suffice it to say, however, that the best any of the PROs can do is get an exact count of performances from some licensees, such as the television networks, get a sample of a larger group such as local radio stations, and use those as an estimate of what songs were performed live in clubs, discotheques, and as background music. The various methodologies are the subject of great debate among the three organizations as to who does the best job of accurately paying their publishers and songwriters. The methodologies all have their merits and shortcomings and no one is perfect, or will ever be perfect because of the virtual impossibility of monitoring all songs played live in clubs. Nightclubs and other live performances account for about 26 percent of performance license fee collections (see Table 3-1).

Once the amount to pay for each song is determined, the PRO divides the payment in half and sends half to the songwriter and half to the publisher. If there are multiple songwriters or multiple publishers the PRO divides the money according to the directions supplied by the songwriters and publishers. If a songwriter specifically instructs the PRO to pay the songwriter's share to the publisher, perhaps because the songwriter is a staff songwriter who has a significant advance to be recouped, the PRO will do so.

Comparing ASCAP, BMI, and SESAC

- Organization: ASCAP is a nonprofit organization run by its "members," the publishers and songwriters. BMI is a corporation owned by broadcasters but which operates on a nonprofit basis. SESAC is a privately held corporation that operates on a profit-making basis for its owners (who are not the songwriter or publisher affiliates).
- Size: BMI claims to represent 180,000 songwriters, composers, arrangers, and publishers. ASCAP boasts 68,000 members of the same kind. SESAC, though clearly the smaller organization with 2,700 affiliates, has become much more aggressive in acquisition of songwriter catalogs in recent years, notably with acquisition of licensing rights to Bob Dylan's and Neil Diamond's catalogs.[31] ASCAP reported receipts of $422.7 million in 1995 and distributed $356.7 million to its songwriter and publisher members.[32] BMI calculates its 1995 collections as $337 million. SESAC does not publicly report its annual receipts but they were estimated at about $8 million before the significant rights acquisitions of the Bob Dylan and Neil Diamond catalogs.[33]
- Kinds of music licensed: Initially SESAC had a stronger hold in Latin and gospel music, ASCAP in "standards," because it was the oldest organization, and BMI in country, R&B, and rock. Now all three organizations compete well in all genres.
- On-line clearances: All three organizations have on-line listings of their repertoire. They also allow on-line clearance of songs by users and listings of new songs by their affiliates. ASCAP and BMI do this by means of their Web pages on the World Wide Web, and SESAC by a bulletin board separate from their Web site.[34]
- "Logging" methodology: A detailed discussion is beyond the scope of this text but important recent changes in methodology for all three PROs indicate that more music from more diverse sources and voices is being logged, and paid royalties. All three organizations have been expanding the scope of their sample and improving its accuracy in recent years. For example, ASCAP began actual monitoring of live performance venues and getting song logs from the top one-hundred touring acts.[35] BMI added college radio stations to its list of stations completing logs. SESAC increased the number of radio formats for which it receives actual airplay information from BDS (Broadcast Data System).[36]

(BDS monitored just under 1,000 stations in 1996, but not in all formats.) All of these changes mean that more songs will be logged and paid for their performances. This means that not only mainstream hits will be logged, but also songs by artists who either do not receive much airplay or who receive airplay on small stations, or less popular formats. This in turn increases the prospect for non-mainstream songwriter/artists to collect performance royalties for their songs and increases the possibility that they can sustain a career.

Broadly speaking, all three PROs get actual program logs from television and radio networks that provide a numerical "census" of airplay. ASCAP *samples* local TV and radio by actually recording broadcasts and deciphering which songs have been played. BMI *samples* by requiring all of its broadcast licensees to complete an actual log, accounting for every song played, once per year for one week. SESAC was the first to use the BDS to obtain actual counts of which songs were performed on stations monitored by BDS and combines that with other information to make their best estimate of performances. Because BDS does not monitor all radio stations, this too is a sample. All of these methods still only provide an estimate of the total number of actual performances for any given song. Some song performances will never be logged. Other songs may have their performances overrepresented in the sample because they are mainstream hits and are performed in all markets. The PROs attempt to adjust for these shortcomings in their methodologies, but none of the systems is perfect.

- Age: ASCAP was founded in 1914 to begin to develop a way for U.S. composers to collect for live performances of their songs. SESAC was founded in 1930 primarily to license European composers' music in the United States. BMI was founded in 1940 to provide broadcasters with music to play when they refused to agree to pay the fees demanded by ASCAP in the 1940 license negotiations.
- Payments: The three organizations debate long and hard about who will pay the most money. There are situations in which either might pay more for a given song than the other two depending on where and how often it was performed. A comparison of average payments on hit songs revealed that the three were within about a seven thousand dollar range of each other out of an average songwriter share of about $140,000. However the PROs reported a range from a low of $114,000 to a high of $194,000 for recent hits (country).[37]

Mechanical Licensing

Although the Copyright Act allows a record company to procure a statutory (compulsory) license to record a musical composition (see discussion in Chapter10), most labels prefer to obtain negotiated licenses from the publishers. The National Music Publishers' Association (then the Music Publishers' Protective Association) established the Harry Fox Agency (HFA) in 1927 to provide a clearinghouse for mechanical rights for the rapidly growing sales of recordings and piano rolls in the

1920s. Now the HFA issues and collects for about three-fourths of the mechanical and synchronization licenses in the United States. By 1995 the HFA represented the catalogs of over 15,000 music publishers and had annual collections of $450 million. The agency charges the member publishers collection fees of 3.5 percent of mechanical royalties collected, 10 percent for motion picture synchronization collections up to a maximum of $250 per song, 4 percent of other synchronization collections up to a maximum of $2,200 per song, 5 percent for electrical transcriptions (recordings that are not for sale to the public) up to $2,200 per song, and 4.5 percent for import licensing. In addition to collecting the fees from the record labels and distributing them to the appropriate publishers the agency conducts audits of its licensees on behalf of the members. The HFA reported audit recoveries of $12 million in 1994.[38] As indicated by Figure 3-4, these collections are distributed to the publishers, who then divide them with the songwriters according to their contractual agreement, usually 50/50. The HFA allows potential licensees to obtain licenses electronically via their World Wide Web site.[39]

Mechanical Rates

Although most mechanical licensing is not through the statutory compulsory license, the rates tend to follow the compulsory rate. Because a large number of the compositions licensed are by songwriter/artists and because these people tend to have controlled composition clauses in their recording agreements (see discussion in Chapter 6), most licenses are for three-fourths of the "statutory" rate. The HFA states that it will not issue mechanical licenses at a rate below the statutory rate without instructions from the publisher, but publishers are often willing to do so, especially when songwriter/artists are involved. The net result is that typical mechanical license rates in 1996 ranged from 5.2125 cents per side to the full statutory rate of 6.95 cents per side. The increase in statutory mechanical rates beginning in 1978 from 2.75 cents (it had been 2.0 cents since 1909) to 6.6 cents in 1994 represented a 240 percent increase, only slightly ahead of the 227 percent increase in the consumer price index for the same period.[40] Total mechanical royalties collections for the same period increased from $148.5 million to $427.2 million, a 288 percent increase. The growth of total mechanical royalties at a rate greater than inflation is

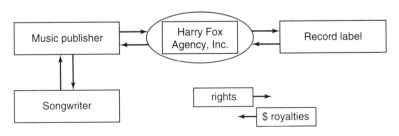

FIGURE 3-4   Mechanical Licensing

accounted for by the "real" growth in sales of recordings during that time period as indicated in Chapter 1. Figure 3-2 indicates the rapid growth of mechanical royalties compared to others in 1990–1994. Performance income increased from an estimated $238 million in 1978 to $575 million in 1994, a 242 percent increase, just ahead of the inflation rate.[41]

Print Publishing

Structure

Total sheet music publishing sales amounted to $3.2 billion in 1994. About $350 to $400 million of that was sold through record stores according to the American Music Conference.[42] Most music publishers, even some of the largest, do not manufacture and distribute print editions of their own songs. Some do not even license print editions of their songs at all. As many as 25 percent of the top one hundred hits do not appear in print editions.[43] Economies of scale in manufacturing and distribution have collapsed print music publishing into a highly concentrated industry with only four major players: Warner Brothers Publications (the print division of Warner/Chappell Music, owned by the Time/Warner conglomerate), Hal Leonard Publishing Corp. (an independent), Cherry Lane Music (an independent), and Music Sales Group (a U.S. company with publishing and retail interests in the UK). A fifth player, C.P.P.–Belwin (formerly owned by Columbia Pictures) was purchased in 1994 by Warner Brothers Publications after Warner lost the EMI Music print rights to Hal Leonard.[44] EMI Music, arguably the world's largest music publisher, has its print publishing done through Hal Leonard, as do Paramount's Famous Music, Disney, MCA, PolyGram, and BMG. The print music oligopoly is even tighter when the songs considered are current hits. The two giant print publishers, Hal Leonard and Warner Brothers Music (individually and in some cases jointly), control roughly equal shares of the sheet music for hit songs.[45] It is unusual to see any other print publisher with sheet music rights to more than one or two songs in the top one hundred.

Print Licensing

Print licensing income amounts to only about 15 percent of total publishing income (Figure 3-1), but the United States has a significantly higher percentage of worldwide print income than it does of other publishing revenues (see Table 3-6). The print publisher typically agrees to pay the music publisher as follows: 35 to 50 cents per copy for sheet music (piano/vocal) if a penny rate and 20 percent of the suggested retail list price (SRLP) if a percentage royalty, and 10 percent to 15 percent SRLP for folios (prorated based on the number of songs the particular music publisher has in the folio). The print publisher may have to pay an additional 2.5 percent to 5 percent for the right to use the recording artist's name on a "personality folio" that is keyed to a particular artist or album. Print rights are usually granted on a nonexclusive basis to the print publisher, with the duration of the license being three to five years.[46]

TABLE 3-6   U.S. Share of Worldwide Publishing Revenues, 1994 (Millions U.S. Dollars)

Source	Worldwide	U.S.A.	U.S.A. Percent
Performance	$2,591	$ 575	22.2%
Phono/Mechanical	$1,810	$ 427	23.6%
Synchronization	$ 459	$ 52	11.3%
Print	$ 535	$ 187	35%
Other*	$ 443	$ 1	0.2%
Total	$5,838	$1,242	21.3%

*Other includes broadcast mechanicals, private copy, reprint, rental, interest investment, and miscellaneous.

Source: National Music Publishers' Association, Inc.

Synchronization Rights

Synchronization rights refer to the right to use music, as the contracts often put it, "in timed relation to visual images." In the early days of attempts to accompany motion pictures with sound, recordings were played while the motion picture was being played and elaborate devices attempted to keep the sound synchronized with the screen action. When the sound became integrated on the film on a separate track it still had to be synchronized because the sound had to precede the image with which it was associated in order for the viewer to perceive the sound as originating at the correct time from the screen. Synchronization rights must be obtained for film, television, and videogram (home video) uses. Licenses are highly individualized, depending on the nature of the use of the song in the film (is it a theme, or featured as in a performance, or simply background?), the amount of the song that is used (a few seconds or wholly), and the stature of the song (is it a recognizable hit or a new song that might benefit from exposure in the film?).

SONGWRITING

"Great songs are about people's hopes, dreams, and aspirations."
—BILL LOWERY[47]

Because, as some people say, "It all begins with a song," why consider songwriters last in this chapter? Because all of the things discussed above have implications for people who want to write songs. With rare exceptions, the songwriters of pop, rock, and R&B hits tend to be the people who perform them or produce them. Even in country music, being a "just plain songwriter" is becoming increasing difficult. A connection with an artist or producer is extremely important. A connection with a music publisher is extremely important. Most publishers will not accept unsolicited demos of songs. To get that contact at the publisher, songwriters can perform in showcases, perform in clubs, work through a performing rights organization, or just knock on doors. A songwriter will have to do these things someplace where a publisher is likely to hear them. Writing with a songwriter who already has songs placed with a publisher is also a quick track to the inside.

As to song content, we have all heard songs on the radio that we think are not very good. Perhaps they just do not communicate with us personally. Perhaps they really are not very good in that they do not communicate very well with anybody. Those songs may not be well crafted in terms of lyrics and structure. The craft of songwriting can be learned. There are numerous books on the subject.[48] The songwriters' organizations in the major cities often have songwriters workshops. The performing rights organizations often have songwriters workshops and seminars. The important thing is to write often and to get feedback from somebody who has some background or experience that qualifies them to judge songs. It is difficult for many songwriters to accept even constructive criticism because the very nature of the early stages of songwriting is that the songs are highly personal statements. There is not much point to complain, "Well, they are *my* songs and I don't care if anybody else will understand them." If that is the songwriter's real perspective then she or he need not be trying to get a publisher or label interested in the songs. If, however, the songwriter would like to use the songs to communicate or share ideas or feelings with a broader audience, then the use of popular music as a communication medium is appropriate. If a songwriter or artist asks others to invest time and money in a message, then the investors need some reasonable assurance that the song or recording stands a chance of recouping the initial investment, i.e., that it is reasonably commercial.

Songwriting is both art and craft. While it is easy to write a song, it is difficult to come up with a song that is well crafted and has enough appeal to get an artist to feel that it could be a hit. Country songwriter Will Rambeaux put it this way: "It takes years to develop that craft to the point where you're writing songs that are good enough for the radio. I know that sounds simple and shallow, but it's not easy to do that, to write songs that have universal appeal."[49]

NOTES

[1] A quote attributed to publisher Lou Levy, founder of Leeds Music, who died in 1995. In Irv Lichtman, "Publishing Legend Lou Levy Dies at 84," *Billboard*, 11 Nov. 1995: 8.

[2] An excellent long-term statistical compilation of publishing revenue data is found in Philip H. Ennis, *The Seventh Stream: The Emergence of Rocknroll in American Popular Music*, (1992): 100.

[3] Paul Ackerman, "New Income Studies Face Publishers as Sheet Music Income Drops," *Billboard*, 15 Jan. 1955: 1.

[4] Paula Dranov, *Inside the Music Publishing Industry* (1980): 8.

[5]Irv Lichtman, "Japan Hops to 2nd in NMPA Survey," *Billboard*, 20 July 1996: 34.

[6]Irv Lichtman, "1995 a Year of Deals, Court Action, and Legislation," *Billboard*, 23 Dec. 1995: 57; Irv Lichtman, "Sony Pub Adds Nile Rogers, Fisher Catalogs," *Billboard*, 17 June 1995: 14; Deborah Evans Price, "Sony Adds to Country Music," *Billboard*, 7 Oct. 1995: 74; Edward Morris, "Hilley Named President/CEO at Sony Tree," *Billboard*, 5 Feb. 1994: 9; Irv Lichtman, "Sony Establishes New Vigor in Market Share," *Billboard*, 17 April 1993: 1.

[7]Jeff Clark–Meads, "PolyGram Takes Globe via London," *Billboard*, 22 July 1995: 36.

[8]Irv Lichtman, "Famous to BMG in Global Shift," *Billboard*, 28 Oct. 1995: 1; Irv Lichtman, "Firth Says BMG Publishing Can Double Biz in 5 Years," *Billboard*, 10 July 1993: 6.

[9]Irv Lichtman, "MCA Music Eyes 'Mid-size' Power," *Billboard*, 4 May 1996: 39.

[10]"Cake, Candles Not Included," *Time*, 31 Oct. 1988: 59.

[11]*See, Mills Music, Inc. v. Snyder*, 496 U.S. 153, at 158 (1985).

[12]Joel Whitburn, *Top Country Singles 1944–1988* (1989).

[13]Joel Whitburn, *Joel Whitburn's Pop Singles Annual 1955–1986* (1987).

[14]Deborah Evans Price, "Writer–Producers Churn Out Hits in Music City," *Billboard*, 20 April 1996: 38.

[15]Warner/Chappel Music creative VP, John Titta, quoted in Melinda Newman, "The A&R Angle," *Billboard*, 3 June 1995: 53.

[16]Ennis, *supra* note 2, at 104.

[17]See, e.g., Melinda Newman, "The A&R Angle," *Billboard*, 3 June 1995: 53; Larry Flick, "A&R Role Expanding for Publishers," *Billboard*, 5 Nov. 1994: 18.,

[18]Chris Morris, "April Sets Mark Milestones for Alanis, Beatles," *Billboard*, 18 May 1996: 12.

[19]Craig Rosen, "MCA Publishing Lands New Talent," *Billboard*, 28 Oct. 1995: 46.

[20]Irv Lichtman, "War Waged on Words: Pubs Expand A&R Role," *Billboard*, 26 Dec. 1992: 22.

[21]For a more detailed discussion of single song and exclusive songwriter terms of agreements see, for example, Al Kohn and Bob Kohn, *Kohn on Music Licensing,* 2nd Ed. (1996); Donald S. Passman, *All You Need to Know about the Music Business* (1994); Sidney Shemel and M. William Krasilovsky, *This Business of Music,* 6th Ed. (1990); Mark Halloran, *The Musician's Business and Legal Guide* (1991); Practising Law Institute, *Counseling Clients in the Entertainment Industry* (1994); Donald S. Farber (ed.), *Entertainment Industry Contracts: Negotiating and Drafting Guide* (1989); and Alexander Lindey, *Lindey on Entertainment, Publishing and the Arts* (1988). Farber and Lindey are loose-leaf publications that are updated annually.

[22]Irv Lichtman, "Strong NMPA Stats in Past Indicate Happy Times Now," *Billboard*, 25 Dec. 1993: 24.

[23]Al Kohn and Bob Kohn, *Kohn on Music Licensing*, 2nd Ed. (1996): 111.

[24]Michael Kosser, "Big Hits Mean Big Money," *American Songwriter*, Jan/Feb. 1995: 34.

[25]Jeffrey Brabec and Todd Brabec, *Music, Money and Success* (1994): 283.

[26]Tom Roland, "Not an Easy Way to Make a Buck," *The Tennessean*, 5 Jan. 1995: E1.

[27]These percentages are assuming that 100 percent is the total amount of ownership available. Music publishers and others often speak of 100 percent songwriter's share and 100 percent publisher's share when mentioning percentages. To avoid confusion it is important to be sure which method is used, 100 percent or 200 percent, as the total available royalties for all parties.

[28]It was called "The Society of European Stage Authors and Composers" when it was founded in 1930, but later changed its name to SESAC, Inc.

[29]Al Kohn and Bob Kohn, *Kohn on Music Licensing*, 2nd Ed. (1996), distinguish between a performance of a composition or several compositions from a dramatico-musical work such as an opera or musical, and a performance that is dramatic in that it is used to tell all or part of a story line being portrayed in a dramatic fashion. Even this distinction would not require a dramatic license for a straight performance of a song which in itself tells a story, such as "Ode to Billie Joe" or "The Wreck of the Edmund Fitzgerald," unless it was done in a dramatic fashion.

[30]*Broadcast Music, Inc. v. Columbia Broadcasting System, Inc.*, 99 S.Ct. 1551, at 1562–1563 (1979).

[31]Irv Lichtman, "SESAC Boosts Profile With Dylan, Diamond Signings," *Billboard*, 4 Feb. 1995: 1; Edward Morris, "SESAC Puts Out Its Welcome Mat," *Billboard*, 26 Feb. 1994: 13.

[32]Irv Lichtman, "1995 Receipts, Distributions Break ASCAP Records," *Billboard*, 24 Feb. 1996: 6.

[33]American Society of Composers, Authors, and Publishers, "Music for Money," ASCAP pamphlet, 1996: 1.

[34]The Web sites: ASCAP is http://www.ascap.org BMI is http://www.bmi.org SESAC is http://www.sesac.org

[35]Don Jeffrey, "ASCAP Revamps Live Show System," *Billboard*, 30 Sept. 1995: 10.

[36]"SESAC, BDS to Monitor More Genres," *Billboard*, 24 Feb. 1996: 12.

[37]Michael Kosser, "Big Hits Mean Big Money," *American Songwriter*, Jan./Feb 1995: 34.

[38]National Music Publishers' Association, *International Survey of Music Publishing Revenues* (1996). National Music Publishers' Association information.

[39]http://www.nmpa.org

[40]Converting the 1978 CPI of 195.4 (1967=100) to 65.26 (1982–84=100), and comparing it to the 1994 CPI of 148.2 (1982–84=100).

[41]Sources: Paula Dranov, *Inside the Music Publishing Industry* (1980); National Music Publishers' Association, *International Survey of Music Publishing Revenues* (1996); U.S. Bureau of Labor Statistics, *Monthly Labor Review*.

[42]Frank DiConstanzo, "Print Strikes Profitable Chord," *Billboard*, 24 Sept. 1994: 64.

[43]Based on a sample of *Billboard's* Hot 100 A–Z listings of the sheet music distributors of the Hot 100 singles chart songs in 1995 and 1996.

[44]Irv Lichtman, "WB Publications Agrees to Buy C.P.P.–Belwin," *Billboard*, 7 May 1994: 6.

[45]See note 42 above.

[46]See, e.g., Kohn and Kohn, supra note 22; Sidney Shemel and M. William Krasilovsky, *More About This Business of Music*, 5th Ed. (1994); Donald S. Passman, *All You Need to Know about the Music Business* (1994).

[47]Bill Lowery is the owner of Lowery Music Group in Atlanta, Georgia and a past president of the National Academy of Recording Arts and Sciences. This is something that the author heard him say publicly on a number of occasions.

[48]For example, Jai Joseph, *Writing Music for Hit Songs* (1989); John Braheny, *The Craft and Business of Song Writing* (1988); Pamela Phillips Oland, *You Can Write Great Lyrics* (1989); Sheila Davis, *Successful Lyric Writing* (1988).

[49]Quoted in Tom Roland, "Not an Easy Way to Make a Buck," *The Tennessean*, 5 Jan. 1995: E1.

4

Live Entertainment: The Third Stream

The power of the popular recording is overwhelmingly evident in the live entertainment business. The vast majority of the income generated in the live performance stream is created by popular artists performing the songs they have recorded. Two important trade publications, *Pollstar* and *Performance*, estimate tour grosses of major artists. *Performance's* list of the Top 50 grossing acts of 1995 contained only three nonrecording artists, Mighty Morphin Power Rangers (East and West editions), magician David Copperfield, and Walt Disney's World on Ice, which accounted for only 5.7 percent of the reported $635.3 million gross ticket sales from the Top 50 acts. The Top 10 grossing tours accounted for 53.4 percent of those ticket sales.[1] *Pollstar* estimated that ticket sales for major concerts amounted to $950 million in 1995 and their top fifty artists (which does not include nonmusical acts) accounted for 78.2 percent of ticket sales. As with recording sales, the majority of the revenues are generated by a small number of the artists.

How big is big? Major acts on the road in 1995 for example, included the Eagles, with fifty-nine shows, over a million attendance, and $65.6 million gross sales. Other shows of interest in 1995 included Boyz II Men, whose 139 shows were seen by nearly 1.5 million people and generated $43.3 million gross sales. The H.O.R.D.E. multiact tour played twenty-three dates with an attendance of over 360,000 and gross sales of $8.3 million. Country/pop act Reba McEntire was the highest grossing solo female artist with forty-one shows, attendance of over 446,000, and sales of $11.9 million. A last noteworthy performer is Luciano Pavoratti. He did three shows, seen by just over 41,000 people, but grossed $4.8 million.[2]

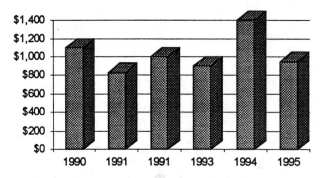

FIGURE 4-1   Touring Grosses 1990–1995 ($ Millions)
Source: *Pollstar,* 31 December 1995 and 31 December 1993.

The live performance income generated by major acts averaged about $1.1 billion per year in 1991–1995. Figure 4-1 shows that major tour income is not very consistent and maintained only a slight upward trend over the 1990–1995 period. The presence or absence of a couple of major stadium tours in a given year can change the gross receipts by as much as 55 percent. In 1994, stadium shows accounted for $143.9 million ticket sales, 10.3 percent of the gross that year compared to 3.9 percent in 1995 (see Table 4-1). Although not all live entertainment is before large audiences it is the large tours that account for the lion's share of the live performance revenues. There is generally, as one would expect, a decreasing share of dollar sales by the sizes of venues (see Table 4-1). *Pollstar* listed nearly 1,500 venues in its 1995 Concert Venue Directory. Even those 1,500 do not account for the thou-

TABLE 4-1   Venue Size and Share of Performance Revenues (Share of 1995 Performance Ticket Sales by Top 10 Venues in Each Size Range)

Venue Size	Top 10 Sales (1995) ($ Millions)	Percent of Total Sales
Stadiums	$ 37.5	3.9
Amphitheaters	$102.8	10.8
Indoor, 20,000 and over	$ 72.5	7.6
Indoor, 13,000–19,999	$ 71.5	7.5
Indoor, 7,000–12,999	$ 39.6	4.2
Indoor, 5,000–6,999	$ 54.7	5.8
Indoor, 3,000–4,999	$ 41.3	4.3
Indoor, under 3,000	$ 41.4	4.4
Clubs, 800 and over	$ 9.9	1.0
Clubs, under 800	$ 5.1	0.5
Total	$476.3	50.1

Source: Joshua Derr, "Year End Charts," *Performance,* 29 December 1995.

sands of small bars and clubs where aspiring musicians play for the "door," for tips, for their supper, or even for free, just for the experience and exposure.

THE MAJOR PLAYERS

There are five roles that must be filled in the live entertainment stream: performer, personal manager, talent agent, promoter, and venue operator.[3] (See Figure 4-2.) The role of the label is discussed later in this chapter. In an idealized situation the performer decides, usually in conjunction with the personal manager, that it is time to do a tour. The manager and performer decide when the tour should be, perhaps in conjunction with the release of a new album. Other details such as what parts of the country to play, what cities, what size venues, and how many dates are roughed out. The manager then contacts the talent agent (a.k.a. booking agent) who has contracted to arrange performances for the artist. The manager gives the agent the details that have been worked out to date and the agent and manager, in consultation with the artist, arrive at a minimum price for the show and some basic terms of a performance agreement. The agent then begins contacting promoters to line up potential dates. The promoters contact venues to see what dates are open for what prices and probably put "holds" on dates that would fit the tour. The promoters then call the agent back and say what dates and venues are available and present the agent with the basics of a deal. As the agent begins putting together pieces of the tour the

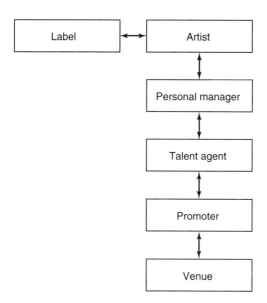

FIGURE 4-2   Concert Promotion: The Players

promoters are notified of any definite dates or at least which holds from the venue operators can be released for some other artist. Finally, when a tour itinerary is fairly firm the agent approaches the manager (and perhaps artist) for approval. If the artist and manager approve the agent begins to issue contracts to the promoters. The promoters then sign contracts with the venue operators. Then the promoters develop plans for advertising and promoting the shows and begin arranging whatever details are called for by the performer's agreement. With luck the performer shows up for the show, the tickets have all been sold, the performance happens without a hitch, and the promoter and artist's representative divide the receipts according to their agreement. That is the ideal world. In the real world things seldom go precisely that way or that smoothly. A closer examination of the roles of the major players will help explain why.

PERSONAL MANAGERS

"An artist's career represents a lot of investment in terms not just of money but of time, energy, sweat and disappointment."[4]

Structure of the Personal Management Business

The business of personal management is run by a large number of firms and managers, who generally manage only three or four acts—very few manage more than a dozen. There is no concentration of market share in the management business. *Performance* magazine's directory lists over 1,300 personal managers and management companies, and *Pollstar's* over 900, in the United States.[5]

What *Does* a Personal Manager Do?

It is difficult, if not impossible, to be a recording artist who performs live without someone at least performing the functions of a personal manager.[6] Personal managers are in charge of developing all aspects of a performer's career. To that end they must possess good "people skills" to be able to work closely with the artist and others in this income stream. They must also possess significant knowledge of the industry and contacts within the industry to be able to create the kinds of opportunities that the artist needs to develop a significant career. In the early stages the personal manager will work with the artist to develop a good live act and performance, giving the performer feedback and constructive criticism. Based on the manager's assessment of the artist's talent and potential the manager will probably develop a career plan that will at least take the artist through the first recording. The career plan will undoubtedly be altered later if the artist achieves substantial success and as other opportunities present themselves. The manager will help the performer become a better songwriter (if he or she is one) by providing feedback on songs or finding or hiring people who can. The manager will attempt to secure the artist a publishing agreement if that is a good possibility. The manager will find an appropriate agent for the artist at the early stages of the artist's career if the artist does not already have an agent. Managers do not generally procure personal appearances, except as ancillary to their job, for the artist. That is the agent's job. In fact, in California, it is illegal for managers to procure employment beyond a recording contract unless they are licensed talent agents. Most managers are not. The managers' most important task in the early stages is to get their artists to the point where they are ready to sign a recording contract, then help them get such a contract.

Once the artist has a recording contract, the manager works to see that the recording is released and is successful. The task probably begins by encouraging the artist to the successful completion of their first master recording. Usually the manager will watch closely the development of the label's marketing and promotion plans and may even assist by hiring independent promotion services or making sure that the artist performs the necessary promotional engagements. The manager will work with the label and the music video director to be sure that the marketing and promotion plans of the label and the video fit the artist's image and music. If the artist got the label deal without a publishing agreement or without an agency agreement, the manager will actively seek those deals for the artist as well. Once touring begins the manager will work to assure that everything goes as smoothly for the artist as possible. If the recording and tour are successful enough the manager does it all over again for a second album and tour.

As the artist's career progresses, the manager must begin to expose the artist to an ever-widening audience. The manager will probably attempt to get talk show appearances for the artist, variety show appearances, and perhaps, if the artist has any acting talent, motion picture and dramatic television appearances. Career growth will require more work from the manager, so the manager will probably expand by outsourcing some functions that the manager had performed at the early stages of the artist's career. Somewhere in this development the manager will probably need to engage the services of a public relations specialist, unless the management company is large enough to provide that service itself. In addition, the manager will probably need to engage the services of a business manager to handle the artist's monetary matters to assure that the income from the artist's peak earning years can be spread out and invested in ways to provide for future stable income.

Finally, the manager will attempt to sustain the artist's career for as long as possible if the artist is willing. Long after most artists have stopped having hit records, they are still able to have successful performing careers. The popular 1990s thing to do was the revival or reunion tour. Major artists from the 1960s, 1970s, and 1980s such as the Eagles, Jimmy Page and Robert Plant (Led Zeppelin), the Allman Brothers Band, and the Beach Boys (to name just a few) had Top 50 tours in 1995.[7]

The manager will help the artist make business and investment decisions that will ensure that the money made during the high earnings phase of a career will be paying dividends for a long time in the future, even through the artist's retirement.

On the "personal" side of the manager's role is that of caretaker, confidant, and surrogate mother. Says Bill Curbishley, the personal manager of Jimmy Page, Robert Plant, The Who, and Judas Priest (and others), "To be a personal manager, you're involved in their marriages, divorces, births, deaths, traumas, dramas, happiness, sadness—all of it."[8]

In order to do these things the manager must believe in the artist's abilities and desire to succeed. The artist must trust the manager implicitly with the details of the artist's career and the manager must be deserving of that trust. When the trust breaks down the relationship rapidly deteriorates. For many artists at a lower echelon of success the breakup simply results in frustration for the manager and a "What have you ever done for me?" from the artist. When the artist has achieved substantial levels of success the breakup can cost the manager literally millions of dollars, especially if the legal and moral trust that the manager holds have been breached. Writer/artist Billy Joel was awarded sums totaling over $2.6 million in separate suits against his former business manager for conversion of Joel's investments in a real estate partnership.[9] Former Beatle George Harrison won an $11.6 million recovery of half of the debt of his film company that the business manager had promised to pay half of but never did.[10] Harrison had won a suit against his former personal manager, Alan Klein, whom Harrison had fired in 1973. Klein later purchased Brite Tunes Music catalog, which contained the song, "He's So Fine." Brite Tunes then sued Harrison, claiming that Harrison's "My Sweet Lord" was a copyright infringement of "He's So Fine." A court ruled against Harrison on the infringement issue. Harrison then won a judgment against Klein saying that a personal manager could not buy the song in order to sue his former client. Harrison wound up owning both songs.[11]

Management Agreements

Although some attorneys refer to a personal management agreement as "air," because the manager usually just promises to exercise "best efforts" to promote the artist's career, there are some "typical" terms.[12] As with most entertainment industry agreements, these tend to be highly negotiated, especially if the artist has much stature. While some managers may be willing to work on an oral "handshake" agreement, most attorneys cringe at the thought of their client, either the artist or the manager, working under such nebulous terms.

- Compensation: Personal managers are typically compensated on the basis of a percentage of the artist's gross earnings. That percentage ranges from 10 percent to as high as 25 percent in some instances. The norm is 15 percent to 20 percent. Allegedly, Colonel Tom Parker, who managed Elvis Presley, received a 50 percent commission. That commission is usually on the artist's gross earnings, but may be restricted to entertainment earnings, further restricted to live appearances, or restricted to earnings from appearances and agreements that the manager made some contribution in obtaining. Advances for which the artist does not receive actual cash in hand, such as recording costs, video production costs, and tour support should not be commissionable. Some attorneys recommend fewer restrictions in order to keep the manager more motivated.

- Duration: Most agreements are for an initial term of one or two years with option years adding up to about five years. The options are usually the manager's but the artist may be able to limit the manager's right to exercise the options unless the artist has reached some plateau of earnings, say $100,000 in year one, $200,000 in year two, and so on.
- Key person (a term slowly evolving from the former sexist moniker "key man"): Personal managers are usually *very* personal to the artist. Even if the artist signs an agreement with a management company, it is usually a particular person who is handling the affairs of the artist and in whom the artist has placed his or her trust. For that reason artists often ask that if the "key person" leaves the firm then the agreement is ended.
- Power of attorney: The manager will usually ask for power to enter into agreements on behalf of the artist. While it may be easier for the manager to be able to sign anything for the artist it is usually advisable for the artist to attempt to limit the power of attorney to routine matters such as short engagements. The manager should seek the artist's approval on all but very routine matters, and the artist and manager should have agreed on the parameters of those routine matters. Whether such detail is necessary in the agreement is a matter of trust.

TALENT AGENTS

The Agent's Role

The primary function of a talent agent is to find employment opportunities for the artist in live entertainment. The agent is the ultimate middle person between the artist and the venue operator or promoter, with an almost purely sales function. Although the agent, strictly speaking, represents the artist and must make the artist's interest paramount, there is also pressure to please the promoter or venue operator. If agents arrange many deals that displease one or the other they will find that they either have no talent to book, or nowhere to book them. The agent has a knowledge of the kinds of performers booked in what venues by what promoters or venue operators. Putting the wrong act in the wrong venue is a double disaster. Agents often know promoters and venue operators "personally," at least over the phone "personally." Most of an agent's work is done over the telephone. Agents usually represent a substantial number of artists, although there may be a particular individual at an agency that is in charge of bookings for a particular artist.

Agency Structure

Talent agents tend to exist in three varieties, depending on the size of the geographic area in which they book talent. Local agents work just in a particular city or small group of cities. They tend to book acts into smaller clubs, parties, and local events. Because the acts they book do not command large talent fees, they have to work fast to keep lots of acts working lots of weeks per year in order to survive. It is most likely that an aspiring artist or group will encounter a local agency first on their rise to stardom. That agent will be one of the first people to pass judgment on performers and to conclude that they are of substantial enough talent to perform in local venues without embarrassing the venue operator, the agent, or themselves. All a local agent needs to be in business is a telephone, an act to represent, a list of clubs to start calling, and perhaps a license (see below for a discussion of agency licensing requirements).

Regional agents can book artists in several, usually adjoining, states. They book some larger clubs and shows and may have the ability to get an act on as an opening act for a larger artist if they have good connections with the promoter. The dream of the regional agent is to hook up with some rising artist who becomes a star and who will take the agent along. Regional agents can book an act into a small tour. The artists represented by regional agents may be just as many in number as for the local agent, but they are usually of higher caliber and more experience. Regional agencies tend to have several agents in the office.

Finally, national agencies are those that can book an act anywhere in the country, and perhaps abroad. They usually will not represent an artist unless that artist already has a recording contract, or perhaps a substantial development agreement with a publisher. They may represent over a hundred artists and have a substantial number of actual agents working at the agency. These national agencies are the ones that work out tours for established recording artists.

Pollstar's Summer 1996 Agency Roster lists nearly 600 talent agencies in the United States. They are not owned by media conglomerates but are independent businesses. That is not to say that they are not dependent on artists who have recording contracts, and other artists who dream of having recording contracts, for their talent. Just like other aspects of the industry, the big money is concentrated in the hands of a few players. The William Morris Agency is by far the largest talent agency in the United States, representing over five hundred artists. On a plateau below that are several agencies representing one hundred to just over two hundred acts. In roughly descending order they are Thomas Cassidy, International Creative Management (ICM), Creative Artists Agency, Famous Artists, Producers, Agency for the Performing Arts (APA), Talent Consultants International, Supreme Talent International, and Monterey Peninsula Artists.[13]

The number of artists an agency represents is not the only measure of its success. The gross bookings in terms of dollars are another good measure. *Pollstar* lists the top ten agencies of 1995 as booking $712.2 million worth of shows (see Table 4-2). That is about three-fourths of the estimated $950 million in major concert ticket sales in 1995. The top five agencies generated over 50 percent of the concert gross.

TABLE 4-2   Top Ten Grossing Talent Agencies (1995)

Agency	1994 Rank	1995 Gross (Millions Dollars)
1. William Morris Agency	1	$159.3
2. International Creative Management	6	121.4
3. Creative Artists Agency	2	97.9
4. Progressive Global Agency	—	76.1
5. Monterey Peninsula Artists	7	61.7
6. Premier Talent Agency	—	58.6
7. The Howard Rose Agency	5	42.0
8. Grateful Dead Productions	8	38.4
9. QBQ	4	37.8
10. Artists and Audience	—	19.5

Source: *Performance*, 29 December 1995: 12.

One could fairly describe the agency industry as approaching a tight oligopoly (the top four firms control 60 percent of the market), but because the top four firms vary from year to year, depending on whose artists happen to be making a major tour (see Table 4-3), the industry is really better characterized as an effective competition that is "somewhat concentrated."

Unlike personal managers, who sometimes do business on a handshake, talent agents almost never do business on a handshake, either with the artists they represent or with the venues and talent buyers to whom they sell. That is partially because they are usually dealing at a distance, over the telephone, with their clients. It is also because they are often subject to specific licensing requirements from the states and/ or the unions.

Agency Licensing

Talent agencies, because they are employment agencies, are usually regulated as such by state laws. Some states, among them California, Florida, New York, Minne-

TABLE 4-3   Top Grossing Agencies 1989–1995

Year	Agency	Gross (Millions Dollars)
1995	William Morris Agency	$159.3
1994	William Morris Agency	203.4
1993	Creative Artists Agency	175.1
1992	Premier Talent	119.6
1991	International Creative Management	103.1
1990	International Creative Management	120.4
1989	Premier Talent	37.0

Source: *Performance*, 29 December 1995: 12.

sota, Texas, and Illinois, require specific licenses to be a talent agent. Most do not. California and New York laws are particularly important because many agencies have their main offices there. Talent agents are known as "theatrical employment agencies" in these codes.[14] The two main labor unions concerned with recording artists, the American Federation of Musicians (AFM) and the American Federation of Television and Radio Artists (AFTRA), also regulate agents in their dealings with the union's members. Generally speaking, a talent agent must be licensed by both the state in which the agency is located and the union that represents the musicians or vocalists booked by the agent.

Agency Agreements[15]

The licensing requirements mean that agency agreements with performers are somewhat limited in their terms:

- Commissions and fees: These are usually 10 percent to 20 percent of the gross payable to the performer. The AFM limits the amount according to the duration of the performance, with 20 percent the limit for one-nighters. Most agencies will agree to limit their commissions to a "standard" 10 percent. The commissions should only be applicable to engagements procured by the agency.
- Duration: The AFM limits booking agents to three-year agreements. If the agent is a "general agent" (one who also books film, television, theater, literary, and so forth) the duration is limited to seven years. As a general rule, the lower the level of agency the shorter the term of the agreement should be, so that when/if an artist gets a recording agreement they can switch to an agency that is capable of booking them nationwide.
- Exclusivity: Agents often ask for exclusive rights, i.e., no other agent can book the artist during the term of the agreement. While this is certainly understandable and "usual" when an artist has reached the national level of agency, it is more questionable at the regional level, and quite undesirable for the artist at the local level.

PROMOTERS

"This is a business for manic depressives."[16]

The Role of the Concert Promoter

Promoters present live entertainment events. To do that the promoter must obtain some talent to present, presumably from an agency, and must have some place to present it, a club or other venue. Like the agent, the promoter is a middle person in between the artist and the audience. But unlike the agent, the promoter takes on a substantial managerial role in the ultimate presentation of the event. Promoters used to be a highly independent entrepreneurial group, working only in one or a few cities, willing to risk substantial losses in order to make substantial profits. They would hear about the availability of an artist from an agent, publication, or the grapevine, contact the agent and the venues for available dates, make a match, and then try to sell tickets. A good show that sold out could reap substantial profits for the promoter and the performer. A show that did poorly in terms of ticket sales could spell disaster, especially for the promoter. The pressure on all parties involved became to reduce their risk of loss but still to share in the high profits that were available for successful shows. The person least able to reduce risk was the local or regional promoter who did not have the resources to spread the risk over a larger number of shows.

The Structure of the Promotion Business

During the 1960s it was common for a local or regional promoter to have a virtual lock on any significant shows happening in "their" towns. They did this by getting "buy back" agreements with agents and managers. The buy back allowed the promoter to be the first to bid on a date for an act's next tour date when they had just finished promoting the current date. The promoters could therefore assure themselves of being able to promote shows most likely to be successful in the future. If they had a profitable show with an artist they would pick up the date for the next tour. If not, they could pass and let someone else do the show. The promoters also worked closely with the venues, securing large numbers of "holds" (a nonbinding agreement to tentatively keep a date open for the promoter and not let someone else book the venue), which effectively kept other promoters from booking that venue.

Beginning in the late 1960s the grip of local and regional promoters on cities began to slip as national promoters, particularly Concerts West, came on the scene.[17] The national promoter could book a large number of dates for a particular tour and spread the risk of a loss on any one or two shows through a larger number of shows. By spreading the risk and being efficient in their operations, the national promoters could offer the artists and venues higher percentages and fees and still make profits themselves. Even when the national promoters would use a local or regional promoter to work out the details for a particular show the local promoter might find themselves getting only a flat fee instead of any percentage of potential profits.[18] Promoters expanded their use of holds to the point that they had exclusive agreements with some venues so that no show could be promoted in the venue unless that promoter did it.

The other pressure on local and regional promoters' profits came from the artists. Major artists and their managers became aware of the high profitability of promoting a successful act. A sellout became a given with some big artists. They reasoned that they should get a higher percentage of the profits from such sellouts. The promoters, however, needed the high profits from the sellouts to cover the high losses from the flops. At the same time the major artists began to put on larger and larger shows. The acts went from requiring the promoter to supply staging, sound, and lights to carrying a self-contained show that only needed a place to play. The artists' expenses skyrocketed. Instead of a van-sized truck for the show and a bus for the artist, fleets of tractor trailers and several buses were necessary to move a show from one venue to the next. The higher cost to the artist of all this personnel and equipment meant that the artists had to demand a larger guarantee (the minimum amount that the promoter had to pay for the artist's performance) for each show in order to meet their daily operating expenses and payroll. By asking for a higher guarantee and a higher percentage of the profits, the artists reduced the profitability for the promoters on successful shows and increased the risk of loss on shows that did not do well. Guarantees for a "shed" or arena show were typically $100,000 to $150,000 in 1996, having increased about 10 percent over the previous few years.[19]

Higher costs, higher guarantees, and bigger shows meant that the shows had to have larger audiences. Shows went from local gymnasiums to basketball arenas to football and baseball stadiums. With larger audiences and the partylike atmosphere that often accompanied the concerts came other headaches for the promoters—potential liability for injury to the fans or the artists or the facilities. Lawsuits for injuries or deaths occurring at concerts became more common with the heavy metal acts of the 1980s.[20] Injuries at rap concerts of the late 1980s and 1990s caused some promoters to cancel shows instead of facing the liability.[21] By the mid 1990s the violent behavior of fans in "mosh" pits and "stage diving" by fans (and even artists on some occasions) raised the specter of even greater liability.[22] The promoter's cost of liability insurance went from pennies per ticket to dollars per ticket over the course of about five years. Increased security measures became necessary. Those factors raised the price of the tickets even higher and decreased the profitability of the shows even further.

The net result of all of these pressures has been the concentration of the promotion business into large regional and national promotion companies. Table 4-4 indicates that the top ten grossing promoters of 1995 accounted for about 54 percent ($510.5 million) of the $950 million in concert sales that year. Looking at concentration ratios for the top four and top eight promoters finds a concentration of 30.2

TABLE 4-4   Top 10 Grossing Promoters, 1995

Promoter	Shows Reported	Gross Sales
1. Cellar Door Productions	481	$83,855,748
2. PACE USA	529	81,280,559
3. MCA Concerts	682	75,579,846
4. Bill Graham Presents	217	46,162,652
5. Delsener/Slater Enterprises	245	40,197,652
6. Metropolitan Entertainment	318	39,880,235
7. Jam Productions	489	37,743,942
8. Belkin Productions	243	35,394,829
9. Haymon Entertainment	120	35,370,528
10. Contemporary Presentations	403	35,178,547

Source: *Performance*, 29 December 1995.

percent and 46.2 percent respectively. The entire top twenty promoters accounted for 73.5 percent of concert sales. These ratios indicate a healthy competition among the major promoters.

Which promoters are the most successful in a given year varies substantially, just as it does with the most successful agents, depending on who is on tour and which promoter has the major tours of a given year. However, there is some stability among the top promoters as Table 4-5 indicates. Three major promoters, Cellar Door Productions, CPI USA, and Metropolitan Entertainment, held the top spot for all but one of the ten years from 1986 to 1995.

Promoter–Artist Agreements

Performance agreements for concerts and club appearances contain two parts. The first part simply sets the fee structure, date and time of appearance, and a few other "basics." The other part is the "rider." This contains the requirements that the artist must have in order to put on the show. From the artist's point of view, compliance with the requirements in the rider is critical to the artist being able to put on a good show for the audience. With a major act the rider will contain details of how much parking must be available for the artist's trucks and buses, how much weight the venue rafters must be able to support so the sound and lights can be "flown," how much and what kind of food needs to be provided for the traveling crew and artist, how much power (A/C) needs to be available and where it needs to be, what local personnel such as musicians, security, follow spot operators, electricians, plumbers, and so on. must be provided, how backstage security is to be handled, and more. The larger the show the more details the rider is likely to contain. The promoter needs to have the rider far enough in advance to be sure there are no problems that the promoter and venue cannot overcome. For example, if a show has a large piece of stage set that cannot be disassembled and must have doors of a certain size to be able to get it into the building, the venue may have to enlarge an entrance, or cancel the

TABLE 4-5   Top Grossing Promoters 1986–1995

Year	Promoter	Shows Reported	Gross Sales
1995	Cellar Door Productions	481	$ 83,855,748
1994	CPI USA/CPI	218	240,298,759
1993	Cellar Door Productions	318	57,679,176
1992	Cellar Door Productions	291	56,314,266
1991	Metropolitan Entertainment	388	51,069,1787
1990	Metropolitan Entertainment	420	51,244,220
1989	CPI/BCL	196	104,801,800
1988	Metropolitan Entertainment*	218	43,162,260
1987	Metropolitan Entertainment*	316	46,466,111
1986	Beaver Productions	160	30,465,974

*Metropolitan Entertainment Group was Monarch Entertainment/John Scher Presents in 1988, 1989.
Source: *Performance*, 29 December 1995: 13.

show. If the roof cannot support the load of the sound and lights, it may have to be reinforced, or the show canceled.

The payment part of the contract typically calls for the artist to get a guarantee of some amount of money and often a percentage of the "gate" (ticket sales revenues). There are several ways of structuring the deal. Artists playing small clubs or opening for other major acts usually just get a flat fee for the show. Typically half of the guarantee or flat fee is paid in advance. It is out of this that the talent agency takes their commission. The amount of the guarantee can go from a few thousand dollars for an opening act to as much as a million dollars for a superstar act on a major tour. The amount is determined by the artist and manager to be enough to cover their expenses plus make what they consider to be a fair profit no matter how many people actually buy tickets. In theory, the artist will get this guarantee even if no tickets are sold. In practice, if sales are going very badly, the artist and promoter will try to work out a compromise. It is not good for the artist's reputation to require the promoters to take huge losses if the artist is not able to attract a good sized audience to the show. Major acts also get a percentage of profits, which usually kicks in after the promoter reaches a "break-even point" (where ticket sales revenues equal the promoter's expenses, including the artist's guarantee). The percentage is highly negotiable, ranging from 50 percent to as high as 90 percent.

THE VENUE

Venue Agreements

The promoter must also enter into an agreement with the venue. The details of that agreement include the venue's rental fee and what other services are to be provided by the venue to the promoter. Arrangements run from the venue providing the facility and nothing more, called a "four walls" deal, to the venue providing significant services in terms of clean-up, ushers, ticket takers, electricians, stagehands, and so forth. Halls may also want either a flat fee, a flat fee against a percentage of the gate (meaning the venue will get whichever is greater, the guarantee or the percentage of the gate), or a guarantee plus a percentage of profits after the promoter's break-even point. Services provided by the venue are usually billed separately but may be included in the flat fee.

In addition to rental fees, the venues can also make money from other things. Venues often charge the artist a percentage of sales from artist "concessions," such as T-shirts, hats, and so forth that the artist has sold at the shows. These percentages can range from nothing to as high as fifty percent. "Ancillary income" for the venue from things such as food and drink sales and parking are usually immune from any percentage participation by the promoter or artist.

The example that follows shows the basic flow of dollars from a show to the venue, promoter, agent, manager, and artist. The figures are based on a number of different specific examples to create a generic kind of concert that does not reflect any particular artist, promoter, venue, or concert. Assume a 12,000 seat arena with potential sales of 10,000 tickets (the show production, stage, and equipment takes up 2,000 seats worth of space). Sales are 89 percent. The venue fee is a flat fee and includes the venue rental plus ushers, security, technicians, and other services provided by the venue. The ticket price is an average. Some seats sold for more than $22.50, some for less. The artist has a guarantee of $50,000 plus 50 percent after the promoter breaks even. The agent has a 10 percent commission. The artist's personal manager has a 20 percent commission. An opening act gets an $8,000 flat fee.

Ticket sales, 8,900 @ $22.50		$200,250.00
Less: ticket sales commission	$ 4,005.00	
Less: venue rental and services	$20,500.00	
Promoter's gross receipts		$175,745.00
Less: opening act	$ 8,000.00	
Less: artist guarantee	$75,000.00	
Less: promotion expenses	$50,000.00	
Available after break-even		$ 42,745.00
Less: artist's 50 percent		$ 21,372.50
Producer's net profit		$ 21,372.50
Artist's income		
Guarantee	$75,000.00	
Plus % after breakeven	$21,372.50	
Artist gross		$ 96,372.50
Less: agency commission	$ 9,637.25	
Less: manager's commission	$19,274.50	
Less: tour expenses	$25,000.00	
Artist's net		$ 42,460.75

This example illustrates a successful show. On the other hand, if only 6,000 tickets were sold, the promoter would face a $21,200 *loss*. It is not uncommon for shows to sell less than 60 percent of the available seats.[23] If the promoter only planned to sell 60 percent, perhaps because the only available venue did not really match the demand for the artist in that market, then all would be well. But the likelihood is that somebody is losing money at 60 percent. That somebody is undoubtedly the promoter.

In-House Promotion

The existence of national promotion of tours and the possibility of ancillary income has led many venues to promote concerts "in-house." In such an arrangement it is really the venue that is promoting the show instead of an independent local or regional promoter. If the venue knows it is going to make a significant amount of money off of the ancillary revenues then it can afford to give the artist a higher percentage above the break-even point. Major artist tours are so self-contained that there is little that a local promoter has to provide that is not usually provided by the venue. Chain ownership of venues, especially of outdoor amphitheaters, makes it possible for the venue owner to book several dates at large venues in significant markets. Again, the local or regional promoter is left out. The majority of club shows are also promoted "in-house." This practice, coupled with the increasing use of national promoters, has led to fewer shows available for local or regional promoters. Sometimes, though, a club will simply rent the facility for a new promoter wanting to break in with a small show.

Ticket Selling

Economic pressures on promoters and venues and the technology of on-line sales in the 1980s and 1990s changed the way tickets are sold to events. It used to be that if someone wanted tickets to a show they had to go to or call the box office or go to some other ticket outlet, such as a record store, that had "hard" tickets. The selling agent for the tickets printed them, and distributed them, and perhaps ran the box office to sell them, for a small commission. Beginning in about 1982 the firm Ticketmaster started selling "soft tickets"—tickets that did not exist at all until printed out by the selling agent's computer when a customer ordered them and paid for them by charge card over a telephone line. The service was much more convenient for the customers than having to go to a location to purchase tickets. Efficiencies in the telephone operations meant that Ticketmaster could sell tickets to many shows at the same time from many locations using networked computers. By the early 1990s Ticketmaster's primary competition, Ticketron, had been bought by Ticketmaster.

In addition to efficient operations, Ticketmaster began to use exclusive selling agreements with venues and some promoters as a means to secure business. The venues and promoters sometimes received a percentage of the service charge added to the ticket price in exchange for the exclusive arrangements.[24] Because the service charge was not part of the gross ticket sales on which the promoter had to pay the artist, it was not subject to the artist's percentage requirements. It was, therefore, a revenue source that did not have to be shared. Independent promoters, in-house promoters, and venues all moved to take advantage of the arrangements. It soon became virtually impossible to play a concert tour without having tickets sold by Ticketmaster. Ticketmaster's service charges increased to from $3.50 to $5.50 per ticket.

Some consumers and artists began to complain. In 1994 the popular group Pearl Jam announced that it wanted ticket service charges held to $1.80 on an $18.00 ticket. Promoters and venue operators complained that their exclusive agreements with Ticketmaster would not allow them to use alternative ticket sellers and Ticketmaster would continue to charge its higher fees. Pearl Jam canceled their summer 1994 tour and complained to the Justice Department that Ticketmaster had a monopoly. At least one legal writer concluded that Ticketmaster's practices did violate federal and California antitrust laws.[25] The Justice Department began an investigation and members of Pearl Jam testified before a Congressional committee. By the summer of 1995, however, the Justice Department had dropped its probe of Ticketmaster's practices without further comment.[26] Ticketmaster reported ticket sales revenues of $1.6 billion for 1995. For its part, Ticketmaster had expanded its operations into promotional partnerships with credit card companies and even a record label. Capitol records began a promotion to give away sampler albums to people who used the Ticketmaster or Capitol World Wide Web sites.[27]

New England concert promoter Don Law went for a share of the ticket revenues in a direct way, starting his own ticket selling company in 1996. Because he had exclusive booking arrangements with a number of venues, he had guaranteed ticket sales and commissions. Service charges for Law's "Next Ticketing" were no lower than Ticketmaster's.[28]

THE LABELS IN THE CONCERT BUSINESS

Live appearances by a recording artist help sell albums. The shows themselves may even be the outlet where the albums are sold. In addition to T-shirts and hats, many artists are now offering their albums for sale at their concerts. One survey reported that 65 percent of the consumers who attended a concert in the last half of 1995 reported seeing the artist's album for sale at the show. Ten percent said they bought the album at the show, another 25 percent bought the album prior to the show. About a fourth of those who did not see the album at the show said they would probably have bought it if they had seen it.[29]

For new artists who need to build an audience through performance, or for an artist who is just beginning to break, the labels may provide tour support in the form of extra advertising and promotional dollars when an artist plays a market or in the form of "shortfall." In the case of shortfall, the label guarantees that the artist will make a certain amount of money per appearance. If not, the label will make up the difference. Even in such cases, the label is not attempting to make money in the concert business, but is hoping that the exposure of the artist through live performances will enhance sales of recordings. Tour support dollars spent by the label are usually recoupable out of artist royalties earned from the sale of recordings.

Several major record labels have entered the waters of the third income stream associated with their recording artists. Consider the following examples of horizontal integration across income streams. In 1990 PolyGram established PolyGram Diversification Division to become involved in local and national concert promotion, artist management, venue ownership and development, and merchandising of artist-related materials such as clothing. PolyGram initially bought a minority interest in promoter Jim Scher's Metropolitan Entertainment.[30] PolyGram later sold its share to Ogden Corporation, a firm with substantial venue management interests. The new firm planned a total integration of record label, music publishing, artist management, concert promotion, and venue management, thereby combining all three income streams.[31] MCA also has a concert promotion division, MCA Concerts, as well as venue management and concert merchandising operations. CBS Records, prior to its sale to Sony, had a deal with Pace Group, which owns amphitheaters, to develop more venues and promote tours.[32] As these examples indicate, there was already vertical integration in the live music stream, with promoters owning and operating venues and venues doing in-house promotion. The notion of promoters owning venues has one of its best examples in Bill Graham's ownership of the Fillmore Ballrooms East and West. Although Graham was killed in a plane crash in 1991, his production company, Bill Graham Presents, was the third top grossing promotion company in 1995 (see Table 4-3).[33]

SPONSORED TOURS

Other businesses with products to sell to people likely to attend concerts have entered the concert business by sponsoring tours for major or even relatively new artists. The sponsor usually provides some underwriting for the entire tour in the form of lump sum or per show payments for the artist and significant promotional money to be spent on radio and television advertising nationally and in markets where the artist is appearing. In return, the artist allows the association with the tour, the use of the artist's name and likeness in advertising, probably agrees to some time for making ads for the sponsor, probably agrees to allow the sponsor to have a presence at concerts in terms of signs or other product placement, and may agree to "meet and greets" backstage where local employees of the sponsor and local buyers of the sponsor's products can meet the artist personally. Companies who sponsor musical events and other shows report sales increases of from 50 percent to 1,000 percent in markets where the sponsored show appears.[34]

THE UNIONS

There is substantial involvement of labor unions in the presentation of live entertainment. The performers themselves are likely to be members of either AFM or AGVA. In addition, IATSE members will undoubtedly be involved in lighting, sound, and stage crews. Finally, the electricians, plumbers, and other craft unions are likely to be involved with the venue as support personnel, particularly in states such as New York and California, where unions are quite strong.

The AFM

The American Federation of Musicians of the United States and Canada is the official name of the AFM. It represents musicians, conductors, arrangers, orchestrators, copyists, and others involved in the preparation and presentation of live music (but not composers). The union has a national organization, which is primarily responsible for the negotiation of national agreements with the major labels (see Chapter 6) and national television and radio networks, and local chapters. The performing musician will be a member of both the national and a particular local. The locals set wage scales for live performances in their areas. The scales vary considerably from local to local depending on the strength of the union in a particular city. The strongest locals are in cities and states where it is legal to have a "union shop," a venue that has agreed with the union to allow only union members to perform there. Because these are primarily the northeastern and north central states and because most musicians will ultimately want to perform there, they will ultimately have to join the union. Even in "right to work" states nonunion musicians may have difficulty at large concerts because union musicians have agreed not to work or perform with nonunion musicians.

The locals and national finance their activities through initiation fees and work dues. When someone first becomes a member they pay a national and local initiation fee. The national fee was $40.00 in 1996 and the local fees vary from local to local, but tend to range around $100.00.[35] Most of that one-time fee goes to the national. Locals may have annual dues as well. Members also pay "work dues" based on the wages they earn as musicians. The amount varies from local to local but ranges from about 1 percent to 5 percent of scale wages. This may be paid by the employer directly to the union or may be paid by the musician.

In addition to setting scale wages the union provides other benefits for its members. Because musicians are independent contractors they usually have no corporate health insurance, life insurance, or retirement benefits unless they arrange for them on their own. The union is able to provide group insurance and retirement plans for its members through its own health and welfare fund and retirement pension fund to which the members as well as the record labels (see Chapter 6) contribute. The union also protects members from employers who do not pay on time. A "defaulters" list names conductors, promoters, and record producers who do not pay.

AGVA

The American Guild of Variety Artists represents singers, dancers, comediennes, and others who perform live. It is one of the "4 As" unions, a group of unions also including the Actors' Equity Association, The American Guild of Musical Artists, the Screen Actors Guild, the Screen Extras Guild, and the American Federation of Television and Radio Artists. The "4 As" nickname comes from the name of the parent union, The Associated Actors and Artists of America. AFTRA is not as important a force in the live performance area, but its impact in record production is discussed in Chapter 6.

IATSE

The International Alliance of Theatrical and State Employees represents nonperformers in theater, television, and film. Its members include stagehands, camera operators, gaffers, lighting technicians, wardrobe people, and others. Most major performance venues have agreements with IATSE to employ union members. Artist performance contract riders often specify the employment of IATSE members.

THE MANAGEMENT TEAM

It is usually necessary for an artist to have more than one person "taking care of business" for them. That is partly because there is need of expertise that is often not available in a single person and partly because it may not be wise to engage a single person, even if she or he did have all the expertise. Certainly an artist who has, or is to enjoy, much success has to have a personal manager. The artist will have to have an agent representing him or her, securing employment and performances. From the artist's perspective the recording industry is a business of providing personal services to everyone from record companies to concert promoters. Most of the arrangements under which the artist will be performing will be under contract. As has been noted in previous chapters and as will be discussed further in Chapter 6, these contractual relationships are often complex and require the services of an attorney familiar with entertainment industry contracts. Finally, because the artist will invariably want/need to audit the accounts of various people with whom the artist has financial dealings, such as record labels, music publishers, agents, and personal managers, the services of an accountant should be retained. These four people, the personal manager, the agent, the attorney, and the accountant, make up the basis of a management team.

It is important for the members of the management team to be independent of each other. For one thing, four independent opinions, each founded on the best interests of the artist, are more likely to generate the course of action most appropriate for the artist to take. This is not to say that all four team members would be consulted on every decision. Attorneys and accountants are legally and ethically bound to represent their client's best interests. Managers also have duties to their clients but they are not as clear cut and well enforced as those of accountants and attorneys. Managers generally cannot be talent agents by law in some states and under union agreements in general.

Conflicts of Interest

Suppose the manager is negotiating the recording contract for the artist. That manager may get a 20 percent commission on all of the artist's income. Suppose that manager needs cash now for the management company. Do you suppose that manager would rather go for a large advance for the artist or for higher royalty percentages? The higher percentages may be in the better long-term interest of the artist but the manager finds a conflict between the manager's interest and the artist's interest. The best way to avoid such conflicts is simply to not be in a position where they are likely to arise. The manager should let the attorney negotiate the agreement, within some agreed-on parameters. Certainly the manager and accountant have to be different people if the accountant may be called on to audit the manager's books.

SUMMARY

The live entertainment income stream is the least consolidated of the three streams. That is not to say that there is not significant consolidation in the agency business or that the trend is not toward consolidation. Although the roughly one billion dollars in annual revenues from concert ticket sales is less than one-tenth of that of the recording industry, it is the stars of the recording industry who are the stars of the live performance stage. Furthermore, the one billion dollars annual sales does not account for the thousands of lounges, bars, restaurants, and clubs that have live entertainment and pay their bands without selling tickets. Live performance is an important part of the career of most recording artists in that it provides a stable, more long-term income than recordings and is an important source of income while waiting for the sale of recordings to reach the point at which advances have been recouped (see Chapter 6).

NOTES

[1]Joshua Derr, "Year End Charts," *Performance*, 29 Dec. 1995: 9; Jane Cohen and Bob Grossweiner, "1995 Year End Analysis," *Performance*, 29 Dec. 1995: 8.

[2]Cohen and Grossweiner, *supra* note 1.

[3]Good general sources for additional information on live performance, touring, and the relationships of the major players can be found in William R. Boswell, *Life on the Road* (1991), which also has good details on production, and in Howard Stein and Ronald Zalkind, *Promoting Rock Concerts* (1979), though the Stein and Zalkind book is getting to be dated.

[4]Personal manager Ed Bicknell, manager of Dire Straits, quoted in Bill Flanagan, "We Three Kings," *Musician*, April 1991: 52, 59.

[5]*Performance Magazine, 1996 Performance Guide: Talent/PM* (1996); *Pollstar, Pollstar Artist Management Rosters 1996*, 2nd ed. (1996).

[6]For additional information about personal managers and their functions, see Xavier M. Frascogna, Jr. and H. Lee Hetherington, *Successful Artist Management* (1990); Mark Halloran, *The Musician's Business & Legal Guide* (1991): 104; Jeffrey Brabec and Todd Brabec, *Music, Money and Success* (1994): 370; Sidney Shemel and M. Willliam Krasilovsky, *This Business of Music*, 6th ed. (1990), Chapter 9; Donald S. Passman, *All You Need to Know About the Music Business* (1994), Chapter 3.

[7]"1995 Top 50 Tours," *Pollstar*, 31 Dec. 1995: 7.

[8]Quoted in Zenon Schoepe, "Management Maven," *1996 Performance Guide: Talent/PM* (1996): 6.

[9]Melinda Newman, "Joel Wins Another Round in Suit vs. Ex-manager," *Billboard*, 20 March 1993: 12.

[10]Chris Morris, "George Harrison Wins $11.6 Mill. in Suit vs. Ex-partner," *Billboard*, 3 Feb. 1996: 13.

[11]Susan Nunziata, "Harrison, ABKCO Suit 'Fine'ally Ending After 20 Years," *Billboard*, 1 Dec. 1990: 80.

[12]For more detailed analysis of management agreements, see, e.g., Mark Halloran, *The Musician's Business & Legal Guide* (1991): 110; Jeffrey Brabec and Todd Brabec, *Music, Money and Success* (1994); Sidney Shemel and M. Willliam Krasilovsky, *This Business of Music*, 6th ed. (1990) Chapter 9; Donald S. Passman, *All You Need to Know About the Music Business* (1994), Chapter 3.

[13]Pollstar, *Summer 1996 Agency Rosters* (1996).

[14]Lionel S. Sobel, "Regulation of Talent Agents and Managers: Registration and Licensing Requirements for Those Who Seek Employment for Entertainment Industry Talent," in *American Bar Association Forum on the Entertainment and Sports Industries 1996 Annual Meeting, Vol II*. American Bar Association, Chicago, IL (1996).

[15]For more detailed analysis of management agreements, see, e.g., Mark Halloran, *The Musician's Business & Legal Guide* (1991): 123; Jeffrey Brabec and Todd Brabec, *Music, Money and Success* (1994): 372; Sidney Shemel and M. Willliam Krasilovsky, *This Business of Music*, 6th ed. (1990), Chapter 9; Donald S. Passman, *All You Need to Know About the Music Business* (1994), Chapter 6.

[16]Regional promoter Philip Lashinsky, speaking in a concert promotion class at Middle Tennessee State University, 20 Sept. 1994.

[17]Melinda Newman, "Colleagues Recall Hulett's Cutting-Edge Tour Biz Work," *Billboard*, 14 Aug. 1993: 10.

[18]Steve Gett, "Promoters Balk at Flat Fees," *Billboard*, 4 Oct. 1986: 1.

[19]"96 Tour Slate Is Heavy on Festivals, Classic Acts," *Billboard*, 13 April 1996: 97.

[20]Anthony DeCurtis, "Concert Insurance Crisis," *Rolling Stone*, 11 Sept. 1986: 15.

[21]Kevin Zimmerman, "Security in the Eye of Summer Storms," *Variety*, 5 Aug. 1991: 56; Kevin Zimmerman, "Rap Braces for Big Chill," *Variety*, 6 Jan. 1992: 89.

[22]Eric Boehlert, "Is Moshing Murder," *Rolling Stone,* 11 July 1996: 19.

[23]A sample survey of concerts in venues of the 8,000 to 12,000 range in *Pollstar*, 26 Aug. 1996 indicated that thirteen of thirty-five shows reported sold less than 60 percent of available tickets. On the "manic" side of the business, twelve of the reported shows sold more than 90 percent of available tickets.

[24]Thom Duffy, "N.Y. Says Concert Ads Deceived Public on Tix Pricing," *Billboard*, 8 Aug. 1992: 10.

[25]Kevin E. Stern, "The High Cost of Convenience: Antitrust Law Violations in the Computerized Ticketing Services Industry," 16 *Hastings Comm/Ent Law Journal,* 349 (1994).

[26]Eric Boehlert, "Play-by-Play Account of Pearl Jam Saga," *Billboard*, 8 July 1995: 85.

[27]"In Other On-line News," *Billboard*, 7 Oct. 1995: 91; Marla Matzer, "Ticket to Ride," *Brandweek*, 8 July 1996: 20.

[28]Greg Reibman, "Boston's Don Law Launches Ticketing Firm," *Billboard*, 3 Feb. 1996: 6.

[29]National Association of Recording Merchandisers, "Soundata Consumer Panel," *NARM Sounding Board* (on-line version), Feb. 1996.

[30]Melinda Newman and Thom Duffy, "PolyGram Enters Concert Biz with Scher," *Billboard*, 6 October 1990: 1.

[31]Paul Verna, "Ogden Acquires 50% of Metropolitan," *Billboard*, 16 Sept. 1995: 5.

[32]See, e.g., "Ontario Place Corp.," *Billboard*, 4 June 1994: 77.

[33]For a good biography/autobiography of Graham read Robert Greenfield and Bill Graham, *Bill Graham Presents* (1992).

[34]Betsy Spethmann, "Sponsors Sing a Profitable Tune with Event Promos," *Brandweek*, 24 Aug. 1994: 20.

[35]American Federation of Musicians, Local 257, Nashville, Tennessee.

5

Relationships to Other Media

As mentioned in Chapter 1, the recording industry has become a major media player not only because of its own size, but also because it has a significant impact on and in other media. Most importantly, popular recordings are the dominant programming content of radio. Broadcasters rely on the popularity of recordings to attract a listening audience. The presence of that audience in turn helps the broadcaster sell advertising time to clients who want their message to reach those listeners. Recordings are also an important part of television programming with the presence of music video channels on cable and the inclusion of significant amounts of popular music and recordings as "background" music in popular television programs. Those programmers and program creators rely on the popularity of recordings and music to attract television and cable viewers in order to sell advertising. Similar uses of popular recordings and music in film attract movie-going audiences and help sell soundtracks and other recordings. Though not as significant as in the electronic media, the recording industry also has an important impact in the print media, especially magazines, with significant consumer and trade publications devoting either the entire publication or substantial content to popular recording artists, audio and recording, and the music business. This chapter details those relationships and their positive, and sometimes negative, effects on those media. The impact on the new media, such as Internet and multimedia, is discussed tangentially in other chapters. Those new media are still in their infancy and the recording industry involvement is often experimental at this time.

RECORDINGS IN RADIO

Overview: A Love/Hate Relationship

It is no secret that radio stations and record companies do not sell the same thing. Get any label promotion people and radio programmers in the same room and the programmers will quickly remind the promotion people that radio programming is to sell advertising, not records. None of the top twenty-five advertisers on radio in 1995 were record labels, or even their conglomerate owners—they were retail, business and consumer services, and automobiles and auto accessories. These advertisers accounted for one-third of radio advertising billings.[1] On the other hand, music obtained by playing records is the predominant format content of 70 percent of all radio stations (see Table 5-1). Those stations rely mainly on the music they play to attract and hold listeners. From the label perspective, radio airplay still accounts for a significant percentage of the exposure of record buyers to new music. 1995 market research revealed that 44 percent of music consumers made their last album purchase because of the influence of radio or television airplay of a record.[2] In the 1970s radio had a stranglehold on the influence of record purchases. At the 1975 NARM Convention, Warner Brothers vice president, Stan Cornyn, lamented the dependency of the recording industry on radio airplay with a speech, "The Day Radio Died." "There is more to promotion than disc jockeys. For promotion men, radio should not be the only game in town. Records should be."[3] A 1977 Warner Communications survey noted, "[T]he 43% of the total population who listen to music [on the radio] for at least 10 hours per week comprise 54% of all buyers and account for 62% of the total dollar market."[4] In 1979, CBS records reported to the NARM convention that 80 percent of singles buyers learned about the records they purchased from radio.[5] Researcher Paul Hirsch concluded that radio programmers were

TABLE 5-1   Growth of Radio Music Formats*

	1986	1995
Stations with music formats†	9,055	11,101
Stations with nonmusic formats	2,681	4,709
Number of different music formats	12	23
Total formats	11,736	15,810

*Only clearly music formats are counted. Thus, foreign language, ethnic, and Indian are not counted as music even though they may contain significant portions of music. The number of formats exceeds the number of stations because a station using a given format for a significant part of the day could report more than one format.

†Music formats in 1986 were Adult Contemporary, Beautiful Music, Big Band, Black, Classical, Country, Urban, Progressive, Top 40, Oldies, Jazz and MOR. In 1995 Rock/AOR, Gospel, Classic Rock, Nostalgia, New Age, Blues, Bluegrass, Folk, Reggae, and Disco were added.

Source: *Broadcasting and Cable Yearbook,* 1986 and 1995.

gatekeepers who preselected the music that listeners and potential buyers would hear.[6]

The Historical Context: 1920s–1955

From the days of the first commercial radio broadcast in 1922 popular music began to have an impact on radio programming. By playing popular music the stations and networks could attract listeners that the advertisers wanted to reach. Most of the programs were not locally produced but were supplied by the networks with which the local stations were affiliated. The programs were produced largely by either the advertising agency, the network (for the sponsor), or by the sponsor itself. Programs with musical content were the most popular. A 1929 survey of the ten most popular programs listed only two nonmusical or musical/variety programs, the comedy series *Amos 'n' Andy* and the dramatic series *True Story,* at numbers four and five respectively.[7] The musical shows usually had live orchestras with guests and regular performers. These programs, together with classical music programs, amateur hours, and a small segment of popular singles programs (with only a 0.7 percent average rating), accounted for just over a 50-percent share of the nighttime radio audience. The dramatic difference between nighttime programming and daytime programming is illustrated by the fact that during the daytime, adult serial drama, talk shows, and juvenile shows accounted for over 82 percent of listenership share.[8] Daytime radio programming in those days was strikingly similar to daytime television programming today.

During the depression it became more of a common practice for local radio stations to fill their non-network time by playing recordings, especially when the quality of the recordings became better with the continued development of electrical recording. (See Chapter 6 for an explanation of electrical recording.) While the music publishers did not particularly care in what form a song was played, live or recorded, the record companies and the orchestras who recorded for the record companies at first took a dim view of airplay of records. They attempted to stop radio stations from playing records by marking the labels "Not Licensed for Radio Broadcast" or "Licensed Only for Non-Commercial Use on Phonographs in Homes. Mfr. & Original Purchaser Have Agreed This Record Shall Not Be Resold or Used for Any Other Purpose." Those attempts ended in a 1940 Federal Appeals Court case in New York.[9] Orchestra leader Paul Whiteman had complained of a radio station (W.B.O. Broadcasting) playing records of his musical performances. Whiteman's label, RCA, joined the suit against the radio station and Whiteman, saying that Whiteman had no interest left in the recordings that had not been contracted away to RCA. The court held that having fixed the recording of Whiteman's performance on records and distributed them to the public, neither the label nor Whiteman could complain if radio stations or others then performed the recordings for the public. At that time there were no statutory rights protecting sound recordings (see Chapter 10). Judge Learned Hand commented, "If the talents of conductors of orchestras are denied that compensation which is necessary to evoke their efforts because they get too little for phonographic records, we have no means of knowing it. . . ."[10]

With the legal path cleared to play more recordings, the radio stations of the early 1940s began to do so. The first "disk jockeys" were born. One of them, Martin Block, who aired a program called "Martin Block's Make Believe Ballroom," realized the future importance of radio to the recording industry. Speaking of radio airplay in 1942, Block said, "If the platter is a good one, the most effective type of direct marketing has just taken place. And sales are sure to reflect the airing of the disk."[11] But it was not until the mid 1950s, when television threatened the death of radio, that records became the mainstay of radio programming. The dramatic, comedy, and variety shows that had been the bulwark of radio programming since the early days of the networks could not compete with the visual impact of the same kind of programs aired on television. Radio stations were going off the air, and advertising revenues plunged. In 1955 *Billboard* reported that playing records was the clear trend for radio programming, noting that records were the programming of 53 percent of stations with power of less than 5,000 watts, and 42 percent of the programming of stations with greater than 5,000 watts power.[12] Even so, popular music was not the primary programming of those stations that did play music. Only 12 percent of the stations that did program popular music played it for seventy-five hours per week (half of the available air time). Twenty-three percent played classical music at least ten hours per week and 16 percent played country music at least twenty hours per week.[13]

Radio Turns to Records

Three other events of the mid-fifties combined with the threat of television to transform radio into a predominantly music medium. The introduction of the 45 RPM single in 1949 by RCA Victor brought an easily handled, nearly unbreakable, inexpensive, high-fidelity recording into the market place. The 45 took less space than the 78 or the LP (introduced by Columbia the year before). The vinyl material was lightweight, especially in the seven-inch format chosen for the 45, compared to the ten- or twelve-inch format for the older 78s. Because the 45 used the same material as the LP but ran at a nearly 50 percent greater speed, it had potentially higher fidelity than the LP. Finally, the 45 was less expensive to purchase than the LP and the players for the 45 were less expensive—factors that would prove attractive to the teen market. Radio initially objected to the 45 single. Many radio stations had built up libraries of 78 RPM ETs (electrical transcriptions). The practice of sending radio stations ETs of programs had developed as a way to distribute high quality recordings of programs, and music, to stations. Most stations paid for the ETs as part of a subscription service from the labels. Most complaints about the 45s died out when the labels began supplying the new 45s free of charge to all but the smallest stations.

Disk jockey Todd Storz was responsible for the second breakthrough that made radio broadcasters and record companies reluctant partners. In 1955 he introduced the Top 40 format on station WTIX in New Orleans.[14] The concept of Top 40 was more than just playing the forty most popular records. That had been being done for some time. What Storz noticed, allegedly at a bar one night as he observed customers playing a couple of jukebox songs over and over, was that listeners wanted to hear certain songs more often than others. He devised a closed play list with a limited number of selections and a rotation that played the most popular songs more often. Now virtually all commercial radio stations with a music format apply this "formula" in one way or another. Many stations have several rotations. How often a record gets played depends on several factors, including such things as the current strength of the recording, whether it is waxing or waning in popularity, whether it was a recent hit (a "recurrent"), or whether it is a hit from several years past. The result was a sound that attracted listeners, and therefore advertisers. *Billboard* noted, "It was Storz who saved radio from death."[15]

Rock 'n' roll was the other "savior" of radio. From 1951 to 1955 sales of recorded music grew a modest 19 percent to about $230,000,000 as reported by the RIAA. The 1956 through 1959 sales figures indicated a growth of more than 125 percent to almost $515 million—largely the result of rock. Rock could also deliver a new radio audience that had not been listening to the predominantly middle-of-the-road formats of the early 1950s. It was an audience that had more money to spend and more leisure time than the youth audience had ever had before. Advertisers were attracted to the potential market that could be reached through rock radio and bought air time. Rock radio prospered. By attracting listeners who were not part of the mainstream radio audience the rock stations were able to succeed quickly in markets where it would have taken years to develop a sizable listenership by eating away at the audiences of several other stations. The existence of the rock format stations created a demand for more music to program. As more music was programmed, more was exposed to potential buyers who then made purchases which benefited the labels.

The availability of records made it possible to produce inexpensive programming at the local level and to sell advertising at the local level. Radio advertising revenues increased over 800 percent from 1940 to 1970, from about $157 million to about $1,257 million. During that same time period the share of advertising revenues produced from local billings (as opposed to national or regional networks, or other national) increased from a mere 28 percent in 1940 to 68 percent in 1970. It was no longer necessary to rely on a network that could afford to hire an orchestra and popular entertainers. Those orchestras and entertainers were available on disc to perform at the spin of a platter. As a result the share of revenues from network billings dropped from 47 percent in 1940 to 4 percent in 1977.[16]

Diversity in Radio Brings Diversity in Music

Table 5-2 illustrates the rapid growth and proliferation of radio stations from a mere thirty in 1922, when the first National Radio Conference began licensing stations, to

TABLE 5-2   Growth of Licensed Radio Stations in the United States

Year	AM stations	FM stations*	Total stations
1922	30**	—	30
1935	585	—	585
1955	2,669	552	3,221
1975	4,432	3,353	7,785
1995	4,945	6,613	11,558

*The first FM permits were granted in 1940.

**Numbers are of licensed, on-air stations (except 1922, when stations were not licensed), not including those under construction.

Source: *Broadcasting & Cable Yearbook, 1995*, B-653, B-655.

over 11,000 stations in 1995. In the forty years between 1955 and 1995, the number of broadcast radio stations increased by 256 percent.

In 1995 radio reached 99 percent of U.S. homes. But not all of the people in the 98 million homes were listening to the same thing. The proliferation of stations brought with it a proliferation of formats. The more stations that existed in a radio market the more they found that they had to have some way to divide the audience pie, and perhaps attract listeners who were not tuned in to the other stations. The stations began to divide the audience pie into smaller shares and look for programming niches. One way to achieve this was by playing different music from the competitors. The demand for different music has led to airplay of a wider variety of music. The radio market has not become homogeneous as some had predicted in the early days of Top 40. In fact, the overall trend for a significant number of years has been to increasing heterogeneity in music available to radio listeners. Even in the decade from 1986 to 1995 the number of radio stations reporting predominantly music formats grew over 2,000 and the number of different music formats reported nearly doubled (see Table 5-1).

The trend towards increasing format diversity in radio is being driven in part by the increasing concentration of ownership in broadcast stations. In the early days of radio the Federal Communications Commission adopted the "duopoly rule." The essence of the regulation was that the FCC would not grant a license to an applicant who already owned or controlled another broadcast outlet in the same area so that the two stations would have overlapping service areas. In the early days of FM the FCC had allowed ownership of AM–FM combinations on the theory that they were not competing services. The rule was changed briefly in 1970 to prohibit AM–FM ownership but that rule was relaxed in 1971 to allow ownership of AM and FM stations in the same market. During the first half of the 1960s many AM–FM combination stations had simply duplicated the AM programming on the FM station. But in 1966 the FCC ruled that jointly owned AM and FM stations had to provide separate programming. FM owners discovered "progressive" rock and music formats that reached audiences beyond the Top 40 and MOR programming common on the

AM dial at that time.[17] By the 1970s FM had become a significant competitor. The reasons were the development of stereo recordings, FM stereo broadcasting, and the widespread use of stereo receivers in homes and automobiles. The FCC first authorized FM *stereo* broadcasts in 1961. At that time the number of AM stations on the air (3,539) exceeded the number of FM stations on the air (815) by more than a four-to-one margin. By 1971 that margin had shrunk to less than two-to-one as the number of FM stations increased to over 2,600 in ten years. By 1983 the number of *authorized* FM stations surpassed the number of *authorized* AM stations for the first time and in 1985 the number of *on-the-air* FM stations surpassed the number of on-the-air AM stations with 4,888 and 4,754, respectively. By 1995 the number of FM stations on the air exceeded the number of AM stations on the air by over 35 percent (6,788 FM and 4,923 AM).[18] Although the FCC authorized stereo AM in 1982 and adopted a standard broadcasting system in 1993, it never caught on. Music programming in stereo had become the dominant content of FM radio. Although there was still significant music content on AM, by 1995 news, news/talk, talk, religious, and sports accounted for more than 35 percent of AM formats. That same programming accounted for only about 16 percent of FM formats.[19]

Less Diversity in Ownership and More Diversity in Programming?

Throughout the 1980s and 1990s the FCC relaxed its rules regarding the number of broadcast outlets in a single market that could be owned by one entity and the total number of broadcast outlets that could be owned by one entity nationwide. In 1988 the Commission began to allow greater overlap between commonly owned AM and FM stations. In 1992 the Commission changed its rules to allow the same owner to operate up to four stations in markets with more than fifteen stations and up to three stations in smaller markets as long as they controlled less than half of the stations in that market. Congress further relaxed the rules with passage of the Communications Act of 1996 (see Table 5-3) with a limit that no single party can own more than half of the stations in a given market. At the same time the national ownership restrictions were relaxing. Since 1953 the FCC rule had been total ownership limits of 7 AM, 7 FM, and 7 TV stations (the 7–7–7 rule). Beginning in 1984 the limits were

TABLE 5-3   1996 Communications Act Radio Ownership Limits

Number of Radio Stations in Market	Maximum Total Stations Allowed One Owner	AM–FM Limits
45 or more	8	5/5
30–44	7	4/4
15–29	6	4/4
14 or less	5	3/3

Source: Section 202(b)(1)(D) of the Communications Act of 1996.

expanded, first to 12–12–12. Then in 1988 radio ownership limits moved to 18–18, then 20–20 in 1990.[20] Finally, the Communications Act of 1996 removed all limits on the total number of stations that could be owned by a single entity.

The relaxation of the ownership limits had the predictable effect. In the early 1990s sale of radio station licenses reached a fever pitch. The reason was the consolidation of ownership into larger and larger chains. Growth-oriented broadcasting owners purchased everything from single stations to entire chains.[21] The removal of all limits by the Communications Act of 1996 led to mega-mergers. Westinghouse Electric purchased CBS, Inc. and Infinity Broadcasting, creating a chain of eighty-three stations. The Infinity deal cost Westinghouse $3.9 billion but raised its market shares in a number of major markets, including San Francisco (19 percent) and Philadelphia (44 percent).[22] In the first half of 1996 mergers totaled more than $5.2 billion.[23]

Radio executives are predicting that the dual trends of format diversity and ownership concentration will continue. "As the market contracts in the number of owners there will be greater program diversity," said Randy Michaels of Jaycor Broadcasting. Another executive predicted that there would be a consolidation down to about fifteen large radio groups over a short period of time.[24] Those predictions are in contradiction to a study, completed before the 1996 Communications Act, which suggested that increasing the total number of stations in a market would have a small effect on the number of available formats for listeners, finding a 10 percent increase in the number of stations would lead to only a less than 2 percent increase in the number of formats. The study concluded, "[R]elaxing ownership rules will generate only small program diversity benefits if only modest increases in either the number of stations or in the incentives to offer different formats or higher quality programming result."[25] The broadcasters' logic that leads to the other conclusion is that as more stations per market are owned by the same entity, that entity will choose not to compete with itself, but rather to be able to deliver to advertisers a larger share of the total market. Theoretical models of mass media, and broadcasting in particular, suggest that advertiser-supported media firms cater to delivering as large an audience as possible. That can be done by programming different stations with noncompeting formats. The noncompeting formats can get a larger total share of the audience by appealing to a larger and more diverse group of listeners. The broadcasting owner can then sell a package deal to advertisers who will buy because they can reach a larger share of the total audience. In 1997 both theories remained to be proven.

The View from the Charts

The growth in the number of music popularity charts in trade publications such as *Billboard*, *The Gavin Report*, and *Radio and Records* (*R&R*) is another indicator of format proliferation and increased diversity. Table 5-4 indicates that each of these three major trades, which report on records and radio programming, increased the number of radio airplay charts by over 100 percent from 1976 to 1996. Although there is a 50 percent overlap of artists and cuts on the various new rock formats, they still manage enough diversity to compete on an overall station sound and attract different audiences.[26] *Billboard* reports similar niche formatting stations are "winning [the] battle against homogenization" in England.[27]

An increase in available information has contributed to local radio programmers being more able to target their particular audiences in their own markets. Until the 1970s the trade popularity charts tended to report only aggregate totals on popularity nationwide. In 1974 *R&R* began publication with a splash when it introduced a section of the publication reporting the actual playlists of the reporting stations. The radio programmers no longer had to rely on calling their friends at other stations in other cities or on possibly "hyped" reports from record company promotion persons. In 1994, local stations no longer had to rely on sales information provided through contacts at local record stores and by the record company promotion personnel. SoundScan, the company that gathers point-of-sale bar code scanning information from thousands of record retail locations, made its reports available to ABC radio networks configured to show local sales.[28] BDS (Broadcast Data Service) began reporting actual counts of times recordings were played, by station, by market. (For a further discussion of the impact of actual airplay reports and actual piece count sales reports on the labels' marketing plans and for a discussion of the development of BDS and SoundScan, see Chapter 7.) Then in 1995 *R&R* began doing call-out research on a regional basis, reporting to the stations particular songs the public wanted to hear more of (favorability), which ones they had heard (familiarity), and which ones they were tired of hearing (burnout). While many stations do their own call-out research, the *R&R* research reached more listeners and gave a better picture of patterns so that a radio programmer could know how long it would take the listeners to "burn out" on a particular record. This was particularly important information to stations in the CHR (Contemporary Hit Radio—the successor to Top 40) format because they tended to play fewer records for their listeners than many other formats. *R&R* compared the advantages of its callout research to retail sales reports saying, "Less than 25% of young adults (CHR's target listeners) will visit a retail sales outlet in a given seven-day period." Listener requests are problematic because, "Less than 10% of a station's listeners will call a request line within a given year." Finally, radio airplay reports from other stations were useful, but tended to focus the programmer's attention inward and could be manipulated [presumably by record company promotion people].[29] From a radio programming perspective it is important to know which recordings the listeners most want to hear. That is not necessarily the same recordings that are the bestsellers. In fact, it is possible to have a record that receives lots of airplay but does not sell well—what record promotion people call a "turntable hit."

Radio Music Listenership

The music preference of radio listeners changed dramatically in the last half of the twentieth century. Several points need to be made about Figure 5-1. Some form of

TABLE 5-4   Radio Popularity Charts 1977–1996

Gavin Report, 1977	Gavin Report, 1986	Gavin Report, 1996
Top 20 (40)	Top 40	Top 40
AC Top 30	A/C Top 30	Gavin Americana (40)
Black Radio (30)	Album Chart (40)	Gavin Country (50)
Country Hits (30)	Country (40)	Gavin AC (40)
	Urban-Contemporary (40)	Gavin A3 (AAA)
		Jazz (50)
		Smooth Jazz (50)
		Post Bop (30)
		Commercial Adult (30)
		College (50)
		Urban (40)
		Rap (40)
		Rock (50)

Source: *The Gavin Report*, May 27, 1977; November 7, 1986; June 7, 1996.

Radio & Records, 1977	Radio & Records, 1986	Radio & Records, 1996
Album Airplay (40)	CHR (40)	CHR/Pop (50)
Singles Airplay (40)	AOR Albums (40)	Pop/Alternative (20)
Country Singles (40)	AOR Tracks (60)	CHR/Rhythmic
Pop/Adult (40)	AC (30)	Hip-Hop (50)
Black Radio Singles (40)	Country (50)	Urban (50)
	Black/Urban	Urban AC (50)
		Country (50)
		AC (30)
		NAC Tracks (30)
		NAC Albums (30)
		Active Rock (50)
		Rock (50)
		Alternative (50)
		Adult Alternative (50)
		Adult Alt. Album (30)

Source: *Radio & Records*, June 11, 1976; June 20, 1986; June 7, 1996.

Billboard, 1977	Billboard, 1986	Billboard, 1996
Easy Listening (50)	Album Rock Tracks (50)	R & B Airplay (75)
Soul Singles (100)	Adult Contemporary (50)	Country Singles & Tracks (75)
Country Singles (100)	Black Singles (100)	Latin Tracks (40)
Hot 100 (100)	Black Singles Airplay (40)	Mainstream Rock Tracks (40)
	Country Singles (1000)	Modern Rock Tracks (40)
	Hot 100 (100)	Adult Contemporary (24)
	Hot 100 Airplay (40)	Adult Top 40 (25)
		Hot 100 Airplay (75)

Source: *Billboard*, May 28, 1976: June 7, 1986; June 8, 1996.

rock continues to be the most listened to music on the radio. Country music has undergone a dramatic increase in popularity as evidenced by both its radio listenership and its sales increases. A 1994 study indicated that country music was the preferred radio format of professionals and managers, among adults with individual incomes of more than $30,000 per year, and among adults with household incomes of more than $60,000 per year.[30] The "Adult Contemporary" of 1996 sounds more like rock than did its predecessor "Pop/Adult" in 1979. Finally, beautiful music, a format whose music accounted for virtually no sales of recordings, has all but disappeared. All of these things bode well for the recording industry. They indicate an increased exposure for more kinds of music that sell to consumers.

Despite all of the foregoing reasons why the record labels should be pleased with radio, they are not. The fundamental problem is that the radio stations, using the Top 40 style format invented by Todd Storz, limit their playlists and only add about three to five new records per week to replace those that have dropped out of the rotation. Much to the frustration of the label promotion people, it is the radio station programmers and their consultants who choose which new records will be added each week. Even with the greater diversity of formats in the rock genre, there are still tight playlists.[31] Country formats were very homogeneous until the mid

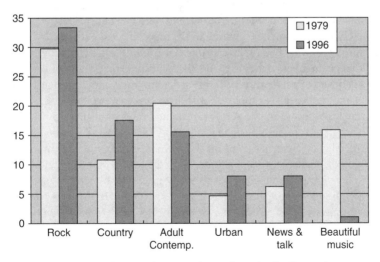

FIGURE 5-1   Radio Audience Share by Kind of Music

Source: *R&R Ratings Report* 1979 and 1996.

Some editorial liberties had to be taken to equate 1979 format terminology with 1996 format terminology. Rock includes Rock and Album Oriented Rock in 1979; it includes Oldies/Classic Rock, Contemporary Hit Radio (CHR), Rock, and Alternative in 1996. Pop Adult in 1979 is equated to Adult Contemporary in 1996. Urban was called Black in 1979.

1990s but even then were slow to move beyond a split between modern country and traditional country. Programmers complained to the labels that all of the product they were given to play was the same. The labels retorted that whenever they tried to get the stations to play something different, the stations complained that it was too different.[32] Radio continues to be a significant source of exposure to recordings and an important marketing tool for the labels. But by the mid 1990s there were also other significant promotion and marketing tools, especially television.

MUSIC AND RECORDINGS IN TELEVISION

Before Music Video

The first public broadcast of a television program was in 1936, but the development of stations, receiving sets, and production facilities was stymied by World War II. Only ten commercial stations were on the air by 1942 and only six of those made it through the war years. Television really took off during the 1950s. In 1950 there were only 5.9 million TV homes, compared with over 42 million radio homes. By 1960 the market penetration of television had almost equaled that of radio with 45.2 million homes compared to radio's 49.5 million homes.[33] Until the mid 1950s the popular music that was on television was primarily on variety shows like Ed Sullivan and Milton Berle. The few music specialty programs usually featured regular performers doing the hits of the day. *Your Hit Parade* was the most successful of these. It was patterned on the radio program of the same name and ran throughout the 1950s. It ultimately became the victim of rock and roll, when the MOR vocalists could not adequately perform the new genre. For the recording industry, the biggest music show of the 1950s was Dick Clark's *American Bandstand.* The show consisted of teen audience members dancing to the hits (and some that were not yet hits but whose labels had paid to get their recordings on the program) and a guest artist or two who lip-synched the vocals to their records. The success of Clark's show at selling records was legendary. Frankie Avalon attributed sales of nearly 1.5 million copies of "Venus" to exposure on *American Bandstand.* The sad truth was that most of the songs Clark played were not even on the *Billboard* charts at the time. He played them because he had some financial interest in the record company, publishing, or artist.[34] Television programs had occasionally produced hit singles, usually their theme songs. The success of the themes from *Peter Gunn* (1955), *Dr. Kildare* (1962), *Charlie's Angels* (1977), *Hill Street Blues* (1981), and *Miami Vice* (1985) proved that popular television programs could generate hit recordings.[35] By the 1980s the variety shows that had helped the music industry early were a dying breed. It was up to music video to show the labels how television again could be used to sell anybody's records, not just those of an artist who was a regular in the show or the artist who had recorded the theme song for the show.

Music Television

The forerunners of the "concept" music videos, in which the primary focus of the audience attention is not a performer doing a performance of the song but rather on other images or some story line, were contained in the TV show, *The Monkees* in the late 1960s. Other 1960s music shows were generally limited to lip-synched performances by the artist in front of some kind of live audience. *Billboard* speculates that the music video had its main origin in the United States with label promotional films that were shot for annual sales meetings. "When the acts weren't available, the film crews would shoot extraneous footage they felt complemented the tune. Conceptual or atmospheric shots would often be intercut with the performance clips."[36]

In the middle and late 1970s the labels began to produce more and more music videos to use for promotion. They were distributed at little or no cost to any TV station that would program them. They mainly aired late at night on local television stations that were grateful to be able to get the free programming and in dance clubs and restaurants. In 1981 Warner Cable started a "Pop Clips" program, the same year that Music Television (MTV) launched. MTV's historic first clip was the Buggles' "Video Killed the Radio Star." It took two years for MTV to reach enough cable audience that it could start showing a profit. By that time video shows were popping up everywhere. "Video friendly" artists whose appearance or material was particularly suited to turn into "short-form" videos became major acts. The "long-form" videos, on the other hand, were concert-length performances. They were typically shot live over a series of two or more concerts and worked for established acts by providing a relatively inexpensive source of singles videos and a program that could then be sold separately to one of the cable channels, such as HBO or Showtime.

None of this made much money as a medium of its own. The primary focus of the music videos, both short- and long-form, was the sale of recordings. For some artists, sales of recordings started immediately after MTV airplay. For others MTV did nothing. Video production budgets began to soar from less than $10,000 per clip in the late 1970s to $30,000 to $70,000 per clip by the mid 1980s. The home sales market was almost nonexistent because the price of home video had not come down below $20.00 per cassette and because home VCR penetration had not risen enough. Some artists who had been successful prior to the video binge discovered themselves displaced by the new video acts. Others found that that their own videos did not come out well. Recording artist Joe Jackson complained that music video devalued the musician and music. "[M]any artists lose their credibility and/or self-respect by coming across as bad actors rather than as good musicians. One result of this is that artists are now being signed for their video potential rather than for their musical talent."[37] The labels that had been paying video production costs as promotional/marketing costs began to ask the artists to help them bear the expense. Music publishers often had to deliver free synchronization licenses for music videos and hope to make their money through the performance royalties generated by the airplay. By

1994 it was "standard" in recording artist contracts that video production costs were 100 percent recoupable from artist royalties, usually from a 50/50 combination of record royalties and video royalties.

The labels, mindful of the difficulty of guaranteeing radio airplay and the problems with payola, sought to gain some control of the MTV rotations. In 1984 they signed deals with MTV whereby MTV paid the labels for providing the programming (i.e., video clips) with cash and advertising time, in return for which the labels were guaranteed a certain number of exposures of clips that the labels picked.[38] The labels and video networks continued to negotiate into the 1990s, with the labels wanting either some form of guarantee of exposure or a payment for the use of the videos. New Country Network in Canada entered deals with the labels to play each video a guaranteed a minimum of thirty performances, with a payment of $150 to the music video copyright owner each time it was performed.[39] The College Music Video channel, which had a monthly three-hour show, paid $550 to $650 per clip and guaranteed at least twenty plays per month. Some labels took the step of getting into ownership of video channels with Sony owning a 19 percent share of the German Viva Music TV channel[40] and PolyGram buying a 50 percent share of MTV Asia.[41]

As the video industry evolved, more cable outlets began to program different genres of music. Country videos began to appear on CMT (Country Music Television) and TNN (The Nashville Network) in 1983. VH-1, originally another Warner–Amex cable channel like MTV, began to program videos aimed at an older demographic in 1985. MTV was notoriously racist, with Michael Jackson being nearly the only minority artist whose videos appeared on the network. BET (Black Entertainment Television) began programming nearly all minority artists, targeting largely an African American audience. The 1990s saw even more diversification in music video programming. Cable channels for classical music, contemporary Christian music, jazz, and even a channel for the Austin, Texas music scene developed.[42]

Meanwhile, the jury was still out on the direct effects of music video watching on music sales. While anecdotal evidence supported direct relationships between music video airplay and sales of a particular recording, the overall results proved mixed. Two 1995 surveys found no correlation between amount of music videos watched and number of recordings purchased. Studies of whether seeing a music video influenced a purchase of a particular recording are inconclusive, with one study reporting that only 6 percent of the respondents said music video influenced their decision and another finding that 25 percent reported video programs as influencing a decision to purchase. Differences in the survey samples and precise wording of questions may account for some of the difference. However, it is clear that music video is still not as important as radio airplay overall in influencing the purchase of recordings. Those same surveys reported that radio airplay was most always or frequently the influence for a purchase by about 40 percent of respondents.[43]

The development of the music video had an important related effect on the way music was used in television programs. In music video the recordings of the artist are often performed while visual images that are unrelated to the actual performance (and many not even feature the artist) appear on the screen. The images may be inspired by the song or may relate a story that the video director imagines the song could support. That kind of use meant that recordings by popular artists could serve a "soundtrack" use for a wide variety of scenes. The recordings were the only or featured audio while some other sequence was happening on the screen. The mid 1980s series *Miami Vice* was one of the early programs to make extensive use of "music videos" woven into the plot. They proved to be an effective way of gaining attention from a younger audience and of promoting recordings. By the mid 1990s such uses were quite common in popular dramatic and comedy series. The labels had found another medium other than radio for reaching their potential audience. Although none of the major recording industry conglomerates own actual television stations in the United States, they all produce programming for television, film, or cable, and the tie-ins are natural.

Selling Music Video

During the 1990s music video sell-through at the retail level began to rise. List prices of music video titles dropped mainly into the $14.95 and $19.95 slots, making them competitive with CDs as a music purchase. That same period saw the rise of more "home theater" stereo VCRs, stereo TV receivers, and speaker systems with TV that could reproduce high quality sound. The RIAA sales data in Table 5-5 reflect the changes in the music video market through the first half of the 1990s. Sales more than doubled, but the dollar value of the sales only increased about 86 percent. That reflects the trend toward lower list prices. Not only did overall music video

TABLE 5-5   Music Video Sales 1991–1995

	1991	1992	1993	1994	1995	1991–1995 % Increase
Total Units (millions)	6.1	7.6	11.0	11.2	12.6	106.6%
Dollar Value at SRLP ($millions)	$118.1	$157.4	$213.3	$231.1	$220.3	86.5%

Source: RIAA 1996 Statistical Survey.

sales improve, but also the top-selling videos had stronger sales. The best selling music video charts in *Billboard* began to contain more and more RIAA certified "gold" or "platinum" videos. The RIAA certification levels are considerably lower for music video than they are for recordings; a gold music video has sales of 50,000 units or $1 million at the SRLP while a platinum music video certification is for sales of 100,000 units or $2 million at SRLP. By 1996 it was not unusual for the *Billboard* "Top Music Video" chart to show over half of its forty videos with at least gold certifications. Because the charts are based on SoundScan data reflecting actual sales by record retailers and record rack locations they are a good representation of the growing strength of the music video market. When *Billboard* went to using the SoundScan data in 1993, it reported a marked increase in the number of country acts on the music video chart and in their chart position. The change was attributed to the fact that rack jobber locations in places like K-Mart, WalMart, and other mass merchandiser chains were reported in the sales data used to compile the video popularity charts for the first time.[44] Keeping music video sales in perspective with the total home video market, the music video share is only about 1.7 percent of the roughly 730 million home video units sold per year in the mid 1990s.[45]

Still, the economic realities of even a gold music video are sobering. By way of example, wholesale on a $20.00 music video title runs about $12.00 ($9.00 on a $15.00 video).[46] Of that $12.00 artist royalties account for about $2.00 (they run 10 percent to 20 percent of wholesale price), manufacturing costs run about $2.00, and distribution costs run about another $2.00. That leaves about a $6.00 margin for the label. Out of that comes any direct marketing expenses, which are usually not high for a music video because it is the video channel exposure and recording exposure that will help sell the video. Even if the entire $6.00 were available, the label's gross profit would be about $300,000. Production costs for five or six short-form videos could easily take 50 percent to 100 percent of that sum. Production costs for a long-form video could take about the same percentage. Suppose production costs come up to $200,000. If half of the production costs ($100,000) are recoupable from artist royalties, the artist will receive no royalties from this video because 50,000 units @ $2.00 royalty is $100,000. Because the video has probably sold because the album has sold, it is likely that the label will be able to recoup the other half of its production costs from the recording royalties due to the artist, leaving it with $300,000 gross profit. The reality, however, is that most music videos will not be sold to consumers at all and the label and artist will have to "eat" the production costs. That, of course, is why the label wants production expenses to be recoupable.

RECORDINGS AND FILM

The recording industry and the motion picture industry have a symbiotic relationship that dates back to the first talkie, *The Jazz Singer*, in 1927. The next year Al Jolson's use of "Sonny Boy" and "Rainbow Round My Shoulder" in his second film generated sales of over a million copies of sheet music. The motion picture companies began to acquire music publishing interests so they could control the music in their movies, making major acquisitions and mergers through the 1930s. Until the mid 1960s the only soundtrack albums that were significant sellers were film versions of Broadway plays that had already proven successful. In 1966 the RIAA certified as gold the soundtrack from *Dr. Zhivago,* the first film soundtrack to achieve that status that was not a Broadway musical. The first gold selling soundtrack that featured significant amounts of pop music was the hit movie *The Graduate,* which featured songs from Simon and Garfunkel. Rock made it big in film in 1970 with the gold soundtracks for *Easy Rider* and *Midnight Cowboy.*[47] But the soundtrack that turned the labels' collective heads was *Saturday Night Fever* in 1977. The movie was made to feature music right from the start with a plot loosely woven around a lowly hardware store clerk who became a disco star at night. The soundtrack had as many as four singles in the charts at once and ultimately sold over 11 million copies in the United States and over 25 million copies worldwide, a number not surpassed by a soundtrack album until 1995 when *The Bodyguard* soundtrack of the Whitney Houston film was certified at over 14 million domestic sales.[48] The notion of a movie that was little more than a vehicle for music was nothing new. The dance musicals of the 1930s, the crooner musicals of the 1940s, and the rock movies of the 1950s, like *Rock Around the Clock* and *Blackboard Jungle*, and the Beatles movies of the 1960s, like *Hard Day's Night,* all drew an audience because they were full of music that the public wanted to hear. They also all helped sell records, especially once the nation had pulled out of the Depression.

In the 1980s and 1990s the marriage of recordings and movies continued but took on a different twist. The labels began viewing movies as sales and promotional vehicles to introduce singles and artists and the movie makers began using them to help reach the movie's target audience. What both movie makers and record labels realized is that the people who go to movies and the people who buy recordings are the same. Coordinated marketing campaigns are the key to the big hits. Singles are usually released four to six weeks ahead of the movie. If the single and music video for the single, which will contain some film footage, are successful, there is a pre-sold audience for the film. The album and movie are then usually released simultaneously to maximize cross-promotional benefits. For the biggest successes the movie and the album are both hits. Sometimes the movie is a hit without the soundtrack doing much, sometimes the soundtrack is a hit without the movie doing much except in home video.

In addition, the songs had moved into a different kind of use. In *Saturday Night Fever* and most other soundtracks, the songs were either totally background or featured a performance by somebody on screen. Music Television showed filmmakers that the songs could also be used as miniature music videos to help tell part of the story or emphasize some mood or theme. That is the way that music has always been used, but the use of the orchestral scores even for action sequences began to be replaced by portions of popular recordings.

The other thing that helped soundtracks in the 1980s and 1990s was the rapid diffusion of video cassette players and home video rentals. Quipped one writer in *Vogue*, "Years ago we bought soundtracks because we liked the music and wanted to be reminded of the movie. Today, we buy soundtracks because we like the music and want to be reminded to rent the movie."[49] Soundtracks like *Dazed and Confused*, a box office also-ran, sold over 500,000 copies because, said an A&M Records executive, "People discovered it at the video store."[50] Typical soundtracks are not one or two artists but more often collections of recordings by nine or ten different artists, some of which may not even be heard in the final version of the film at all, or be heard so briefly that no one can remember where or when the music appeared. Record companies use small independent movie makers to help introduce their newer "cutting edge" artists. The filmmaker gets a soundtrack, the likes of which they could not otherwise afford, and the artist gets exposure that just might launch a career. Even though those kinds of movies show mostly in large cities or on college campuses the exposure can be significant. Major U.S. films also drive soundtrack sales in Europe. In Germany, for example, soundtrack sales account for 3 percent of record sales.[51] In 1996 *Billboard* launched a special soundtrack column, "Nothin' Like the Reel Thing."[52] Arista Records President, Clive Davis, summed up the movie–music marriage: "It's always been about the same thing: a merger of music within the context of a film. One drives the other. It's a marriage of mediums."[53]

It is also a marriage of corporate profits. All of the six major conglomerates that own record labels also own film production interests.[54] Time Warner owns Warner Brothers studios, Lorimar Television productions, and HBO. MCA (Seagrams) owns Universal Pictures. Sony, where movie revenues were $3.1 billion and recording revenues were $5.6 billion in 1995,[55] owns Sony Pictures and Columbia Pictures Entertainment. PolyGram sold its major film interest, MGM/United Artists in 1993, but still owns Interscope Communications, Island Pictures, and Working Title Films. In 1995 film revenues made up 14 percent of PolyGram's sales. Bertlesman, A.G. owns primarily European film, television, and radio interests. EMI purchased Filmtrax in 1990 and owns Thames Television. The exact nature of the working relationships between the various "groups" and profit centers within each of the conglomerates needs to be examined more closely. One might ask, for example, whether Sony Pictures and Columbia Pictures feature Sony Music artists or songs more than those of other labels or publishers?

RECORDINGS AND THE PRINT MEDIA

The impact of the recording industry on print media and the impact of the print media on the recording industry has not been a subject of much study or debate. Music/entertainment magazines have been described as a "major niche" in the magazine industry,[56] but their influence on the sale of recordings is problematic. A

1995 *Billboard* article concluded: " While it's unlikely that there will ever be a fully quantifiable way to measure the impact that consumer music magazines have in selling records or influencing airplay, the one certainty is that no one wants to live without them."[57] Their direct influence on the purchase of recordings has been variously rated at 3 percent,[58] 3.7 percent,[59] and 7.4 percent[60] of respondents to various surveys who said they were motivated to purchase a recording by a print ad or review. When people are asked about how they first heard about a recording that they have purchased, one study indicated that 4.5 percent heard first from a review and 2.4 percent heard first from a print media advertisement.[61] Record reviewers do not have a very high opinion of their effects on the record buying audience either. On a scale of 1 through 5 (with 5 being the highest degree of influence) the critics rate their influence as an average of 1.9 with almost 49 percent rating their influence in the lowest category, a one.[62]

The effects on consumers are probably much more indirect. If magazines serve a function of correlation, bringing together sometimes disparate parts of a news story or a culture, then reviews of performances or recordings and articles about recording artists in publications help readers place an artist within the context of the magazine's general editorial slant. The magazine itself is also situated within the context of either the entire culture or the particular subculture about which the magazine writes.[63] For example, an article or review in a hip-hop publication such as *The Source* serves to clearly identify the artist with the hip-hop subculture and legitimize that artist to the readers. Many of the publications below, even specialty publications like *Mix*, have reviews or recordings or feature articles about how some artist made their latest recording, and are potential publicity sources.

Sizing Up Print

Magazines are typically divided into two broad classes depending on whom they serve, either consumers or businesses. The business publications are often referred to as "trades." There are music and recording publications of both types. An additional useful split for purposes of our understanding is that of music business and audio.[64]

Trade Publications

Music Business Publications

The publications classified as "business" for music run a wide gamut. There are half a dozen educators' publications like *The American Music Teacher*, another half dozen specialist instrument publications like *Drum Business,* and approximately seventeen publications in core recording industry/music business areas, such as *Billboard, Variety, Amusement Business, Pollstar,* and *Radio and Records.* Putting this category into the context of total magazine sales, the top ten *Standard Rate and Data Service* (*SRDS*) trade publication categories (which do not include music and music

TABLE 5-6   Revenue Production of Music-Related Publications (1995)

Publication	Revenues (in Thousands)	Total Circulation	Folio 500 Rank
Rolling Stone	$146,045	1,180,000	26
Stereo Review	$ 31,511	450,000	156
Spin	$ 27,209	453,000	175
Billboard	$ 24,631	45,000	198
Daily Variety	$ 20,485	27,000	229
Audio	$ 13,594	115,000	304

Source: "The Folio 500," *Folio,* 1 July 1996: 51.

trades) measured by total circulation have a combined circulation of 26.1 million.[65] The combined circulation of the music business publications is about 650,000, only about 2.5 percent of the total for the top ten groups.[66]

The leading recording industry publication is *Billboard*, sometimes referred to as the "Bible" of the recording industry. It began circulation in 1894 as *Billboard Advertising,* a trade publication covering the outdoor advertising and bill posting business. Because lots of bills involved circus and other live performers, it naturally evolved into carrying news of those businesses as well. By 1900 *The Billboard* recast itself as covering "the Great Out-Door Amusement World." It moved indoors in the first decade of the twentieth century adding coverage of vaudeville, film, and theater. Gradually, coverage of the music business increased. Coverage of the outdoor fair and carnival business continued until 1961 when the parent company split off *Amusement Business* for that purpose and focused *Billboard Music Week* entirely on the music business.[67] With an audited circulation of over 43,700, it has the largest readership of the music business publications. It is a moneymaker, too, bringing in over $234 million in 1995, enough to rate it in the top 200 of *Folio* magazine's "Folio 500" annual chart. Table 5-6 shows which other music related publications also ranked in the "Folio 500." *Billboard* is a *trade* publication, providing news and features of interest to those on the inside of the business. Its editorial slant is generally positive. It is an important chronicler of news events and information about the industry. There is a section of reviews as well as the infamous charts (see earlier discussion in this chapter) that track the success of recordings in achieving airplay and sales. *Daily Variety* (usually just referred to as *Variety*) is broader in scope and covers the entertainment industry in general, including recordings, television, movies, and theater. Other significant music business publications are *Radio and Records, Pollstar, Performance, Music Trades Magazine,* and *Music and Sound Retailer.*

Audio Publications

Business publications about audio include those dealing with recording, sound reinforcement, audio/video applications, consumer audio trade publications, and even two scholarly journals from the Audio Engineering Society and the Society of Motion Picture and Television Engineers. *Audio Video International* and *Mix* have the largest circulations, with about 70,000 and 40,000, respectively. Some of the publications such as *Mix* and *Pro Sound News* review artists' recordings, concerts, or video productions and can be sources of publicity within a segment of the industry.

Collectively the audio and music business trade publications have a combined circulation of about 560,000. *Folio*'s top ten categories of trade publications had a combined circulation of 26.1 million in 1995. The smallest category in the top ten, restaurant and food service trades, had a circulation of about 950,000.[68] Recording industry trade publications amounted to less than 2.2 percent of total trade publication circulation.

Consumer Publications

Recordings

Rolling Stone is the king of the music-related consumer publications. Its annual revenues put it in the top thirty of *Folio* magazine's "Folio 500" listings. National publications with large circulations, other than those inserted in Sunday newspapers, such as *USA Weekend* and *Parade,* tend to have circulations in the three to seven million range. (Notable exceptions are *TV Guide* and *Reader's Digest*, with circulations over 13 million and 15 million, respectively.) *Rolling Stone*, with nearly 1.2 million in circulation, heads the category of music/style publications. Others with circulations over 100,000 are *Spin* (progressive rock), *Request* (all contemporary), *Vibe* (urban), *Jazziz* (jazz), *Hit Parader* (rock), *Pulse* (Tower Records/contemporary), *Rap Sheet* (rap), *Release* (Christian), *The Source* (hip-hop), *BAM* (contemporary), *Bone* (contemporary), and *Country Music* (country). Publications for all styles of music exist, from bluegrass, to black gospel, to opera, to metal.

Audio

Consumer audio publications account for a combined circulation of about 1.4 million. Almost one-third of that circulation is accounted for by the venerable *Stereo Review*. It heads a group of nine publications about hi-fidelity home and auto equipment. These publications are important because the main drive for consumers' interest in home audio and auto audio is the availability of high quality recordings. Two of the consumer publications are targeted at the semiprofessional, home and project recording environment. *EQ* and *Recording* are closer to the recording industry core function of the creation of recordings. They encourage people without major recording contracts or the resources provided by the labels to create their own recording studios. By supplying the encouragement and some "how to" information, these publications contribute to a growing pool of recording talent at the margins of the industry. They are the new artists, the specialty artists, the independent label artists who can survive on selling 100,000 or less units and playing club dates. It is from their ranks that many new sounds and future mainstream acts often emerge.

Collectively, the recording industry consumer publications have a total circulation of about 6.6 million. Putting this in perspective, the *SRDS* top ten consumer categories (which do not include music) have a combined circulation of about 301.3 million. The tenth ranked category in consumer publications is business publications, with about 7.2 million combined circulation.[69] So, recording industry magazines are probably less than 5 percent of total magazine circulation. The direct conglomerate connection to recording industry publications is generally missing. Although Time Warner has a large magazine publishing division, it does not publish any recording industry magazines but focuses primarily on larger circulation publications such as *People* and *Time*. The question remains of whether Time Warner publications may feature or review artists on Time Warner labels more than those on other labels.

SUMMARY

Part 1 has focused on an overview of the recording industry. It has grown from a notion of a business machine invented by Edison into a major entertainment medium, surpassing some of the more traditional mass media and rivaling others in economic significance. It is a cultural phenomenon, with impact on a wide variety of behavior from dance, to social group definition, to clothing. Yet the exact nature of the cultural effects are debatable and not yet uniformly agreed on. Rather than enter the cultural debate, Chapter 1 set the stage for an economic analysis of the industry, using an approach that followed the three income streams generated by recordings and recording artists: the sale of recordings, the sale and performance of songs, and live performances by musicians. An understanding of these three streams leads to a better understanding of how the industry functions and why it functions the way it does.

Chapters 2, 3, and 4 then examined each stream in turn, its economic structure, functions, and relationships to the other two streams. There is a strong trend towards concentration of ownership and market share in each of the three streams. Particularly in the recording and music publishing streams the "big six" have acquired labels and music publishing companies at a rapid rate. Yet, this trend is not having the predicted effect on lack of diversity of recordings and music. To the contrary, there is a trend towards more market share by independent labels. There is a trend towards more small music publishing companies owned by writer–artists and producers. The large corporate interests often let others take the risks of production and creativity and become involved more in the distribution and marketing of the final products.

This both stabilizes the income and cash flows of the larger entity, and encourages smaller entities to enter the market because they have some hope of effectively selling and collecting for the sale and use of their recordings and songs.

Part 2 examines in detail three important components of the recording stream: the production of recordings, the marketing of recordings, and the retail sale of recordings. In production, the diffusion of technological means of production and its reduced cost is encouraging small firms and musicians to actually produce their own recordings, leading to more diversity in the recordings available. In marketing, the development of more marketing media and methods for recordings and a decreased reliance on radio is broadening the reach of the record companies. Similarly, the availability of more detailed marketing information developed through SoundScan and BDS allows labels to more carefully market to niche audiences. As time passes, that should allow labels to be less reliant on the smash hit and more reliant on having more smaller hits in smaller markets. Not that there will not be an impetus to get the big hit and cash in on its financial rewards, but that there will be an increased emphasis on steady income from smaller markets. That is part of how independent record companies survive and sometimes prosper. Finally, in the retail sector, two trends are important to increased diversity of product availability; the growth of average record selling location size and a trend to very large "megastores" allows greater depth of inventory so consumers have more choice in the individual stores, and the continued strength of the independent retailers, despite the growth of chains and megastores, helps insure continued availability of some specialty genres. Used CDs, despite label opposition, are another viable way for more consumers to access more music because of the reduced prices of used CDs. The restructuring of the industry, brought about by technological advances and economic considerations, continues.

NOTES

[1]"Study Reveals Top Advertisers," *Billboard*, 13 April 1996: 85.

[2]National Association of Recording Merchandisers, "Soundata Consumer Panel," *NARM Sounding Board*, March 1996 (retrieved from NARM's internet site, http://www.narm.com).

[3]Reprinted in "The Day Radio Died," *Music Retailer*, April 1975: 29.

[4]Warner Communications, "The Prerecorded Music Market: An Industry Survey," reprinted in *NARAS Institute Journal*, 2, 1 (1978): 77.

[5]CBS Records, "Today's Singles Buyer," distributed at the NARM Convention.

[6]Paul Hirsch, *The Structure of the Popular Music Industry,* University of Michigan Institute for Social Research monograph (1969).

[7]Edgar A. Grunwald, "Program Production History 1927 and 1937," in *Variety's 1937–1938 Radio Directory* (1937).

[8]Ibid.

[9]*RCA Mfg. Co., Inc. v. Whiteman*, 144 F.2d 86 (2d Cir. 1940).

[10]Ibid. at 90.

[11]"The Bionic Radio," *Billboard*, 21 May 1977: RS-71 (Century of Recorded Sound Special Issue).

[12]Ibid. at RS-96.

[13]"Radio Meets the TV Challenge and Re-invents Itself," *Media Week, Radio 75th Anniversary Supplement*, 4 Sept. 1995: Supp. p. 20.

[14]R. Serge Denisoff, *Solid Gold* (1975) notes the 1955 date at 233. Russell Sanjek and David Sanjek, *American Popular Music Business in the 20th Century* (1991) notes it as KOWH, Omaha at 109.

[15]"The Bionic Radio," *Billboard*, 21 May 1977: RS-71 (Century of Recorded Sound Special Issue).

[16]Data from "Radio Billings 1935–1974," *Broadcasting Yearbook* (1976): C-298.

[17]See generally, R. Serge Denisoff, *Tarnished Gold* (1986); Phillip H. Ennis, *The Seventh Stream: The Emergence of Rocknroll* (1992); Russell Sanjek and David Sanjek, *American Popular Music Business in the 20th Century* (1991).

[18]"Record of Radio Station Growth Since Television Began," *Broadcasting & Cable Yearbook* (1995): B-655.

[19]"U.S. and Canada Radio Programming Formats," *Broadcasting and Cable Yearbook* (1995): B-592.

[20]T. Barton Carter, et al., *The First Amendment and The Fourth Estate*, 6th ed. (1994): 609–619.

[21]See, e.g., "Sage Acquires Stations," *New York Times*, 26 June 1996: C3-national; "Chancellor Agrees to Buy 8 Radio Stations, *New York Times,* 16 May 1996: C4-national; "American Radio Merging with Henry Broadcasting," *Broadcasting and Cable*, 25 March 1996: 14; Cheryl Heuton, "The Large Get Larger: SFX Purchase of Liberty Continues Run on Stations in Big Markets," *Mediaweek*, 4 Dec. 1995.

[22]"The New Empire of the Air," *U.S. News and World Report*, 1 July 1996: 10.

[23]Elizabeth H. Rathburn, "The Reordering of Radio," *Broadcasting & Cable*, 1 July 1996: 6.

[24]Donna Petrozzello, "Radio Group Heads Foresee Consolidation, Format Diversity," *Broadcasting & Cable*, 24 Oct. 1944: 3.

[25]Robert P. Rogers and John R. Woodbury, "Market Structure, Program Diversity, and Radio Audience Size," *Contemporary Economic Policy,* Jan. 1996: 81.

[26]Cara Jepsen, "Mainstream Rock Updates Itself," *Billboard*, 20 April 1996: 91.

[27]"U.K.'s Niche Stations Willing Battle Against Homogenization," *Billboard*, 13 April 1996: 85.

[28]"ABC Radio, SoundScan to Feed Sales Info to Affiliates," *Billboard*, 16 April 1994: 85.

[29]Tony Novia, "Is CHR an Endangered Species?" *R&R*, 10 May 1996: 28.

[30]Phyllis Stark, "Interep Studies Country Listeners," *Billboard*, 2 April 1994: 69.

[31]Donna Petrozzello, "Alternative Rock in the Mainstream," *Broadcasting & Cable*, 20 May 1996:51.

[32]Chuck Taylor, "Format Issues Tackled at Gavin Seminar," *Billboard*, 24 Feb. 1996: 90.

[33]*Broadcasting & Cable Yearbook 1986:* G-16.

[34]See, e.g., R. Serge Denisoff, *Tarnished Gold* (1986): 238; Russell Sanjek and David Sanjek, *American Popular Music Business in the 20th Century* (1991): 173–175.

[35]Joel Whitburn, *Joel Whitburn's Pop Singles Annual 1955–1986* (1987).

[36]Deborah Russell, "Video Kills the Radio Star," *Billboard 100th Anniversary Issue 1894–1994*, 1 Nov. 1994: 196.

[37]Joe Jackson, "Video Clips: A Personal View," *Billboard,* 16 June 1984: 10.

[38]Tony Seideman, "Four Labels Ink Vidclip Deals With MTV," *Billboard,* 23 June 1984: 1.

[39]Edward Morris, "NCN Cites $1.1 Mil Paid for Use of Music Videos," *Billboard,* 29 May 1995: 26.

[40]Dominic Pride and Melinda Newman, "MTV Deal Marks Strategy Shift for Sony," *Billboard,* 12 Nov. 1944: 5.

[41]Mike Levin, "PolyGram NV Buys 50% of MTV Asia," *Billboard,* 29 April 1995: 5.

[42]Deborah Russell, "No Art to making Vid a Class Act," *Billboard,* 11 June 1994: 56; Deborah Evans Price, "Benson, Z Music's Retail Team-Up," *Billboard,* 20 May 1995: Jeff Levenson, "BET to Bow Jazz Network," *Billboard,* 2 Oct. 1993: 8; Deborah Russell, "Austin Scene Spawns Vid Network," *Billboard,* 7 May 1994: 44.

[43]Recording Industry Marketing Research Class, Middle Tennessee State University, *Music Videos and Record Store Customers* (a 1995 study for the Music Video Association).

[44]"Music Video Sales Chart Moves to SoundScan Data," *Billboard,* 24 April 1993: 6.

[45]Seth Goldstein, "Managing Ever-Changing Sell-Thru," *Billboard,* 6 Jan. 1996: 43.

[46]Al Stewart, "Suppliers Weigh $14.95 Vid Prices," *Billboard,* 1 April 1989: 1.

[47]Recording Industry Association of America, *Gold and Platinum Record Awards* (1984).

[48]Susan Nunziata, "Bodyguard Album, Single Soar at Sales Counters," *Billboard,* 16 January 1993: 10; Top 200 Albums Chart, *Billboard,* 29 July 1995.

[49]George Kalogerakis, "Keeping Score," *Vogue,* May 1996: 170.

[50]Brett Atwood, "Indie Film Soundtracks Help Expose Modern Rock Acts," *Billboard,* 8 Oct. 1994: 8.

[51]Wolfgang Spahr, "Movie Soundtracks Start Moving Units in Germany," *Billboard,* 17 Sept. 1994: 50.

[52]"There's 'Nothin' Like the Reel Thing,'" *Billboard,* 18 May 1996: 4.

[53]Quoted in David Seay, "The Sound of Movie Music," *Billboard,* 3 April 1993: S3.

[54]Source: *Standard and Poor's Stock Reports,* unless otherwise noted.

[55]Sony Corporation, *1995 Annual Report,* on-line version, at http://www.sony.co.jp.

[56]Charles P. Daley, Patrick Henry, and Ellen Ryder, *The Magazine Publishing Industry* (1997): 9.

[57]Melinda Newman, "Consumer Music Mags Win Clout," *Billboard,* 23 Dec. 1995: 1, at 105.

[58]Melinda Newman, citing a 1994 study in "Consumer Music Mags Win Clout," *Billboard,* 23 Dec. 1995: 1

[59]Geoffrey P. Hull, *Atlanta Record Buyers Survey* (1977) (Georgia State University: 1977).

[60]R. Serge Denisoff, citing a 1984 study in *Tarnished Gold* (1986): 289

[61]Geoffrey P. Hull, *Atlanta Record Buyers Survey* (Georgia State University: 1977).

[62]Previously unpublished results from the survey discussed in Robert O. Wyatt and Geoffrey P. Hull, "The Music Critic in the American Press: A Nationwide Survey of Newspapers and Magazines," *Mass Comm Review,* 17, 3 (1990): 38.

[63]See, e.g., Melvin L. DeFleur and Everette E. Dennis, *Understanding Mass Communication,* 4th ed. (1991): 127.

[64]Unless otherwise noted, circulation figures and publication information are obtained from Standard Rate and Data Service's (SRDS) *Business Publication Advertising Source*, July 1996 and *Consumer Magazine Advertising Source*, July 1996.

[65]"The Folio 500," *Folio*, 1 July 1996: 53.

[66]The figure was arrived at by adding all *SRDS Business Publications* category 99 (Music and Music Trades) for which circulation figures were given, plus *Variety* and *Radio and Records,* plus appropriate selections from category 122 (Radio, TV, Video).

[67]Ken Schlager, "On the Boards, 1894–1920," *Billboard 100th Anniversary Issue* (1994): 18.

[68]"The Folio 500," *Folio*, 1 July 1996: 53.

[69]"The Folio 500," *Folio*, 1 July 1996: 52.

Part 2

Recording Industry Core Functions

The next three chapters examine in detail the two core record company functions: the acquisition of masters and the marketing of those masters. Chapter 6 explores the ways a label can acquire masters, primarily focusing on the label's efforts to find recording artists, sign them to contractual obligations to record masters, and produce those masters. Chapter 7 analyzes the ways labels market their recorded products, using the "four Ps" approach to focus on product lines, promotion, place of sale and distribution, and pricing. Although most labels do not sell their recordings directly to consumers, retail, the final phase of marketing, is critical to the industry. It is especially important because sales of most recordings are through specialty stores or through specialty rack jobbers who provide recordings to mass merchandiser's record/electronics departments. Chapter 8 provides a closer look at record retailing.

6

Production and the A&R Function

In order to be a record company a label must acquire rights to market master recordings. This chapter deals with all the ways a label can perform one of its two basic functions—the acquisition of masters. This is the A&R (artist and repertoire) function. The labels can either create the masters themselves, or have somebody else do it for them. A&R is about taking and reducing risks—knowing when to take and when not to take risks, and knowing how to reduce the risk of making a poor choice. Like most things in business, higher risks are usually associated with higher rewards if there is success. The label can engage in the higher risk, but greater reward, activity of having new masters created for it by acquiring exclusive recording rights from artists and having those artists make master recordings. As an alternative, the label can acquire masters that have already been finished from smaller production companies or labels thereby reducing risk by knowing what the finished product will sound like, and perhaps by having some marketing track record on a small scale. The label can acquire masters that have already been successfully marketed in some manner and attempt to repackage, remaster, or in some way create a recording that is a new and different assembly of the older masters. There the initial risk of recording and marketing has already been taken and a market established. "Greatest hits" and "essentials" packages and digital remasterings of older analog recordings are examples of this method.

FINDING AND RECORDING NEW TALENT

New or Used?

It is often said that the lifeblood of a record label is new talent. Without infusions of new recordings that excite consumers to purchase them a label as an entity, or the industry collectively, fails to advance. As noted in Chapter 1, it may even fall into a state of decay towards entropy. Strictly speaking, a label does not have to find talent that has never been recorded before or that has never had a record released on a major (or any other) label. A label can acquire talent by "buying" established talent from other labels when the artist's contract with the former label has expired. That is an expensive proposition for two reasons. First, the artist is already established and will therefore demand a large advance per album. When Island Records signed Janet Jackson from Columbia in 1995 she was reportedly given a five million dollar per album advance, plus 25 million dollars just for signing her new contract.[1] When Clive Davis at Columbia signed a ten album deal with Neil Diamond for four million dollars in 1971, it was a major deal.[2] The reward of such deals is that the label gets an artist who can already sell millions of records without the label having to pour hundreds of thousands of dollars into marketing and a slow development process. The risk is that the label may have acquired the talents of the artist at, or after, the artist has peaked, never to be as successful again. In which event, the huge advances may never be recovered. Several 1990s megadeals did not bear as much fruit as the labels might have wished, notably Michael Jackson's $60 million deal with Sony Music, Madonna's $60 million deal with Warner Brothers, and ZZ Top's $35 million deal with RCA. One way that the labels hedge their bets with such large deals is to make any per album advances contingent on sales performance of the prior albums. In some instances the total package might wind up actually costing only about half or less of its initially reported value.[3]

There are some good reasons to sign and develop new artists: (1) their royalty rates and advances will be much lower because they are an unknown quantity in terms of how many records they can sell, and (2) if successful they will be obligated to the label for a significant number of future albums. New artists do not have sufficiently strong bargaining positions based on track records of sales to negotiate for a high royalty per album and a high advance per album. If such an artist is successful, the label will obtain a much higher profit per copy sold because their artist royalties will be substantially less than those for an established artist. A typical new artist contract usually requires a royalty of 60 percent to 70 percent of what a superstar can command (see discussion of royalties below). If a new artist nets roughly $1.00 per unit sold, then a superstar probably nets $1.70 or as much as $2.00 per unit sold. A label would rather sell a million units of the new artist and take home an extra $700,000 profit. The problem is that there is much less certainty that the new artist will sell that million units. In fact, there is a likelihood that the artist will sell substantially less than that. In fact, the likelihood is that the new artists will probably not sell enough for them to recoup their advances (that does not necessarily mean the label will not have made a profit on the sales, see discussion in Chapter 7).

The other reason for developing a new artist into a major artist is that they will be obligated to make more records for the label than the already developed superstar. A typical new artist deal will call for eight to ten albums over the life of the agreement. A major artist deal will probably be from four to six albums. So, with a new artist who becomes successful the label will probably be able to keep the artist under contract for the most successful part of their recording career—typically no more than five to seven years.

Finally, since the recording industry runs primarily on popular musical tastes, it is imperative to be seeking and signing the next new sound, the next hit. A label can only rest on its laurels and current acts for so long. After a while, new faces and new sounds catch the public's attention and purchases. The formerly reliable sales from the established acts begin to drop and the label has no new blood under development to take up the slack. It happened to Columbia about the time that Clive Davis took over in the mid 1960s. They were relying on Broadway cast albums and a few Middle-of-the-Road artists to make up most of their sales—missing the important new wave of rock artists. It happened to RCA in the mid 1970s—relying too much on John Denver and a couple of other artists who were passing their peak. No label is immune. There has to be attention paid to what is new, on the streets, in the small clubs, and on the local, regional, or custom labels. That is the job of the A&R department.

Who Has "Good Ears"?

How does an A&R person know whether a particular new artist will be a hit? They don't. Industry people say, "You have to have good ears." People with good ears become producers and A&R vice presidents. We know they have good ears because they signed or found the latest hit artist. Of course, that is an after-the-fact test. If that same artist had "stiffed" (done very poorly on their first album sales) the person who found them obviously did not have good ears. Whatever good ears are, they are a product of listening to lots of popular music, not only what is being recorded now, but to what is not being recorded yet. Ear training for A&R people is going to clubs, and listening to demos from bands, personal managers, and publishing companies. It is knowing social trends. It is knowing some history of popular music, for example when a sound or artist that has not been heard in a while might be given a new twist that suddenly fits in. And, by the way, it is a little bit of luck. Hearing the next big act and signing them before some other label does may be simply the result of being in the right place at the right time. The solution to improving the odds is to be in lots of places, lots of times. Knowing the timing of the next sound that will capture the public's fancy and what that sound will be is partially a product of hearing lots of music and talking to lots of people. Those are the reasons why being "on the street" is important to the A&R function.

Money Matters

A label will usually be able to spend only a limited amount of money recording and promoting its artists. Based on the cash flows predicted on past experience and knowledge that there have to be some new artists being signed, most labels set aside a certain amount of money to develop new artists. If they know it will take $150,000 to record an album, and another $150,000 to introduce it to the market, then the number of new artists that can be signed by that label is the number of $300,000 "lumps" the label can afford to spend from its current budget.

The label will want to reduce the risk of spending $300,000 on a new artist whose record turns out to be a stiff. New talent can be drawn from the pool of artists who have proven themselves in live performances. Live performances sell records. An artist with a great live show that really gets an audience excited will probably be able to sell more records than one with a mediocre live show. That is why A&R people want to hear and see an artist perform before signing them.[4] That is why artists and managers often set up "showcase" performances where the artist can play for a select crowd of influential record company, radio, and other people. An artist who can make a good visual appearance will also sell more recordings because of the impact that MTV and other video channels have on record sales. That is why A&R people may even want to see some video on an artist they are thinking about signing. A&R people don't like to sign artists who do not already have a personal manager—someone else who has already invested time and money, who is an industry insider, and who believes the artist has the talent and drive to become a success. A&R people do like to sign artists who sound like somebody else who has just broken a new sound. The risk there is that the label will be trying to get into a market that is already too crowded. A&R people do like to sign artists who have publishing deals in which a music publisher has invested substantial amounts of money in the development of the artist's writing abilities. A&R people like to hear a high quality demo so that they can get a very good idea of what this artist will sound like on a finished master. All of these are ways for the label to minimize the risk that they will invest several hundred thousand dollars and come up with nothing.

Another way to minimize the risk, but still retain an option to record new artists, is to enter a "development deal" with the artist. These deals are a step short of a full recording contract. A label may feel that the artist has potential but is not quite ready to record, perhaps because she or he needs to work on songwriting, live performance, or recording techniques. In that case, the label may decide to offer the artist an agreement whereby the artist promises to remain available to enter an exclusive contract with the label in exchange for working on whatever deficiency the label feels exists. The artists will usually be given an advance to do a demo recording of three or four songs to showcase their abilities in the studio. The advances for these recordings are rather small, usually in the $4,000 to $6,000 range. These advances are recoupable from any royalties earned under a recording agreement that may be signed later. (See discussion and example later in this chapter about advances, royalties, and recoupment.) The label substantially reduces its financial risk compared to a full album contract with the new artist and reduces the risk that someone else may find and sign this potential hit artist first.

ARTISTS' RECORDING CONTRACTS

At its most basic level, a recording agreement between an artist and a label is a contractual arrangement between the two parties based on an exchange of promises. The artist promises to make recordings for this label, and for no other (an exclusive agreement), in exchange for the label's promise to pay the artist royalties based on the sale of those recordings, when and if those sales occur. What the two parties both want to do with the agreement is to minimize their risks and maximize their profits. To that end recording agreements are highly negotiated. There are a lot more points of concern to both parties; that is why the agreements are likely to be thirty to sixty pages in length.

Bargaining Position

The critical factor deciding who has the upper hand in the negotiations is the relative bargaining power of the two parties. That boils down to a question of size—the "size" of the artist and the size of the label. A new artist with no track record of sales has very little bargaining power compared to the superstar whose last album sold five million copies. The new artist is all risk to the label—all unknown. From the artist's perspective the size of the label is a factor. A major label has marketing know-how and money to spend on delivery of an album to the public. A major label also has lots of artists and it is possible to get lost in the shuffle. A smaller, independent label does not have the marketing resources but the artist will be more important to the small label because the label does not have a large artist roster. What the artist wants to minimize risk is commitment from the label. What the artist wants to maximize profits is high royalties and advances. What the label wants to minimize risk is ways to get out of the deal (i.e., less commitment). What the label wants to maximize profits is lower royalties and advances. The conflicts are obvious. There is no "standard" agreement, but there are provisions standard to most contracts.[5]

Commitment—A Two-Way Street

The labels minimize risk in artists' recording contracts by trying to build in ways to get out of the deal at every stage.

1. The label will delay signing the contract at all. This gives them more time to make up their minds and to see if anything better comes along.
2. The label may decide not to record the artists once they are signed. The label may want to do this because they found some other artist who really gets them

excited, or because they are running out of money to invest in new recordings, or because the artist in question has committed some major public relations problem, such as the married Christian music artist who was having an affair with a band member, and the label does not want to try to market albums in the face of the negative publicity. The label will therefore try to get into the contract a "play or pay" clause that lets the label not even hold recording sessions at all, just pay the artist a single session union wage as if the session had been held. That is a lot cheaper than all the costs associated with a production.

3. The label may not accept the finished master or refuse to release it. Even if they have paid recording and studio costs, the label may feel they should cut their losses by ceasing to put money into the project now rather than market what is going to be an obvious (to them) stiff.

4. The label may release the record but only put a minimum amount of marketing money into it, figuring if the record begins to make waves on its own strength, then they will invest some money in marketing.

The artist wants the label to guarantee everything instead of allowing the label to have options to quit the project. At a minimum, from the artist's point of view, one is not much of a recording artist if there are not recordings available to the public. Even new artists can usually get a label agreement to record a minimum number of "sides" (single songs) or perhaps an entire album. A guaranteed release clause, usually only available to a middle level/established artist or higher, does not mean that the label must release a recording—only that the artist can get out of the agreement if the label fails to release the album within a certain time. It is even harder for the artist to get the label to commit to spending a certain amount of money on marketing. If the artist can get such a guarantee the label will try to get the artist to underwrite part of the expense by making the marketing guarantees 50 percent to 100 percent recoupable from the artist's royalties. Even if an artist could get all of these guarantees in the contract, there can be no guarantee that the label will do any of this with enthusiasm—just as there is no guarantee that the artist will record with enthusiasm.

Just as the label will seek to minimize its commitment to the artist, it will try to maximize the commitment of the artist to the label. This usually happens in the clause dealing with the recording obligation. Typically a new artist will be obligated to record as many as seven to ten albums, total. The label has the option to require each successive album, or drop the artist. The label gets to decide which to do, usually on a yearly basis or within a certain length of time after release of the previous album. The artists can be required to record the total number of albums. What artists would like is being required to record fewer albums, so they could get out of the deal and possibly go to a different label at a much more lucrative arrangement after a few years. (Artists, of course, always assume they will be successful. That is the kind of ego it takes to be a recording artist.) In reality, what most often happens is that the initial deal with the new artist gets restructured after (if) the artist has a reasonable amount of success. Then they are "established" artists and less of a risk to the label because they have a track record of album sales. This renegotiation process will invariably result in a more lucrative contract for the artist with the same label, but also in a commitment of more albums.

Why would a label be willing to renegotiate? Why not just say, "Hey, you made this agreement, now stick to it!" Simply because an artist who is upset with the label over the fairness of their recording agreement is not likely to produce a very enthusiastic recording for the next album. Keeping the artist happy is about the only way the label has of being sure they can get more good albums. They cannot force the artist to record a good album or even record at all. About all the label can do is get a divorce and maybe prevent the artist from making a new "marriage" with another label until the duration of the original contract is over.

Royalty Rates and Deductions

Paying artists royalties for exclusive recording arrangements goes all the way back to Enrico Caruso's arrangement with Victor records in the early 1900s. His 1904 contract called for a royalty of forty cents per disk (equivalent to more than five dollars per disk in 1995 prices), and an advance of $4,000. Sales of his recordings totaled into the millions and his income from recordings is estimated at $2 million to $5 million.[6] In 1995 dollars that would be equivalent to total earnings of $26.8 million to $67.1 million—earnings as good or better than some of the superstars of the 1990s. In the 1950s typical royalties were 5 percent of retail list, paid on 90 percent of sales. By the 1960s they began to move up, driven by the popularity of rock and roll and the growth of record sales, with *Billboard* reporting nearly a dozen artists with royalties exceeding five percent.[7] By the mid 1970s new artist royalties pushed up as high as 8 percent of retail list. If the royalty included the producer's royalty in an "all in" deal, new artists could expect to start in the 10 to 12 percent range.[8] By the mid 1990s the all-in deal was the norm. Typical rates for new artists ranged from 9 to 13 percent, for established artists from 14 to 16 percent, and for major artists from 16 to 20 percent; superstar artists sometimes exceeded 20 percent.[9]

But those royalty rates are not as lucrative for the artist as it might first appear. First, they are paid only on records sold. Because most records are sold on a 100 percent return privilege, there is no guarantee that shipment of a million recordings means that a million have been sold. A substantial number may end up being returned to the label by retailers and subdistributors. Artists receive no royalties for promotional copies and others that are given away to dealers and wholesalers as incentives or discounts. Some labels define "sales" to be 85 percent of shipments. In a practice that goes back to the days when records were made of shellac and easily broke, some labels pay on only 90 percent of sales to account for "breakage." Of course CDs and cassettes seldom break. Both of these are just ways for the label to reduce its royalty costs by paying less. Also, virtually all labels deduct from the list price a "container charge," typically 20 percent for tapes and 25 percent for compact discs. This supposedly is to cover the cost of the manufactured product itself. Compact discs do not cost $4.00 (25 percent of typical $15.98 list price) to manufacture, one to two dollars for the disc, box, and all inserts is closer. The deduction is just a way to pay the artist less per unit, and increase the label's profits per unit.

Advances

Advances are prepayments of royalties. They are highly negotiable. Some artists get paid an advance on signing the contract. Most get paid an advance on delivery and acceptance by the label of the master. As the artist earns royalties these advances are "recouped" (deducted) from earnings. The advances are nonreturnable, meaning the artist does not owe them to the label, and if no records sell, or not enough to recover the advance from the artist royalties, then the label is simply out the difference. That is the label's risk. The labels also include as "advances" things such as recording costs, producer fees, all or half of the video production costs if a music video is made, and even some marketing expenses such as independent promotion, or other marketing guarantees demanded by the artist. Recording and production advances are often included in a lump sum "recording fund." If the artist does not spend all of the recording fund advance on actual recording costs then any remainder can be paid to the artist, which in effect will amount to an advance for the delivery of the master.

A Gold Record and a Bounced Check

So how much would an artist really make on an album that went "gold" (sold 500,000 copies)? Suppose this is a recording by a new artist with an all-in rate of 12 percent. The producer has a royalty of 3 percent, which is deducted from the artist's all-in rate, making the artist net rate 9 percent. For the sake of simplicity, suppose the sales are all CDs with a list price of $16.00 (rounded for the sake of more simplicity). After the 25 percent packaging deduction, the artist is paid 9 percent of $12.00, or $1.08 per disc sold. Even if the 500,000 is net sales after returns, the artist will only be paid on 85 percent or 90 percent of those. Because this is a new artist, assume 85 percent. That means the artist gets $1.08 for 425,000 discs, or $459,000.

Now, about those recoupable advances. Recording fund advances for a new artist depend on the genre of the music and stature of the artist, but suppose this is a new rock/pop artist with a fund of $200,000. A careful artist may have been able to hold on to as much as $50,000 of that to actually put in their pockets. Assume the label did two music videos, at a cost of $50,000 each, which is one-half recoupable from album royalties. The label spent $100,000 on marketing expenses, half of which are recoupable. Because this is a new artist, the label will probably withhold payment on 30 to 50 percent either of royalties otherwise due or of the number records counted as shipped as a "reserve against anticipated returns." The reserve is to protect the label from the possibility of paying out royalties on records that appear to be "sold" but are later shipped back as returns from retailers and sub distributors. For the sake of simplicity, assume this artist's 35 percent reserve is out of royalties otherwise earned. Here are the calculations:

"Net sales" (85% of units shipped)		425,000
Times base rate per unit		x $1.08
Gross royalties earned		$459,000
Less: reserve (35%)		(160,650)
Net earned by artist		$298,350
Less recoupments:		
Recording fund	$200,000	
Video (50%)	50,000	
Promotion (50%)	50,000	
Total recoupable		($300,000)
Net due artist		($ 1,650)

This artist is in an "unrecouped" position. They don't owe the money back to the label but neither have their royalties accumulated yet to the point that they cover all of the advances. Furthermore, those unrecouped advances are "cross-collateralized." They may be recovered from any other income earned by the artist from the label. So, if still not recouped when the next album comes out, they will be deducted from royalties due from sales of the second album, in addition to the other recoupables directly attributable to the second album. The label cannot keep the reserves indefinitely. When the label "liquidates" (pays out) the reserve, usually over three or four accounting periods (up to two years), the artist will get the $160,650. Over a two-year period this artist kept $50,000 from the recording fund advance plus $160,650, a total of $210,650. Is $105,325 per year a lot of income? Suppose this artist is a four-piece band. Each member gets $26,331.25 per year *before* taxes. Because recording artists are self-employed they have to pay their regular income taxes plus the additional self-employment tax of over fifteen percent (their share of social security taxes plus the share normally paid by the employer). This band had better hope they make money from their live appearances, which have been made more profitable by the exposure from the gold album. Unfortunately, the only unrealistic number here is the number of albums sold for a new artist. SoundScan reported that only 148 titles sold more than 250,000 units in 1995 (out of over 17,000 new titles released) and that the average new release had 1995 sales of only 9,134 copies.[10]

Publishing Rights and Controlled Compositions

Many recording artists write or cowrite the songs that they record. All labels have affiliated music publishing companies. They would like to have artists who are also songwriters sign publishing agreements with those affiliates. To *require* the artist/ writers to do so would probably be a restraint of trade (though this has not been confirmed by a court opinion). However, the label can encourage the artist to sign with the label music publishing affiliate, and it is possible that an artist who is willing to do so will have more leverage in negotiating the recording or publishing agreement. The label's argument is that the existence of the recording, which they paid for and will promote, gives the artist/writer the chance to record the songs. Then it is sales of the recordings and airplay of the recordings that generates most of the publishing income. Many established artists who are also writers have their own publishing companies and are able to retain their own publishing rights. In most such cases they would pay a regular music publishing company a fee to either copublish or to administer the writer's company. That fee ranges from 10 percent to 25 percent of collections through the administrative company. Of course, the administration or copublishing could be through the label's publishing affiliate.

Since the 1909 Copyright Act record companies have had to pay the music copyright owner, usually a music publisher, a mechanical license fee for the right to make and sell copies of a recording of the song. From 1909 to 1978 that rate was two cents per song, per copy. (See Chapter 10 for further discussion.) From the label's point of view, mechanical royalties are a per-album expense, just the same as the pressing costs. As would any manufacturer, the label would like to control or reduce these expenses. As early as the mid 1970s the labels, spurred by the probable increase in the "statutory rate" to two and three-quarter cents in the new copyright law, began to seek ways to limit their mechanical license fees. What they came up with is a contractual provision that has caused much controversy but is now the norm—the "controlled compositions" clause. Because the recording and music publishing income streams intersect when the artist is a singer/songwriter or a self-contained group, the labels are able to control their expenses at the expense of the publishing stream.

A controlled composition is one written, owned, or controlled in whole or part by the artist (or probably the producer as well, especially in a producer–label agreement). The clause requires the artist/songwriter to license such compositions to the label at a specified rate, typically three-fourths of the "statutory rate" at the time of release. In addition, the labels often put a limit on the total mechanical royalties payable per album of about ten times the controlled composition rate. Here is the kicker: Any mechanical royalties paid in excess of the limit are recoupable out of artist recording royalties. It is not unusual for CDs to contain eleven or twelve songs and exceed the limit of total mechanical royalties. So, an artist/writer who puts twelve songs on an album would have just put two on "for free." A particular problem arises when the artist cowrites with other songwriters. In such cases the other writers are either forced to take the reduced rate on their shares of the songs, or the artist is forced to allow the label to take any difference between the full rate and the controlled composition rate out of his or her own royalties. Those results caused an uproar among artist/writers and cowriters when country artist Randy Travis released an album full of cowritten songs and his label refused to pay the cowriters the full statutory rate, even though Travis initially thought they would get the full rate. He ultimately agreed to pay them the full rate with the differences deducted from his own royalties.[11] The NSAI (Nashville Songwriters Association International) formally petitioned (to no avail) most of the major labels to drop the clauses from their contracts, especially as they applied to cowriters.[12]

How would all of this work? Suppose the artist has a controlled composition rate of 75 percent of the statutory rate. That rate in 1996 was 6.95 cents per song or 1.3 cents per minute of playing time, whichever was greater. For sake of simplicity, assume the per song rate applies. That means the label will only pay 5.2125 cents per song and a maximum of 52.125 cents per album. If the artist records eleven of his or her own songs, either the eleventh must be licensed for free, or the record royalties go down by 5.2125 cents per copy. If the artist got all of the mechanical royalty, that would not be too bad, a trade-off of songwriter royalties with recording artist royalties. More likely, the artist, as a songwriter, will not get 100 percent of the mechanical royalties. If the songs are owned by a music publishing company that is not the artist's company the writer will usually get 50 percent of mechanicals after the publisher/writer split. Even when artists/writers own their own publishing companies, they would probably be paying someone else to administer the company and still get only 75 percent to 90 percent of mechanicals after the administration fee. If the artist/writer cowrote with other songwriters, then those other writers would have to be willing to take the reduced rate and limits, or the artist would have to be willing to pay them a full rate, then have the label take the difference out of the artist's record royalties. All of the percentages, amounts, and limits in the controlled composition clause are highly negotiable if the artist has any stature, and are particularly important points for artist/writers.

Video Rights

The birth of Music Television (MTV) in 1981 caused labels to add yet more pages to their artists' contracts to deal with the creation and ownership of rights to music videos and other video performances of the artist. Initially many labels paid for all of the video production costs of the music videos. But that increasingly expensive proposition, coupled with the fact that the videos themselves were little more than promotional tools, albeit valuable tools, caused a shift to having the artists pay part or all of the production costs as "advances." By the mid 1990s it was customary to recoup half of the video production costs from recording royalties with the other half recouped from video royalties. Some labels would allow recoupment of all video production costs from video royalties. But as a practical matter for most artists, video royalties never approached half of the $30,000 to $100,000 production costs for the typical single song music video. However, for concert-length videos, usually shot live, the production costs per minute were substantially less and a market existed from the cable services such as HBO, Showtime, Cinemax, and others to show the video as programming. It is over creation and use of such nonpromotional music video productions that most of the difficult negotiations occur.

The labels prefer to view the music videos as "recordings" and say that they have exclusive rights to all the artist's "recordings." The artists say those exclusive rights are limited to phonograph recordings, or perhaps promotional music videos, but not to concert-length performances. To counter that the labels often ask a right of first refusal, to allow them to make the same concert video on the same or slightly more favorable (to them) terms if they wish. Royalties earned for the sale of a video tend to be about equal on a per copy basis to the royalties earned for the sale of a record. If the videos are sold through licensees then the artist usually gets 50 percent of net label receipts.

Union Agreements: AFM and AFTRA

Two unions have significant impact on recordings. The American Federation of Musicians of the United States and Canada (AFM) and the American Federation of Television and Radio Artists (AFTRA) have agreements with all major labels and most independents that require certain scale payments to nonroyalty performers on all recordings sold by the label. The labels require that all of their artists join the appropriate union. The AFM required payment to a musician in a standard three-hour recording session in 1995 was $263.81. A maximum of fifteen minutes of music could be recorded. The rates, set in the Phonograph Record Labor Agreement, include provisions for overdubs, premium hours, and a wide variety of other issues. The union leader on the session and the record producer make sure that all musicians are credited and proper payments made to the union, including a contribution of 10 percent of total wages to the union pension fund and a $15.00 health and welfare fund payment for each musician.

The AFM has two other agreements with the record labels, the Phonograph Record Trust Agreement and the Phonograph Record Manufacturers' Special Payments Fund Agreement. The first requires that the label pay about 0.3 percent of the suggested retail list price (SRLP)[13] of each recording sold to a fund that is used to provide free live musical performances for the public. The Special Payments Fund is a pot of money that is generated by the labels paying another percentage of the SRLP[14] of records sold, about 0.5 percent. This fund is then distributed to all musicians who performed on master recordings according to how many masters each recorded. The total of both payments is less than 1 percent. It is important to the recording artist to not allow the label to deduct these charges from the record royalties payable to the artist. Whereas the union scale wages are recording costs, the per copy charges are not.

Background singers and other vocal performers are under the AFTRA agreements with the labels. In 1995 the AFTRA Code of Fair Practice for Phonograph Records required soloists to be paid a scale wage for master sessions of approximately $120 per hour or per song (side), whichever was greater. Group members are paid on a sliding scale depending on how large the group is—the bigger the group, the less each member is paid. AFTRA also requires the labels to make contingent payments of 50 percent of minimum scale for the master session vocalists when certain sales plateaus are reached. There are seven steps that go from 125,000 units up to 1,000,000 units, and total up to 3.5 times the original scale. Like the per unit AFM payments, these should not be considered recording costs to be charged against the artist's royalties.

RECORD PRODUCTION

Q: "How many producers does it take to make a hit record?"
A: "I don't know . . . what do you think?"[15]

Whether it takes an actual individual identifiable as a "producer" to produce a
hit record, or any other record, is perhaps debatable. It does require somebody performing the functions that in most instances are relegated to a record producer. The
producer may be the artist. The producer may be somebody in the A&R department
at the label. The producer may be an independent producer hired by the artist or label
to help deliver the finished album to the label. Sociologist Simon Frith argues that
the production of popular music is a process "that fuses (and confuses) capital, technical, and musical arguments."[16] It is the record, not a song or music, that is the final
product, and it is the producer that is at the center of the creation of that product.

Producers have one goal, whoever they are: to complete a finished, marketable
recording. The producer must bring together the talent and the physical and monetary resources necessary to create a master recording. The producer must serve two
masters to do that—the artist and the label. The producer must possess good ears for
hearing hit songs and performances, good people skills for getting the best performances out of artists, engineers, musicians, and label personnel, and good creative
instincts to add to the chemistry of a recording project.

Producer Functions

Producers provide input into the process of the creation of recordings on three levels.

1. They perform A&R functions by finding talented artists to record, finding good
   material to record, and by matching artists and material.
2. They are managers of the production process: arranging and supervising recording sessions, hiring studios, musicians, and engineers, getting the best perfor-

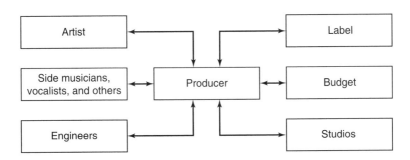

FIGURE 6-1   Producer Responsibilities

mances out of those people, supervising the creative aspects of the recording and mixing process to get the best sounding recording, supervising and approving the mastering and references—all with the goal of producing a recording that is marketable and at the same time is a good representation of the artist's abilities and any messages that the artist wishes to convey with the recording.

3. Producers perform business functions: budgeting the recording sessions and process, making sure the recording process does not go over budget, and making sure proper tax, withholding, and union forms are completed.

Kinds of Producers

At one time virtually all producers worked directly for record labels. They were "A&R men." They worked on salaries. They found the perfect songs for the recording artists, most of whom did not write their own songs. They set up recording sessions, hired arrangers to make create musical parts for trained musicians to perform, then listened as they and the artists plied their crafts for a few "takes" (tries at recording the song), then picked the best one for release. With rock and roll came artists who had great amounts of creativity and energy, but sometimes lacked great musical skills. They needed someone who could nurture their performances in a studio. With multitrack recording came the possibility of taking just a few musicians and turning out a recording that sounded like it had fifty people singing and playing on it, when it really only had four.

All of these developments meant that a producer had to take on a much more creative and managerial role. Rock artists did not want producers who were label employees, even though some of those people were quite talented. It was too "corporate" for the rock image. The independent producer became the norm. Producers began to be paid a royalty on the sales of albums, just like artists. Reportedly this began with Snuff Garrett, a producer in the late 1950s and 1960s, who was the first to ask his label for a royalty—a penny per album.[17] Artists began to produce, or coproduce, their own recordings out of ego, out of a desire to be more in control of the creative aspects of their recordings, and out of a desire to keep more of the available money. Some successful producers became label executives, but retained their production deals. In those instances the producer/executive (not to be confused with an executive producer) would typically be paid a royalty on sales of those artists produced, and a salary in their capacity as executives (usually in the A&R department, but sometimes label presidents).

Independent producers work under a variety of contractual arrangements with artists and labels. Sometimes an independent producer will find a potential recording talent, sign the talent to a deal to make a demo in the hopes that the producer can then succeed in getting a label to sign the artist, and producer, to a full-blown recording contract. In such instances the producer may even go so far as to release the recording on the producer's own label, aiming to either start a small record company or create some local sales and excitement to better attract the labels. In both of these instances the independent producer is performing valuable A&R functions: finding and recording new talent that may later get introduced to the public through a small or even major label.

Independent producers may also be hired by artists or labels to produce recordings or artists under contract to the label. In those instances, the label has done the A&R function of finding the talent, and the producer has the function of bringing a recording to fruition.

Recording artists, particularly after several successful records, may be allowed to produce themselves. In practical terms that usually means that the artist becomes almost totally in charge of the creative aspects of the production process, but will still need someone, an associate producer, or a coproducer, to be in charge of the business aspects of the process. Artists who successfully produce themselves have usually proven themselves capable of producing marketable recordings and making the creative decisions that go into those recordings. It is also possible that new artists who have produced themselves can get recording contracts based on the strength of their demos alone, though this is rare. The label still prefers to have an experienced person in charge of the business aspects of the production process. With the advent of project studios owned by the artists and producers themselves, the 1990s saw a movement to artists and producers being even more in charge of their production, leaving only the marketing to the record companies.

Producer Pay

Producers' royalties range from 2 to 5 percent of SRLP and are generally paid on the same terms as those of recording artists. They are also paid advances per side, or per album, depending on whether the deal is for a certain number of singles or for an album. Singles advances run in the $1,000 to $5,000 range and album advances in the $12,000 to $25,000 range. The size of the advance depends primarily on the experience of the producer and whether that producer also producers other important artists for the same label. Assuming the artist has an all-in royalty, the producer's royalty is paid out of the all-in royalty. This can lead to a variety of complex situations regarding recoupment of artist and producer advances, when the producer gets paid, and possible double recoupment of the producer's advance as a recording cost from artist royalties, and as an advance under the producer's royalties. These complexities are just more reasons why artists and producers are well advised to have music industry attorneys negotiate their arrangements with the labels.

Stages of Production

While much production actually takes place in the recording sessions there is also work to be done in the preproduction phase of the process and in a postproduction phase. In preproduction, the songs are selected, studios reserved, arrangers hired, session musicians and singers arranged for, engineers hired, the production concepts of the songs and album decided on by the artist and producer, and (for budget-minded producers and artists) rehearsals held. In the production stage, tracks are recorded, overdubs are recorded, and the songs are mixed down to a finished master, ready to be delivered to the label. The postproduction phase is likely to have duties shared between the actual producer and the A&R department for the label. Tasks such as getting correct liner notes, credits, lyric sheets, and licenses/clearances when needed for samples and for the songs themselves are usually carried out after the production is completed. The producer will also oversee or approve creation of master tapes and discs for manufacturing into cassettes or CDs. Alternate mixes for dance clubs or radio or singles are made. The producer may consult with the label's marketing department or product manager over which cut should be the first single released from an album.

Production Budgeting

One of the producer's responsibilities will be to submit to the label a budget for the production of the recording(s). The sizes of the budgets vary from less than $50,000 to hundreds of thousands of dollars. One of the factors contributing to the variation is the genre: jazz is usually recorded live, with just a few takes so studio time and musician time are minimal; country can be simple or elaborate, with budgets approaching pop or rock in some instances; rap can be very inexpensive, especially if the rappers have their own rhythm tracks already created in a project or MIDI studio; rock can be very expensive, especially if the artist wants to write the songs in the studio, work out arrangements in the studio, and/or is not really a very good musician/vocalist. In some respects, the budgets end up being governed by how many recordings the label thinks it can sell of this particular artist. An artist who can sell 200,000 copies on a good album cannot be allowed to spend as much on production as an artist who can sell three million albums. Particularly in rock and pop, album advances are intended to cover production and leave some money left over for the artist. It is usual for albums after the first to have the per album recording fund advance increase substantially so that the artist has a larger production budget with which to be creative, and so the artist will have more money to take home after all production expenses are paid.

   If the production costs exceed the budget, the producer has put the label in a difficult situation. If the project is nearly completed and is worth releasing, the label is just about forced to come up with more money. The label may, however, have a contractual right to demand that any over-budget amount be repaid immediately out of the producer's or artist's album delivery advance, if there is one. It is almost always possible to spend a few more thousand dollars to work on a track or a mix just a little more. One of the producer's jobs is knowing when to say "when." Money is not the only factor determining when a production is "finished." The label has deadlines for delivery of the master so that the release date can fit into a certain schedule decided to be best not only for this album and artist, but for all of the label's upcoming releases.

Creative Controls

The trend in recording contracts and production contracts is to let the artist and producer make most of the creative decisions, especially if they are experienced and have delivered satisfactory masters in the past. So, selection of songs, selection of studios, selection of musicians and vocalists, selection of engineers and assistants, and selection of the producers themselves is usually up to the artist working in concert with the producer. At most, some labels want a right to approve these decisions. In such cases the producers and artists can usually successfully demand that approval cannot be unreasonably withheld.

Master Delivery Requirements

Both producers and artists are contractually obligated to deliver masters that are satisfactory to the label. The difficult problem is what standard of satisfaction is to be applied. The label would like to insist that the masters be "commercially acceptable." After all, the label is in the business of selling records. Artists and producers, on the other hand, do not like the label to be second-guessing their creativity. They would insist that the master merely be "technically satisfactory." The impasse can often be cured with language that says the label will accept an album that is at least as technically and commercially satisfactory as the previous album or other albums by artists of similar stature on this label. Whatever the language in the contract, it would be unusual for a label to reject an album when the artist and producer have made a serious effort. Acceptability standards most often come into play when artists attempt to throw together an album simply to meet their recording obligations, in the hope of getting out of the contract.

ACQUISITION THROUGH LICENSING

Instead of going through all the grief of finding artists, finding producers, and risking the inevitable stiffs, a label could get all or part of its masters by licensing them from other labels. Rhino Records, for example, sells significant numbers of albums that are repackages and remasters of older recordings. Rhino does careful research on the artists and songs, careful remastering, and produces Grammy-winning albums. The Musical Heritage Society also does this in the art/classical music field.

The label could also acquire masters that already exist by licensing or purchasing them outright from some smaller label or production company. In the 1990s this was a particularly popular approach in rap music. Some labels such as K-Tel sell albums like "The Greatest Hits of 19xx" that are simply collections of masters licensed from the labels that had the original artists and original hits. In those cases the releasing label pays the original label a per-copy royalty per cut, usually three to five cents.

STUDIOS AND RECORDING ENGINEERS

No discussion of production could be complete without at least an overview of the recording process as it involves studios and recording engineers. The recording gear and the people who operate it have become an integral part of the creative process in the production of master recordings. The diffusion of recording technology through lower costs and greater availability to musicians has created a situation in which the production process has become more "democratized." More people are able to afford and to produce high quality recordings and the conglomerates are in much less than total control of the production of recordings.

Studios Then and Now

Studios have not always been studios. In the late 1800s and early 1900s they were often referred to as "labs." The first professional disc recording studio was set up in Philadelphia in 1897 for recording the Berliner discs. A lot of early recording was done by taking the recording machines to locations that were convenient to the artists and setting up in some hotel or warehouse. In fact, Caruso's first major recordings were done in a hotel in Milan, Italy in 1902. He cut ten master cylinders in one day. Prior to 1902, when the making of molds for cylinder mass production was finally a viable procedure, every cylinder was an original or a direct dub of an original. When recording facilities were set up for cylinders they often involved the performers singing into a set of horns, with each attached to a different cylinder cutter. As many as twenty could be recorded at once. Of course the performer had to repeat the performance many times. Those who could perform steadily and repeatedly found plentiful work. One source called them "durable citizens with lungs of brass."[18] The number of times a performer had to record were referred to as "rounds." The studios were small, often barely able to hold more than a dozen musicians and the recording machines.

Until the advent of electrical recordings in 1925, all recordings were acoustic. The sound pressure energy from the performer had to be transferred into mechanical energy that moved a cutting stylus to make a groove in the master disc or cylinder. Isolation from surrounding background noise was not critical because it would not likely be picked up from the recording horns, much less then reproduced by the consumer's playback machine. But the electrical process, which captured the sounds in a carbon microphone and converted the sounds to electrical energy that could be amplified to run an electromechanical cutting lathe, meant much greater frequency response. The response range improved to 200 Hz to 9,000 Hz—almost two and one-half octaves greater than the purely mechanical systems. The microphones were also more sensitive than acoustic horns and necessitated more isolation from outside sounds. Studios more like modern ones began to develop.

World War II caused the development of more high quality amplifiers, radios, microphones, and most importantly for the recording industry, the practical development of recording tape. Tape could be easily edited and it became possible to "construct" a recording by splicing together bits and pieces of a performance or of several performances. Bing Crosby was the first to utilize this important ability for the creation of his network radio show in 1948. Later, multitrack recording made it possible to break down the construction of the recording into even more components, one track per instrument. Fewer musicians were needed to produce a complex recording and the importance and size of the control room grew. Steve Jones points out that the increasing amount of control over time, timbre, and all of the musical and sound elements of the recording became integral to the process.[19]

Audio Engineers

As the importance of the control room grew, so did the importance of the recording engineer—the person who ran all of the machinery that controlled the sound. At one time, for example, the effect of reverberation (the "echo" effect of sound bouncing around in a room and gradually dying out after the initial sound was made) was only possible to create by actually having a room into which the sound could be fed and allowed to reverberate, or by recording live in such a room with some microphone available to pick up the reverberant effect. With digital delay it is possible to simulate many different rooms and echoes and control many different aspects of how that "room" sounds with an electronic "box" no bigger than a ream of paper. More sophisticated devices meant a higher level of technological expertise was required from the engineers. Because of their knowledge of and ability to control all of the technology of recording, the engineers began to take on more of a creative role in the process.

The Industrial Model

Although it had always been possible to do location recordings, the assemblage of a large number of cylinder or disc cutters in the early days, the use of expensive amplifiers and disc cutters not available to the general public, the need for isolation from outside sounds, and the required presence of a significant number of skilled players and vocalists, dictated an industrial model for the recording process. By analogy, the studio was a "factory" where capital and labor were gathered together to complete a product. Not until the 1970s, when good quality multitrack recording equipment, known as "semiprofessional," became available to consumers was there significant diffusion of the recording process away from the factory/industrial model. By the mid 1990s high quality recording was possible with digital multitrack recorders available for the semiprofessional market. The MIDI (Musical Instrument Digital Interface) and sequencing revolution meant that complex sounds and even orchestral arrangements could be created by single musicians. The diffusion of recording technology does not necessarily create more high quality recordings, any more than the diffusion of water color paints creates more great water color paintings, but it does give more creative people ready access to the possibility of creating quality recordings and it has had a significant impact on the studio business and recording processes.

By 1995 70 percent of professional studios reported at least some degree of competition from home-based private production studios. Twenty-eight percent of respondents reported "very much" competition from the home studios.[20] In many instances the artists and producers used these home facilities to create basic synthesis tracks or work out arrangements so that when they did go to the higher end professional studio, they spent less time and money. The label practice of paying advances in the form of a "recording fund" where the artist and/or producer keeps what is left after expenses encourages such a reduction of expenditures. Also, the labels often approved the practice of the artist charging recording time and expenses from the artist's own facilities toward the recording costs. Artists are then in a position to set up their own studios and recover the cost through their own recording budgets. After a few albums, the studio is paid for.

This same practice has lead established and superstar artists to build their own top of the line studios to be used in their own productions. These facilities are most commonly known as "project rooms." Again, 70 percent of studio owners said in 1995 that they felt at least "some degree" of competition from such rooms, with 24 percent reporting "very much" competition from the project studios owned by producers or artists.[21] A fairly typical path of development is for a small private studio to develop into a project studio, which then begins to book commercial clients and then turns into part-time commercial studio. Even the major artist-owned studios sometimes begin to book outside clients. A problem with project studios is that they are often built in homes in residential neighborhoods. When they become commercial they run afoul of zoning restrictions and tax laws.[22]

Kinds of Studios

While the lines of distinction between professional and semiprofessional, and private, project, and commercial are blurring, the latter classification system still has some usefulness in understanding the studio business. Private studios tend to be small in size and track capability. They are usually owned by aspiring artists, songwriters, or producers and seldom book any outside time. They most often use top of the line semiprofessional equipment and may have as much as twenty-four track digital capability though they usually exist in the sixteen track and under range.

Commercial studios are those that are primarily used by "outside" clients and are in the studio business for profit. These studios are primarily twenty-four track and higher. They may be analog or digital formats, though the majority, about 55 percent, have multitrack (at least twenty-four track) digital recording capabilities.[23] They charge the higher rates, with twenty-four track analog studios charging from $85 to $120 per hour, and the twenty-four track digital studios charging from $107 to $165 per hour. These rates are 65 percent to 100 percent higher than their sixteen track or less counterparts.[24] A fair characterization of the smaller commercial studios is as "demo" studios for music recording or professional for small advertising clients. Some "world class" studios charge as high as $300 per hour.[25]

Project studios, to distinguish them from private studios, are most often owned by established artists and producers. They have all the capabilities of the commercial studios and some are as well equipped as the best commercial facilities. They tend to be twenty-four track (or more) digital format rooms. They are used primarily by the owners for producing their own recordings (projects) but may sometimes be rented to outside clients.

Studio Business Survival

The recording studio business is centered in five geographic locations: New York City, Los Angeles, Nashville, Chicago, and Southeast Florida (Orlando to the Keys). Any city of over about 100,000 has at least one commercial studio catering primarily to advertising clients. Private studios are as widespread as aspiring artists and writers, but the bulk of the recording for released masters, major client advertising, and film is done in these five areas. In 1994, average annual income for studios in these centers ranged from a high of $425,000 in New York City to $333,000 in Southeast Florida. Los Angeles incomes tend to be very near the New York City incomes, which tend to be about $70,000 per year higher than the incomes in Nashville, Chicago, or Southeast Florida. A four-year trend analysis reveals that the Los Angeles and New York annual incomes tend to fluctuate the most, dependent on the larger recording budgets in major recording artist and film contracts. A four-year income range in the New York City and Los Angeles studios is from a high of $473,000 to a low of $390,000. The other three centers are more stable, hovering near $350,000 per year over the 1990–1994 period.[26] Nationally, the average for all studios' income was reported at $256,000 in 1995.

Profile of the Typical Recording Studio

Most studios have only one control room (67 percent), are about ten years old, are equipped with MIDI (70 percent), are 24 tracks or more (55 percent), earn most of their income (58 percent) from music recording (advertising and broadcast recording revenues are a distant second at 13 percent), and are booked an average of 180 hours per month.[27] Note that this last figure is an average of about forty-two hours per week, just in case one is inclined to think that recording engineers do not work long hours.

By the mid 1990s recording studios as businesses were faced with difficult times. A *Pro Sound News* article summed up the problem: "In a nutshell: traditional studios find that they cannot raise their rates to offset the cost of equipment demanded by an increasingly sophisticated clientele that does more and more of its recording outside of those same studios."[28] In response, a number of studios started their own record labels or began manufacturing audio gear, in addition to providing other ancillary services, such as tape duplication or postproduction of audio for video.[29]

Recording Engineers

The task of the recording engineer is to operate the equipment that captures, and in some instances creates, the sounds that the artist and producer want on the recording. To that end the recording engineer is more of a technician than an "engineer" in the sense that the term is used in other professions. In addition to a thorough understanding of the specific equipment that they operate, most engineers find useful a basic level of knowledge in the areas of electronics, acoustics and sound, and music. Recording engineers must also possess the ability to work with and get along with people, some of whom will have quite large egos and be difficult to work with. Engineers must have "good ears" capable of discerning often subtle differences in sounds and understand how those differences will contribute to or detract from the overall sound which the artist and producer are trying to create. Engineers must also be capable of making creative decisions. The producer or artist may not be at every recording session for a particular project. The engineer will then have to decide what is the "best" sound for the purpose. Even when the producer or artist is present, they will often ask the engineer what they think about a particular track or sound. Sometimes they want real advice, sometimes they only want their egos stroked.

Recording engineers are often classified based on their knowledge, experience, and skill into four groups: senior engineers, assistant engineers, freelance engineers, and maintenance engineers. Senior engineers are usually associated with a particular studio. As their name implies they are the most knowledgeable and experienced engineers available at that facility. Even when an artist or producer brings their own favorite independent engineers to a session, the presence of a senior staff engineer from the studio is usually necessary to help with knowledge of the ins and outs and particular quirks of the studio and its equipment. Assistant engineers, also known as second engineers, often work primarily at one studio or primarily with one particular independent engineer. Freelance engineers tend to be senior level engineers who have a track record of recording successful albums with established artists. They work in studios wherever their artists want to work. They may have worked with the artist in the early days of the artist's career, they may have been doing the live sound reinforcement for the artist, but in some way, the artist has become convinced that this particular person is helpful in getting the sound that the artist wants on record. Maintenance engineers have the most electronics expertise. They tend to be associated with one particular studio, but some successfully freelance their time among several smaller studios. Engineers are usually paid on an hourly basis as indicated in Table 6-1. The table numbers represent averages, and *Pro Sound News* reported that salaries ranged from a low of $6.60 per hour in some cities for assistant engineers to a high of $26.60 per hour for maintenance engineers in the Los Angeles area.[30]

TABLE 6-1   Recording Engineers' Hourly Pay Rates

	Average Hourly Pay
Senior Engineer	$16.80
Assistant Engineer	$ 8.80
Freelance Engineer	$19.70
Maintenance Engineer	$22.00

Source: "1995 Studio Business Operations Survey," *Pro Sound News*, September 1995.

Organizations

Three industry professional organizations are of particular interest to studio owners and audio engineers: the Society of Professional Audio Recording Services (SPARS), the Audio Engineering Society (AES), and the Society of Motion Picture and Television Engineers (SMPTE). SMPTE is the older organization, having been formed in 1916 as the Society of Motion Picture Engineers. Its membership consists of engineers involved in the creation of "motion pictures, television, computer imaging, telecommunications, and the related arts and sciences." Among other things, it helps set technical standards for those areas and publishes the technical journal, *The SMPTE Journal*. The members of the AES are involved in the creation of audio and recording devices and the creation of recordings and live sound reinforcement. AES, like SMPTE, is an international organization, publishes a technical journal, *The Journal of the Audio Engineering Society,* and helps set technical standards for its industry. AES was founded in the mid 1940s. The newest of these organizations is SPARS. It was founded in the 1970s to represent professional studio owners as a trade organization. For more information on all of these organizations visit their World Wide Web sites listed in the Internet Appendix.

Going to School

Two factors, the complexity of recording and the popularity of recordings in general, have led to the growth of preparatory programs for recording engineers. The equipment has increased in complexity and sophistication to the point that it is very difficult to come in off the street and pick up the necessary knowledge in an apprenticeship situation. Under the "apprentice" type system that had developed in the 1960s and 1970s, someone who wanted to learn audio would show up at a studio, convince the owners of their desire to work and be assigned to help keep the studio clean. After a while they could usually convince the engineer to teach them something about some of the equipment. They learned on the job by doing. In addition, the increased sales of recordings and a growing interest in popular music in general has led to the increased interest of young people in careers in recording and the music business.

Those two factors prompted a significant number of institutions to offer programs which aim to provide some of the necessary training. There are well over 200 and perhaps as many as 300 institutions offering some kind of training in audio engineering and/or the music business. The programs range from seminars and short courses, often at studios seeking to sell their down time, to full-blown four-year bachelor's degree programs. The providers range from individual studios, to schools of the arts, to major colleges and universities. At all levels, there are some very good programs and some that are not very good. There is no industry certification or accreditation process for these programs and students need to investigate carefully the range of alternatives and compare the relative merits of various programs to the student's particular needs. The two most thorough listings are in the *Mix Master Directory* published by *Mix Magazine*, and the Audio Engineering Society's *Directory of Educational Programs*.[31]

These audio and music business programs began to develop in the early 1970s and by the mid 1990s a number were quite sophisticated. They, like the studios themselves, have benefited from the diffusion of lower priced high quality recording equipment and technology. While having a degree or certificate is not a requirement of being a recording engineer or a label promotion person, many of these programs place interns in the slots formerly occupied by apprentice-type learners. They also provide entry-level personnel who do possess the base level knowledge required of assistant engineers and employees. A study for NARM found that over 65 percent of NARM affiliates (including labels, retail, wholesale, and distribution firms) would give preference to graduates of a music business program when hiring new employees.[32] Some studios and recording industry businesses will not hire entry-level employees that have not been through one of the audio or music business programs, in part simply because there are quite a few students from these programs seeking employment and employed in the recording industry. There is a professional organization of college faculty who teach in such programs called the Music and Entertainment Industry Educators Association (MEIEA), which promotes the development of college audio and music business programs. During the late 1980s the Recording Academy (NARAS) launched its "Grammy in the Schools" program to pique the interest of high-school students in the recording industry.

SUMMARY

Technological advances are making it more possible for musicians and bands to record and distribute their music to wider audiences. On one front, the advances in low cost, high quality "home recording" equipment mean that many bands and musicians can afford their own recording gear or to go to a low-cost demo studio. The equipment available enables them to make high quality recordings without having to go through any record company or pay studio rentals of hundreds of dollars per hour. Lower costs in the manufacturing of compact discs now mean that these same bands can make CDs in small numbers. Typical prices for custom orders of 500 run from $800 to $1,500, depending on whether the packaging is four-color, the number of pages in a booklet, and so forth. The same quantity of cassettes would cost about 40 to 60 percent of the CD cost.[33] The Internet makes possible distribution by individual bands and musicians (or by very small labels) of their recordings to a worldwide audience. While the electronic distribution of an entire album is not practical at the time of this writing, samples of cuts can be distributed and the album can be promoted for direct sale. This should ultimately mean that more recordings of more music will be available to more people.[34]

NOTES

[1]David Thigpen, "Are They Worth All That Cash?" *Time*, 29 January 1996: 54.

[2]Clive Davis, *Clive: Inside the Record Business*, (1994).

[3]David Thigpen, *supra* note 1.

[4]For an interesting description of an A&R person's job, see "A&R—A Week in the Life," *Musician*, Aug. 1994: 31.

[5]Several excellent books explore in detail the ins and outs of recording artist agreements are: Donald S. Passman, *All You Need to Know About the Music Business* (1994); Mark Halloran, *The Musician's Business and Legal Guide* (1991); Sidney Shemel and M. William Krasilovsky, *This Business of Music* (1990). More legalistic publications are: Donald C. Farber (ed.), *Entertainment Industry Contracts: Negotiation and Drafting Guide* (1995); Alexander Lindey, *Lindey on Entertainment, Publishing and the Arts* (1996); Practising Law Institute, *Counseling Clients in the Entertainment Industry* (1994, annual seminar handbook). Farber and Lindey are loose-leaf publications updated regularly. All of these sources and personal experiences have been used in preparation of this chapter.

[6]Russell Sanjek and David Sanjek, *American Popular Music Business in the 20th Century* (1991): ix.

[7]Bob Rolontz, "Artist Pressure Liberalizing Standard Record Contracts," *Billboard*, 19 December 1960: 2.

[8]Jay L. Cooper, "Current Trends in Recording Contract Negotiations," *NARAS Institute Journal* 2, 1 (1978): 14.

[9]Halloran, and Passman, *supra* note 5.

[10]SoundScan data through the Bluegrass Music Discussion Group on the Internet via Ken Irwin of Rounder Records.

[11]Edward Morris, "NSAI Blasts Controlled Composition Clause; Group Seeks Full Royalties for Songwriters," *Billboard*, 15 January 1994: 8.

[12]Ibid.

[13]The agreement has a maximum SRLP of $8.98 for tapes and $10.98 for CDs.

[14]Again, there are maximum SRLPs applicable of $8.98 for tapes and $10.98 for discs.

[15]Record industry inside joke. That's the producer's answer to any question about how good a recording, or track, or whatever, is.

[16]Simon Frith, "The Industrialization of Popular Music," in James Lull, ed., *Popular Music and Communication,* 2nd ed. (1992): 50.

[17]Passman, *supra* note 5, 135.

[18]Daniel Marty, *The Illustrated History of Talking Machines* (1981): 146.

[19]Steve Jones, *Rock Formation* (1992).

[20]"1995 Studio Business Operations Survey," *Pro Sound News*, September 1995: 20.

[21]Ibid.

[22]Dan Daley, "The Big Shift: When Personal Studios Go Public," *Mix*, February, 1996: 98; Jim Mandrell, *The Studio Business Book*, 2nd ed. (1995): 4.

[23]"1995 Studio Business Operations Survey," *Pro Sound News*, September 1995: 18.

[24]Ibid., 19.

[25]Mandrell, *supra* note 22.

[26]"1994 Pro Sound News Recording Studio Operations Survey," *Pro Sound News*, September 1994: 28.

[27]"1995 Studio Business Operations Survey," *Pro Sound News*, September 1995: 18–20.

[28]Dan Daley, "Studios Develop Coping Skills as Margins Shrink," *Pro Sound News*, February 1996: 14.

[29]Ibid.; "Music Studios Face Challenges of the '90s," *Pro Sound News*, April 1996: 1.

[30]"1995 Studio Business Operations Survey," *Pro Sound News*, September 1995: 18–20.

[31]*The Mix 1996 Master Directory* lists 180 colleges and universities offering at least some course work in audio and 112 proprietary institutions offering some training in audio. The 1994 AES Directory of Educational Programs lists forty-nine providers of seminars and shout courses, twenty-five programs leading to some form of certification of diploma, forty leading to an associate's degree, sixty-seven leading to a bachelor's degree, and twenty-two graduate level programs. The AES Directory is available on the Internet at the AES home page at http://www.aes.org

[32]Thomas W. Hutchison and James A. Progris, "Study Shows Music Biz Graduates are Given Top Priority," *NARM Sounding Board*, Nov. 1996: 8.

[33]Check the advertising in magazines like *Musician* and *Electronic Musician*.

[34]See, for example, Mary Cosola, "Going Global," *Electronic Musician*, Dec. 1996: 52.

7

The Marketing Function

THE FOUR PS OF MARKETING

Marketing is a term that encompasses a wide variety of activities. The American Marketing Association defines it as "the process of planning and executing conception, pricing, promotion, and distribution of ideas, goods and services to create exchanges that satisfy individual and organizational objectives."[1] Marketing is said, at a simpler level, to involve four functions, each beginning with the letter P: Product, Pricing, Promotion, and Place (distribution).[2] The objective of these functions for most firms is usually stated as the "marketing concept"—the creation and delivery of a "product" (broadly speaking) that will satisfy consumer needs at a price that will allow a profit to be made for the organization.[3]

Most record labels, even the major labels, think of marketing less broadly. The product creation is basically the A&R and production function. The "marketing" department at most labels includes primarily the sales, promotion, and publicity functions. Distribution is either through a branch operation of the parent organization, through independent distribution, or through a branch operation by agreement between an independent label and the branch distribution organization. Which of the basic marketing functions a label may choose to perform itself is a management decision. However, all of the functions must be performed by somebody. At its broadest, the definition of marketing includes retailing, since that is the final "place" of delivery of the product to the consumer. Retailing is discussed in Chapter 8. A&R and production was discussed in Chapter 6. A description of the market for recordings, who is buying, what they are buying, and why they buy, was a significant part of Chapter 1 and should be reviewed at this time. What this chapter will do is discuss the labels' attempts to reach that market, specifically including those aspects of product, price, promotion, and place that are not dealt with elsewhere. In so doing, the discussion will cover a broader range of activities than most labels would refer to as "marketing."

Recording industry products, albums, singles, and music videos by recording artists, are generally what marketing people would call "highly differentiated." That is, no two products are really alike and each has a built in uniqueness because of the performances by the artist, producer, engineers, and others, and the compositions which are recorded. Unlike, for example, the cereal industry, which spends millions of dollars to convince us that company Y's brand of cornflake cereal is different from and better than that of competitor X, the record industry does not focus on product differentiation in its marketing. That is the job of the A&R department. The marketing departments either assume or are told that the A&R department has done its job and delivered a highly differentiated product that the marketing department is then told to sell. The marketing departments of the labels focus their efforts on product awareness. They figure that, if the consumer is aware of a particular recording and has heard it, then the uniqueness and special appeal of that recording will be enough product differentiation. The labels do not spend marketing dollars and efforts to convince potential buyers that a particular angst-ridden Generation X band is better than that of their competitor, or that a particular "hunkey," black-hatted, country male singer is better than that of the competition. They simply let the recordings speak for themselves.

The problem with relying primarily on product awareness for a marketing program is that the product must, in fact, be highly differentiated. While no one would argue that any two recordings were not differentiated somewhat from each other, the question is whether the consumer perceives that differentiation, and whether that differentiation is enough to make the consumer want to purchase the new recording. If the consumer does not perceive significant differences between two recordings, then the consumer will figure, "I already have an album like this, why do I need another one?" That phenomenon explains why, when the labels flood the market with artists that sound, look, and perform too much alike, the consumers slow down their overall levels of purchasing.

PRODUCT

Product considerations have two dimensions for record labels: the style and quality of the artist recorded and the packaging of the final recorded product. Both of these considerations must be keyed to consumer taste and demand but also need to fit the other "products" which the label is offering. There is no intention of offending artistic sensibilities by referring to recordings as "product." One might argue that such an appellation depersonalizes the artistic performance recorded but the labels use the term for the sake of simplicity and that is a good enough reason to use it here as well.

Style of the Music

Recalling Figure 1-1, four genres dominate the sales of music: Rock, Urban/Rap, Country, and Pop/Easy Listening account for over 78 percent of the market. This is the mainstream market for recordings. Here the sales potential is the greatest and here the competition is the greatest.

What happened to country music in the 1990s is a good example of the competitiveness of these mainstream markets. The country music market grew rapidly in the early 1990s. By 1996, 30 percent of music buyers reported purchasing country music over a six-month period. White females were noted as most likely to purchase country music. Younger consumers (16–17) made nearly twice as many purchases as the older buyers.[4] The popularity of country music spurred growth with more labels and artists competing for a share of the larger market. Country radio also grew with more stations in almost every market competing for listeners who preferred country music. That, of course, led to many more country releases vying for spots on the radio stations' playlists. The country radio stations found themselves in a much more competitive environment for listeners so they became much more careful about which records were added and the number of records that were added to playlists. "There's just not enough space for all these records," said one country radio station music director.[5] Country promotion and marketing had become just as competitive as pop/rock.

Specialty Markets

The shares of the other genres outside of the mainstream remained fairly stable during the 1990s as indicated by Figure 7-1. For the most part sales of the specialty genres indicated have varied by no more than plus or minus one percentage point since 1990.

The decline in the sale of jazz recordings does appear to be rather consistent through the period, but also rather slow. This is partly attributable to the fact that the first year on the chart, 1990, was a relatively high year for jazz sales. For most of the previous decade jazz sales had hovered around three percent of the total. It must be pointed out that the RIAA's research data is from a sample, not from SoundScan, and is accurate only within 2 percent according to their statisticians. At this relatively low level of sales, a 2 percent variance could make a significant difference. One might be curious, for example, why the multiplatinum hit soundtrack form *The Bodyguard,* which sold about ten million copies in 1993, did not have some effect on the soundtrack sales numbers. The probable reason is that even sales of 10 million units only represents about 1.2 percent of total shipments that year. It is also quite likely that some consumers in the RIAA interviews simply reported purchases of *The Bodyguard* as pop or urban.

A specialty category showing some surprising gains during the 1990s is the "Original Broadway Cast" album. Some of the big Broadway hits of the 1950s and 1960s saw a resurgence in popularity during that time with more frequent touring

Specialty Genre Sales 1990-1995

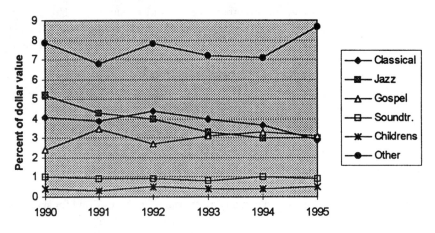

FIGURE 7-1 Specialty Genre Sales 1990–1995

Source: Recording Industry Association of America.

casts and local performances. In 1996, 12 percent of consumers in one survey said they had purchased an original cast album during the past year, an increase of four percentage points from previous data from 1990. Original cast albums tended mostly to be purchased by the forty-five and over group, perhaps because that group is affluent enough to afford the often "pricey" live performances. NARM reported that the SoundData Consumer Panel showed the age category in second place for the purchase of original cast albums to be the 18–20 age bracket.[6]

The Christian/Gospel market is a bit puzzling. While consumers indicate a strong interest in Christian music, with just over 25 percent of consumers saying they "strongly like" or "like" it,[7] the data would indicate that those likes are not being translated into sales. The RIAA reports Christian sales under the more general Gospel category. Perhaps people are reluctant not to say they like Christian music. Christian artists began appearing on the *Billboard* Top 200 album chart as soon as SoundScan data from Christian bookstores was added to the database because the predominant source of sales is not through mainstream record outlets but through Christian bookstores. The Christian Booksellers Association represents most Christian bookstores. A handful of major Christian artists appear in the Top 200 Albums chart, and some even sell as many as 50,000 to 80,000 units during their first week of release. One Christian label executive stated, "Mainstream retail is still driven by mainstream radio, mainstream video, and all the promotional things that happen. . . . I think if we've done anything, we've overestimated our core consumers that shop at mainstream stores."[8] One analyst of the Christian and Gospel market attributes the lack of sales partly to the fact that, "For other performers, the music comes first and foremost; for the gospel performer, music is secondary to the ministry . . . presenting the Christian message to the public."[9]

Repackaging

The value of a hit album does not end once it drops off the charts after the first year or so. By that time production costs and initial promotion and marketing costs are already recouped. These recordings are usually referred to as "catalog" product. They remain available to retailers through the record label's catalog of current products. An accepted industry definition is that current product sales are those taking place within fifteen months of release and that catalog sales are those taking place fifteen months or more after release. NARM estimates that catalog product so defined accounts for 43.4 percent of record sales based on dollar volume.[10] Since catalog usually has a lower SRLP and wholesale price than current "front line" product, this would indicate that in terms of units purchased, catalog product probably accounts for more than half of all recordings sold. If an artist continues to have success the catalog sales of earlier albums inevitably pick up with subsequent current hits.

Continued success also opens up the possibilities for a "Greatest Hits" package. Greatest hits are popular with consumers who have recently discovered an artist who has an extensive catalog. They are popular with consumers who may have had the hits on an older format, say tape or vinyl, and who want to convert to CDs but don't want to replace their entire album collection. The Soundata Consumer Panel information from NARM reports that one-third of music buyers had purchased greatest hits albums during a ninety-day period, a figure that was consistent with a prior ninety-day period. Nearly three-fourths of those buying the greatest hits albums had at least one other record by that artist.[11]

An elaborate form of the greatest hits package is the "boxed set." These are usually reserved for artists with long careers or who are historically significant. They frequently include not only greatest hits, but some previously unreleased tracks. Usually there are two or three discs with elaborate packaging, biographical material, photos, interviews and other material not usually accompanying a standard release. In 1996 a reported 20 percent of consumers of recordings had purchased a boxed set, compared to 30 percent in 1995. NARM speculates that boxed sets are most popular with older consumers, "probably due to the wide variety of older artists that publish these sets and the higher cost."[12]

Configuration

Configuration of the recording is yet another variable of the product dimension. Changing and multiple configuration questions have made life difficult for the record labels since discs and cylinders both appeared. Then questions turned to the size of the discs, later to questions of speed of the discs, to album or single, then mono or stereo, then 8-track or vinyl, then cassette or 8-track or vinyl, then cassette or vinyl or CD, then CD or cassette or enhanced CD. Ever since the appearance of the true long-playing album on a single disc in 1948, records have existed in at least two formats, single and album.

Singles

The decision whether to release a given cut as a single is one of the more difficult for the label. The single is primarily a promotional tool. It is what most radio stations actually play, though many also play cuts off of albums. The release of a single signals which cut the label will promote. Finally, it is also a product to sell. Figure 7-2 indicates that the popularity of singles as an item to purchase has declined fairly steadily since 1973. Vinyl singles had all but disappeared by 1995, declining to 10.2 million units shipped—less than 1 percent of total recordings shipped that year. The cassette single, or "cassingle," had replaced the vinyl sales to some extent, but popularity continued to decline. SoundData research indicated that only 16 percent of buyers had purchased a cassette single within a six-month survey period and only 11 percent had purchased a CD single. The majority of singles buyers are African American. African Americans purchase cassette singles nearly twice as much as non-African American buyers. Only 25 percent of the singles buyers reported taping singles to put on collections with other recordings. There is a significant amount of dual ownership with singles buyers. One-third of singles buyers also own the album. Most (65 percent) of those purchase the single before buying the album, indicating that the single is a factor leading to purchase of the album. Thirty-five percent those

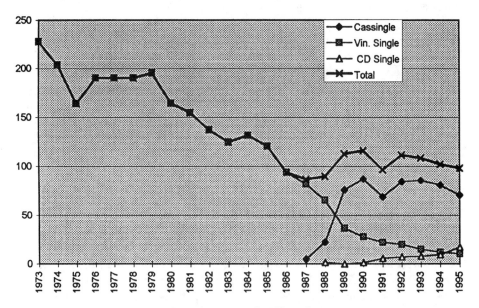

FIGURE 7-2   Singles Sales 1973–1995 (Millions)

Source: Recording Industry Association of America.

who bought CD singles and the album report buying the album first. That compares to 20 percent of cassette singles buyers who purchased the album first.[13]

There is evidence that price was part of the reason for declining single sales. In 1995 consumers were paying an average price of $4.24 for a cassette single and $5.67 for a CD single. During the latter half of 1993 some labels began deeply discounting CD singles to retailers. By late 1995 and the first half of 1996 the practice had become widespread. Labels had also been lowering the SRLP for singles during 1995. CD singles had a suggested retail list of $3.49 by mid 1996. At the same time, store prices had fallen to about three dollars. The stated retail and wholesale prices, however, often bore no relation to the price actually paid by the retailer. Labels frequently gave "free goods" to retailers purchasing singles, effectively discounting the cost of the single to as low as ninety-nine cents, and even lower in some cases. Those free goods were in addition to the usual practice of giving three to five singles to stores to get them to stock the single if it was receiving local airplay. The usual free goods practice for singles had been to ship free goods in a 3:7 ratio. That meant that out of every ten singles received by a retailer only seven were paid for, or from the other perspective, 30 percent were "free."[14] A retailer who paid an average of ninety-nine cents for a single would be getting slightly more than half of their singles as "free goods" and paying the regular wholesale price for the others. To lower the effective wholesale price to forty-nine cents apiece, as was done in some cases, the retailer would only be paying for one out of every four singles received from the label. The effectively lower wholesale prices enabled the retailer to reduce the price paid by the consumer while maintaining a reasonable profit margin. The labels and artists do not fare so well. A one-to-one free goods ratio would result in the label just breaking even, barely covering manufacturing costs and royalties for the two singles. It is important to note that the recording artists do not receive any royalties for recordings given away as "free goods" and usually have a lower royalty rate (often 75 percent of their album rate) for singles. An artist with a base royalty rate of 10 percent SRLP would make about only twenty cents per CD single sold at a $3.49 SRLP.

SRLP	$3.49
Less: 25% packaging deduction	.87
	$2.62
Times royalty (75% of 10%)	.075
Net royalty per unit sold	$0.1965

The promotional value of the heavy discounting got mixed reviews. Most artists' managers and even artists did not appear concerned about the singles royalty situation. They wanted the single sales for the promotional and emotional value of having a highly charted single. Most radio programmers only used sales as one component of their decision whether to play a single, or which rotation to play it in. They would also factor in listener requests, their own (or *R&R*'s) call-out research, and even video airplay. Label executives began to complain that the heavy discounting was too costly. *Billboard* quoted one as saying, "God forbid you have a hit; you can go bankrupt. It can cost you half a million dollars."[15] Capitol records dropped the $0.99 discounted price. Other labels felt compelled to continue to compete. *Billboard*, meanwhile, began to reconsider how much single sales should be counted in calculating chart position in its Hot 100 Singles and Hot R&B Singles charts. By mid 1996 the publication was experimenting with a chart that reduced singles sales from 40 percent to 20 percent of the points available to a record and increased the importance of airplay information gathered from BDS.[16] Since African Americans are heavier consumers of singles, that would quite likely reduce the overall number of rap and urban cuts in the Hot 100 Singles chart as well as reduce their relative chart positions.

Consumers, however, reacted positively to the lower single prices, particularly for CD singles. The RIAA reported that CD singles sales increased over 128 percent in terms of units, and over 76 percent in terms of dollar value for the first half of 1996 compared to the first half of 1995.[17] (See Figure 7-3.) The disparity between percentage increases for unit sales and the dollar value of those sales is accounted for by the lower list prices. Sales of vinyl and cassette singles continued to decline in 1996, dropping 3.5 percent and 7.6 percent respectively during the compared periods. These figures would indicate that CD singles demand is responsive to CD player penetration and is fairly price "*elastic*" at the current range of prices (i.e., a given percentage reduction in price will result in a larger percentage increase in sales).[18]

Another factor in increasing singles sales was an actual change in the configuration of the product. The traditional "single" contained two cuts, one on each side of

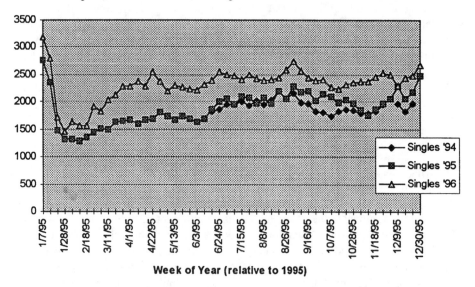

FIGURE 7-3 Weekly Singles Sales 1994–1996 (Thousand Units)

Source: *Billboard*, "Market Watch" (SoundScan data) 17 June 1995–28 Dec. 1996.

a vinyl disc or tape. With CDs it is possible to add additional music without substantially increasing the manufacturing cost of the single, assuming that the additional cuts have already been recorded. In 1995 the labels began to market more "maxi" singles (also known as CD–5s), with the "single" and additional nonalbum cuts on them. The nonalbum cuts were usually remixes, club or dance versions, or material not included on the album for some reason or another, or perhaps a live version of an album cut. The additional tracks therefore differentiated the maxi single from the album and made it a sellable item. *Billboard* reported that maxi singles sometimes made up a significant portion of CD single sales. For example, 57,000 of the 102,000 singles sold for Smashing Pumpkins' *1979* were the maxi singles. The signs of success for the maxi single follow a similar trend in the U.K.[19]

Albums

Another place where price is important is in the "mid-line" and "budget line" categories of albums. Industry estimates placed sales of these lower priced albums at 16 to 18 percent of total unit sales in 1995 and 1996.[20] SRLP on these products was typically $11.98 to $12.98 for CDs and $7.98 for tapes in the mid-line category, and $9.98 for CDs and $5.98 for tapes in the budget category. Wholesale prices for these products run $7.00 to $8.00 for CDs and $4.50 to $5.00 for cassettes on mid-line, and about $6.50 for CD and $3.00 for tapes on budget lines.[21] For the majors, these price lines are often used for deep catalog for artists who still have current releases or for artists who have not had recent releases. Solid selling mid-line albums in 1996 included: Beastie Boys, *Licensed to Ill*; James Taylor, *Greatest Hits*; Tracy Chapman, *Tracy Chapman* (debut album); Patsy Cline, *12 Greatest Hits*; Carole King, *Tapestry*; Guns N' Roses, *Appetite for Destruction*. All of those albums were priced at SRLP of $11.98 and all are multiplatinum, with certified sales ranging from four million for Tracy Chapman to thirteen million for Guns N' Roses. Typical strong selling budget albums in 1996 included: Janis Joplin, *Greatest Hits* and Hank Williams, Jr., *Greatest Hits, Vol. 1*. Both of those were priced SRLP at $9.98 and had certified platinum status with lifetime sales of over two million and one million respectively.[22] Reissues on CD are another important part of the lower priced catalogs. For example, Patsy Cline's *Twelve Greatest Hits* was a strong 1996 seller with certified sales of over two million.[23] Often consumers will replace vinyl discs or buy CDs for the first time for recordings that they may have wished they had purchased before. All major labels report that moving albums to mid or budget pricing increases sales significantly. For example, WEA reported shipping over 90,000 units on a *Best of Jimmy Durante* budget album and PolyGram 500,000 units on mid-line Beastie Boys, *Licensed to Ill*. In addition to the regular labels offering these products, there are several labels that specialize in them. Rhino Records, K-tel, Collectibles Records, and Essex Entertainment, for example, frequently package greatest hits compilations either by artist, genre, or year to sell at budget prices. K-tel reports more than 500 titles available at budget prices and Essex over 800 budget titles.[24]

PRICE

The price of albums is one thing on which the labels do not compete very much. They behave as oligopolists in a market in which there is high product differentiation and tacit coordination of prices, but there is no outright cartel or price collusion. Although WEA Distribution has the largest market share, it is not a clear price leader making changes with the other majors following suit. Any of the majors appear to be able to step out as the first to make pricing adjustments. For example, in 1993 WEA lowered wholesale prices across the board on its various CD SRLPs, but moved some individual albums up to a higher price SRLP, and therefore a higher wholesale price. Their $15.98 list and $16.98 list CDs were reduced from $10.30 to $10.18 and $10.88 to $10.67 respectively.[25] In late 1995 PolyGram Distribution (PGD) was the first distributor to lower wholesale prices on CDs in response to retailers' demand for more margin in the price wars that had developed between the retail record chains and the mass merchants. PolyGram Distribution's $16.98 list CDs were reduced from $10.65 to $10.50 wholesale and the $17.98 CDs list from $11.39 to $11.00 wholesale.[26] Note the similarity of wholesale prices between WEA and PGD for the $16.98 SRLP albums prior to PGD's adjustment. Wholesale price differentials of a few pennies among the majors have been the norm in the industry for a long time. In 1955, for example, wholesale prices for $3.98 list price vinyl albums varied among the majors by only a few cents, from $2.45 to $2.48. Singles prices for $0.89 list singles varied by only three cents among the majors, from $0.52 to $0.55.[27] In 1979 list prices for the $7.98 vinyl album lines ranged from $4.00 to $4.11.[28]

Price and Demand

While the overall prices of various SRLP lines do not vary much from label to label, there is often movement of albums by particular artists from one category SRLP to another. Moving individual albums up or down to a different SRLP suggests that the labels are very aware that there is high product differentiation in the eyes of the consumer, based on the particular artist and particular album. In other words, when a consumer goes to purchase a recording they wish to purchase a particular current recording or a recording by a particular currently popular artist, not just *any* recording. Two studies bear this out. A study published in 1978 found that "taste" (as measured by the popularity of singles from the album) was the most important factor in the quantity of an artist's album demanded. The second most important factor was exposure of the artist/recording as measured by a combination of radio airplay and live appearances during the time of release. The artist's status (measured by the success of the previous album) was found to be the third most significant factor. A factor measuring submarket appeal (the ability of the record to cross over into or out of a submarket such as Country or R&B) was found to be more important than price of the album, the last factor of significance. "Price," said the author, "does not seem to be a significant detriment to sales, reinforcing the opinion of some in the industry that 'the public will pay for what it wants, even though it may bitch about the higher cost.'"[29] In another study, conducted by a record retail chain in the early 1980s, the price of a popular artist's new record was varied at two outlets of the chain that were in the same city. At one store the album was placed on sale as is common with new releases. At the other store it was carried at the regular "shelf" price of other nonsale albums in the store. After a week, the two stores switched their pricing. At the end of the two weeks the store managers compared sales and found that there was essentially no difference in sales of the "hot" new product at the sale price or at the shelf price.[30]

This is not to say that there is not an overall interest in price by consumers. As the previous discussion about CD single prices indicates, consumers are responsive to categorical price changes. When vinyl LP list prices were raised across the board from $5.98 to $6.98 in the mid 1970s, the industry estimated a 14 percent drop in unit sales due to the 16.7 percent increase in price.[31] By the 1990s the industry appeared to have found a more workable mechanism to adjust prices and avoid lost sales. They introduced a new price point (usually higher) by setting it for the new release of a hot artist. If the album proves popular the public is usually willing to pay the higher price. Then other new albums by hot artists can be introduced at the new higher price. Soon, the higher price becomes the norm for new albums by major artists. The older price may be maintained as a catalog price for older albums before moving them back to a mid-line price as discussed above.

Consumers do appear to be willing to pay a higher price for CDs in general. When CDs were first introduced in the early 1980s, suggested retail list prices ran about $19.00 and wholesale prices about $11.75. As volume of production, sales, and demand increased the labels began to drop their SRLPs and wholesale prices. By mid 1984 SRLPs had fallen to $15.98 and wholesale prices to around $10.00.[32] As more CD manufacturing capacity came on-line and the volume of sales continued to increase, the cost to manufacture the CDs dropped from nearly four dollars per disc when CDs were first introduced to less than a dollar a disc by 1995.[33] Wholesale prices, however, did not continue to decline. Wholesale prices crept back up to about $10.65 as the typical SRLP rose to $16.98 by 1995. Although there was some consumer complaining and a lawsuit by an independent record store alleging price collusion by the major labels, the answer to the question of why CDs cost so much was simply, as *Consumer Reports* put it, "Because people are prepared to pay more for compact discs."[34] In mid 1996 two consumers in Knoxville, Tennessee filed an antitrust suit alleging that the major labels had "coerced and cajoled" stores into keeping prices high.[35] It should also be noted that the average price paid by consumers for CDs had fallen to a low of about $12.00 in 1990 and remained near $13.00 for the first half of the 1990s. Since Figure 7-4 reflects RIAA figures for all CDs, it is likely that part of the reason for the decline and stabilization is that significant numbers of purchases were of lower priced catalog product at mid-line and budget price points.

In marketing terms, the perceived value of the CD is significantly higher than that of the cassette. The components of that perceived value are many. CDs do have

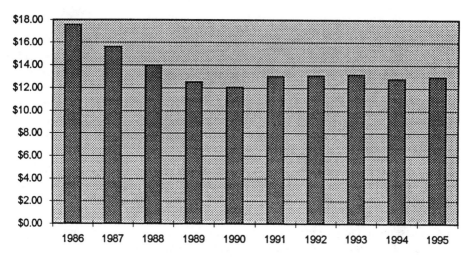

FIGURE 7-4 Average List Price of CDs Shipped

Source: Recording Industry Association of America. Computed from RIAA shipment and dollar volume figures.

significantly higher quality of sound. They do not get hung up in and destroyed by their players nearly as often as tapes. They do not wear out as quickly as tapes. The players allow more flexibility than most tape players, allowing the listener to quickly shuttle back and forth between cuts, or even between CDs with the players capable of loading multiple CDs. Most CD players allow the listener to program the order of the cuts they hear or to leave out certain cuts when playing the discs. Most cassette players do not. The technology developed by Phillips and Sony gave consumers a highly desirable product for which they have been willing to pay a higher price.

Price and Profit

As a result of declining manufacturing costs and stabilized wholesale prices the profit margins of the record labels rose. Consider the example below. The calculations operate on several assumptions: SRLP is $16.98, manufacturing costs of a completed disc with all graphics and inserts, shrink-wrapped and ready to sell is about $1.00, distribution charges amount to about $1.50,[36] artist and producer royalties (all-in) are 20 percent in the high cost example and 11 percent in the low cost example, the CD royalty rate is 100 percent of the base rate in the high cost example and 75 percent in the low cost example, mechanical royalties are for twelve cuts at full "statutory" rate (6.95 cents per cut) in the high cost example and at 75 percent rate in the low cost example. Even in the high cost example, the label ends up with a gross margin of $4.62 per disc and over $1.50 more, most of which comes out of artist and producer royalties in the low cost example.

TABLE 7-1   Low-Margin and High-Margin CD Example

	Low Margin (High Cost)	High Margin (Low Cost)
Wholesale price	$10.50	$10.50
Less: Manufacturing costs	$ 1.00	$ 1.00
Artist and Producer royalties	$ 2.55	$ 1.12
Mechanical royalties	$ 0.83	$ 0.62
Distributor charges	$ 1.50	$ 1.50
Gross margin	$ 4.62	$ 6.26

In the above example, if the CD were priced at a $17.98 list price, the wholesale price would be about fifty cents higher (using the PolyGram earlier figures). The only item that would increase would be the artist and producer royalty, because they are based on the price of the record. That increase would be twenty cents in the high cost (low margin) example and nine cents in the low cost (high margin) example. Certainly, then, there is a logic as far as the label is concerned to raise prices in order to increase profits. The concern must be that they could price themselves out of the market or create an even greater demand and market for used CDs (see Chapter 8).

Minimum Advertised Prices

In a move that tied price with promotion, the labels in the 1990s began to threaten retailers with the loss of co-op advertising money if they advertised product for sale at less than a certain minimum price. The Minimum Advertised Price (MAP) policies varied among the major distribution companies, but each distributor set prices for each category or list price of product. If a retailer advertised the product for sale below that price then the label might go so far as to stop all advertising funds for all product from that distributor for a period of time (WEA's policy), or just cut off funds for that particular record for a period of time (BMG's policy).[37] Theoretically the store could still sell a recording for less than the MAP, as long as it did not advertise that price using money that the label had provided. The labels put the policies in place to help regular record retailers who found themselves in price competition with some nonrecord retail chains such as Best Buy, Circuit City, Lechmere/Montgomery Ward, and Target, which used the low-balled prices on CDs as loss leaders to entice people into their stores to purchase electronics and other merchandise. As the price wars intensified in the last quarter of 1995 the labels began enforcing or strengthening their policies. By June 1996 *Billboard* reported, "Thanks to the majors' new-found resolve on MAP, prices of hit CDs at discount chains rose by $2 to $11.99 over the last month."[38] Meantime, NARM reported that the average price paid by their Soundata Consumer panel during December 1995 through February 1996 was $13.64, up from $12.71 from the previous survey.[39]

PROMOTION

"There is no accounting for taste."

The driving force behind the labels' promotional efforts is the well-founded belief that the consuming public is unlikely to purchase a recording until they have heard the album or a cut from it. The exposure can take the form of radio airplay, MTV (or other video channel) airplay, live performance by the artist, sampler album, record store listening station or kiosk, or record store airplay. Advertising, record reviews, and other forms of exposure that do not result in the public being able to hear the record receive a secondary priority. They promote an awareness of the existence of the album as opposed to knowledge of its content. These secondary promotional methods may help, especially if the artist has had previous success and has a following. Print advertisements have some limited impact. Only 4 percent of the Soundata panel reported purchasing the last recording they saw advertised. A larger percentage, about one-third, reported seeing newspaper ads for specific records at specific stores.[40]

Radio

Radio is still the primary means of promotion for most labels for most albums that would be considered popular mainstream. (For a discussion of television and MTV as promotion mediums, see Chapter 5.) The important fact is that it is no longer almost the *only* means. While only 44 percent of consumers report purchasing their last album because they heard a song on the radio or television,[41] it is well to remember that nearly half of the recordings purchased are catalog product, which is much less likely to be the subject of radio or music video airplay. Chapter 5 discussed the basic relationship of radio and the recording industry. The primary job of any record promotion person is to get radio airplay. Except with follow-up albums and singles by hit artists, very few singles or albums are played "out-of-the-box." Airplay has to be built up from stations in smaller markets or from smaller stations in large markets. Once the record proves to be popular enough larger stations will consider playing it. If enough stations play the record and if that begins translating to sales, the label will push to maximize the radio exposure in a concentrated effort to produce the highest possible chart position—an effort that the label hopes will maximize sales. A radio airplay hit that does not translate into sales is referred to as a "turntable hit."

Promotion people are either label employees or independent. Independent promotion people were often hired when the label promotion department had too many releases to try to promote at once. Also, independent promotion people were sometimes hired by the artist, manager, or music publisher directly to help the label staff. Expenses of independent promotion are often split between the label and the artist or even 100 percent paid for by the artist as a recoupable expense. How expensive is independent promotion? *Rolling Stone* reported that in the mid 1990s a new method of promotion was developed by independent promotion people—the radio station exclusive.[42] The independent promotion person would pay a significant sum of money to a radio station in exchange for the station promising to talk *only* to that promoter. The cost of such an arrangement to the indie promoter can be up to $50,000 a year. Record labels pay independent promotion people on the basis of records "worked" per week at a cost of $500 to $700 dollars with a bonus for every radio station that adds a record. If an independent promoter has a station as exclusive, then every label that has that promoter under contract will pay the promoter for every record the station plays, whether the promoter had anything to do with it or not. The new breed of independent promotion persons, concluded *Rolling Stone*, "are essentially lobbyists who cultivate close relationships with key programmers and make money schmoozing them on behalf of the labels."[43] The end result of all of this is that labels may spend $25,000 or more in independent promotion fees to start a "modern rock" single. Chapter 11 deals with the involvement of label and independent promotion people with payola as a method of insuring radio airplay.

Samplers

The use of samplers is another method to get more product into the hands of consumers to try to get them interested in particular artists and recordings. Samplers are made available through record stores, magazine offers, radio stations, through direct mail, or via the World Wide Web. About 30 percent of the Soundata panel of consumers had received music samplers in 1995. About one half received their samplers unsolicited through the mails. Most of the consumers (80 percent) who got the free samplers listened to them. The most significant statistic was that 21 percent of those who heard a sampler reported purchasing music as a result. If those percentages were applied to all music consumers it would amount to about 5 percent of all music consumers.[44] Many of the labels' home pages on the World Wide Web have short samples of recent releases and product information on-line. It is also possible to request samplers at many of the home pages. See the Internet Appendix in this book for URLs of label home pages.

Listening Stations

A related way to get consumers to hear the recording is to place it in some sort of listening station at the record stores. Listening stations were becoming more common in the mid 1990s, having all but disappeared during the 1970s and 1980s. Thirty-seven percent of the Soundata respondents said their favorite store had a listening station in late 1995.[45] Ninety percent of those using listening stations reported that it "somewhat" or "very much" influenced their decision to purchase. Other research supports that conclusion and notes that listening station users are more likely to purchase an additional record because of listening station use. Additionally, 70 percent of consumers say it is "somewhat important" to preview music at a listening station before purchasing. Those who do not use listening stations tend to already have their minds made up about what to buy before entering the store.[46]

PLACE

The place analysis must include the physical (or cyber) place where the customer purchases the recording, the mechanisms used to distribute the recordings to those places, and the place *in time* that the recordings are purchased. Chapter 8 deals with retailing by independent stores, chain stores, and mass marketers. Distribution and place in time are discussed below.

Distribution

Figure 7-5 depicts the basic product flow from major or independent label to retail store. Each player in the system has distinctive characteristics that can be easily described, but consolidation of functions at some levels makes the actual system much more complex.

At their most basic, the functions are as follows:

Independent label: a record company not owned by one of the majors that has its records manufactured and shipped to various independent distributors around the country. The label or the distributor may handle promotion and sales activities. Some independents have distribution deals with majors or are partially owned by majors, in which case their albums go through branch distribution.

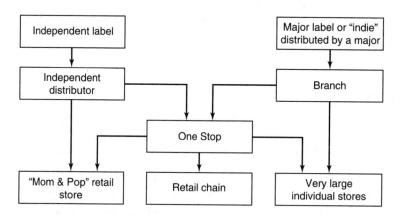

FIGURE 7-5   Distribution System

Major label: a record company owned by one of the six conglomerates that has its own branch distribution system. Note that even a small label, if it is owned by one of the big six, could be considered a "major" label for this purpose, to distinguish it from a true independent label (see below). A major has records manufactured and shipped to its branch locations for further sale to independent one-stops or to chain-owned one-stops. Sometimes a very large single retail account or store can "buy direct" from the branch.

Independent distributor: buys records from independent labels, usually several or all, and sells those labels to retail stores and to one-stops that handle all lines. Typically independent distributors are also one-stops.

Branch distributor: sells only the labels manufactured by its corporate owner or other labels that the owner has agreed to distribute. The branch distribution companies are: WEA (TimeWarner), UNI (Seagrams-MCA), Sony Distribution, BMG (Bertlesman), PGD (PolyGram), and EMD (EMI).

One-stop: sells all labels. It purchases records from branches and from independent distributors. It sells records to individual stores whether they are independent "mom and pop" stores or individual locations of retail chains. Many chains are serviced by an in-house one-stop. One-stops began by servicing singles to jukebox operators. Because they handled all labels a natural evolution for them was to begin selling to retailers and to begin their own rack jobbing operations as well.

"Mom and Pop" stores: are single stores or very small chains. The "Mom and Pop" comes from the notion that they are sole proprietorships or family owned, though that is not necessarily the case. They usually buy from one-stops for the ease of being able to purchase all records from a single source and because the branch operations will not sell labels distributed by the majors directly to small stores. Because the one-stop must make a profit, the small retailer ends up paying a higher price for records.

Retail chain: a group of stores with a common owner. Most chains buy from a one-stop that is owned by the same parent company as the chain. Individual stores usually have authority to buy from a local one-stop when "emergency" product shortages hit on a very hot product and the store would not be able to get resupplied fast enough by the company one-stop.

Very large individual stores: may sometimes buy directly from branch operations if the branch will allow it. Otherwise, such stores are often part of chains that buy from their chain one-stops.

The distribution system within the recording industry has evolved through several phases. Initially each label was in charge of its own distribution. As the number of releases and labels increased so did the need for a middle person who could handle several labels and deal directly with the retailers. That caused the birth of independent distributors. During the rock and roll explosion of the 1950s and 1960s independent labels flourished and so did the independent distributors who sold those labels. By the end of the 1960s the major labels felt the need to compete more effectively and bolstered their own distribution systems, moving into a stronger branch system. During the 1970s and 1980s the largest independent labels, such as Motown, Arista, A&M, and Chrysalis, were purchased by the majors. With very little product flow through their own operations the independent distributors were forced to begin to handle all labels, taking on the functions of a one-stop. As one-stops they also discovered the profitability of record retailing and many opened their own record store chains. Record store chains discovered the profitability and other benefits of having their own company owned one-stop. Because they carried all lines, one-stops also began to service rack locations. The lines of distribution began to crisscross and functions became merged, especially at the ownership level of one-stops. In the 1990s a resurgence of independent labels brought renewed life to the independent distributors. While branch distribution through the "big six" still controlled about 80 percent of records sold, Figure 7-6 indicates that the share of the independents grew substantially in the 1990s.

Although the branch distribution systems control the lion's share of the market it is interesting to note that the various majors are not equally strong in all markets. For example, Figure 7-7 indicates a nearly 10 percent lead by WEA over its nearest competitor in the country market. On the other hand WEA's share of the R&B market (Figure 7-8) is a virtual tie with BMG for third place, behind PGD by about 7 percentage points. (The charts are based on SoundScan data published in *Billboard* and SoundScan did not gather separate information on the R&B market until mid 1993.)

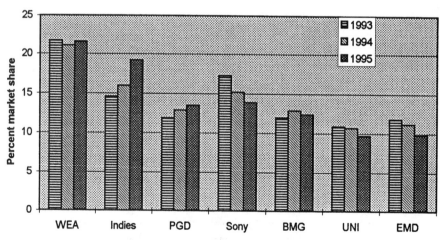

FIGURE 7-6   Total U.S. Market Share by Distributor

Source: *Billboard,* 20 Jan. 1966: 55; 21 Jan. 1995; 54.

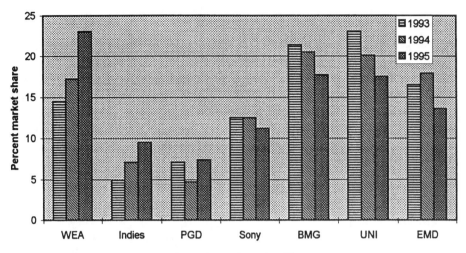

FIGURE 7-7   Country Market Share by Distributor

Source: *Billboard,* 20 Jan. 1966: 55; 21 Jan. 1995: 54.

Product Availability

From a marketing perspective, it is important for a label to remember that not all places that sell records sell all records. For a record to sell it has to be available at the place where the consumer is looking for it. That is why if a record is getting airplay in a particular town the label must make sure that the stores in that town that are likely to carry that particular record do have copies of it. Soundata information indicates that 44 percent of record consumers will try to find a record elsewhere if it is not available at the store they first try. That is good news for the label, but bad news

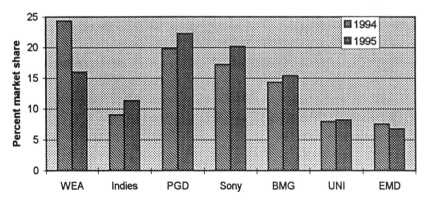

FIGURE 7-8   R&B Market Share by Distributor

Source: *Billboard,* 20 Jan. 1966: 55; 21 Jan. 1995: 54.

for the store. Thirty-seven percent of buyers said they would buy nothing. That is bad news for both the label and the store.[47] Two industry practices try to keep the lack of product availability from causing a loss of sale. First, the labels will often give free goods to the retailers to encourage them to stock the record. Second, records of new acts are often sold on a 100 percent returnable basis. That is important because the labels do have policies that allow a retailer (or distributor) to return only a limited percentage, typically 15 percent, of orders. Records that are 100 percent returnable are not counted towards the return limits, so they are sort of like getting the records on consignment. That 100 percent returnable practice was introduced by RCA in 1957.[48]

Product Placement

Place also means placement in the record store. Most retailers rent the high visibility and high traffic spaces in their stores, particularly special sale displays for hot or new products and "end caps" at the end of aisles, to the labels. Such displays are effective in promoting impulse purchases. Fifteen percent of music buyers report making unplanned purchases because of displays. The most effective single type of display is the end cap, influencing 40 percent of those impulse buyers. The least effective in-store means of prompting impulse buys is reportedly posters, and artist cutouts.[49]

Place in Time

Labels work hard to plan their release dates. They want to spread out the recordings they release so that their promotion budgets can be spread out. They will attempt to second-guess the competition in order to not release an album that might directly compete with some other label's album that may be by a "bigger" artist. They try to avoid releasing new acts the same week as a major act because the major act will demand all of their promotion resources. A label promotion person may have to push a record by a major artist whose record was expensive to produce and who is demanding the label's attention instead of a record by a new artist. Finally, the label will frequently try to have important releases in the fourth quarter of the year in order to capitalize on the Christmas buying season.

The Season to Be Jolly

There is no doubt about it. Sales of recordings, like many other things, soar during the roughly five to six weeks between Thanksgiving, at the end of November, and early January. Figure 7-9 indicates that sales of albums begin to pick up significantly about the week before Thanksgiving. (The dates in Figure 7-9 are issue dates of *Billboard*. The SoundScan data contained in the issues is about ten days to two

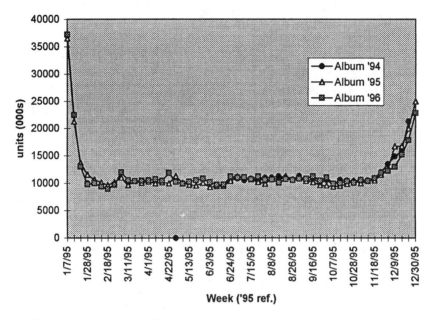

FIGURE 7-9   Weekly Album Sales 1994–1996

Source: *Billboard,* "Market Watch" (SoundScan data), 17 June 1995–28 Dec. 1996.

weeks old at the time of release.) By the week of Christmas sales are at their peak for the year— about three times their previously weekly average of 11 million units per week. By the end of the second week in January they are back at their old average. That old average is quite consistent during the non-holiday season.

How much of the total sales are accounted for by the holidays? A tally of SoundScan figures from *Billboard's* "Market Watch" feature for a nine-week period beginning with the week of Thanksgiving and ending with the third week in January indicates that 195.6 million albums were sold. That accounts for about 27 percent of the total year's sales of 715.2 million albums. That 27 percent was sold in about 17 percent of the year. Certainly that is an impressive sudden jump in the rate of album sales, but it is not near the 40 percent of total sales that some label executives believe occurs in the Christmas season.[50] A *Billboard* columnist pointed out that a problem with releasing so many major albums in the fourth quarter means that they compete with each other for sales and none has the attention of the buyers for very long. In addition, any albums by new artists that are released in the fourth quarter are competing with releases by the major acts for the discretionary dollars of consumers. Finally, if a late release has the "wrong" single picked to be the one to promote then the album will not be able to get a second chance because it will be too late to change marketing directions once the error is discovered.[51]

ENTERING THE INFORMATION AGE

The recording industry has been accused of having difficulty with marketing. "Success in the record industry is basically believed to be a combination of luck, timing, hard work and the great man theory. Only hard work is a controllable force."[52] Labels would often work under the "shotgun" approach—shooting out a lot of releases, hoping that some would be hits. They would try to outdo each other at making the most noise about their current releases. The results were often nothing but "hype" (short for hyperbole)—exaggerated claims of the quality and value of a particular artist's record. Beginning in the 1970s the labels began to put more effort into marketing plans, creating separate plans for each release, and hiring product development specialists to work with the artist and producer to develop a marketing plan suitable to the particular record. The problem was that they lacked essential information about the extent and nature of their market. Was it teens? Who was buying recordings? Why did they buy them? Late 1970s studies by NARM, Warner Communications, and CBS Records began to examine the nature of the market.[53] Still, the industry lacked hard information on sales patterns, buying preferences, and trends.

Universal Product Code

In 1979 the labels began to use Universal Product Code (UPC) identification on all of their releases. Each UPC "bar code" uniquely identifies the label (manufacturer), the specific selection, and the configuration (tape, CD, cassingle, vinyl single, and so on). The bar code can be read by laser and other light scanners and the data then recorded in a computer. Once all recordings were bar-coded a retailer could know exactly how many pieces of exactly which products had been sold in a given day, month, week, or year. Information such as price could be looked up by computer/ cash registers attached to a local database and automatically printed on a receipt. The implications for precision in inventory management at the retail and wholesale levels were not lost on the industry. A NARM report for rack jobbers stated:

> In the broadest terms, UPC offers rack jobbers the benefits of comprehensive, timely and accurate management information with which they can more effectively control their businesses. If well used, a UPC system can improve operational performance, allocate resources more wisely, and enhance the return on investment.[54]

SoundScan

As more retailers and rack jobbers began to use point-of-sale scanning devices that read the UPC and tracked sales, it became possible to gather actual sales data on a national basis. In 1989 market researcher Mike Shalett began SoundScan, a company that worked out agreements with retailers to gather their point-of-sale (POS) data, compile it, and make national sales reports available to retailers, distributors, record labels, and others in the industry who needed to know actual piece count data. The data could be broken down by artist and title, by market, and by retail location. Armed with SoundScan information a label could know if their purchase of display space in a chain of retail stores was having any noticeable impact on sales. Retailers could watch sales in other stores or other markets to look for opportunities or trends in consumer purchases. All kinds of data on the effects of test marketing, advertising, and other promotional tools became available.

SoundScan made its biggest splash in 1991 when *Billboard* added SoundScan data to its calculations for determining chart position in the Pop Albums (Top 200 Albums) and Top Country Album charts. By that time SoundScan was gathering data from over 2,000 retail locations, including many of the major national record store chains and the Handleman Company, the nation's largest rack jobber.[55] The use of SoundScan data had an immediate effect on the charts, moving popular country albums into higher positions, moving artists on some independent labels into higher positions, and moving some new pop/rock acts off the chart entirely. Within a week the major labels were complaining that the new actual sales data might not be fair to new acts, for whom the labels desired a good chart performance. The sample of retailers, said the majors, was too heavily weighted in favor of artists who sold at major mall chains and rack jobber locations, and did not accurately reflect enough sales through independent stores and smaller chains. Shalett simply said that other outlets would be added as soon as they had the data gathering capabilities and could work out arrangements with SoundScan.[56] Many independent labels had a more positive reaction. Those that sold pop product, particularly rap and dance, had better chart numbers than in prior years. Tommy Boy Records CEO Tom Silverman commented, "SoundScan is a great thing for indies—we realize we're a bigger part of the industry than we thought we were."[57] Independent labels with specialty product did not chart well in early SoundScan charts because they tended to sell through specialty shops and very large full-line stores that were not well represented in the early SoundScan data base. Alligator Records president, Bruce Iglauer noted, "When more full-line stores that don't do their buying off the charts come on line, it will be a marvelous thing for the industry."[58] The sudden appearance of more independent labels in the charts and the increasing share of the charts belonging to independent labels (see earlier discussion), in the words of a Cheetah Records executive, "Legitimized indie labels, proved we're a factor in the industry. The indies never had the money to market like the larger labels."[59]

As the use of POS technology became more widespread, more sales outlets were indeed added to SoundScan's data base. By 1997 SoundScan was gathering data from over 14,000 retail locations.[60] In addition, the use of actual sales data continued to enter more charts. Eventually SoundScan figured into the computing of the *Billboard's* Hot 100 Singles (11/30/91), Bubbling Under the Hot 100 Singles (12/5/92), R&B Singles Sales (7/11/92), Hot R&B Singles and Bubbling Under Hot R&B Singles (12/5/92), Top R&B Albums, Top Pop Catalog Albums (5/25/91),

Top Reggae Albums (2/5/94), Top Jazz Albums (12/4/93), Top Contemporary Jazz Albums (12/4/93), Hot Dance Music (8/28/93), Billboard Latin 50 (7/10/93), Top Christmas Albums (12/7/91), Top Music Videos (4/24/93), Hot Rap Singles (12/4/93), and The Billboard Classical 50 (12/4/93).[61]

The depth of marketing information that is available through SoundScan is impressive. Labels (and other users such as personal managers, agents, music publishers, and concert promoters) can access national sales information by region, by specific Designated Market Area (DMA), by store, and more. Summary reports on sales by configuration and store type in addition to sales charts are also available in most music genres. Users pay annual fees ranging from about $5,000 per year to over $80,000 per year, depending on the size of the client's annual sales.[62] The availability of such detailed information makes more detailed marketing plans possible. All of this was the result of the bar coding that began in 1979.

Broadcast Data Systems

Data availability through new technology also had a significant impact on a record company's ability to monitor actual radio airplay. Broadcast Data Systems (BDS) was formed as an affiliate of *Billboard*'s BPI Communications to create a computer driven method of monitoring actual radio airplay. Prior to 1990 radio airplay charts had been compiled from airplay information provided by the music and program directors at radio stations that were contacted by the chart compilers, *R&R*, *Billboard*, *Gavin Report*, *CashBox*, and others. The performing rights organizations either sampled airplay by recording (ASCAP) or by having the stations list which songs were performed (BMI), or by using the charts themselves as an indication of airplay (SESAC). BDS is described by *Billboard* as:

> a proprietary, passive, pattern-recognition technology that monitors broadcast waves and recognizes songs and/or commercials aired by radio and TV stations. Records and commercials must first be played into the systems computer, which in turn creates a digital fingerprint of that material. The fingerprint is downloaded to BDS monitors in each market. Those monitors can recognize that fingerprint or "pattern," when the song or commercial is broadcast on one of the monitored stations.[63]

The monitors then transmit data back to BDS headquarters for compilation. BDS sells the information to SESAC, the labels, advertisers, and others needing that specific airplay information. In 1994 the system was improved to reduce the number of "unrecognized" songs. The BDS monitors would capture all airplay on a separate unit. Any song not recognized would be transmitted back to headquarters in Kansas City, Missouri where it could be compared to a master library containing more "fingerprints." Songs not recognized by the master library (said to contain several million patterns) could then be listened to by actual persons for recognition and counting.[64]

Billboard first began using BDS information in March 1990 for the Hot Country Singles chart. By late 1990 *Billboard* and *R&R*, its major competitor in the radio airplay chart business, were in a war of words over which system provided a more accurate accounting of actual airplay. *R&R* contended that the two systems had discrepancies of as many as thirty plays for a song in some locations, with *R&R* picking up the greater number of plays. BDS countered that discrepancies were accounted for partly due to doctored playlists that radio people were providing *R&R*, some methodology differences with both systems, and some software problems of the early BDS system. The lure of actual data had a very strong appeal to music publishers. "It's obviously a purer system if it really monitors what's really being played," said a BMG music publishing executive.[65] *Billboard* pressed BDS information into more of its radio airplay charts, including The Hot 100 (singles) (11/30/91), Bubbling Under the Hot 100 (12/5/92), Top 40 Radio Monitor/Hot 100 Airplay (12/8/90), Top 40/Mainstream and Top 40/Rhythm Crossover (10/3/92), Hot R&B Singles and Bubbling Under Hot 100 R&B Singles (12/5/92), R&B Radio Monitor (7/11/92), Hot Adult Contemporary (7/17/93), and Modern Rock Tracks (6/12/93).[66] In early 1995 BDS merged with its former competitor, Competitive Media Reporting, to form a new entity under *Mediaweek* parent, VNU.[67] BPI, the parent of *Billboard* and BDS, had been purchased by VNU, a Dutch company, in 1994.[68]

As the BDS monitors were in place in more markets the labels began to use them to monitor not only airplay, but the success of their label and independent promotion people. RCA announced a plan to pay independent promoters for Top 40 adds only after the records had appeared in the station's Top 35 for a week, as measured by BDS. Other labels began to follow suit.[69]

Computer technology has also had a direct impact on consumers. As record stores got larger in terms of square feet and number of different albums stocked, it became more and more difficult for the consumer to locate the product they wanted unless it was a mainstream hit. With thousands of titles and artists it also became impossible for store personnel to know the inventory in detail. As a result some stores began putting a kiosk in the store where the consumer and clerk could access the store's database of recordings available and in stock to find out if a particular recording or particular artist was in stock and where in the store it would be located. By 1996 over 40 percent of music buyers were using kiosks as listening stations or as look-up stations.[70]

Market Research

Other market research methodologies have risen and fallen in the labels' favor. For example, one survey research company sends out albums to a group of one hundred country music buyers, asking each a number of questions about the albums. That data is then assembled into a report for the label buying the service, and is used in helping to decide what singles to release or promote. Focus groups, a less expensive methodology, often help a label identify a particular appeal or turn-off that some cut might have. These methods sometimes hit, sometimes miss. For example, a focus group told RCA that the group Alabama's *Mountain Music* was too much like rock and roll. The album became one of the group's biggest sellers. Other albums or cuts are projected to be hits, but turn out stiffs. Most labels want at least some kind of information other than their own marketing department's gut feel. As one researcher put it, "Competition has stiffened and labels need as much ammunition and information as they can get."[71]

SUMMARY

Even with additional information, the labels still face a marketing dilemma. They sell products that are highly differentiated and rely on consumer taste preferences for success. It is difficult to predict how consumers will react to a particular album or artist. Following the current trends leads labels to release more of the "same old, same old," which leads to less than enthusiastic consumer response. Trying to anticipate trends and "new waves" is risky and still may not receive an enthusiastic consumer response. Yet, the best consumer response and the most profit can be made from taking the risks. What the marketing information can do for the labels is help the marketing department reduce the risk and get the most return from the risks that the A&R department has already taken.

NOTES

[1]American Marketing Association Board of Directors, 1985. In J. Paul Peter and Paul H. Donnelly, Jr., *Marketing Management: Knowledge and Skill,* (1986) 1.

[2]See, e.g., Jim Willis and Diane B. Willis, *New Directions in Media Management* (1993): 299.

[3]See, e.g., Stephen Lacy, et al., *Media Management* (1993):251; J. Paul Peter and James H. Donnelly, Jr., *Marketing Management: Knowledge and Skills* (1986): 9.

[4]"Soundata Consumer Panel," *NARM Sounding Board,* Aug. 1996 (on-line version).

[5]Peter Cronin, "Country Labels, Radio Adjust to Reality of Boom," *Billboard,* 29 April 1995: 1.

[6]"Soundata Consumer Panel," *NARM Sounding Board,* Sept. 1996 (on-line version).

[7]Ibid.

[8]Reunion Records President Terry Hemmings quoted in Deborah Evans Price, "Christian Music Searches for Sales Strength for Its Journey," *Billboard,* 13 Jan. 1996: 1.

[9]Don Cusic, *Music in the Market* (1996): 127–128. For insight into the gospel and Christian music industry see Cusic's, *The Sound of Light: A History of Gospel Music* (1990).

[10]National Association of Recording Merchandisers, *Annual Survey Results 1995* (1996): 6.

[11]"Soundata Consumer Panel," *NARM Sounding Board,* Sept. 1996 and June 1996 (on-line versions).

[12]Ibid.

[13]"Soundata Consumer Panel," *NARM Sounding Board,* Dec. 1995 (on-line version).

[14]Mark Halloran, *The Musician's Business and Legal Guide* (1991): 253.

[15]Ed Christman, et al., "Discount Singles Spark U.S. Cost/Benefit Debate," *Billboard*, 31 August 1996: 1, 133.

[16]"Billboard Examining Hot 100 Revamp," *Billboard*, 31 August 1996: 133. The Billboard Hot 100 chart, because it combines sales and airplay factors, must weight how much to count sales and how much to count airplay. Sales points are assigned on the basis of the relative sales of the recording that week and airplay points are assigned on the basis of relative total airplay that week. The more points a record receives, the higher its chart position.

[17]Don Jeffrey, "CD Singles, Music Vids Lead Modest Growth," *Billboard*, 31 August 1996: 1.

[18]To be precise, assuming that the previous discounting structure often resulted in a $1.50 wholesale price and the new structure often resulted in a $0.99 wholesale price and the resulting increase in sales was 128 percent, the elasticity would be 4.27, a high price elasticity. Of course, the assumptions made to reach this result are rather broad. Even assuming that some of the increased demand is the result of CD player penetration, it is likely that the demand for CD singles still has a price elasticity significantly greater than one. That would mean that decreases in price, for example, of 5 percent, would result in increases in sales of greater than 5 percent.

[19]Craig Rosen, "CD Singles Spurred by Addition of Non-Album Cuts," *Billboard*, 30 March 1996: 5.

[20]Steve Traiman, "Off-Price Millions: The Secret in the Vault," *Billboard*, 13 April 1996: 50.

[21]Ed Christman, "EMI–Capitol Creates Marketing Arm," *Billboard*, 13 April 1996: 5.

[22]"Top Pop Catalog Albums," (chart), *Billboard*, 12 Oct. 1996: 83.

[23]Ibid.

[24]Christman, *supra* note 20.

[25]Ed Christman, et al., "WEA Reduces Wholesale Prices on CDs," *Billboard*, 13 March 1993: 9.

[26]Ed Christman, "PGD Reduces Boxlot Prices, Boosting Retain Profit Margins," *Billboard*, 23 Dec. 1995: 5.

[27]"Price List Reflects Firmer Structure in Cost of Disks," *Billboard*, 15 June 1955: 5.

[28]"WEA Raises LP & Single Basic Prices," *Billboard*, 30 June 1979: 3.

[29]Alexander Belinfante and Reuben R. Davis, Jr., "Estimating the Demand for Record Albums," *Review of Business and Economic Research*, (Winter 1978–1979): 47, 51.

[30]An unpublished report to the author from a graduate of the Recording Industry program at Middle Tennessee State University who was one of the store managers involved. The name of the manager and chain are withheld by request.

[31]Belinfante and Davis, *supra* note 29.

[32]"CD Prices Start to Tumble," *Billboard*, 7 July 1984: 1.

[33]Susan Nunziata, "CD Plants Expand in Anticipation of Business Boom," *Billboard*, 25 July 1992: 6.

[34]"CD Prices: Why so High?" *Consumer Reports*, Feb. 1996: 17.

[35]David Hinkley, "Suit Calls CD Prices a Steal—for Companies," *New York Daily News*, 11 July 1966, New York Now section: 2 (LEXIS).

[36]Neil Strauss, "Pennies That Add Up to $16.98: Why CDs Cost So Much," *New York Times*, 5 July 1995, Final edition, C-11 (LEXIS).

[37]Ed Christman, "MAPing the Route to Consistent Pricing," *Billboard*, 30 March 1996: 59.

[38]Ed Christman, "MAP Policies Bring Price War Cease-fire," *Billboard*, 1 June 1996: 3.

[39]"Soundata Consumer Panel," *NARM Sounding Board*, June 1996 (on-line version).

[40]Ibid.

[41]"Soundata Consumer Panel," *NARM Sounding Board*, Mar. 1996 (on-line version).

[42]Eric Boehlert, "Pay to Play," *Rolling Stone*, 22 Aug. 1996: 34.

[43]Ibid.

[44]"Soundata Consumer Panel," *NARM Sounding Board*, Dec. 1995 (on-line version).

[45]"Soundata Consumer Panel," *NARM Sounding Board*, Jan. 1996 (on-line version).

[46]"Don Jeffrey, "Survey, Listening Posts 'Important' to Customers," *Billboard*, 8 June 1996: 1.

[47]"Soundata Consumer Panel," *NARM Sounding Board*, Aug. 1996 (on-line version).

[48]"Victor's LP Offer Sets Trade Buzzing," *Billboard*, 30 Dec. 1957: 11.

[49]"Soundata Consumer Panel," *NARM Sounding Board*, Jan. 1996 (on-line version).

[50]Geoff Mayfield, "Between the Bullets," *Billboard*, 23 Dec. 1996: 106.

[51]Ibid.

[52]R. Serge Denisoff, *Solid Gold* (1975): 180.

[53]Geoffrey P. Hull, "The Aging of America: The Recording and Broadcasting Industries Awareness of Shifting Demographic Patterns," *NARAS Institute Journal,* 1, 1 (1977): 3.

[54]National Association of Recording Merchandisers, *What UPC Means to the Recording Industry* (1979): 20.

[55]"Billboard Debuts Piece Counts on Two Music Charts," *Billboard*, 25 May 1991: 1.

[56]Ken Terry, "Labels to Billboard: Balance New POS Charting System," *Billboard*, 1 June 1991: 1.

[57]Quoted in Moira McCormick, "SoundScan: Boon or Bane for Indies," *Billboard*, 21 Mar. 1992: I4.

[58]Ibid.

[59]Ibid.

[60]SoundScan promotional materials.

[61]"Chart Histories," *Billboard 100th Anniversary Issue 1984–1994*, 1 November 1994: 262–273.

[62]SoundScan promotional materials (1996).

[63]"New Technology Will Strengthen Accuracy of BDS," *Billboard*, 1 July 1994: 1.

[64]Ibid.

[65]Charles Fleming and Kevin Zimmerman, "Charts Off Course," *Daily Variety*, 31 Dec. 1990: 1.

[66]"Chart Histories," *Billboard 100th Anniversary Issue 1984–1994*, 1 November 1994: 262–273.

[67]"BDS, CMR to Merge Services," *Mediaweek*, 23 Jan. 1995: 41.

[68]"Dutch Conglomerate VNU to Purchase BPI Communications," *Billboard*, 22 Jan. 1994: 3.

[69]Eric Boehlert, "Labels Put New Spin on Indie Promo; Many Eye BDS Data for Payment Plans," *Billboard*, 22 Jan. 1994: 1.

[70]"Soundata Consumer Panel," *NARM Sounding Board*, Mar. 1996 (on-line version).

[71]Tom Hutchison, quoted in Tom Roland, "Record Labels Debate Research," *The Tennessean*, Business Section, 5 June 1995: 1.

8

Retailing:
Software on Hard Copies

OVERVIEW

The development of record retailing, its place in the recording industry, its state in the mid 1990s, and its future are best understood by keeping in mind the function(s) that retailers play in any industry. Retailing is the selling of goods and services to the ultimate consumer. In particular, record retailing occupies a place in the sale of goods to ultimate consumers for *personal* (as opposed to business or industrial) use. The retailer provides valuable functions for both the manufacturers and distributors, and for the consumers. For the manufacturer, the retailer is the final stop in the distribution chain. The retailer provides one last opportunity to influence consumer purchases at the point of sale. The retailer provides important information on what is selling and what consumers want. And, most importantly, the retailer provides the manufacturer with the purchase dollar, without which there would be no multibillion dollar recording industry.

From a consumer point of view, the retailer provides a place to purchase the music. This is generally a physical place, such as the corner or mall record store, but can also be a "place" such as a catalog for direct purchase through a record club or place in cyberspace from an on-line service. By 1995 NARM estimated that there were over 25,000 different places to buy music recordings, with about 16,000 of those being record specialty stores.[1] The retailer helps the customers sort through merchandise, provides a selection of inventory from which the customers can choose, and provides information to help the consumers get the recordings that they want.

What *do* consumers want in record stores? One survey found that 49 percent of record buyers cited selection as the "most liked" feature of buying locations, while price was second place (16.5 percent), location fourth (9.2 percent), and "other" third (9.8 percent). ("Other" appeared to be factors involving the store atmosphere.)[2] These top four image components then accounted for almost 85 percent of the most liked features of record selling locations. They remain the primary image factors by which record stores seek to differentiate themselves from their competitors.

RECORD RETAIL: 1890 TO 1950

The Early Years

In the 1890s cylinder recordings were sold by mail order from the manufacturer (label). By 1895 Emile Berliner had established the first store to sell disk recordings in Philadelphia. Columbia opened its first phonorecord "parlor" in Washington, D.C. about the same time. Most recordings were sold to the parlors, which used the cylinders and disks in "coin-ops"—machines that customers could use to play their favorite recordings. There were not many machines sold for the home market because they were too expensive for most consumers. But as the century turned the prices of the players fell from around $150.00 each to as little as $35.00 or less. Consumers became owners of phonograph players in significant numbers and stores that sold the players also sold the recordings. Columbia, Victor, and Edison, the makers of the players, were also the makers of the recordings and sold both through the same outlets. The manufacturers became labels because they simply had to provide software to drive the sales of their hardware, much as the radio manufacturers later would establish radio stations and networks to provide programming for the receivers they were attempting to sell. There was also significant mail order business direct from the labels. The manufacturers thus were in total control of the system. They sold the machines to play the recordings, made the recordings, and sold the recordings direct to consumers through mail order and through company-owned retail outlets. This scheme of vertical integration has had few rivals before or since.[3]

The End of Monopolies

When the Edison, Victor, and Columbia patent monopolies ended in 1917, a number of other labels sprang up, Okeh (a 1920 Columbia subsidiary selling primarily blues and minority, and later hillbilly recordings), Brunswick, Pathe, Vocalion, and Emerson. The presence of other labels created the need for stores to sell recordings of several labels and the independent record store was born.

Depression and Recovery

The 1930s saw the collapse of the recording industry into a few major labels, the establishment of significant connections with broadcasting, and the near death of record retailing. In 1929, Victor Talking Machine had been purchased by RCA, the electronics and broadcasting firm, later to become RCA Victor. Columbia collapsed into American Record Corporation (ARC), along with a number of other labels, and reemerged in 1938–1939 when CBS, the electronics and broadcasting firm, purchased ARC. In England, a 1930 merger of Columbia Graphophone with Gramophone (His Master's Voice/HMV) and Parlophone created Electric and Musical Industries, Ltd. (EMI). Decca, a British company founded in 1929, ended up with the U.K. rights to the ARC Group. In 1934, U.S. Decca was formed. These labels formed the core of four of the labels that became the "majors" in the United States and internationally: RCA Victor, Columbia, EMI, and MCA.

The broadcasting connection was important because radio stations in the 1930s began to play more and more recordings instead of having live orchestras. The recordings were much less expensive to program. Radio became both a market for the recordings (because at that time the stations purchased the records they played) and a promotional tool for the exposure of the recordings to the public.

The other savior of the recording industry in the 1930s was not retail—it was jukeboxes. The coin-operated machine for playing recordings was introduced in 1927 and by 1930 there were 12,000 in use. In the Depression, most people had to be content for their musical entertainment to listen to a radio or go to some place that had a jukebox. The machines became immensely popular. By 1936, there were 150,000 of them, consuming 40 percent of all records sold that year. By 1939, the 300,000 jukeboxes consumed 30 million 78s per year, well over half of all records sold. They continued to be a significant factor right through the war years and the early 1950s. Overall, jukeboxes proved particularly important to the spread of the popularity of country music.

Independent retailers became more important during the 1940s and 1950s. A pent-up demand for recordings during the war years led to sales of 350 million records in 1946, up from 130 million only four years earlier. Important new labels, MGM, Capitol, Mercury, Atlantic, and others, formed during the forties.

The explosion of record sales and record labels brought on by the advent of rock and roll in the mid 1950s also brought on significant developments in record retailing. With so many new labels to keep up with and so much near instantaneous demand for the hits as heard on the local radio station, the mom and pop record shops simply could not keep up. Into their places stepped rack jobbers, retail chains, superstores, and megastores.

RACK JOBBERS

> "What the rack jobber did was they really
> made it easy for people to buy records."[4]

The first record rack jobber, Music Merchants, began by setting up racks of discount records in drugstores, supermarkets, and variety stores in 1952. They sold the Top

15 hits. John and David Handleman, destined to become the nation's largest rack jobber operation, soon entered the business along with others. The rack jobber was a subdistributor, like the one-stop, and got a 10 percent discount from the wholesale price paid by retailers. As the public appetite for records expanded, so did the racks' business. They had to provide more than a single 4.5 foot metal rack of Top 15 hits. They either ran entire leased record departments in department and mass merchant discount houses, or provided all of the stock, fixtures, inventory control, pricing, and serviced virtually everything else except sweeping the floors and running the cash register. By selling only the hit records they were able to sell at a high volume and therefore at a lower price than the other retailers. In addition, they had a 100 percent return privilege with the labels. If they overbought or guessed wrong on what would be hot, the label would take it back. Rack locations accounted for about 18 percent of all sales in 1960, by 1965 a third of all sales, and by the mid 1970s, 80 percent of all records sold were through the rack jobbers. They provided people with lots of places (location convenience) to purchase the most desired recordings. They also provided the kinds of locations, discount mass merchandisers, and other large retail stores such as Sears, where people were likely to be. A 1994 poll found that 60 percent of the sample had visited a K-Mart in the last thirty days (Wal-Mart scored a close second with 57 percent).[5] That is the same reason why record store chains flocked to shopping malls in the late 1970s and 1980s. It is not, however, convenient to go to a mall just to buy a record. A free-standing store or strip center is a much more convenient for a single purchase.

Shipped Out Platinum, Came Back Gold

The rack jobbers provided the labels with a way to sell larger quantities of records to a single buyer. Label executives said the racks allowed them to move "tonnage" of product. That was the good news. The bad news was that the racks, with their 100 percent return privilege often returned tonnage of product. Executives coined the expression, "shipped out platinum, came back gold." (Translation: orders for 1 million copies, returns of 500,000 copies.) Copies of the Bee Gees/Peter Frampton soundtrack album for the film of *Sgt. Pepper's Lonely Hearts Club Band* appeared in cut out bins for years after its ill-fated 1978 release.

The other problem that the rack jobbers presented was that they could not stock a very deep inventory. A typical store would stock 8,000 to 10,000 titles,[6] while a typical rack location (record department) would have only 500 to 1,000 titles. The majority of sales, as much as 70 percent, typically were generated from only the top 200 titles.[7] In the early stages of development of a market for a particular recording the racks would not stock the product. A new recording had to be showing significant signs of consumer acceptance before the racks would stock it unless it was from a well-established artist with a good sales history. On the other hand, since the majority of the business is sales of hit product, one could argue that the rack jobber provided the consumer with a preselection of the music that the consumer was most likely to want.

The Handleman Company

Like most of the recording industry in the 1980s, rack jobbing consolidated with the largest accounts getting larger and one company, Handleman, getting more of the accounts. In 1991–1992, Handleman acquired its largest rack competitor, Lieberman Enterprises. By the mid 1990s Handleman was the largest single retail account in the recording industry, followed by the chain retailers, Musicland Group, Blockbuster Music, and Trans World Music.[8] Handleman serviced over 22,000 rack locations, primarily in K-mart and Wal-Mart (those two accounted for about 65 percent of Handleman's sales), with some of the locations being leased departments where the rack jobber supplied everything, including personnel, to run the department. Handleman's typical leased departments, called "Entertainment Zone," were about 1,400 square feet and included 5,000 SKUs of CDs, 3,500 of cassettes, and 2,000–3,000 of home video. In these leased departments, the rack jobber owns the product until the customer buys it. The rack jobber pays a rental based on a fee per square foot plus a percentage of sales. In the more typical rack situation, the retailer buys the product from the rack jobber, but it is the rack jobber who supplies all of the fixtures, keeps track of stock selection, ordering, and replenishment. Like many other recorded music retailers in the 1990s, Handleman expanded its rack sales to include books, home video, and computer software, reporting sales as music (53 percent), video (38 percent), books (5 percent), and computer software (4 percent).[9]

THE CHAIN GANG

Chain Retail Record Stores

The desire of the consumers for a larger selection of recordings, the development of the shopping mall as a center of shopping convenience, and the overall increase in the demand for recordings (noted in Chapter 1) influenced the growth of the record retail chains. That growth was dramatic from the mid 1970s into the early 1990s. As Table 8-1 indicates, the number of record stores (which does not include rack locations) more than doubled in a fifteen year span from 1977 to 1992. This was at a time when other related stores such as musical instrument and radio/TV/Electronics stores were decreasing in number.

TABLE 8-1   Record Store Growth

Census Year	Record Stores	Musical Instruments	Radio/TV/Electronics
1977	3,655	5,748	24,752
1987	6,272	4,690	18,892
1992	7,924	4,149	17,324

Source: U.S. Department of Commerce, Census of Retail Trade.

TABLE 8-2   The Growth of Record Retail Chains (Units per Firm)

Census Year	Mom and Pop (1 Unit)	25 or More Units	100 or More Units
1977	2,026	8 firms account for 580 establishments	1 firm accounts for 218 establishments
1987	2,635	22 firms account for 2,562 establishments	6 firms account for 1,656 establishments
1992	2,923	20 firms account for 4,064 establishments	12 firms account for 3,648 establishments

Source: U.S. Department of Commerce, Census of Retail Trade.

Once the chain retailers began to grow, they grew both in number of firms, number of locations, and in power. In 1977 the largest firm, the only chain with more than 100 units, accounted for just under 10 percent of the locations. (See Table 8-2.) By 1992, the large chains (100 plus units) accounted for 46 percent of the stores. More than half of the nearly 8,000 locations were accounted for by chains with at least twenty-five locations. Even though the number of "mom and pop" single store locations grew, their share of the stores had dropped from 60 percent in 1977 to 37 percent in 1992—still a significant factor, but not a dominant force in the industry.

Most significantly, the concentration of the retail record store business in a few major chains characterized the record retail business by the mid 1990s. In 1977 it took the fifty largest retail chains to control 50 percent of the retail stores. By 1987 that number had dropped to a point where the eight largest firms controlled just under 50 percent of the stores. By 1992, 41 percent of the store sales were controlled by the four largest firms. Although this would still quality as "effective competition," as discussed in Chapter 2, there was clearly a trend toward a tight oligopoly in the record store business.

TABLE 8-3   Concentration Ratios of Largest Chains (Percent of Total Record Store Sales)

Census Year	4 Largest Firms	8 Largest Firms	20 Largest Firms	50 Largest Firms
1977	20.4	28.9	39.0	49.5
1987	34.5	49.3	63.9	72.8
1992	40.9	57.8	70.0	76.2

Source: U.S. Department of Commerce, Census of Retail Trade.

The Weakest Link

All was well in the retail chain business until the mid 1990s. At that time a combination of factors led to significant problems in chain management.

1. The overall growth of record sales leveled off.
2. The chains became overextended.
3. Price competition became fierce.
4. Other "places" to buy records began to compete more effectively, including record clubs, rack jobbers, and other nonrecord store outlets.
5. Some consumer dollars were channeled off into the purchase of used CDs.

Overall Growth of Record Sales

The sales of records through stores had grown steadily and consistently since 1979. The stores had participated in this growth to the detriment of rack locations through the 1980s. Furthermore, this growth of overall sales and of chain share of the sales was real. Until 1995 record store sales grew even accounting for inflation. But in 1995, when total unit sales dropped about 1 percent (down to 1,113,100,000 units from the 1,122,700,000 units of the previous year), the slight increase (2.1 percent) in dollar value of shipments was nullified by an approximate 3 percent inflation. As Table 8-4 indicates, the result was an actual decrease in retail store sales in constant dollars.

Overextended Chains

As the sales bloom faded from the recording industry rose, music retail chains discovered they were trying to run too many outlets in marginal locations. Yet, they continued to open or acquire new stores at a rapid rate. Musicland announced it would open thirty Media Play superstores in 1994. In 1993 the company opened

TABLE 8-4 Sales Growth of Record Stores (Adjusted for Inflation by Consumer Price Index, 1984 = 100)

Year	CPI for Entertainment Commodities (1984 = 100)	Record Store Sales in Constant Dollars (millions)
1977	69.0	$1,775
1987	110.5	$3,325
1992	131.3	$4,123
1994	136.1	$4,699
1995	140.0	$4,579

Sources: U.S. Dept. of Labor, *Monthly Labor Review;* and Recording Industry Association of America.

fifty-one music stores and closed thirty-five.[10] Blockbuster Music acquired 270 music stores from the Super Club, including Record Bar, Tracks, and Turtles stores.[11] Even small chains were in the act, with Hear Music adding five stores to a seven store chain in 1995.[12] By 1995 the five largest record store chains operated 2,854 record stores (see Table 8-5).

Problems were close at hand as growth turned into retrenchment for the chains. Camelot Music, the fourth largest retail chain, dropped below four hundred stores, closed eighteen early in 1996, and went into Chapter 11 reorganization later that year.[13] Musicland announced it would close at least fifty stores in 1996 and was in Chapter 11 reorganization.[14] Blockbuster Music closed thirty stores in 1995–1996.[15] Trans World closed 190 stores and went into Chapter 11 reorganization.[16] Chapter 11 of the "bankruptcy" ("bankruptcy" is no longer a term used in the code to describe a debtor) code permits a debtor to go to court to ask for time to restructure its operations to allow it to pay off its debts. If the creditors and bankruptcy court approve the plan then any creditors are stayed from foreclosing on any debts pending the completion of the reorganization plan.

Competition to get into the shopping malls tended to bid up the rent paid by the mall music retailers. While they had been paying 9 percent to 12 percent of store revenue to the mall owners in the 1980s, the chains, in their desire to get the mall locations, had bid that up to 14 percent to 17 percent in the 1990s. As rents went up, profit margins went down

Price Competition Problems

In the early 1990s the mall record merchants had been getting a premium price for their CDs, as much as a dollar or two over list price. During the mid 1990s the concept of the megastore, featuring a huge selection of recordings, videos, books, and computer software had emerged. The megastores often located in vacant building supply or grocery stores, keeping construction costs down. They would offer product at $10.99 or $11.99, not much margin on a new disc that would cost the

TABLE 8-5   Largest Retail Chains

Musicland Group	861 stores	Musicland, Sam Goody, Discount Records
Trans World Entertainment	700 Stores	Record Town, Tape World, Coconuts, Saturday Matinee, Abraham/Strauss
Blockbuster Music	540 stores	Blockbuster, Music Plus, Sound Warehouse, Turtles, Tracks, Record Bar
Camelot Music	405 stores	Camelot Music
Wherehouse Entertainment	348 stores	Wherehouse

Source: Billboard's *1995 Record Retailing Directory*.

retailer about $10.72. Other nonmusic merchants began using music as a loss leader, to draw customers into the store. Circuit City, primarily an electronics and appliance retailer, often sold CDs below cost at $9.99. Wal-Mart offered CD titles as low as $8.88. One writer noted that the average price paid by the customer for a CD had fallen 63 cents since 1990 while the average wholesale price paid by the retailer had risen 43 cents since 1991. SoundScan surveys reported that, of the 10 percent of music consumers who purchased recordings at the electronics store discounters such as Best Buy, Circuit City, and Fry's Electronics, two-thirds said price was the primary reason.[17] As the old saying goes, you can't sell at a loss and make up the difference on volume. The music-only retailers had nowhere to make up the loss. The competition offered lower prices, often in locations surrounding malls, and in many instances a greater selection.[18] Figure 8-1 indicates the extent to which alternative outlets eroded the record stores' market share from 1988 to 1995.

A *Rolling Stone* article hit on another not so obvious problem, calling many of the 6,000 plus record retail outlets a "huge bore." Commented the writer, "The hip, funky record stores of the Sixties gave way to the carnival like emporium stores of the Seventies, but with wide scale corporate consolidation of the music business during the last decade, retailers have decided to play it safe . . . and boring."[19] Store atmosphere, one of the four significant factors to consumers mentioned earlier, had declined. The article reported a NARM survey that showed that 34 percent of record

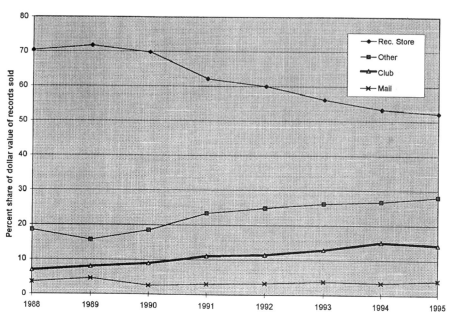

FIGURE 8-1   The Declining Record Store Share

Source: Recording Industry Association of America.

buyers were not able to find what they wanted at record stores and an earlier Warner Music Group survey found that only 35 percent of buyers were "very satisfied" with their stores.

The chains were being effectively competed with on all four of the most important factors in choice of retail record store. The megastores and superstores had greater selection and the mom and pop specialty stores still catered to real specialty audiences. The electronics store discounters and some of the mass merchants were effectively competing on price. Mall locations are only convenient for mall shoppers. Free-standing stores are more convenient for shoppers just out to buy recordings. Finally, the mall locations had become bland, look-alikes—leaving store atmosphere to the mom and pop stores and the free-standing chain stores.

INTERNATIONALIZATION OF RECORD RETAILING

Just as the recording industry became more internationalized in the 1980s with the emergence of the six multinational record/entertainment conglomerates, the record retail end of the industry internationalized in the 1990s. Large U.S. chains began to open stores outside of the United States. Large foreign chains, particularly from the United Kingdom, began to compete in the U.S. market.

U.S. Chains Abroad

In most foreign territories where U.S. chains have opened up stores they are competing with HMV and Virgin from the U.K. as well as each other and, of course, the domestic independents and chains. Japan was a particularly favorite target of these retailers in the 1990s, partly due to the fact that 70 percent to 80 percent of the retail record outlets in Japan were independent record shops. That is similar to the situation that existed in the United States in the 1960s and invited the rapid growth of chains in the 1970s and 1980s. The most aggressive U.S. retailer in foreign markets is Tower Records. Tower has thirty-three stores in Japan, and one to three stores each in Taiwan, Hong Kong, Singapore, Thailand, and Korea.[20] Most are large stores in the 6,000 to 10,000 square foot range.[21] The Musicland group, through its Sam Goody name, also competes in the Pacific Rim market as well as the U.K. The Sam Goody name will be licensed to retailers by the Japan Record Sales Network (JARECS). JARECS is owned by a consortium of record labels in Japan.[22]

Foreign Chains in the United States

The most significant British invasion of the U.S. record industry since the Beatles is the expansion of two of the U.K.'s largest record retailers on American soil. The retail arm of EMI Music ("HMV" stores) and W.H. Smith ("The Wall" and "Virgin Retail" stores) have both opened stores in the United States. HMV is a 330-store international chain that began in London in 1921. It now operates stores in the U.K.,

Canada, Japan, Hong Kong, Australia, Germany, and the United States. Into 1996 HMV had focused its fourteen stores and new store openings on the eastern U.S.[23]

By the mid 1990s WHS Music, the wholly owned U.S. subsidiary of W.H Smith, operated over 167 outlets in the U.S. under the names of "Our Price" and "The Wall." They are small to medium-sized stores averaging about 3,500 square feet. Competing on the large store end of the spectrum, W.H. Smith and Blockbuster Music operated Virgin Retail in the U.K. as a 50/50 joint venture.[24] In the United States and elsewhere, Virgin Megastores are in the over 10,000 square foot category. In fact, the Virgin Megastore that opened in Times Square in New York in May of 1996 became the world's largest record store at 70,000 square feet, topping the prior Virgin and world record 60,000 square footer in London. The Times Square store, developed at a cost to Virgin of about $15 million, needed to generate $21 million of sales per year just to break even.[25] The U.S. operation of Virgin is a 25 percent W.H. Smith and 75 percent Blockbuster Music joint venture.

INDIES: THE "MOM AND POP" STORES

"There is no competing with the big guys. . . .
You can only offer something different."[26]

The independent, single, "Mom and Pop" store remains an important segment of the retail end of the recording industry. Such stores provide entrepreneurs with entries into the industry. They provide customers with locations where the chains might not wish to build or might have overlooked. They often provide customers with niche stores catering to special catalogs or oldies. They frequently sell used CDs. They provide a means for local talent to distribute their recordings locally (although many chain managers also have the option of picking up a local album on consignment).

The numbers of the indies barely grew at all while the chain explosion took place. Table 8-2 indicates a modest growth of about 39 percent for single unit firms from 1977 to 1992. During that same period the total number of stores grew 117 percent (see Table 8-1). And, while one cannot assume all indies are sole proprietorships instead of corporations, there were 994 sole proprietorship establishments in 1977 and 1,061 in 1992.

Creating a Niche

Independent stores tend to be smaller than the chain locations, most in the 2,000 to 4,000 square foot range, some even smaller. Therefore they cannot stock the breadth of titles that the chains do. However, they frequently do stock a deep catalog in some specialty area such as jazz, country, rap, reggae, alternative, or imports. With a special inventory they develop sales personnel that are particularly knowledgeable in that genre of music, a fact that many customers appreciate. The special inventory also enables them to create a store atmosphere that is geared to particular kinds of customers, not the generic mall browsers that chains cater to. As mentioned at the beginning of this chapter, these "other" kinds of image components are important to significant numbers of record buyers.[27] Most of the independents do not compete on price. They feel that their deep inventory is worth a higher price. As one indie owner put it, "So, pay me for having it."[28] The possibility of selling used CDs is also important to independent stores. Many of them do carry used CDs and the used business accounts for anywhere from 15 percent to 100 percent of their business.[29] Out of deference to the major distributors, many chains do not carry used CDs. The independent store, however, is much more likely to buy from a one-stop or independent distributor and so is not so much concerned with how the majors feel about their used CD business.

Table 8-6 indicates other important differences between the individual store units in chain operations and the typical independent record retailer. Chain stores average about 2.6 times the sales of the indies. Chain stores are able to do this more efficiently as far as payroll is concerned, spending about 4 percent less of their sales on payroll than the indies do, even though they utilize more employees to do so.

An examination of Figure 8-2 indicates just how little, in some respects, the mom and pop stores changed from 1977 to 1992. The nearly doubling of sales per unit indicated in Table 8-6 is virtually flat sales when adjusted for consumer price index changes between 1977 and 1992 into constant (1982–1984 = 100) dollars. The chains enjoyed real growth in sales per store until the early 1990s when price competition, and other factors discussed above, cut into chain store volume.

RETAIL MANAGEMENT CONSIDERATIONS

For the most part record store managers face the same problems as other retailers. However there are some considerations specific to the recording industry that are

TABLE 8-6   Comparison of Chain and Mom and Pop Stores

Census Year	Sales Per Unit		Payroll % of Sales		Paid Employees	
	Mom and Pop	Chain	Mom and Pop	Chain	Mom and Pop	Chain
1977	$188,986	$437,246	11.1	10.0	3.3	7.1
1987	$308,376	$857,254	12.3	8.7	4.2	8.8
1992	$362,644	$959,852	13.4	9.4	4.1	9.7
1977–1992 % change	+ 91.9	+120	+20.7	–6	+24.2	+36.6

Source: U.S. Department of Commerce, Census of Retail Trade.

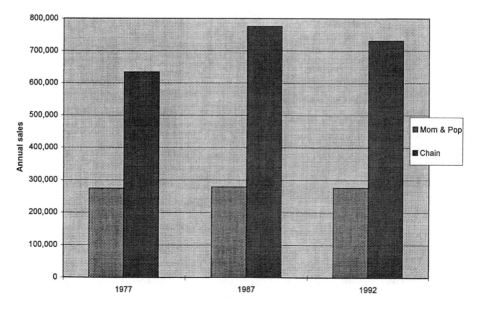

FIGURE 8-2   Sales Per Store (Constant Dollars, 1982–1984 = 100)
Source: Department of Commerce, Census of Retail Trade.

worth mentioning because they are particularly headaches for record retailers. Most of these would fall under the general heading of inventory management; multiple configurations, packaging, shrinkage, and breadth of inventory.

Multiple Configurations

Multiple configurations have been a fact of life in record retailing since the days of cylinders and discs. Later it was 78s, 45s, and LPs, with the latter being available in 10" and 12" formats. Often the same selection or album was available in multiple formats. Next it was 45s, LPs, and 8-tracks. There is wide speculation in the industry that one reason retailers were quick to delete eight-tracks from inventory in favor of the cassette was that they simply did not want to have to carry the same album in three formats. By the mid 1990s, most retailers found themselves carrying the same albums in Compact Disc and cassette form, and the same singles in CD and cassette form. Retailers proved to be as lukewarm as consumers were to the mini-disc and DCC tapes of the early 1990s.

Packaging

Packaging is important to retailers for four reasons.

1. Packaging determines the size of the recording and therefore the amount of space that a unit takes up. The more space taken up by a package, the fewer units the retailer can fit into the store, so the smaller inventory can be carried.
2. Changes in packaging, such as when CDs quit being sold in 12" × 6" cardboard boxes, affect the way the store fixtures that hold the products have to be built. Often, a change in packaging that affects the size of the product will result in an expensive refixturing of part of the store.
3. Smaller packages, such as cassettes and compact discs, are less likely to make effective display items. The 12" × 12" LP cover was an effective package that could convey lots of information and have a visual impact because of its size. In fact, manufacturers often supplied retailers with blank album jackets or cardboard "flats" (which had only the album cover on one side) to use in creating store displays. With CDs and cassettes the point-of-purchase display material provided by the labels must be a different size and often different shape from the product package. This makes it more difficult for the customer to link the display to the item.
4. CDs and cassettes without packaging that makes them larger than they need to be are easily slipped into pockets and stolen.

Shrinkage

Among all retailers, audio and video stores have the third highest rate of "shrinkage" (merchandise that was supposedly purchased by the retailer, but which disappears from inventory), 2.73 percent. Shoplifting accounts for 45 percent of music and video shrinkage, while employee theft accounts for 40 percent, administrative and bookkeeping errors for 13 percent, and vendor fraud for 2 percent. That is why over 80 percent of music retailers use some form of inventory tagging theft prevention system and why they have lobbied the manufacturers to tag items at the pressing plant.[30]

Breadth of Inventory

The 1990s development of the "megastore" that carries a large inventory of recordings, plus a large inventory of home video products, plus a large inventory of paper and audio books, plus a large inventory of computer software and CD-ROM titles, forced record retailers to diversify their inventories. As the number of computer systems with CD-ROM capabilities pushed 20 million in the mid 1990s record stores began to consider stocking CD-ROM music, education, and entertainment titles.[31] The presence of audiobooks in CD format and the presence of more audiobook labels with music industry ties encouraged record retailers to begin carrying this line of merchandise.[32] The presence of high profit margins in sheet music and songbooks encouraged many record retailers to carry print music, as well as recorded music. By 1994 music books (folios) sold for $17.00 to $25.00 with luxury editions, often containing CD-ROMs, priced as high as $60.00 and $75.00. Titles were usually not discounted and sold at a 40 percent to 50 percent profit margin. The lower margins on CDs made music books attractive to some retailers.[33] In deciding how much precious retail floor space to allocate to which kind of product, record retailers were becoming aware of what one audiobook executive noted, "People who buy records don't just buy records."[34]

USED CDS

Although there had been limited resale of used recordings at back-yard sales, flea markets, and some specialty used record stores catering to serious collectors, it was not until the advent of the compact disc that the used record business became widespread and of concern to the record labels and artists. In a compact disc the sound quality of a used copy is usually the same as a new copy unless the disc has been so damaged as to be unplayable. While sales of new CDs soared from 22.6 million units in 1985 to over 727 million units a decade later in 1995,[35] consumers and some mom and pop retailers discovered the value of used recordings. They could be purchased from consumers who were tired of them or in need of quick cash for anywhere from three to five dollars apiece and resold for about twice that amount. With the price of new discs running in the fifteen dollar range (except for sale items), the sound of used discs being equal to the sound of new discs, and some items no longer being available as new discs, the used disc market grew rapidly.

From a strictly legal perspective, there is nothing in the copyright laws to prevent someone who owns a copy of a CD or other recording from selling it to someone else, either a store or another individual. The "first sale doctrine" allows "the owner of a particular copy or phonorecord lawfully made . . . , or any person authorized by such owner . . . without the authority of the copyright owner, to sell or otherwise dispose of the possession of that copy or phonorecord."[36] Rental of sound recordings is specifically prohibited under the Record Rental Amendment of 1984.[37] The copyright laws now prohibit the owner of a copy of a sound recording from disposing of a particular copy for purpose of direct or indirect commercial advantage by rental, lease or lending, or "any other act or practice in the nature of rental lease or lending."[38] Some industry spokesmen claimed that the sale of used recordings was just another way to rent the recordings, where the customer could buy the disc one day then return it a few days later for credit or cash.[39] However, a survey sponsored by the National Association of Recording Merchandisers (NARM) found that only 9 percent of the buyers of used CDs said they purchased the product to tape it then sell it back.[40] Similarly, the sale of used CDs was only a sideline for most recording retailers. Only 18 percent of stores surveyed had more than 50 percent of their inventory in used product, while 64 percent of the stores had 25 percent or less of their inventory in used recordings. One could reason that, since the vast majority of the used CD sales would go to legitimate activities, then it would not be likely that the entire practice of selling used CDs could be stopped.[41]

Sharing the "Blame" for the Used CD Market

Retailers cited several reasons for the growth of the used CD market:

1. Customers want it because the price of a new CD is too high.[42] That was born out by the NARM survey, which found that 82 percent of used CD purchasers said the reason they bought the used CD was because it cost less.[43] Even some label executives acknowledge this. "There's a perception on the public's behalf that compact discs, particularly at traditional retail, are priced too high. The industry, I don't believe, has responded very favorably to that perspective and people want a bargain," said David Blane, Senior Vice President of Polygram.[44]

2. There is more profit, i.e., a higher margin, on the sale of used CDs than on new CDs.[45] A typical used CD is sold for at least twice the purchase price with a profit of anywhere from three to six dollars, creating markups ranging from 83 percent to 177 percent and dollar margins as high as $6.65.[46] Retailers typically pay the labels about $11.00 for new CDs and sell them for prices in the neighborhood of $16.00 if they are not on any special sale—a markup of 45 percent and a margin of about $5.00.[47]

3. Labels set up tight returns policies on opened CDs, usually only accepting a 1 or 2 percent return.[48] That makes it difficult for retailers to return product that has been opened for airplay in the stores, a particular problem because many stores now have a policy of allowing a customer to hear any product before buying. That led some large record retail chains to open up independent used CD stores to dispose of the opened product. They discovered the business to be profitable and began to consider selling used product in their main "name" stores.[49]

4. Label promotion persons and radio station personnel sell promotional copies, which they obtain at no cost, to used CD outlets to make some quick cash. Label and radio people agreed that such practices exist, but disagreed on the size of the practice.[50] The NARM survey found that 32 percent of all titles purchased were promotional copies.[51] Strictly speaking, the sale of promotional copies does violate the copyright laws. Because the labels purport to have given the copies to the radio stations for promotional purposes only and, to have retained title they have not transferred ownership of the copy and, thus those copies are not subject to the first sale doctrine. On the other hand, many promotional copies are given to the radio stations with the intention that they be given away to consumers. It would be difficult to argue that giving the recording to a consumer does not constitute transfer of ownership. One can reasonably argue that recordings are loaned to the radio stations so the station will play them on the air, but contending that they are being "loaned" to consumers who are contest winners at radio stations and whose identities are unknown to the labels is a difficult case to make. Note that, whether the artist is paid royalties on these copies (which they are not) is irrelevant to a discussion of whether it is legal for a store that has obtained a copy to sell it. The artists must take up their concerns with the labels because all they have is a contractual right to be paid by the

TABLE 8-7   Why People Sell Used CDs

Don't listen to them anymore	37%
To generate cash	13%
Don't like the disc anymore	27%
To make room for new CDs	7%
Tired of the same CDs	7%
Received as gift	2%
To tape, then sell back	9%

Source: Soundata survey reported in *Billboard*, 2 October 1993: 4, 112.

label. An artist would have to show that the label knew its promotion staff was selling promotional copies and either participated in the process or did nothing to stop it.

5. Customers want used CDs because the quality of CDs do not deteriorate in used copies, so the customer can feel confident when buying a used product that it will sound as good as a new copy of the same recording but cost less.[52]

Pressure Points

Prior to late 1992, when some major retail chains started to get into the used CD business, the labels had generally ignored it as a small percent of business, confined mostly to mom and pop stores.[53] But in December of 1992 three major chain retailers, Wherehouse, Hastings, and LIVE Specialty, announced plans to begin carrying used product in some or all of their stores.[54] By summer of 1993 four of the six major distributors, Sony, WEA (Warner, Elektra, Atlantic), CEMA (Capitol–EMI, later to become EMI Music Distribution or EMD), and Uni (MCA, Geffen, and GRP), announced that they would no longer provide co-op advertising money to chains or stores that sold used CDs. Sony said "The sale of used, bootleg or counterfeit product . . . is detrimental to our industry, unfair to the artist, publisher and manufacturing company, and ultimately both your customer and ours, the consuming public." The WEA announcement stated that sale of used CDs diminished the perceived value of the new product.[55] PolyGram (Polygram, Mercury) and BMG (RCA, Arista), the other two major distributors, did not participate in the co-op pull-out.[56]

TABLE 8-8   What Used CD Sellers Do with the Money or Trade

Take the cash	32%
Buy more used CDs	35%
Buy new CDs	30%
Buy a new cassette	4%

Source: Soundata survey reported in *Billboard*, 2 October 1993: 4, 112.

Later CEMA began to refuse to take *any* returns of opened CDs.[57] Country superstar artist, Garth Brooks, got on the bandwagon, announcing that he did not want his new album sold to any store that sold used CDs.[58] Said Brooks, "I'm against anyone who sells used CDs and if I have my way, we won't send any product to them, not just CDs, until they find a way to compensate those writers and publishers and all involved with the record."[59]

The retailers fired the next round. In 1993 they formed an ad hoc trade group, the Independent Music Retailers Association (IMRA), to petition the FTC to investigate the withholding of co-op advertising money as a possible unfair trade practice. Then, in July of 1993, the 339-unit chain Wherehouse Entertainment and IMRA filed suits in Federal District Court against CEMA, WEA, Uni, and Sony Music distributors. The suit alleged that the distributors were violating antitrust laws by conspiring to withhold advertising dollars from stores that sold used CDs.[60] By September the air had cleared. The distributors agreed to reverse their policy of withholding advertising money as long the money was not used to promote the sale of used CDs.[61] The IMRA suit was finally settled in 1994 for $2 million. That payment from the labels was to be distributed among the 300 retailers in the IMRA class action to make up for lost co-op advertising money. The labels also agreed to a payment of about $250,000 to cover the costs of the litigation. The terms of the Wherehouse suit settlement were not disclosed.[62]

For his part, Garth Brooks was still not happy. He recanted his statements as they applied to small stores selling used CDs of rare albums. "My bitch and gripe is when mass retail takes over used CDs," Brooks told a press conference, adding that the chains would kill the independents. Meanwhile a number of stores were boycotting Brooks's newest album, which arrived in the middle of the controversy. Remarked one small retailer, "Garth can't be the person to decide who can sell used and who cannot."[63]

The Federal Trade Commission was not happy, either. It launched a separate investigation into price-fixing and the used CD problem against all six major distributors. One distributor executive was quoted as saying, "We thought they were satisfied. . . . Now it looks like they'll be checking into the books. Nobody here wants that."[64]

RECORD CLUBS

The record club is a method by which the label can sell direct, or almost direct, to the customer. As such, it is competing for consumers' record purchase dollars with other means of retail. Columbia started the first record club, Columbia House, in 1955. At that time there were not record selling outlets everywhere and clubs represented a way to reach a customer directly, without having to sell to a middle man. Without a wholesaler in between them and the customer, the label could sell at list price, and therefore at a higher profit margin. Capitol and RCA started their own clubs in 1958. By the end of 1959 clubs had nearly two million members, with Columbia at 1,300,000, RCA at 600,000, Capitol at 250,000, and Diners Club at 125,000.[65]

Columbia moved to distribute not only its own labels, but those of Warner Brothers, A & M, Kapp, and Vanguard through exclusive club distribution licenses, meaning that those outside labels sold through Columbia House could not be distributed through the other clubs. Former Columbia president, Clive Davis, noted, "The Record Club, in turn, was turning a nice profit and controlling something like 60 to 70 percent of the industry's mail order business."[66] The other clubs complained, and the Federal Trade Commission launched an antitrust investigation in 1962. The investigation ended with Columbia agreeing not to use exclusive club licensing for outside labels. That meant that labels that did not have clubs could have their records distributed through any, or all, of the clubs that they could agree with. The record retail stores and rack jobbers also complained that the clubs were competing unfairly with dealer sales—a complaint that had not gone away as late as the 1996.[67] Club sales declined from their nearly 15 percent of sales in the 1950s and 1960s to a low of 6.8 percent in 1988. They then proceeded to climb back up to a high of 15.1 percent in 1994 and 14.5 percent in 1995 (see Figure 8-1).

The price competition between retail stores, the general stagnation of sales in 1995, the decline of the chain retailers, and the frustration of the retailers and labels over the sale of used CDs sparked renewed controversy about the record clubs. By that time there were two clubs that controlled the majority of the direct sales business: Columbia House, jointly owned by Sony Music Entertainment (Columbia's parent) and Warner Music Group (a subsidiary of Time Warner), and BMG Music Service, owned by BMG Entertainment (RCA's parent). These two clubs shared about 64 percent of the club sales market with Columbia House netting sales of about $615 million and BMG Music Service netting sales of about $500 million.

Both clubs ran incentive plans to entice members to join by giving them eight to as many as twelve CDs free if they agreed to buy one to four at the regular club price. The clubs could do this for several reasons, all having to do with their cost of goods sold. First, manufacturing costs for CDs had fallen to about one dollar per disc. Because the clubs actually manufacture their own copies of the discs under a license from the labels their pressing costs are low. Secondly, the clubs do not pay royalties to the artists or labels on any of the "free" records. They do pay the music publishers on all product sold, but at a reduced rate of usually 75 percent of the statutory mechanical rate. When the clubs do pay the labels, it is usually a royalty of 10 to 25 percent of the suggested retail list price (SRLP). The labels then pay the artists out of what they receive from the club, usually half of the artist's royalty rate, or a maximum of one half of what the label receives from club sales. The economics of the situation is simple. The direct cost to the club on a "free" incentive or bonus record is about $1.50 to $1.60 per disc. For a disc sold at full list the club's direct costs are about $3.20 to $5.50, including label and mechanical royalties and manufacturing costs. Even if the club only sells one of every three discs distributed, that is a gross margin of at least $10.50 (assuming a $15.98 list) on the sold copy, less costs of $3.20 for the free copies leaves a gross margin of $7.20 for each sold disc. A retail store has a maximum gross margin on the same disc of about $6.50 (wholesale of about $10.50 on a CD with a $15.98 SRLP) if it is sold at full list price—an occurrence that is not very common. If the retailer is trying to move the discs at a more common sale price of $11.99 or $12.99, the margin is reduced to $1.50 to $2.50. The clubs counter that they have heavy advertising costs, estimated to be as high as $150 million per year.[68]

Partially in response to the retailers' complaints, and partly in response to their own growing feelings that the clubs actually do take away more profitable sales at retail stores and rack locations, several labels, Disney, Virgin, MCA and Geffen, abandoned the clubs in 1995 and 1996. The clubs' parent labels often contend that the club sales are "extra," reaching people who would not otherwise buy records. However a 1995 NARM survey revealed that 72 percent of club members are "heavy" buyers—the same kind of people who frequent record stores. To make matters worse, another NARM survey found that club product accounted for about 11 percent of used CD sales, thus competing twice with the retail store—once as a club purchase and again as a used CD.[69]

FUTURE OF RECORD RETAILING

*"No one can predict with any certainty
the future of the media world."
—JOHN PAVLIK[70]*

In 1996 there were at least five sites on the World Wide Web offering a computer-based shopping service for recordings. Most offered large catalogs, and catalog search by title, artist, or genre. Some even offered samples of the albums, artist biographies, and reviews.[71] In such instances, the "place" utility of the merchandiser becomes the computer user's home or office. That is a convenience that is hard to beat. Early response to these sites was small. NARM reported that in 1995 only 1 percent of the Soundata panel had actually purchased recordings on-line.[72]

In early 1997 Camelot Music announced an ambitious foray into Web retailing. The ailing chain announced it would make its entire CD inventory available for on-line sale directly to customers. Each cut of the 80,000 titles would have a thirty-second preview sound bite—1.2 million soundbites![73]

The End of Record Stores?

The labels, record clubs, and web services could all sell direct to the consumer, bypassing the retail store. They could even utilize digital delivery of the recording to the purchaser's computer or recorder once enough fiber optic is in place to meet the demand of the high density information transfer that is required. These methods of retailing recordings will probably develop parallel to the in-place retail system, just

TABLE 8-9   Record Store Hierarchy, 1995

Store Size	Size in Square Feet	Average Number of Employees	Average SKUs	Average Annual Sales
Small	1,000–2,499	5.4	33,200	$752,000
Medium	2,500–5,999	6.8	50,500	$1.2 million
Large	6,000–11,999	11.1	78,500	$1.96 million
Superstore	12,000–20,000	19.4	122,900	$3.2 million
Megastore	over 20,000	36.6	281,500	$6 million

Source: NARM data reported in "NARM Survey: Average Record Store Sale Dropped Almost $5 Over Last Three Years," *Billboard*, 20 July 1996: 44.

as the rack jobber and record club did earlier. It seems likely that many people will still desire to possess an object that contains the recording and that can exist outside the confines of their computers. One of the redeeming features of the cassette was its portability. Now consumers take their music everywhere and take portability of their music for granted. The CD has become just as portable as the cassette. In 1995 audio hardware manufacturers were looking to a huge nearly untapped market for CD playback units in autos. Maybe the computer will become as portable and as inexpensive as the personal stereo or "boom box." Maybe. Still, there would be the desire to go out, to encounter other people, and to touch a copy of the recording (in whatever format).

By 1995 record stores had evolved into a five-tiered structure, based on size: small, medium, large, superstore, and megastore (see Table 8-9). There will undoubtedly be fewer medium and small record stores in malls and strip centers. Those that do survive will be larger in an effort to compete with the multimedia "megastores" in both breadth and depth of inventory. Those two trends had become apparent by 1995. There will also continue to be independent record stores, usually small and medium-sized, that cater to special niches in terms of location, inventory, and ambiance. The independent stores survived the onslaught of the chains, they can survive the onslaught of the cybermerchants as well.

NOTES

[1]"State of the Industry," (NARM President Ann Leiff's remarks at the 1995–1996 NARM Convention), *NARM Sounding Board*, May 1995 (on-line version).

[2]Geoffrey Hull, *Atlanta Record Buyers Survey*, Georgia State University (1976). The survey did include rack locations but was dominated by stores.

[3]General sources are: Russell Sanjek and David Sanjek, *American Popular Music Business in the 20th Century* (1991); Guy A. Marco (ed.), *Encyclopedia of Recorded Sound in the United States* (1993).

[4]Former NARM President Jules Malmud, quoted in R. Serge Denisoff, *Tarnished Gold* (1986): 212.

[5]"Soundata Consumer Panel," *NARM Sounding Board* (December 1994): 10.

6 NARM Survey, 1981.

[7]"A Guide to Profitability, " *Music Retailer* (July 1975): 34, 50.

[8]Ed Christman, "Blockbuster to Add Super Club to Expanding Retail Portfolio," *Billboard*, 16 October 1993: 5.

[9]Handleman information from: *Moody's Handbook of Common Stocks* (Winter 95–96); *Standard and Poor's Stock Reports* (February 1996); Lisa Gubernick, "We Are a Society of Collectors," *Forbes*, 24 July 1989: 80; Ed Christman, "2 Deals Alter Rackjobbing Landscape," *Billboard*, 12 February 1994: 5; Seth Goldstein, "Direct Moves Pinch Levy Home Ent.," *Billboard*, 18 July 1992: 6.

[10]Don Jeffrey, "Musicland Reports Double-Digit Profit Hike in '93," *Billboard*, 12 February 1994: 85.

[11]Ed Christman, "Blockbuster to Add Super Club to Expanding Retail Portfolio," *Billboard*, 16 October 1993: 5.

[12]Ed Christman, "The Positive Sounds of Hear Music's Expansion," *Billboard*, 4 March 1995: 64. (Hear Music is a Boston-based chain with stores spread out across the country in a number of major makets, most recently opening stores in California.)

[13]Ed Christman, "More Downsizing at Camelot," *Billboard*, 13 April 1996: 68.

[14]Ed Christman, "Musicland to Shutter More Stores," *Billboard*, 20 April 1996: 72.

[15]Ed Christman, "Alliance Breathing Easy after Failed Metromedia Merger," *Billboard*, 18 May 1996: 52.

[16]Ed Christman, "The Brass Tacks of Camelot Music's Financial Restructuring," *Billboard*, 3 February 1996: 62.

[17]"Soundata Consumer Panel," *NARM Sounding Board*, Jan. 1996 (on-line version).

[18]Margaret Webb–Pressler, "The Unsound of Music," *Washington Post*, 29 April 1995: C1; Ed Christman, "Closings Reveal Chinks in Chains' Long-Term Strategies," *Billboard*, 28 October 1995: 66; and "Can Retail's Shaky Health Be Cured?" *Billboard*, 23 December 1995:1.

[19]Jeffrey Ressner, "You Can't Always Get What You Want," *Rolling Stone*, 3 September 1992: 13, 80.

[20]Tower Records advertisement, *Billboard*, 18 May 1996: APQ-29.

[21]Steve McClure, "Tower Records to Open in Seoul," *Billboard*, 9 July 1994: 39.

[22]Steve McClure, "Sam Goody Joins Japan's Retail Wars," *Billboard*, 2 July 1994: 80.

[23]Jeff Clark–Meads, "HMV's 75th Year Marked by Celebration, Expansion," *Billboard*, 16 March 1996: 1, 116.

[24]Dominic Pride, "W. H. Smith Plans to Add More Bricks to the Wall," *Billboard*, 4 September 1993: 12.

[25]Ed Christman, "Million-Dollar Times Square Gamble by Virgin Megastore," *Billboard*, 4 May 1996: 54.

[26]Mary Mancini, Owner of Lucy's Record Shop, Nashville, Tennessee, quoted in Carrie Borzillo, "Unable to Compete with Chains, Indies Offer Alternatives," *Billboard*, 30 March 1996: 66.

[27]The following articles describe typical examples of indie stores: Jim Bessman, "At the Heart of Cajun Country, Floyd's Record Shop Has Finger on Region's Pulse," *Billboard*, 20 January 1996: 61; Pat Hadler, "Rap, Vinyl Fans Boogie to Columbus' Groove Shack," *Bill-*

board, 7 January 1995: 78; Tom Phalen, "Easy Street Stores a Family Affair," *Billboard*, 20 November 1993: 93; Don Jeffrey, "Atlanta's Wax 'n' Facts Is Hip—and Hot," *Billboard*, 17 July 1993: 93; Ed Christman, "D.C.-Area Indie-Intensive Record Shop Is Ready to GO!" *Billboard*, 5 June 1993: 73.

[28]Borzillo, supra note 26.

[29]Kevin Stander (spokesman for the Independent Music Retailers Association, commentary), "Used CDs Integral to Industry," *Billboard*, 14 August 1993: 4.

[30]Don Jeffrey, "Shrinkage Ebbs At Music/Vid Stores," *Billboard*, 26 November 1994: 63.

[31]Brett Atwood, "Multimedia in Stores," *Billboard*, 30 March 1996: 59; Steve Traiman, "Finally, Retailers Get Smitten by 'CD ROMance'," *Billboard*, 25 February 1995: 76.

[32]Trudi Miller Rosenblum, "Audiobooks Aimed at Record Stores," *Billboard*, 15 July 1995: 61.

[33]Frank DiConstanzo, "Print Music Strikes Profitable Chord," *Billboard*, 24 September 1994: 64.

[34]Seth Gershel, Vice President Simon & Schuster Audio, quoted in Trudi Miller Rosenblum, supra note 32.

[35]R.I.A.A., 1995 Year End Statistics.

[36]17 U.S.C. § 109.

[37]P.L. 98–450, 98 Stat. 1727, 98th Cong., 2nd Sess. (1984).

[38]17 U.S.C. § 109(b)(1)(A).

[39]See, e.g., Michael Diamond, "Music Companies Try to Crack Down on Sales of Used CDs," *Gannett News Service*, June 17, 1993 (LEXIS).

[40]"Both Retailer, Label Claims Backed by Used-CD Survey," *Billboard*, 2 October 1993: 4, 112.

[41]That is the theory that the U.S. Supreme Court applied in declining to prohibit the copying of broadcast television programs on home VCRs in *Sony Corp. v. Universal City Studios, Inc.*, 464 U.S. 417 (1984). Considering the question of whether the manufacturers of VCRs could be liable as contributory infringers the Court stated, "The sale of copying equipment, like the sale of other articles of commerce, does not constitute contributory infringement if the product is widely used for legitimate, unobjectionable purposes." Although the used CD retailer would be more directly liable under the specific terms of the statute, the overall logic applies.

[42]Jesse Hamlin, "Big Labels Declare War on Used CDs," *San Francisco Chronicle*, Wed., 16 June 1993, Daily Datebook Section, Pg. D1 (LEXIS), quoting Wherehouse record store chain Vice President for Marketing, Bruce Jesse; Brian Kaberline, "Used CDs Are Good and Cheap—Unless You Manufacture New Ones," *Kansas City Business Journal*, 18 June 1993: Sec. 1, Pg. 1 (LEXIS); John MacDougall, "Small Record Stores Feud with Big Distributors Over Used CDs," *Houston Business Journal*, 21 June 1993: Sec1, p. 1 (LEXIS).

[43]*Billboard*, supra note 40 at 112.

[44]Morning Edition, *National Public Radio*, 14 July 1993 (Transcript, LEXIS).

[45]Kaberline, supra note 42, estimating that the profit on a used CD is twice that of a new product; MacDougall, supra note 42; Ed Christman, "3 Big Chains Test Used-CD Waters," *Billboard*, 5 December 1992: 1.

[46]Based on purchasing a used product for $6.00 and selling it for $10.99, or purchasing for $3.60 and selling it for $10.95; Hamlin, supra note 42.

[47]Neil Strauss, "Pennies That Add Up to $16.98: Why CDs Cost So Much," *New York Times*, 5 June 1995, Late Edition, Sec C, P. 11 Col. 1. (LEXIS).

[48]Christman, supra note 45; Craig Rosen and Ed Christman, "Retailers Sound Used CD Alarm," *Billboard*, 7 December 1971: 1.

[49]Christman, supra note 45.

[50]"Radio, Promo People Said to Sell CDs," *Billboard*, 7 December 1995: 79.

[51]*Billboard*, supra note 40.

[52]Hamlin, supra note 42; Kaberline, supra note 42; Chuck Philips, "Wherehouse ups ante in Used CDs," *Los Angeles Times*, 29 June 1993: Calendar: Part F; Page 3 Col. 1. (LEXIS).

[53]Rosen and Christman, supra note 48.

[54]Christman, supra note 45.

[55]Michael Diamond, "Music Companies Try to Crack Down on Sales of Used CDs," *Gannett News Service*, 17 June 1993 (LEXIS).

[56]Hamlin, supra note 42; Jeffrey Jolson–Colburn, "Merchandisers Call for Study on Used CDs," *Dallas Morning News,* Thursday, 17 June 1993: Today section, p. 14C; MacDougall, supra note 42.

[57]Christman, supra note 45.

[58]"Brooks Delivers Used-CD Ultimatum," *Billboard*, 10 July 1993: 6.

[59]Ibid.

[60]Craig Rosen, "Wherehouse Suit Hits Used CD Policies," *Billboard*, 31 July 1993: 8.

[61]Craig Rosen, "Used CD Rivals Near Truce," *Billboard*, 11 September 1993: 1.

[62]Kelly Greene, "Local Retailers Win Settlement in Battle Over Used CDs," *Business Journal-Charlotte*, 11 July 1994: section 1, p. 1 (Lexis); "Dispute between Music Companies and Record Store Owners Over Sale of Used CDs Is Settled," 15 *Entertainment Law Reporter*, April 1994: 26 (LEXIS).

[63]Rosen, supra note 61.

[64]Adam Sandler, "FTC Subpoenas Record Distribs in Used CD Case," *Daily Variety*, 3 May 1994: 1.

[65]Bob Rolontz, "Disk Clubs Zoom to 2 Mil Subscribers," *Billboard*, 5 October 1959: 1.

[66]Clive Davis, *Clive: Inside the Record Business* (1974) 19.

[67]General record club information sources: R. Serge Denisoff, *Tarnished Gold* (1986) 211, 212, 219; Sidney Shemel and M. William Krasilovsky, *This Business of Music*, 6th ed. (1990), 60–62; Russell and David Sanjek, *American Popular Music Business in the 20th Century* (1991).

[68]See generally, Ed Christman, "Disney Records Pulls Out of Record Clubs," *Billboard*, 3 February 1996; Ed Christman and Don Jeffrey, "Record Clubs Focus of Closed-Door Meeting," *Billboard*, 23 March 1996: 1; and "Record Clubs: An Inside Look at an Evolving Enterprise," *Billboard*, 30 March 1996: 1.

[69]"Both Retailer, Label Claims Backed by Used-CD Survey," *Billboard*, 2 October 1993: 4.

[70]John V. Pavlik, *New Media and the Information Superhighway* (1996): 394.

[71]Rick Ayre, "Five Virtual Record Stores," *PC Magazine*, 28 May 1996: 56.

[72]"Soundata Consumer Panel," *NARM Sounding Board*, Jan. 1996 (on-line version).

[73]Catherine Applefield Olson, "Camelot Music Unveils Ambitious Web Site," *Billboard,* 11 Jan. 1997: 68.

Part 3

The Legal Environment of the Recording Industry

The three-income-stream model of the recording industry is reflected in a variety of ways in the legal issues and structures in the industry as well as in the strictly economic issues and structures. Songwriters create songs to be performed by the recording artists. The recording artists perform for recordings sessions and for live events. Record companies capture the performances of artists and producers on sound recordings. All of these "products" are rather ephemeral and difficult to control either to prevent piracy or to enhance their value by controlling the supply. For those reasons the recording industry is particularly prone to utilize legal methods in attempts to gain control over the production of those products, the supply of those products, the distribution of those products, and the income generated by those products in each of the three streams. For instance, a record label will seek to lower its costs per unit sold by attempting to limit the amount of mechanical royalties paid to the music publishers whose songs are recorded. Labels will attempt to negotiate licenses with music publishers at a favorable rate, lower than the "statutory" rate provided by the Copyright Act. The label will also attempt to get the recording artist to lower the rate on "controlled compositions," those compositions written or owned or "controlled" in whole or part by the artist. The label will attempt to have recording costs and some promotion costs considered as "advances," and hence recoverable ("recoupable") out of the artist's royalties. Music publishers seek new writers who have the potential to become recording artists. If the writers do become artists, then the publisher will have a ready-made outlet for recordings of that writer's songs to generate mechanical and performance royalties. Artists and writers attempt to control their own music publishing to obtain a larger percentage of the royalties in the music publishing income stream. It is often through legal structures such as copyright, or recording, publishing, or management agreements, that each player in one of the major income streams attempts to gain some manner of control over or participation in one of the other streams.

9

Copyright Basics in the Recording Industry

The recording industry runs on its copyrights. Without the protection against unauthorized use of recordings and songs, two of the three income streams (sound recordings and music publishing) would be a mere shadow of their current size. Though not intended to be a broad summary of copyright law, this chapter does address the basics of copyright law as they apply to the recording industry and a number of specific copyright law provisions and issues of great importance to the recording industry. It is crucial to remember throughout this chapter that most recordings involve two separate copyrightable works—the actual recording itself and the work (usually a song) recorded. Chapter 10 details the significant differences, but for present purposes it is still important to know that there are separate copyrights in the recording and the song.

For the record companies copyrights have always been a "good news/bad news" affair. Copyright, at least as the law stands now, protects the recordings created by the labels. It gives record companies a means to fight piracy of their recordings. It gives them, indirectly, a means to fight bootleg recordings of their artists' performances. Pirate and counterfeit recordings detract directly from sales of the legitimate product because the consumers think they are purchasing the same thing as the legitimate recording, it is just less expensive. In economic terms, the pirate recording is a direct substitute for the legitimate recording. Bootleg recordings compete for the same discretionary consumer dollars that a consumer might spend to purchase a recording of a particular artist, but are often not a pure substitute because the label will not have released a recording of that particular performance. The label may not have even released any "live" recordings of that artist at all. As far as the consumer is concerned, there is some substitution, just not pure substitution.

The "bad" news is that the labels are also users of the copyrights belonging to others. Most notably, the labels record performances of musical compositions (songs) and manufacture and distribute copies of those recordings to the public. Whenever a recording is sold it is not only a copy of the performance of the artist as captured on the master recording, it is also a copy of the song that was performed. Therefore the label must have permission (in the form of a mechanical license) from the owner of the copyrights in the song, usually a music publisher. Like most other things in copyright, permission is easy to obtain—just bring money. The mechanical license fees paid by the labels to the publishers would typically be sixty to seventy cents per album, about 7 percent of the wholesale price of a compact disc and about 10 percent of the wholesale price of a cassette. If the labels can reduce the cost of a mechanical license just one cent for each song recorded, about ten cents per album, they can shift $100,000 into the profit line for a million seller. Most mechanical licenses between the labels and the music publishers are negotiated either through the Harry Fox Agency or directly with the publisher/owner of the copyright. Copyright Arbitration Royalty Panels adjust the "statutory rate" around which the negotiated rates tend to move.

DURATION OF COPYRIGHT

Copyrights in sound recordings last as long as those in any other work. The basic provisions currently allow for copyright protection for the life of the author plus fifty years. If there are multiple authors then the fifty years does not start to run until the death of the last surviving author. Most commercially released sound recordings are created as "works made for hire" for the record companies. In that case the label is considered the "author" for copyright purposes. Because businesses do not have a "life" that will meet a certain natural end, the duration of copyrights for works made for hire is stated as seventy-five years from the year of first publication, or one hundred years from creation, whichever ends earlier.[1] That means that sound recordings are protected in the United States for longer than most other nations protect them. The standard for World Trade Organization (WTO) members is fifty years, and some countries protect sound recordings only for twenty-five years.[2]

In 1995 legislation was introduced in Congress to change the duration of copyrights in the United States to parallel that in European Union nations. The proposed new law would move to life-plus-seventy years instead of the current life-plus-fifty years. Twenty years of additional protection would also be added to the renewal term of pre-1978 copyrights, making it sixty-seven years instead of forty-seven years. Twenty years would also be added to protection for works made for hire, extending their terms to ninety-five years from first publication or one hundred and twenty years from creation, whichever ends earlier. The times for executing termination rights, generally thirty-five to forty years after the transfer, would not be changed.[3] There is strong impetus in the copyright community for passage of the legislation and it is likely to become law.

When copyrights expire the work protected goes public domain—that is it becomes available for anyone to use without permission of the previous copyright owner. One of the rationales underlying copyright law is to grant a "monopoly" to copyright authors so they can make money and be encouraged to create more works, but that the monopoly should only last for a limited time. At the end of that time the public is served by the work becoming available to anyone, without need for a license, and therefore at a lower price. Thus, more of the arts are available to more people.

P.D. or Not P.D.?

The public domain status of recordings is a complex matter. Prior to 1972 sound recordings were not protected by federal copyright law. They were protected under a patchwork of state laws. Theoretically, those pre-1972 recordings will never be public domain in the strict sense of the word. Most of the state laws do not contain a time when their protection ends. Recordings created after February 15, 1972 (the effective date of the sound recording amendment) were subject to federal protection and that federal protection preempted any state laws. For those recordings the duration of copyright would be a twenty-eight-year original term, and a forty-seven-year renewal term—a total of seventy-five years.[4] Because none of the sound recording copyrights would have expired before renewal was made automatic in 1992 they will all get the full seventy-five years. So, none of the copyrights for recordings made between 1972 and 1978 will expire before the end of 2047. (Copyrights expire at the end of the calendar year in which they would otherwise expire.[5]) The duration of copyright was changed to life of the author plus fifty years in 1978 but because most sound recordings are works made for hire their duration is seventy-five years from first publication, just as it was from 1972 to 1978.

Even when copyrights of the sound recordings do begin to enter the public domain in 2048 that does not mean that the copyrights in the works recorded will necessarily be expired. Because one could not make a copy of a sound recording without copying the work recorded at the same time there are two copyrights to be considered. Most musical compositions, and any literary or dramatic works likely to be recorded, will be operating under the "life plus fifty" rules. It would then be necessary to know who the authors were and exactly when they had died in order to know whether it was safe to copy a particular recording, even if the recording was known to be public domain.

FORMALITIES: NOTICE AND REGISTRATION

The current copyright laws recognize the existence of copyrights in works from the moment they are "created," i.e., first fixed in some tangible medium of expression. Formalities, such as publication of the work with the appropriate copyright notice and registration, are no longer necessary to secure basic copyright protection. That is the same standard used in most other nations, particularly those that have joined the Berne Convention for the Protection of Literary Property or the World Trade Organization (WTO). The 1994 General Agreement on Tariffs and Trade (GATT) treaty that set up the WTO requires its members to apply Berne Convention standards in their copyright laws. There are, however, reasons why some formalities are still of importance to the recording industry, particularly in the United States.

Notice

The copyright notice for sound recordings is different from that for other works. For most works that notice consists of (1) the symbol ©, or the word "Copyright," or the abbreviation "Copr."; (2) the year of first publication; (3) the name of the copyright owner. For sound recordings the notice requirement is (1) the symbol ℗ (often referred to as the "circle P" notice); (2) the year of first publication of the sound recording (not the work recorded); (3) the name of the sound recording copyright owner (usually a record label). The "circle P" notice is required by the Rome Convention[6] for protection of sound recording copyrights on an international basis. One typically sees notices on albums, whatever format, that have both the © and ℗ notices because the labels are claiming copyright in both the recording and the supplemental artwork, liner notes, and so forth that are part of the packaging of the recording.

The Case of "Boogie, Chillen"

A 1995 court decision regarding formality requirements for recordings of some pre-1978 works may have the effect of casting some songs into the public domain. Under the 1909 law a copyright notice was required to be placed on copies of published works.[7] Prior to publication works were protected by common law copyright and some kinds of works, including musical compositions and dramatic works, could be protected by federal copyright registration even if unpublished. When a work was published it lost common law protection. If the publication was without the required notice, it lost federal protection. Without common law or federal protection the work then became public domain. The 1908 case of *White-Smith Music Pub. Co. v. Apollo Co.*[8] held that a piano roll, and by implication a phonorecord, was not a copy of a work because the work could not be visually perceived from that kind of device. Music publishers had therefore assumed that copyright notice for songs was not, therefore, required on phonorecords of the songs. In 1973 a federal district court in New York upheld that view.[9] However the Ninth Circuit Court of Appeals declined to follow that precedent and in *La Cienega Music Company v. Z .Z. Top*[10] held that distribution of pre-1978 recordings of John Lee Hooker's "Boogie, Chillen" was a publication of the song and if the records did not contain a proper copyright notice for the song, the song would become public domain unless it had previously been registered. The U.S. Supreme Court refused to hear the case. Because literally thousands of recordings had been released without copyright notices for the songs recorded on them the music publishing companies were in an uproar at the prospect of thousands of songs suddenly being in the public domain. The publishers are attempting to get Congress to alter the copyright law to "fix" the problem but the exact nature of the "fix" is going to be difficult because it would potentially have a retroactive effect. The notice dilemma is not a problem for recordings released between January 1, 1978 and March 1, 1989 because the copyright law at that time only required notice on "publicly distributed copies from which the work can be visually perceived."[11] For the most part, then, there was no need for a notice for the song copyrights on the recordings unless the lyrics were reprinted on the sleeve, liner notes, or booklet. Even then, that notice would usually accompany the lyrics and still would not be on the label of the recording itself. Beginning March 1, 1989 notice was no longer required. That change was made in order for U.S. copyright law to comply with the Berne Convention.

Registration

The statute specifically states that "registration is not a condition of copyright protection."[12] However, registration is necessary in order to sue for infringement for works when the United States is the country of origin.[13] The owner can register at any time, including after the discovery of an infringement, it is just that the suit cannot commence until there is a registration.

Registration soon after the creation of the work is desirable for a number of reasons. If the work is registered within five years of first publication, the registration is considered as *prima facie* evidence of the validity of the copyright and the information contained on the registration form.[14] That means the burden of proof would shift to the other party to prove that the copyright owner and author were not as claimed on the registration—a tactical advantage.

Perhaps more importantly, the copyright owner cannot get certain remedies for the infringement unless the work was registered *prior* to when the infringement began. Awards of statutory damages (see below) or attorney's fees cannot be made for published works unless registration is made within three months of publication or prior to the infringement if the infringement is later than three months after first publication.[15]

Registration of musical compositions is accomplished on form PA (for works of performing arts) and registration of sound recordings is on a form SR. Both are obtainable from the Copyright Office directly by mail, via the "forms hotline" telephone number, or on the Internet.[16] Electronic registration is not yet available but is being developed. The fee in 1996 was $20.00 per form.

Although record companies fought a long battle for recognition of sound recording copyrights (see Chapter 10), they often do not take full advantage of the protection provided through registration. Independents in particular, but even the majors on nonhit products, often fail to register their recordings. The lack of registration within five years of publication will mean that the registration, which would still be required in order to sue for infringement, will not be considered *prima facie* evidence establishing the validity of the copyright. Nor would the label be able to collect court costs and attorneys' fees, or statutory damages. They would have to prove their exact losses and the infringer's exact profits, and pay their own costs and attorneys' fees. A spot check of deposits in 1993 revealed at least a 15 percent noncompliance with the deposit requirements.[17] Deposit with the Library of Congress is required for all works published in the United States, even if the works are not registered.

Registration of copyrights in sound recordings may be proving a bigger benefit to bands and musicians without label deals than it is to the labels. In 1971 the Librarian of Congress estimated that there would be 15,000 sound recording registrations per year.[18] As Figure 9-1 indicates, the registration of published sound recordings, presumably mainly from the major labels has been slow to reach that 15,000 per year pace. On the other hand, the registration of unpublished recordings, more likely from unsigned bands and artists, exceeds that of published recordings. Given the growth of home studios and other small professional "demo" studios this trend is likely to continue.

Registration Tips for Unsigned Bands and Songwriters

A special feature of the sound recording registration form, SR, allows the owner to register both the recording and the underlying musical composition (or other work) recorded. The only catch is that the same person(s) must be the owners of the copyrights of both works. This is particularly useful to unsigned bands or songwriters who either publish their works on their own labels or who simply wish the comfort of a registration. The only caveat is that in a band it is likely that all the members of the band, and additional persons including any audio engineers or producers, are all

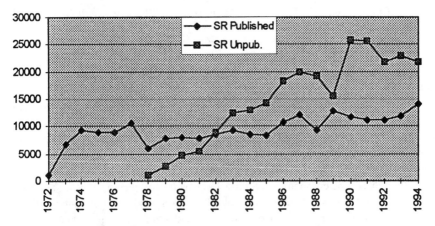

FIGURE 9-1 Sound Recording Copyright Registrations

Source: Annual Reports Register of Copyrights and Librarian of Congress.

probably "authors" and owners of the copyright in the sound recording. Whereas those same people would probably not be the writers of all the individual songs on an album or demo recording.

A feature of both sound recording registration and musical composition registration (as well as other classes of works) is the registration of collective works. This feature can be turned to the advantage of the performing artist or songwriter who does not have a recording or publishing contract, hence a label, producer, or publisher to look out for their copyrights. Multiple works can be submitted in one registration as an unpublished collection, such as "The Songs of Geoff Hull, 1996." Whether on a demo tape or in some sort of "folio," the single registration would protect all of the individual compositions or recordings in the collection.[19] They would not be indexed by their individual titles in the Copyright Office records but even that could be accomplished by later filing a Supplemental Registration, form CA, which lists the individual titles and refers back to the previous collection registration. So, the typical unsigned band or songwriter could register, say, ten songs for the price of two registrations instead of ten, $40 instead of $200. In fact, the Copyright Office recommends this practice.

THE "FAIR USE" LIMITATION AND PARODY

All works are limited by a section of the copyright act generally referred to as "fair use."[20] That section permits uses such as "criticism, comment, news reporting, teaching (including multiple copies for classroom use), scholarship or research" as fair uses, and not infringements provided they meet certain criteria. Although an extended discussion of fair use is beyond the scope of this book, it is important to understand fair use in trying to answer questions of sampling and parody in musical works and sound recordings.

The Fair Use Factors

There are four factors to be considered in determining whether a particular use is a fair use and all of them must be considered in any given case. Just because a use is for educational purposes, for example, does not necessarily mean it is a fair use. How the use weighs on the other tests may tip the scales of justice towards infringement. Below is the statutory language of each part of the test and a brief commentary.

1. "The purpose and character of the use, including whether such use is of a commercial nature or is for nonprofit educational purposes." Here the uses listed in the first part of the fair use section—criticism, comment, news reporting, teaching (including multiple copies for classroom use), scholarship, or research, plus satire or parody—and general private noncommercial use are more likely to be

considered as fair uses. Uses that change, alter, or make the work into a new work or somehow "transform" the work are more likely to be considered "fair."

2. "The nature of the copyrighted work." Generally, factual works are less likely to receive protection than entirely creative works. Presumably, the reason one creates a factual work is to spread the information. Facts themselves are not protected by copyright.

3. "The amount and substantiality of the portion used in relation to the copyrighted work as a whole." This test has both a qualitative and a quantitative aspect. Taking the "hook" out of a song, even if it is as short as eight notes, may be a significant taking. Taking only a few hundred words out of thousands may be significant if the words taken were a crucial part of a book.

4. "The effect of the use upon the potential market for or value of the copyrighted work." Fair use tries to balance the possible benefit to society (as opposed to the user of the protected work) that results from the use versus the potential harm to the copyright owner. Generally, harm is measured in economic terms such as lost sales, lost licensing revenues, and even lost opportunities. The more the work created by the claimed fair use provides a substitute for the original work, then the less likely the use is to be deemed "fair."

The Case of "Oh, Pretty Woman!"

Although there are certainly conceivable fair uses of sound recordings there have not been any cases that have addressed that issue. However, there are significant cases involving questions of fair use of musical compositions, most notably in the areas of satire and parody. In 1994 the U.S. Supreme Court decided that parody of musical compositions could be a fair use in *Campbell v. Acuff-Rose Music, Inc.*[21] Luther Campbell's 2 Live Crew had made a parody rap version of the Roy Orbison/William Dees song, "Oh, Pretty Woman." Campbell's version used the famous guitar riff that introduces and is used throughout the song, portions of the melody, and a few lines of the lyrics of the original. Although the Court did not definitively say Campbell's version was a fair use, they said,

> *2 Live Crew's song reasonably could be perceived as commenting on the original or criticizing it, to some degree. 2 Live Crew juxtaposes the romantic musings of a man whose fantasy comes true, with degrading taunts, a bawdy demand for sex, and a sigh of relief from parental responsibility. The later words can be taken as a comment on the naiveté of the original of an earlier day, as a rejection of its sentiment that ignores the ugliness of street life and the debasement that it signifies. It is this joinder of reference and ridicule that marks off the author's choice of parody from other types of comment and criticism that traditionally have had a claim to fair use protection as "transformative works."[22]*

The Court sent the case back to the district court to determine whether the repeated use of the bass/introductory riff was excessive and whether the parody version damaged the market for a straight rap version of the song. The Court cautioned that "this is not to say that anyone who calls himself a parodist can skim the cream and get away scot free."

JOINT AUTHORSHIP/JOINT WORKS

It is common practice in the recording industry for people to collaborate on the songs they write or the recordings they create. The songwriting teams of Rogers and Hart, Lennon and McCartney, Ashford and Simpson, and many more are legendary. Popular groups work together to create the recordings that they make. This is all well and good, but the copyright law creates some presumptions about people who create works together that might not be what the authors have in mind. If two or more authors create a work with the intention that their contributions be merged into a single unitary work, even if the work contains interdependent parts, such as melody and lyrics, then their work is deemed to be a "joint work."[23] If a work is a joint work, then each author owns an equal, undivided share unless there is some agreement among the authors that otherwise spells out the ownership shares. So, if one person writes a melody and another writes lyrics with the intention of creating a single song, then each owns half of the entire work (i.e., an undivided share) instead of one owning the rights to the lyrics and the other owning rights to the melody. Each author may authorize the use of the work, but is under a duty to account to the other authors for their fair shares or any royalties or revenues received. These things are fine if they are what the authors intend. If they intend otherwise, they would have to have a written agreement spelling out their arrangement.

The situation with bands becomes even more complicated. Suppose one band member comes up with the idea for a song, creates a verse and chorus and basic melody. That member then presents the unfinished song to the other members of the band. Together they find a "groove" and work out an arrangement suitable for their musical style. Perhaps some of the other band members contribute a lyric, line, or make some suggestion to modify the melody. The bass player comes up with a bass part. The drummer works out a drum part to anchor the song rhythmically. How many authors are there of the song? How many authors are there of the sound recording that the band later makes as a demo? If the person who had the original idea and wrote some of the basic parts of the song intends all contributors to be equal authors, and if the other contributors intend to be equal authors, then they have a joint work. Notice this has to be what *all* the parties intend, not just the people who later added small parts to the song. There are also court decisions that hold that each person's contribution, to be deemed a joint author, must be "significant." What is "significant"? Some courts say that contributions must be copyrightable to count as acceptable for the creation of a joint work. Generally, the "head" arrangement that a group of musicians makes for a popular song is not considered as copyrightable. So, unless the members of the group have made a significant contribution to the melody and lyrics then they are not "authors" of the song. Presumably they could have a written agreement that any songs created by the group were to be deemed joint works. Problems are likely to arise when there is no agreement and someone who thinks they are an author, such as the drummer, attempts to claim his or her share of the song after the group has split up (as it almost surely will).

Joint authorship in the sound recording is a bit more clear-cut. Under most circumstances all group members will have made a significant contribution to the recording. They are, therefore, all joint authors of the recording, because it is pretty clear that they fully intended to create a recording in which all had participated. If the recording is made for a label under a "standard" recording artist contract, the label will assert that the recording is a "work made for hire" and that it is the "author" for copyright purposes and copyright owner.

WORKS MADE FOR HIRE

A significant issue for both record labels and music publishers, and the artists (and producers) and songwriters respectively who create the works for the labels and publishers, is whether the works created are "works made for hire." Generally, works made for hire are works created by employees within the scope of their employment, and certain kinds of commissioned works for which the parties have agreed in writing that the work is a work for hire. There are two significant results of a work being considered made for hire. First, the employer, not the person who created the work, is deemed to be the author for purposes of copyright. That means no further transfer of rights is necessary. It happens automatically. More importantly, the person who created the work does not have any termination rights in the work. Thus, in works made for hire, the creator of the work does not have a right to "recapture" the copyrights after a period of time (thirty-five to forty years). The employers can then be totally sure that they will own the copyrights for their entire duration (seventy-five years from first publication or one hundred from creation, whichever ends earlier). (See discussion below on termination rights.)

While that might seem simple enough on its face, the application has proven quite troublesome to the courts. The statute defines "work made for hire" as:

1. *a work prepared by an employee within the scope of his or her employment; or*
2. *a work specially ordered or commissioned for use as a contribution to a collective work, as a part of a motion picture or other audiovisual work, as a translation, as a supplementary work, as a compilation, as an instructional text, as a test, as answer material for a test, or as an atlas, if the parties expressly agree in a written instrument signed by them that the work shall be considered a work made for hire.*[24]

The Case of the Homeless Statue

After reviewing the language and legislative history of this provision, a unanimous Supreme Court in *Community for Creative Non-Violence v. Reid* [hereinafter, *CCNV v. Reid*][25] concluded, "Congress intended to provide two mutually exclusive ways for works to acquire work for hire status: one for employees and the other for independent contractors. Second, the legislative history underscores the clear import of the statutory language: only enumerated categories of commissioned works may be accorded work for hire status."[26] The Supreme Court in deciding *CCNV v. Reid* concluded that the appropriate test of whether someone was an employee or not under the works made for hire provisions of the Act were "principles of general common law agency."[27] Although drawing from a number of federal cases, the Court referred to the *Restatement (Second) of Agency* §220(2)[28] [hereinafter *Restatement*] for a "nonexhaustive" list of factors used in determining whether a worker is an employee or an independent contractor. The Court specifically listed thirteen factors, including "the hiring party's right to control the manner and means by which the product is accomplished [. . .] the skill required; the source of the instrumentalities and tools; the location of the work; the duration of the relationship between the parties; whether the hiring party has the right to assign additional projects to the hired party; the extent of the hired party's discretion over when and how long to work; the method of payment; the hired party's role in hiring and paying assistants; whether the work is part of the regular business of the hiring party; whether the hiring party is in business; the provision of employee benefits; and the tax treatment of the hired party [citations omitted]."[29] The Court then cautioned, "No one of these factors is determinative."[30]

Analyze the typical contractual and other working conditions of a recording artist and a "staff" songwriter. You will probably conclude that in many instances it is probable that recording artists, particularly those who are given freedom to create and even produce their own recordings, are probably not "employees" of the record company. On the other hand, a songwriter who uses staff writing rooms, demo rooms, and recording facilities at the music publisher's place of business may very well be creating works for hire as an employee, without meaning to do so. Both of the situations have recently raised work for hire questions in the legal literature, but neither one has been litigated. Nor has a court determined the validity of the label claim that the recordings are contributions to collective works and therefore may be work for hire by agreement, as their recording contracts say.

TERMINATION RIGHTS

In an effort to correct the many problems that had developed with copyright renewals under the 1909 copyright law, Congress created a new right for authors in the 1976 revision—the right of termination of transfers. This right, as was the earlier renewal right, is designed to give authors, or their heirs, a right to recapture the copyrights after a period of time. The theory is that when authors initially bargain away their copyrights for long periods of time, the value of the copyrights is not known because they have not stood the test of the marketplace and for that reason "beginner" authors are not in a very good bargaining position with publishers and labels. That certainly holds true for new recording artists, as discussed in the chapter on recording artist contracts. The statute, therefore, allows the authors to "recapture" their copyrights after a period of time during which the initial transferee, usually a publisher or label, has had ample time to exploit the work.

The termination "window" begins after thirty-five years after the transfer and runs for a five-year period. (If the transfer includes the right to publish, the termination window begins after forty years after transfer or after thirty-five years after first publication, whichever begins earlier.) During this time the termination may be effected by written notice to the transferee (owner) signed by a majority of the owners of the termination interest. Those people are the author(s) themselves, or if an author has died prior to serving the termination notice, the author's surviving spouse and children, or if a child has died, that child's children (the author's grandchildren of the deceased child). The people owning a majority of the termination interest must agree to end the transfer. The surviving spouse owns 50 percent and the children the other 50 percent percent. They must notify the transferee no more than ten and no less than two years before the effective date of termination that they are exercising their right to end the transfer and recapture the copyrights. If notice, number of people, and date of termination all fall within the requirements of the statute, then the authors or their heirs regain control of the copyrights. There is nothing that the transferee can do to prevent this. The statute even states that a termination may take place even if the author has contracted not to do it![31]

TERMINATION PROBLEMS

For the record companies, the combination of problems with viewing the recordings as works made for hire and the existence of termination rights may mean that recording artists and/or producers can end the labels' rights to own the copyrights in the master recordings after thirty-five years. The value of masters that are thirty-five years old was illustrated in 1995 with the release of a collection of Beatles recordings from the early 1960s. Capitol Records shipped more than four million units of the "Anthology" collection in late 1995. It debuted at number one in the *Billboard* album chart the next week with reported sales in the United States alone of over 800,000 copies in one week.[32] Needless to say, the labels would not be pleased to lose the rights to such valuable products. Termination rights litigation between recording artists and their labels for control over the copyrights in their master recordings made and transferred in 1978 will likely begin in 2003. That is the first year in which notices of termination rights in sound recordings could be sent by the artists.

The record companies are putting lots of effort and language in their recording agreements to try to prevent the artists from recapturing, or, more correctly, terminating the transfers, of the sound recording copyrights. Particularly, the labels claim that the recordings are "contributions to collective works" under the second part of the work for hire definition above. The labels require artists to agree to that fact and state that the recordings are works made for hire. Again, while this may seem logical on its face, the statutory definitions of collective works, the legislative history of the statute, and court decisions interpreting the work for hire and other provisions cast doubt on the labels' claim. It is sure to be litigated, probably around 2003, when the first termination notices from artists are likely to arrive at the record companies. On the music publisher and songwriter side of the question, the litigation is also likely to be in 2003 when some unsuspecting songwriter attempts to terminate the transfer to a music publisher only to find that the publisher counterclaims that the work was made for hire because the songwriter was really an employee of the publisher.[33]

THE "MANUFACTURING CLAUSE" AND PARALLEL IMPORTS

The recording industry is a particular beneficiary of a provision of the copyright laws that is little known outside of the publishing and recording industries. It goes by the name of "the manufacturing clause" because it originally required that English-language books or periodicals had to be manufactured in the United States in order to achieve full copyright protection. From its birth in 1891 it was quite simply a trade barrier designed to protect United States publishers and bookbinders from foreign competition.[34] Although the clause requiring manufacture in the United States to enjoy full copyright protection was abolished when the United States joined the Berne Convention in 1989, part of the clause continues to this day.

The surviving language prohibits the importation of copies of works of U.S. copyright owners without permission. Such an unauthorized importation is an infringement of the distribution right. The clause is particularly effective in stopping the importation of "gray market" goods—those which have been legally manufactured outside of the United States for distribution *outside* of the United States. Although the copyright law says nothing about goods themselves, it does speak to copyrightable materials that may be part of the goods (such as labels) or boxed with the goods (such as instruction manuals). In some respects the manufacturing clause is a better deterrent to gray market goods than trademark law.[35] For the recording and music industry it prevents the distribution of what are referred to as "parallel imports."

Domestic Problems

Parallel imports are a problem for the U.S. recording industry for several reasons. These goods, which are lawfully manufactured outside of the United States for sale outside of the United States, return a lower profit per copy than copies made in the United States and sold in the United States by the U.S. label. Often, in foreign manufacturing arrangements, the U.S. label gets only a royalty that is 8 to 17 percent of the retail list price in the foreign country. This is far less than the margin on the records made and sold domestically. Some products are on different labels outside of the United States.[36] And, when the dollar is particularly strong relative to the foreign currency, these imports can be purchased by a retailer or distributor at a substantially lower price than the domestic product. If they can be sold alongside the U.S. product at the same or a slightly lower price, then the distributor and/or retailer can make more money selling the import than they can by selling the domestic product.

Not only does the U.S. record company lose money when copies of parallel imports are sold instead of domestic copies, so does the recording artist who is often paid at a one-half royalty rate for copies made outside of the United States. So also do the music publisher and songwriter because they, too, are usually paid at a one-half or other reduced royalty for copies made outside of the United States.

Parallel import products are often available in configurations that are not manufactured domestically. For instance, European discs often contain more material than U.S. recordings. Some artists or recordings may not even be available at all from a U.S. manufacturer. Nonetheless, if the U.S. owner of the copyrights in either the sound recording or the musical composition objects, the importation may be stopped.[37] This was a particular problem in the first couple of years of CD manufacturing. When there were only one or two plants in the United States, they could not keep up with demand. Some retailers, such as Tower Records, began to purchase parallel imports simply to meet the demands of their customers. They were forced to stop selling the imports and had to wait until U.S. manufacturing capacity could catch up with demand.

Foreign Problems

The growth of international trade in copyrighted works in general and in particular because of the reduction in trade barriers under the World Trade Organization has increased the problem of parallel imports to a worldwide scale—particularly in Europe. Since the creation of the European Union in 1993 parallel imports have been vexing labels in Europe. The EU made it illegal for one country to prohibit parallel imports from another EU country. Parallel imports, or cross-border trans-shipments as they are also called, became legal—and a way of business for some. Labels can no longer make marketing plans on a country-by-country basis because retailers and distributors may buy copies of albums from other EU nations at savings of up to $4.00 per CD in places like Germany, where the value of the Mark is stable and high. There, a German wholesaler can buy a CD from Italy or the Netherlands at a $2.00 per copy savings. These savings can be passed on to the retailers who are facing fierce price competition. In Belgium estimates are that 10 percent to 20 percent of hit product is "parallel."[38] While the labels would clearly prefer to be able to set prices on a country-by-country basis, and the EU policy is clearly for "one price," there are economists who argue that for overall delivery of maximum consumer welfare a regional pricing basis would deliver the best economic results.[39]

POOR MAN'S COPYRIGHT

It is not unusual to hear people, particularly musicians and songwriters, refer to "poor man's copyright." Prior to 1978 that was a common law copyright concept. The notion of common law copyright is that the author of a work ought to be the first to be able to decide whether to disclose the work to the public. Until such time as a work was published, the rights in the work belonged to the author. Hence, common law copyright became generally known as the "right of first publication." On publication the work was eligible for statutory copyright protection if published with the copyright notice and/or registered (for dramatic and musical works, whether published or not). Because registration cost money ($6.00 to $20.00 most recently), some people chose not to register their unpublished works (and some unpublished works could not be registered) but rather attempted to establish some kind of evidence of ownership and creation of the work by mailing it to themselves registered mail, depositing copies with some writers' protective organization, and so forth. These nonstatutory devices became known as "poor man's copyright." Whether *poor* should be taken to refer to the typical author's impoverished state or to the quality of evidence resulting from these practices is open to question.

Under the 1976 Act, copyright in any work exists on the first fixation of the work in a tangible medium of expression. Because common-law protection is specifically preempted on first fixation, the only thing left for common law to protect is a work until it is first fixed. There would not be many works that would come under those terms—perhaps a musical performance by some jazz musicians or a poem or song written and kept "in the head" of the author. Furthermore, registration is no longer a requirement for federal protection. If an impecunious author chooses not to register to save the $20.00 fee, then the "poor man's" alternatives still exist as a means to attempt to create evidence of authorship and ownership. However, registration is *prima facie* evidence of the existence of the copyright and its validity as stated on the registration form.[40] Registration prior to the infringing acts is necessary to get statutory damages and court costs and attorneys' fees. Registration is required in any event, for U.S. works or non-Berne country works, prior to any court action for infringement.

A good rule of thumb to follow is that if the author or copyright owner is going to distribute copies to the public or place the work where it is likely to be accessible to members of the public, or where the owner does not really know who will have access to the work, then registration is the best approach. Relying on "poor man's copyright" is a bit risky in those circumstances.

SUMMARY

This chapter has dealt with general aspects of the copyright law as they apply to sound recordings and musical compositions. For the most part, those general aspects apply to works in the recording industry the same as they apply to all works, regardless of their nature. However, there are some particular twists of the copyright law specifically written to deal with some aspects of sound recordings and musical compositions that must be explored in some detail in order to understand how the recording industry attempts to mold the copyright laws to its advantage. They are discussed in Chapter 10.

NOTES

[1]17 U.S.C. § 302(c).

[2]Geoffrey Hull, "The GATT and the Media: How the Uruguay Round of the General Agreement on Tariffs and Trade Affects Media in the United States," paper presented at the Southeast Colloquium, AEJMC, Law Division, March, 1996. The Uruguay Round of the General Agreement on Tariffs and Trade, Trade Related Aspects of Intellectual Property Rights, Article 14 (1994). The Treaty of Rome (International Convention for the Protection of Performers, Producers of Phonograms and Broadcasting Organizations) only requires twenty-five years.

[3]"Copyright Term Extension Act of 1995," H989 and S483, 104th Cong., 1st Sess. (1995).

[4]17 U.S.C. § 304.

[5]17 U.S.C. § 305.

[6]The International Convention for the Protection of Performers, Producers of Phonograms and Broadcasting Organizations, adopted at Rome on 26 October 1961. It is worth noting that the United States is unusual in that it protects sound recordings fundamentally the same as other literary or artistic works, whereas most nations treat rights in phonograms and rights for performers as "neighboring rights."

[7]Copyright Act of 1909, § 10.

[8]209 U.S. 1 (1908).

[9]*Rosette v. Rainbo Record Manufacturing Corp.*, 345 F. Supp. 1183 (S.D.N.Y. 1973).

[10]44 F. 3d 813 (9th Cir. 1995).

[11]17 U.S.C. § 401(a).

[12]17 U.S.C. § 408(a).

[13]17 U.S.C. § 411.

[14]17 U.S.C. § 410(c).

[15]17 U.S.C. § 412.

[16]Register of Copyrights, Library of Congress, Washington, DC 20559-6000; forms hotline is (202) 707-9100; fax on demand (not forms but other information) (202) 707-2600; Internet address is http://lcweb.loc.gov/copyright/copy1.html

[17]Bill Holland, "Labels Lose Legal Ground Over Lax Library of Congress Filings," *Billboard*, 27 February 1993: 1.

[18]H.R. Rep. No. 92-478, 92d Cong., 1st Sess. (1971) at 9.

[19]See, e.g., *Szabo v. Errisson*, 68 F.3d 940 (5th Cir. 1995).

[20]17 U.S.C. § 107.

[21]114 S.Ct. 1164 (1994).

[22]114 S.Ct. 1164, 1173.

[23]17 U.S.C. § 101.

[24]17 U.S.C. § 101.

[25]490 U.S. 730 (1989).

[26]Ibid., 747–748.

[27]Ibid., at 751.

[28]*Restatement (Second) of Agency* (1957).

[29]490 U.S. at 751.

[30]Ibid., at 752.

[31]17 U.S.C. § 203.

[32]"Sales of Beatles Set Give Retailers Hope," *Billboard,* 2 December 1995: 5, 106; Don Jeffrey, "Holidays Bring Retail Optimism," *Billboard*, 9 December 1995: 3, 93.

[33]The 2003 date is because the termination provisions provide for a maximum of ten years' notice to be sent to the copyright owner. Because the earliest termination cannot happen until after thirty-five years after the transfer and because termination rights did not exist until the 1976 Copyright Act took effect January 1, 1978, the earliest transfers that could be terminated would be those made in 1978. Thirty-five years after the transfer is 2013 for the effective date of termination, minus ten years notice—2003. 17 U.S.C. § 203.

[34]H.R. Rep. No. 94-1476, 94th Cong., 1st Sess., 164–171 (1976).

[35]David Nimmer & Melville Nimmer, 2 *Nimmer on Copyright* § 8.12[B][6] (1995).

[36]Roman Kozak, "Court Ruling Hits U.S. Importers," *Billboard*, 7 August 1982: 1.

[37]Two important cases involving sound recordings are *Columbia Broadcasting System, Inc. v. Scorpio Music Distributors, Inc.*, 569 F.Supp. 47 (D.C. Pa. 1983), and *BMG Music v. Perez*, 952 F.2d 318 (9th Cir. 1991). The landmark case involving the musical compositions is *TB Harms Co. v. JEM Records*, Inc., 655 F.Supp. 1575 (D.N.J. 1987).

[38]Jeff Clark-Meads, "No longer banned, parallel imports cause woes for EU," *Billboard*, 5 August 1995: 1.

[39]David A. Malueg & Marius Schwartz, "Parallel imports, demand dispersion, and international price discrimination," 37 *Journal of International Economics*, 167 (1994).

[40]17 U.S.C. § 410.

10

Copyright in Sound Recordings and Songs

SOUND RECORDINGS

Pre-1972—A Recording Is Not a Song

Phonorecords, the objects on which sounds are recorded, have been around in some form or another, cylinder or platter, since before the turn of the twentieth century. They had become a significant enough commercial commodity that by 1899 an estimated 3,750,000 copies were being sold each year. That number reached 27,500,000 per year by 1909, the year of the copyright law revision that gave the music publishers the mechanical right.[1] At that time the estimated number of phonographs in the United States was put at 1,310,000 and total sales of phonograph recordings since 1889 was estimated at 97,845,000. During the decade between 1899 and 1909 recordings had become big enough business, and the means of manufacturing had become widespread enough, that the labels had begun to feel the effects of unauthorized copying of their recordings. The labels sought relief from Congress in the form of legislation amending the copyright law that would allow copyright in their recordings. At the same time, the music publishers were complaining that the copies of their songs embodied in the phonorecords should not be sold without some compensation to the owners of the copyrights in the musical compositions—a proposition that the labels would have preferred to reject. The labels maintained, and a decision of the United States Supreme Court in *White-Smith Music Publishing Co. v.*

Apollo Co.[2] backed up their position, that a recording that utilized some mechanical device, such as a piano roll or cylinder or disc recording to reproduce the song, was not a copy of that song, because it could not be visually perceived from the mechanical reproduction. The difficulty with that position was that the labels could not very well maintain that this noncopy of the song should be entitled to some copyright protection of its own. The labels became much more concerned over the prospect of having to negotiate a license for every song they recorded and abandoned the argument that sound recordings should be copyrightable. Then they could maintain, with straight faces, that recordings were not copies of songs and that, therefore, the music publishers and songwriters were not entitled to any right to object to those copies being sold. The labels said that their own rights in the recordings were adequately protected by unfair trade laws.

An additional complication was the state of the piano roll and player piano manufacturing industry. In 1899 the Aeolian Organ Company, the largest manufacturer of player pianos, sold 75,000 mechanical pianos and pianolas. By 1921, near their peak of popularity, an estimated 342,000 such devices were sold. The Aeolian Company was not only a manufacturer of the pianos, but also of the rolls of music needed to make them perform. As it became clear in 1908 that Congress was going to give music publishers a right to control mechanical reproductions of their songs, it was reported that the Aeolian company had begun to enter into arrangements with many of the largest music publishers to be the exclusive manufacturer of piano rolls of their compositions. Fearing that they might create an Aeolian monopoly, Congress responded to pleas of the other piano roll manufacturers to make the mechanical right subject to a compulsory license. The effect of the license was to be that once a musical composition copyright owner had allowed one party to make a mechanical reproduction of a song, then anyone else might do the same thing provided the publisher was compensated. At the urging of Congress, the record companies, pianola manufacturers, music publishing companies, and authors' groups arrived at a compromise that became the compulsory mechanical licensing provision of the 1909 Copyright Act. Although the labels complained that the statutory rate of two cents per copy was too high, they were pleased to have a guaranteed way to be able to reproduce recordings of popular songs without having to negotiate over a royalty rate.

The labels, and the songwriters and publishers, continued to be at odds over the creation of a copyright in sound recordings through the 1920s. A series of bills introduced in 1912, 1925, 1926, 1928, and 1930 all contained provisions for copyright for sound recordings. All were met with opposition on the grounds that it was not fair to require a compulsory license from the writers and publishers for their songs and give the labels an unfettered right in their recordings. None of the proposals were met with much enthusiasm by Congress.

In 1932 a new player, the broadcast industry, emerged as an important force in the discussions. For the first time the National Association of Broadcasters came forward to oppose the creation of copyrights in sound recordings, contending that

small broadcasters would be hurt if record companies were given a public performance right. Better, said the broadcasters, to limit the sound recording rights to
"dubbing" or duplication. With the record companies, music publishers, and broadcasters all at odds over a copyright for sound recordings, no further progress was
made through the 1950s.

Enter—The Pirates

The introduction of 8-track tape cartridge player in the early 1960s meant that there
was a convenient way for people to take and play prerecorded music virtually anywhere. Recordings could now be played in automobiles or at a picnic with simple
equipment that could reproduce reasonable sound quality. The tape cartridge caught
on rapidly and by 1974 there were 6.7 million 8-track tape players (including auto
and home) shipped in the United States by the hardware manufacturers.[3] The volume of tape sales had risen to 112 million units that same year. At the same time the
volume of sales of vinyl records had risen to 480 million units (including singles and
albums).[4]

The introduction of the tape players also meant that now it was possible to reproduce recordings in tape cartridges relative easily. Tape duplicating equipment
was much less costly than record pressing equipment, easier to use, and the product
much easier to handle. Without the technological barriers to entry into the market,
significant numbers of unauthorized duplicators began manufacturing cartridge
tapes. By 1971 the volume of unauthorized tape sales had risen to an estimated 100
million per year—about one-third the sales volume of legitimate tape recordings.[5]

The record companies were nearly powerless to stop it. A 1955 case[6] had determined that recordings were not directly copyrightable under the 1909 copyright law.
Although music publishers had rights in the songs being copied on the pirate recordings, they did not have an effective remedy for several reasons. The music publishing rights on any one album amounted to only about twenty cents (ten songs at the
then two-cent-per-copy "statutory" mechanical royalty rate). Furthermore, those
royalties were often divided between different publishers because the copyrights in
the songs recorded did not always belong to the same publisher. So, the publishers'
interest per copy was not as high as that of the labels, which were losing about $1.80
gross margin per copy. Additionally, some of the pirates claimed that they could
make the copies legitimately under the provisions of the compulsory mechanical
license. Once the copyright owner of the song had allowed a recording of the song to
be made and distributed any one else was allowed to make a "similar use" of the
song if they paid the two-cent-per-copy royalty.[7] The federal courts had split in deciding cases as to whether a "similar use" meant that a new recording had to be made
with new musicians, and so on, or whether that phrase meant that a total duplication
could be made. So, even if the publishers might desire to stop the piracy they could
be kept from any remedies if the pirate simply paid the compulsory mechanical license fee. Many pirates included labels on their recordings with statements such as
"All royalties required by law have been paid." Sometimes that was true, more often

it was not. Finally, the penalties available for criminal copyright infringement were only at the misdemeanor level—a small fine and up to one year in prison. Some pirates simply considered these "inconveniences" part of the cost of doing their business.

There was a push for legislative relief at both the state and federal level. For their part, the labels had been actively lobbying the individual states to pass antipiracy legislation. However, by 1971 only eight states had done so. Congress had been considering a total revision of the copyright law since 1962 but appeared unable to reconcile all competing interests. A provision protecting sound recordings was included in the 1966 version of the new law passed by the House of Representatives, but it failed to pass the Senate before a new House was elected.

1972–1977—A Sound Recording Is Still Not a Song

In late 1970 the labels got Congress to consider an amendment that would separate the issue of sound recording copyrights from the rest of the revision process. After some compromises on the extent of rights afforded to the owners of the new sound recording copyrights, the legislation passed in 1971, and became effective February 15, 1972. The primary compromise was that there be no right of public performance associated with the sound recording. The broadcasters, particularly radio broadcasters, whose programming consisted substantially of playing recordings on the air, objected to the possible requirement that they pay a royalty to the record companies. Their primary argument was that they already paid the music publishers through the performing rights organizations of ASCAP, BMI, and SESAC, and that their airplay of the recordings was the primary vehicle by which the labels gained the promotional exposure necessary to get consumers interested in buying the records. If the broadcasters had to pay it would be unfair, said the broadcasters, to allow the labels to profit twice from the airplay, once from the sale of the records which the airplay promoted, and once from the payment of a performance royalty by the broadcasters to the labels. Congress also specifically noted in the legislative history, but not in the language of the statute itself, that the new copyrights were not meant to stop home recording from broadcasts or copying other recordings for private noncommercial use. The state antipiracy laws that the labels had worked so hard to get would be allowed to remain in effect until 2047.[8]

The legislative history also noted that the new rights in recordings were specifically subject to the "First Sale Doctrine,"[9] which states that, once the copyright owner has unconditionally parted with a legitimately manufactured copy of the work, the disposition of that particular copy can no longer be controlled. Future disposition could include resale or rental. Due to the fact that vinyl records were easily damaged and worn out and that there was not a very large installed base of home recording equipment, the record rental business was not a significant threat to the recording industry in the early 1970s. (A decade later the situation had changed and the labels and publishers joined forces again to gain passage of the Record Rental Amendment of 1984, see below.)

The music publishers joined with the labels for this legislation. Piracy was hurting their royalties from the sale of legitimate copies of the recordings and Congress added that unauthorized reproduction of a sound recording was also unauthorized reproduction of the recorded work. So the publishers now also had a remedy to fight record piracy, having discovered that both income streams were negatively impacted by the sales of pirate copies.

1978–Present—A Sound Recording Is *Still* Not a Song

Exclusive Rights

Rights in sound recordings are not as broad as rights in other kinds of works. The Copyright Act gives copyright owners five exclusive rights for most works:

- To reproduce the work in copies or phonorecords;
- To prepare derivative works based upon the copyrighted work;
- To distribute copies or phonorecords of the copyrighted work to the public by sale or other transfer of ownership, or by rental lease or lending;
- In the case of literary, musical, dramatic, and choreographic works, pantomimes and motion pictures and other audiovisual works, to perform the copyrighted work publicly; and
- In the case of literary musical dramatic and choreographic works, pantomimes, and pictorial, graphic, or sculptural works, including the individual images of a motion picture or other audiovisual work, to display the copyrighted work publicly[10]

While these rights are stated rather broadly, they are subject to a number of limitations by way of specific exemptions and the overall "fair use" exemption as explained in Chapter 9.

Limitations of Rights

A simple perusal of the rights listed indicates that sound recordings are not in the lists of works having rights of public performance or public display. Although a 1995 amendment gives sound recording copyright owners a limited right of public performance for digital audio transmissions (see below) that right is quite narrow. In fact a section of the Copyright Act specifically limits sound recording copyrights to those of reproduction, distribution, and the creation of derivative works.[11] It is also clear that the rights apply only to the actual sounds captured on the original recording. Thus, one could make another recording that imitated or attempted to sound just like the original recording as long as the new one was made by hiring new musicians, singers, engineers, and so on. and making an entirely independent recording. Unless the makers of the "sound alike" recordings failed to secure mechanical licenses to make recordings of the songs or marketed the recordings in some way that misled consumers to think that they were the original recordings by the original artists, in violation of unfair competition laws, the sound-alikes would be perfectly legitimate. The narrow definition of the rights in sound recordings has led various members of the recording industry, particularly the labels, to frequently ask Congress for changes in the laws to shore up their rather limited protection.

Record Rental

With the Record Rental Amendment of 1984[12] the record labels and music publishers in the United States avoided the significant losses of revenues that had occurred when record rental became big business in Japan. By the early 1980s cassette decks had become relatively popular in the United States, having been introduced and become widespread in Japan some years earlier. In 1983, for instance, cassette sales reached 237 million units, surpassing LP sales (210 million) for the first time. Although not as large an enterprise in the United States as it had become in Japan, record rental loomed as a significant threat to the sale of LPs and cassettes by the labels. In 1981 what had been a "mom-and-pop" kind of business took on alarming proportions for the labels when the first major record retail chain did a trial run at record rental.[13] A customer could rent an LP for about $0.99 to $2.50, purchasing a blank cassette from the same place, take the disk home, tape it, and return the rented disk to the store the next day, having copied the album on to tape. The only copy sold by the label was the one originally sold to the rental store. Even assuming some wear and tear on the rental disk, it could be taped many times before becoming unrentable, thereby supplanting sales by the label. In 1983 there were an estimated 200 rental shops in the United States. Although there was a coalition of rental store owners, blank tape manufactures, tape deck manufacturers, and some consumers established to lobby against the legislation, Congress ultimately decided that the potential threat to the labels, music publishers, recording artists, and songwriters was great enough to require action. In Japan, sales of prerecorded albums had dropped precipitously as the rental business mushroomed.[14]

At the present time the practice of record rental exists in only two developed nations, Japan and Switzerland. It is forbidden for nations who are members of the World Trade Organization unless there is a system of remuneration for the labels, publishers, artists, and writers in the particular country.[15] The U.S. labels (and other nations) and Japan agreed to a payment of $6.24 million to compensate for rentals occurring in 1992 through 1994. A per copy royalty of about $3.10 is to be paid for each copy delivered to rental outlets for 1995 through 1996, and a new agreement is expected to be in place in 1997.[16]

The Record Rental Amendment of 1984 amended the Copyright Act to create an exception to the first sale doctrine by allowing owners of sound recording copyrights to prohibit rental of phonograms. It prohibits, "for purposes of direct or indirect commercial advantage . . . the rental, lease, or lending, or . . . any other act or practice in the nature of rental, lease, or lending."[17] There is an exemption for nonprofit lending by nonprofit libraries or educational institutions. If a label does decide to allow rental they are required to compensate the music publishers with a percentage of the rental revenues.

Home Recording

The growth of the cassette hardware market also brought another problem for the recording industry—home taping. The issue had been raised in Congress during the hearings surrounding the creation of sound recording copyrights in 1971, but the legislative history indicated that the new copyrights in the sound recordings were not intended to prohibit home taping for noncommercial purposes. There was no similar language in the legislative history of the 1976 Copyright Revision Act on the same sound recording provision so it became unclear to some whether Congress had meant to prohibit home taping. In 1977 a survey commissioned by Warner Communications found that 21 percent of the U.S. population over the age of ten taped recordings either off the air from radio broadcasts or from prerecorded albums and tapes. What concerned the industry the most at that time was the fact that those who taped were also those who spent the most money on prerecorded music. Concluded the survey, "It is abundantly clear that people who use tape recorders for recording music are more likely to be buyers of prerecorded music, and on average, spend more money for prerecorded music than people who don't have access to a tape recorder, or have the recorders but don't use them to tape music. This, however, does not imply that "home tapers" would not spend even more money on prerecorded music if tape recorders did not exist."[18]

By 1980 the International Phonogram Federation (IFPI) added its voice, stating that home taping was becoming as big a concern as piracy, estimating losses due to the combination as "in the millions." The IFPI urged a legislative fix to the problem, but saw that as a "long and tortuous path."[19] In 1982 home taping losses were set at $2.85 billion per year, with $1.13 billion coming from taping of recordings already owned by the taper and the rest coming from taping recordings borrowed from others, from broadcasts, or from live events. Forty-five percent of the tapers said they taped to avoid buying the product. And, although the lower quality of prerecorded tapes was thought to be an incentive to make home tapes, only ten percent of tapers said they taped to get a better quality recording. The reasons most often cited for taping were convenience (40 percent) and to use in car or office (35 percent). Tape recorder penetration had increased almost 25 percent in the three years from 1977 to 1980 with almost half of the population over the age of ten having recorders in their homes.[20]

The legislative fix sought by the industry was long and tortuous, indeed. Formidable opposition from the tape recorder manufacturers, the blank tape manufacturers, and a "right to tape" citizens group repeatedly fought the labels to a standstill. In a decision not directly on audio home taping, the U.S. Supreme Court held that taping broadcast television programs off the air for private, noncommercial, time-shifting purposes was "fair use" in *Sony Corp. v. Universal City Studios, Inc.*[21] This decision weakened the labels' arguments on the applicability of the existing law to prevent home taping.

In the meantime, digital recordings on compact discs had become extremely popular. By 1987 sales of CDs reached about 100 million units, nearly equaling those of vinyl albums. That same year digital audio tape recorders (DAT recorders) were introduced and the prospect loomed of generation after generation of near-perfect tape reproduction of CDs. The tape manufacturers wanted to introduce their machines into the U.S. market. The labels threatened potentially long and costly litigation against the manufacturers of the machines as "contributory" copyright infringers. By June 1991 the parties had come to an agreement that they took to Congress.[22] The proposal became the Audio Home Recording Act of 1992, as passed September 22 that year.[23]

Audio Home Recording Act of 1992

The Act represents a compromise between the parties in interest. It provides that:

1. Analog and digital home taping for private noncommercial purposes is exempt from liability for infringement;
2. The manufacture and sale of analog and digital home recording devices is exempt from liability for infringement, but the manufacture and distribution of digital recording devices and blank digital recording media is subject to a compulsory license issued by the Copyright Office;
3. All home-type digital recorders must contain some sort of anticopying system that prohibits the user from making more than single generation copies;
4. A compulsory license is used to generate royalties for the owners of the sound recording copyrights and the musical composition copyrights. The royalties are collected from the distributors of recorders and blank media based on wholesale prices and the number of units sold. For recorders the royalty is 2 percent of the wholesale price. For blank media it is 3 percent of the wholesale price. The royalties are collected by the Copyright Office quarterly and distributed according to a specific statutory scheme by the Librarian of Congress;
5. Royalty distribution is to be as follows: The total available for distribution is divided into two funds, a sound recording find (two-thirds of the total) and a musical works fund (one-third of the total). The labels get 60 percent of the sound recording fund and the artists, including provisions for background musicians and vocalists, get the remaining 40 percent. The music publishers and songwriters split their share of the royalties fifty/fifty. When all is said and done the shares of the total fund are indicated in Table 10-1.

For 1994 the royalties collected amounted to over $410,000—not much when compared to the $191 million dollars collected that same year for secondary transmission licensing from cable systems.[24] Still the labels felt that digital home record-

TABLE 10-1   Distribution of Audio Home Recording Act Royalties (Percentages Slightly Rounded)

Labels	38.40%
Featured artists	25.60%
A.F. of M. members	1.75%
A.F.T.R.A. members	0.90%
Music Publishers	16.70%
Songwriters	16.70%

Source: 17 U.S.C. § 1006.

ing would become prevalent over time and that this was an appropriate beginning to compensate for the losses due to home taping.

Digital Audio Performance Rights

As noted before, the record labels had been attempting to get a performance right for their recordings since the 1909 law. They did not succeed until they got the regular broadcasters, television and radio, to drop opposition to the legislation by exempting traditional broadcast performances, even if the broadcasters later developed digital broadcast systems.[25] Congress ultimately passed the "Digital Performance Right in Sound Recordings Act of 1995."[26]

The new right only applies in cases of *digital* transmissions that are through noninteractive subscription background music services or that occur in interactive services such as those that might happen when a consumer orders a "digital delivery" of a copy of a specific recording requested by the consumer via Internet, satellite, or other means. The legislation envisions the rights owners and users negotiating licenses and setting their own rate structure but provides for a compulsory licensing system if the parties fail to reach an agreement. If the owners and users cannot agree on rates, the Librarian of Congress may convene a Copyright Arbitration Royalty Panel (CARP) to set a rate structure.

Whether the licenses are negotiated or compulsory, the division of the sound recording performance royalties between the labels and performers is dictated by the statute as follows:

50 percent to the labels,

45 percent to the recording artist(s) featured on the performance,

2.5 percent to the American Federation of Musicians to be distributed to nonfeatured musicians, and

2.5 percent to the American Federation of Television and Radio Artists (AFTRA) for distribution to nonfeatured vocalists.

MUSICAL COMPOSITIONS

Initial Copyright Ownership—a Song Is a Song

Copyrights in musical compositions, or songs, usually belong to music publishers. The publishers acquire the rights from songwriters with a transfer of copyright ownership. Copyright initially belongs to the person who creates the work, the author, and that copyright begins from the moment the work is "fixed in a tangible medium of expression." That is to say, as soon as the song is written down, recorded, taped, or otherwise put into some medium from which it can later be perceived or reproduced, the federal copyrights and protection for them springs into existence. Only if the work is never "fixed" would it be protected under state or common law.

Copyright in Musical Arrangements

Although it is quite clear that musical arrangements of musical works are generally copyrightable, the situation is not as clear with the arrangements of songs that are often found on popular recordings. The compulsory mechanical license (see below) gives the licensee, the record company, the right to create an arrangement "to the extent necessary to conform it to the style or manner of interpretation of the performance involved," but that arrangement cannot alter the basic melody or character of the song and is not copyrightable as a derivative work.[27] Because the typical negotiated mechanical license often tracks or incorporates by reference the statutory language for the compulsory license, most recorded arrangements of pop songs would not be copyrightable.

The Case of the "Satin Doll"

A recent court case testing that proposition involved the copyrights in the famous jazz composition and recording "Satin Doll" by Duke Ellington. "Satin Doll" was originally written as an instrumental by Duke Ellington in 1953. That year a "lead sheet" showing the melody was registered with the Copyright Office. A version with harmony and revised melody was recorded by Ellington and released in 1953 on Capitol Records. Billy Strayhorn (actually his estate) claimed copyright in the arrangement as recorded. The court refused to hold that there could never be copyrightable arrangements of harmony. Instead the court sent on to trial the question of whether the particular harmony was sufficiently original to qualify for protection. [28]

The Case of the "Red, Red Robin"

A case which *did* decide that the usual piano–vocal arrangements made by publishers and the usual arrangements made by musicians in a recording were not copyrightable involved the 1926 song, "When the Red, Red Robin Comes Bob-Bob-

Bobbin' Along." The Court concluded that even when the publisher worked from a simple lyric and melody "lead sheet" from the songwriter there was not enough creativity in a "stock" piano–vocal arrangement to qualify it for copyright as a derivative work. "There must be more than cocktail pianist variations of the piece that are standard fare in the music trade by any competent musician. There must be such things as unusual vocal treatment, additional lyrics of consequence, unusual altered harmonies, novel sequential uses of themes—something of substance added making the piece to some extent a new work with the old song embedded in it but from which the new has developed. It is not merely a stylized version of the original song where a major artist may take liberties with the lyrics or tempo, the listener hearing basically the original tune."[29] This is not the sort of thing that members of bands who do not write the basic melody or lyrics of a song like to hear. It is, however, something that they, and the band members who *do* write the lyrics and melodies should be aware of.

Compulsory Mechanical License

Even though the vast majority of mechanical licenses issued by music publishers in the United States are negotiated and not compulsory, it is important to understand the workings of the compulsory (a.k.a. "statutory") license. Many mechanical licenses are pegged to the statutory rate. The existence of certain features of the statutory license establishes the parameters around which many of the terms of a negotiated license are set.

Availability of the Compulsory Mechanical License

The compulsory mechanical license is available for the manufacturing and distribution of "phonorecords" of nondramatic musical works to the public. (A license to do the same thing, but not for public distribution, would usually be referred to as a "transcription license.") The phonorecord is the material object, be it compact disc, cassette tape, or other device, in which both the sound recording copyright and the musical composition copyright are fixed when a recording of a song is made and distributed. In the United States, licenses for reproduction of songs in videos (motion pictures or music videos) are referred to as "synchronization" licenses. In many other places in the world, video or "videogram" licenses would also be called "mechanical licenses"—a source of some confusion.

A record company could obtain a compulsory mechanical license for a song once the music publisher had allowed a recording of the song to be made and distributed to the public. So, while a music publisher could control who could make the first recording of a song, after that any record company or artist could make a recording of the same song by using the compulsory license.[30] Even when the compulsory license is available, its terms are not viewed with much favor by record companies. They would prefer to negotiate a lower rate, less frequent payments, and different accounting for returns. So, because first-time recordings of songs would require negotiated licenses, and because the labels desire to have terms more favorable than the compulsory license, there are not many compulsory licenses issued.

Statutory Rate

When the compulsory mechanical license was created in the 1909 revision of the copyright law the rate was set in the statute as two cents per copy. It remained at that rate until 1978. Since 1978 the rate has been changed numerous times through procedures set up in the Copyright Act (see Table 10-2). Even though the rate is now

TABLE 10-2   Compulsory Mechanical License Rate Changes

Date(s)	Rate	Authority
1909–1977	2 cents per copy	Copyright Act of 1909, § 1(e)
January 1, 1978	2.5 cents per copy or 0.5 cents per minute whichever is greater	1976 Copyright Act, § 115
January 1, 1981	4 cents per copy or 0.75 cents per minute, whichever is greater	1980 Copyright Royalty Tribunal rate adjustment proceeding
January 1, 1983	4.25 cents per copy or 0.8 cents per minute, whichever is greater	1980 Copyright Royalty Tribunal rate adjustment proceeding
July 1, 1984	4.5 per copy or 0.8 cents per minute, whichever is greater	1980 Copyright Royalty Tribunal rate adjustment proceeding
January 1, 1986	5 cents per copy or 0.85 cents per minute, whichever is greater	1980 Copyright Royalty Tribunal rate adjustment proceeding
January 1, 1988 to December 31, 1989	5.25 cents per copy or 1 cent per minute, whichever is greater	1980 Copyright Royalty Tribunal rate adjustment proceeding, based on consumer price index, Dec. 1985 to Sept. 1987.
January 1, 1990 to December 31, 1991	5.7 cents per copy or 1.1 cents per minute, whichever is greater	Adjustment based on consumer price index, Oct. 1987 to Oct. 1989.
January 1, 1992 to December 31, 1993	6.25 cents per copy or 1.2 cents per minute, whichever is greater	Adjustment based on consumer price index, Oct. 1989 to Oct. 1991.
January 1, 1994 to December 31, 1995	6.6 cents per copy or 1.25 cents per minute, whichever is greater	Adjustment based on consumer price index, Oct. 1991 to Oct. 1993.
January 1, 1996 to December 31, 1997	6.95 cents per copy or 1.3 cents per minute, whichever is greater	Adjustment based on consumer price index, Sept. 1993 to Oct. 1995.

Source: Copyright Office, Licensing Division.

determined by Copyright Arbitration Royalty Panels, it is still referred to in the industry as the "statutory rate." Labels often "get a rate" below the statutory rate, most often 75 percent of the statutory rate.

Other Compulsory Mechanical Provisions

The statute also requires that the compulsory licensee (the record label) file a notice of intention to obtain a compulsory license with the copyright owner. It requires that payment be made for each record "distributed," meaning the label has "voluntarily and permanently parted with its possession." To account for the fact that recordings are usually sold subject to return by the purchaser, the Copyright Office has made regulations further defining *distributed* to mean the earlier of when revenue is recognized by the label from the sale of the record, or when nine months has passed from the date of shipment.[31] The labels would prefer to be able to withhold some payments as a reserve against anticipated returns for a longer period. Payments are to be made monthly, instead of quarterly as preferred by the labels.

Performing Rights and Music

Public performance rights are particularly important in the recording industry. Income from public performances is the largest source of revenue for music publishing (as discussed in Chapter 3). Public performance rights in musical compositions were first added to the copyright laws in 1897 but did not take on particular significance until the 1909 copyright revision, in part because minimum damages established by the statute began at $100 for the first performance and went to $50 dollars for subsequent unauthorized performances or whatever "as to the court shall appear to be just."[32] During the 1909 revision process the provision for civil liability for public performance was amended to apply to public performances "for profit," the idea being to not have liability for church groups, school children, and other such groups. ASCAP was formed in 1914 to begin a systematic way for publishers and writers to collect revenue for public performances and by 1917 had landed a test case in the U.S. Supreme Court on the issue of just what constituted a "for profit" public performance.

The Case of "Sweethearts"

Composer Victor Herbert, one of the ASCAP founders, found his songs from the operetta *Sweethearts* being performed in Shanley's restaurant by professional singers and musicians for the enjoyment of the diners. Shanley argued that he was not charging the patrons to hear the music so the music was not "for profit" within the meaning of the statute. In a brief opinion, Justice Holmes explained that the public performance right did, indeed, apply to such situations because the music really was being performed for the profit of the restaurant, regardless of whether an admission fee was charged. "The defendant's performances are not eleemosynary. They are part of a total for which the public pays, and the fact that the price of the whole is attributed to a particular item which those present are expected to order, is not important. . . . . If music did not pay it would be given up. If it pays it is out of the public's pocket. Whether it pays or not the purpose of employing it is profit and that is enough."[33]

Public Performances and Exemptions

The current copyright law defines public performances broadly. "Publicly" means,

1. at a place open to the public or at any place where a substantial number of persons outside of a normal circle of a family and its social acquaintances is gathered;
2. to transmit or otherwise communicate a performance . . . to a place specified in clause (1) or to the public. . . ."[34]

So, private clubs and most broadcast, closed circuit, or cable transmissions are covered. Although the words "for profit" were dropped from the public performance right in the 1976 revision to broaden the application of the right, a number of specific exemptions were added, generally at the behest of groups representing the special interests who wanted exemptions. These exemptions apply to nondramatic performances, that is those in which the songs are not used in some manner to accompany a dramatic presentation or to tell a story, such as an opera or Broadway musical. The list below paraphrases the statute and covers, out of the ten specific exemptions in the statute, those most interesting or most significant to the recording industry. For details on these and the other exemptions, refer to the statute.[35]

- Performances by instructors or pupils in the course of face-to-face teaching at nonprofit educational institutions;
- Performances in transmissions for educational broadcasting from government or nonprofit educational institutions;
- Performances in the course of religious services at a place of religious worship or assembly;
- Noncommercial performances (other than in transmissions) when there is no payment to musicians or promoters, and either no admission charge, or the proceeds are used for charitable, religious or educational purposes;
- Public reception of transmissions on single sets of the kinds of receiving devices commonly found in the home if there is no admission charge and no further transmission;
- Performances in stores selling recordings where the purpose is to promote sale of recordings and there is no admission charge and no transmission.

There are frequently amendments proposed to the law to exempt other performances, usually by special interests who simply do not want to have to pay for performance licenses. Congress then finds it must balance the economic and political interests of the copyright owners with the economic and political interests of other groups.

Infringement and Remedies

Civil infringement suits (as opposed to criminal prosecutions) are rare for sound recordings copyrights because imitation of sounds is specifically allowed by the statute. So, "sound-alike" recordings are not infringements. The most common civil copyright infringement action for sound recordings is for sampling. The general civil remedies are discussed later in this chapter in the section dealing with musical composition infringement.

SAMPLING—"THOU SHALT NOT STEAL"

Sampling, sometimes also called "digital sampling," is the process whereby a recording artist or producer takes a small piece from a previous recording, digitizes it (the actual sampling process) so that it can be manipulated by computer sequencers and MIDI instruments, and puts it back into a new recording or song. Sampling is commonplace in most genres of music, particularly in rap and urban dance music. Everything from James Brown's famous yells to the rare congas as heard on the "Miami Vice" theme have been sampled and used by other musicians and producers to make new recordings, not that imitate the original, but that build the actual originally recorded sounds into what is often a very new and different work. There is no question that the use of samples in the creation new works can be, and often is, quite creative. The problem is that unless the sampling and new use is done with the permission of the owners of the copyrights in the sampled works, then copyright infringement is the likely result.

The Case of "Alone Again, Naturally"

The very first sampling case to go all the way through to a court decision was in 1991. It set the tone for future sampling discussions and set into motion a flurry of label, artist, producer, and publisher sampling agreements and clauses. Rap artist Marcel Hall (a.k.a. Biz Markie) used three words from a Gilbert O'Sullivan recording and song, "Alone Again (Naturally)." Hall, his attorneys, and Warner Brothers Records (the distributing label for Hall's Cold Chillin' Records) knew that they should obtain a sampling "clearance" (license) for the use of the three words in the song and their accompanying music, but for reasons not clear from the court record, they released the Biz Markie recording anyway, even though Gilbert O'Sullivan's publishing company, Grand Upright Music, Ltd., had refused the license. Federal District Court Judge Duffy's curt opinion quoted the *Bible*'s commandment, "Thou shalt not steal," and chided the defendants for their "callous disregard for the law and for the rights of others."[36] The settlement caused Warner Brothers Records to physically remove all of the offending recordings from the marketplace, pay heavy damages, and brought a rather abrupt end to Hall's career.

Sample Once—Infringe Twice

Sampling exposes the labels to copyright infringement charges on two possible fronts—the sound recording copyright owners and the song copyright owners. First, whenever *any* sound is taken from a recording made after February 15, 1972, there is a likelihood that there is a violation of the sound recording copyright. Whether the sound is an artist's moan or yell, a drummer's kick drum sound, or a hot guitar lick, there is no doubt that the previous sounds are taken. The copyrights in the recordings of those sounds usually belong to the label that did the original release. So, one label will have to ask another label for permission to use the sample. Permission can usually be had unless there is some problem with the artist not wanting to allow sampling. Permission, however, comes at a price. A typical sampling license from a label would cost anywhere from a one-time flat fee of $1,000 to $5,000 (typically) up to more than $25,000, to a share of up to 50 percent of the new sound recording copyrights. This depends greatly on the significance of the sample taken and the extent to which it is used in the new recording. If the sample also takes any of the words or melody of the song a second sampling license must be obtained from the copyright owner (usually the music publisher) of the original song. The price there is about the same as for the sounds themselves.

These days, labels and music publishers not only have departments dedicated to tracking down copyright owners and obtaining sampling licenses for their artists who do lots of sampling, but also to chasing down other labels who may have used a sample of one of their recordings or songs. The cost of the sampling licenses is usually deducted from the artist's royalties. The licenses can add up to large sums of money or losses of significant percentages of copyright ownership. Artists who do heavy sampling are frequently quite creative, but they end up costing themselves considerable sums of money. The potentially high costs of sampling and loss of ownership of rights have made some labels a bit gun-shy of artists who use lots of sampling. However, judging from the number of recordings that use sampling, the necessity for licenses did not stop uses of samples, creative and otherwise.

INFRINGEMENT AND REMEDIES—"YOU STOLE MY SONG!" EVERY SONGWRITER'S NIGHTMARE

"Get a hit, get an infringement suit" is a not uncommon saying in the music business. Instances of alleged infringement are common for two reasons.

1. There are some charlatans who think they can make a quick buck off of someone else's success. There was not really an infringement, but they figure if they claimed that there was and sued, they might get a settlement and a few thousand dollars.

2. Lots of popular songs do sound a lot alike. There are form and style constraints in much of popular music. There are only so many ways to arrange notes in a melody.

Given those two factors, it is quite possible that two composers could create works that did, indeed, have similarities, even without ever having seen or heard the other's work. In that case one is likely to think that they have been infringed by the other.

Fortunately, for music publishers and record companies, it is rather difficult to prove infringement in court. The person claiming infringement must be able to prove two things:

1. That they are the author or owner of the copyrights in the work claimed to be infringed. That is usually not too difficult because a copyright registration form is *prima facie* evidence of the validity and ownership of the copyright.
2. That the other party copied their work. To show this the plaintiff must prove that the other party somehow had access to their work and that the two works are "substantially" similar. The access is fairly easy to prove if the original work enjoyed widespread public distribution or performance but can be quite difficult in the plaintiff's work was unpublished.

"Substantial similarity" means the works must be similar in more ways than simply style or an occasional few notes. There is an old saying that one can copy up to four bars of music and not be infringing. Not so! In the case of *Saturday Night Live*'s parody of the "I Love New York" song and advertising campaign, the copying of four notes of the original composition were held to be an infringement. NBC and *Saturday Night Live* were ultimately allowed to use the song because their use was deemed to be a fair use since it was a parody of the original.[37]

The Case of "How Deep Is Your Love"

"Substantial similarity" by itself is not enough to prove infringement. A fellow named Ronald Selle sued Barry Gibb and the other Bee Gee brothers for an alleged infringement by the song "How Deep Is Your Love." The two songs were so similar that Barry played the plaintiff's song on a piano in the courtroom and thought it was his own. But the court ruled that because the plaintiff's song had not been published or performed publicly anywhere that the Gibb brothers could have heard it, there was no reasonable possibility of access so there could be no infringement.[38]

The Case of "My Sweet Lord"

The infringing songwriter does not have to have done the dirty work intentionally. George Harrison apparently fell victim to being familiar with the hit song "He's So Fine" as performed by the Chiffons. He wrote his song, "My Sweet Lord," that was similar in structure, much of the melody, and some of the lyrics. Similarities even existed down to accidental grace notes in the two songs. Harrison testified that he did not deliberately copy "He's So Fine." Said the judge, "[Harrison], in seeking musical materials to clothe his thoughts, was working with various possibilities. As he tried this possibility and that, there came to the surface of his mind a particular combination that pleased him as being one he felt would be appealing to a prospective listener; in other words, that this combination of sounds would work. Why? Because his subconscious knew it already had worked in a song his conscious mind did not remember. . . ."[39] Even though convinced that Harrison did not deliberately copy "He's So Fine," the judge ordered him to pay $1.6 million in damages. Through rather protracted litigation and a complex settlement, the rights to "He's So Fine" in the United States, United Kingdom, and Canada ultimately ended up with Harrison for the sum of $270,020.[40] But the principle of subconscious infringement, every songwriter's nightmare, had ended up a permanent part of copyright law.

NEW DIRECTIONS FOR COPYRIGHT?

Much has been written about whether the existing copyright system can serve effectively into the twenty-first century. New media, new methods of creating works, and new delivery systems are certain to stretch the existing notions of copyright, authorship, and fair use. Copyright law has always been changing in response to new technology. It was a new technology, the invention of movable type by Johannes Gutenberg in 1456,[41] that made possible the mass reproduction of copies of a work. One must remember that the notion of controlling the right to reproduce copies of works began as a method of censorship in England in the late 1400s and 1500s. The crown wished to control who could print books and other materials in order to control the content of those books. Only certain printers were granted licenses or "patents" to print. And only those printers who produced publications to the king or queen's liking were likely to get a license.

By the early 1700s it was not political turmoil that resulted in the passage of the first copyright act, the Statute of Anne of 1710, but rather the needs of commerce. By the early 1700s there were enough competing printing presses in England so that when any printer began to publish a book, it was soon pirated in England (and the colonies). To get some protection from piracy the printers went to Parliament and requested a statutory privilege in the name of themselves and the authors of the works. Parliament noted,

> *Printers, Booksellers, and other Persons have of late frequently taken the Liberty of Printing, Reprinting, and Publishing, or causing to be Printed, Reprinted, and Published Books, and other Writings, without the Consent of the Authors or Proprietors of such Books and Writings, to their very great Detriment, and too often to the Ruin of them and their families. . . .*[42]

TABLE 10-3   Copyright Law Changes and the Recording Industry

1790	First U.S. Copyright law protects books, charts, and maps
1831	Musical works first protected
1856	Dramatic works first protected, including public performance rights
1897	Public performance rights for musical works protected
1909	Mechanical rights for musical works added; unpublished musical works could be protected by registration
1912	Motion pictures first protected
1972	Sound recordings first protected
1978	All works created, whether published or not, are protected. Jukebox performance rights protected. Compulsory mechanical license rate subject to change by the Copyright Royalty Tribunal (later the Librarian of Congress)
1982	Piracy of recordings and motion pictures made a felony with increased fines and jail terms
1984	Record rental prohibited
1992	Audio Home Recording Act exempts home copying and places a royalty on digital recorders and blank digital media
1994	Antibootlegging rights for performers of live musical events
1995	Digital public performance rights for sound recordings, digital delivery rights for sound recordings and the musical works embodied in the phonorecords

Source: Various statutory provisions, Title 17 U. S. Code; and R. Gorman & J. Ginsburg, *Copyright for the Nineties* (4th ed.) 1993.

The right to make copies (copy, right?) was extended to authors and those who took their rights from those authors for the purposes of preventing piracy and "for the Encouragement of Learned Men to Compose and Write useful Books." These two-fold purposes, protecting commercial interests and protecting authors so that they will be encouraged to create more works, have been the significant driving forces for copyright law ever since.[43]

In the United States, those purposes are written into the Constitutional authority for Congress to make copyright laws. Article I, Section 8, Clause 8 empowers Congress to make laws "To promote the Progress of Science and the useful Arts, by securing for limited Times to authors and Inventors the exclusive Right to their respective Writings and Discoveries." Even considering only changes to copyright law that directly affected the recording industry, as listed in Table 10-3 it is clear that many changes have been effected in reaction to new technologies, new media, and new methods of utilizing works.

Everyone Is a Manufacturer and Distributor

It is no longer necessary to have a printing press to reproduce a book, a film studio to copy a motion picture, or a record pressing plant to make a copy of a phonorecord.

The photocopiers, VCRs, and audiocassette decks that are in the homes of many have moved manufacturing out of the hands of the capitalists and into the hands of the consumers.

Mass production allowed copyright owners to control their works at the point of production or distribution. One license issued to one producer was sufficient. When there are thousands of users and thousands of copyright owners, as is the case in musical performance rights, an intermediate agency is needed to keep track of all of the users and to distribute appropriate royalties to all of the many copyright owners. When the number of users and manufacturers reaches into the millions, as is the case with photocopiers and cassette decks, the copyright owners are faced with a dilemma. They must either prohibit the users from making copies or using the works in unauthorized ways, find another control and licensing point in the distribution or manufacture or some part of the process, or allow the uses and hope to make their profits through more easily controlled uses. Motion picture copyright owners are contemplating requiring digital video disc systems to have a system in the playback hardware that prohibits copying, either single or serial copies.

The recording industry has tried the approach of allowing analog and digital home taping but placing a royalty on the devices that allow digital recording, thus finding a different point in the manufacturing process where the control is easier to accomplish. Instead of attempting to license the manufacture of the copy of the recording, which occurs in the private homes of millions of consumers, the industry licenses the manufacture of the recorders and blank media, which still requires mass production technology and only has a few producers to contend with. For the individual consumer, the barrier to entry into the market of being a manufacturer of high quality copies of recordings is low—the cost of a cassette deck, a CD player, and a blank tape. The consumer is not concerned with being able to make thousands of copies per hour or per day. One or two copies is probably all the consumer wants.

The other method is to control delivery of the work itself—that is what the digital delivery of phonorecords provision passed in 1995 does. The provider of the soft copy (which the consumer converts into a hard copy) purchases the license and keeps track of how many digital deliveries have been made so that the copyright owners can be appropriately compensated. Whatever approach is used, the trick is to find a point in the manufacturing or distribution chain at which the copyright owner can exert some control (licensing) over the process that ultimately leads to the consumers making their own copies.

Everyone Is an Author

With a computer and a laser printer, anyone can produce copies that would have made Gutenberg proud. With a computer and MIDI setup anyone can produce high quality orchestral recordings that would have made Beethoven proud. Of course, these people can also author new works. They may not possess the creative writing or composing talent to produce great works, but they can produce copyrightable works easily. They can even distribute copies of these works electronically without the need to secure the services of a production plant. To John Pavlik's framework for media analysis, which concentrates on the way media content is "gathered, processed and produced: transmitted; stored; and retrieved and displayed,"[44] we need to add "created."

Where Is the Editor?

There is one problem with a world where "everyone" is an author or composer. With the publisher, who had access to the means of mass production through investment of the necessary capital, serving as a filter, only those works that the publishers thought worthy would reach the public. The merits and benefits of having a filter or censor in the information stream are debatable. On the one hand some voices and meritorious works may never be heard or seen. On the other hand we did not have to open millions of oysters in order to find a pearl. With so many avenues of free expression open to the public at large we might like to have an editor or publisher do some filtering for us—to select which oysters are likely to contain pearls before we begin opening, or even to present us with a nicely strung set of pearls. Of course, we do have to compensate the publisher or record company for all of the work of opening all of those nonpearl-bearing oysters. If everyone with a computer can produce a book and everyone with a fairly simple MIDI setup can produce a sound recording, and then make it available for the rest of the public (distribute it) through the Internet, we are still going to need music publishers, record companies, and patrons of the arts to help us decide which works are deserving of our attention, whether because of artistic merit or simply because of a mass appeal.

Highway Robbery on the Information Superhighway

> *"There are just too many holes in the Internet."*
> —ED MURPHY, PRESIDENT/CEO OF NATIONAL
> MUSIC PUBLISHERS' ASSOCIATION[45]

The Case of the "Unchained Melody"

In late 1993 the recording industry became one of the first media to challenge copyright infringement on the "information superhighway." A class action lawsuit on behalf of 141 music publishers against CompuServe, H&R Block's on-line service provider, raised the specter of an on-line service provider being liable for the infringing activities of its clients. Frank Music Group, one of the plaintiffs and owners of the copyright in the musical composition "Unchained Melody," which had become popular at the time because of its inclusion in the movie *Ghost,* said that electronic versions of the song were being created by users using MIDI equipment and sound cards in computers, and uploaded to a CompuServe music database. From there thousands of users could download a copy of the song to play, or keep it for use on their own computers. CompuServe had turned down a request to pay $25 to $100 for each downloaded copy of the song. The National Music Publishers' Association and Frank Music claimed that CompuServe should be liable as a contributory infringer, even though the initial infringer was the person who made the unauthorized version and then attempted to distribute it to the public through the bulletin board.[46] CompuServe ultimately settled the dispute by agreeing to pay over $500,000 for the alleged infringements and to pay a license fee for each copy downloaded in the future. Whenever a CompuServe user wants to download a MIDI file of a song, the service issues a mechanical license for the song to the user. CompuServe keeps track of the licenses issued and then pays the Harry Fox Agency royalties that are then distributed by the HFA to the copyright owners.[47]

Who Is Liable?

When there is an on-line provider like CompuServe, there is a control point for the copyright owners to attack. However, when the access is via the Internet, who is responsible? In the litigation surrounding former Church of Scientology minister Dennis Erlich and the distribution of unpublished Scientology documents through on-line services, one court concluded that the service provider, in that case NetCom On-Line Communications Services, and the operator of the bulletin board where the documents were posted can be liable as contributory infringers. To be liable as a contributory infringer the operators must have knowledge of the infringing activity and induce, cause, or contribute to the infringement. Failure to act in the face of notice could constitute participation in the infringement. The court stopped short of making the provider responsible for screening all postings. The court further held that NetCom could not be liable as a contributory infringer because, even though it could control the conduct of subscribers, it did not receive any direct financial benefit from the infringement, only a monthly service charge for the service in general.[48]

Both ASCAP and BMI are involved in licensing music performances on the Internet and other on-line services. The first Internet performance license was issued by BMI to On Ramp, Inc. in April of 1995. Even before passage of the Digital Performance Rights Act in 1995, the Harry Fox Agency had licensed OmniBox, an interactive music provider, for digital delivery of copies of songs licensed by HFA.[49]

Is Copyright Passé?

While some may contend that these new delivery methods and difficulties portend the end of copyright as we know it, or that copyright is being taken over by the commercial enterprises,[50] it is well to remember two things. Copyright law has always had to change to cope with new technologies. From engraving to the still photograph to the motion picture; from sheet music to phonorecords to digital deliveries, copyright law has evolved over the course of over 280 years. As the white paper on the National Information Infrastructure points out, there is no reason to expect it will be unable to evolve to cope with new technologies.[51] Secondly, a core purpose of copyright law in the United States has always been encouraging authors to create works, which are for the general benefit of society, by making it possible for them to make a living while so doing. "By giving authors a means of securing the economic reward afforded by the market, copyright stimulates their creation and dissemination of intellectual works."[52] If everything becomes free in some sort of Internet utopia, then the only ones creating new works will be hobbyists, not persons engaged full time in the creation of new works. While this might seem more "democratic," we should ask ourselves would there be a *Ninth Symphony* if Beethoven had not had a patron? Would there be a *Madame Butterfly* if Puccini had not worked with G. Ricordi & Sons music publishing company? Would there be a "Yesterday" if the Beatles were dock workers in Liverpool? Would we have heard Coolio's "Gangsta's Paradise" or Alanis Morissette's "Jagged Little Pill" albums? How would we be aware of these works without record companies, music publishers, and performers who rely on copyrights to make their labors worthwhile financially? The three income streams need copyrights to exist in order to provide us with the recordings, songs, and performances we enjoy and appreciate.

NOTES

[1]See, generally, Barbara Ringer, "The Unauthorized Duplication of Sound Recordings" (1957), *Study No. 26 for the Senate Committee on the Judiciary, Copyright Law Revision, Studies Prepared for the Subcommittee on Patents, Trademarks, and Copyrights*, 86th Cong., 2d Sess. (1960); Harry G. Henn, "The Compulsory License Provision of the U.S. Copyright Law," *Study No. 5 for the Senate Committee on the Judiciary, Copyright Law Revision, Studies Prepared for the Subcommittee on Patents, Trademarks, and Copyrights*, 86th Cong., 2d Sess. (1960).
[2]209 U.S. 1 (1908).
[3]"57th Statistical Issue and Marketing Report," *Merchandising*, March 1979: 31.
[4]Recording Industry Association of America, *Inside the Recording Industry: A Statistical Overview 1987*, 4.
[5]H.R. Rep. No. 92-487, 92nd Cong., 1st Sess. (1971).
[6]*Capitol Records, Inc. v. Mercury Record Corp.*, 221 F.2d 657 (2d Cir. 1955).
[7]1909 Copyright Act, Title 17 U.S. Code §1(e).
[8]17 U.S.C. § 301(c).
[9]Embodied in the current Copyright Act as 17 U.S.C. § 109.
[10]17 U.S.C. § 106.
[11]17 U.S.C. § 114(a).
[12]P.L. 98–450, 98 Stat. 1727 (1984).
[13]Irv Lichtman, "King Karol Tests Disk Rental Idea," *Billboard*, 16 May 1981: 1.
[14]H.R. Rep. No. 98–987, 98th Cong., 2nd Sess., 2 (1984).
[15]Uruguay Round Agreements Act, Statement of Administrative Action, P.L. 103–465, reprinted in 6 U.S. Code Congressional and Administrative News (108 Stat.) 4040, at 4281. The Agreement on Trade-Related Aspects of Intellectual Property Rights (TRIPS), Art. 14 prohibits commercial rental of phonograms.
[16]Jeff Clark-Meads, "10-year Dispute Over Japanese Record Rental Business Settled," *Billboard*, 29 April 1995: 5.

[17]17 U.S.C. § 109(b).

[18]Warner Communications, Inc., "The Prerecorded Music Market: An Industry Survey" in *NARAS Institute Journal* Vol. 2, No. 1, 1978: 78.

[19]Adam White, "Villain: Home Taping," *Billboard*, 5 January 1980: 3.

[20]Sam Sutherland, "Taping Losses Near $3 Billion," *Billboard*, 3 April 1982: 1.

[21]464 U.S. 417 (1984).

[22]H. R. Rep. No. 102–873(I), 102nd Cong., 2d Sess. 1992.

[23]P.L. 102–563, 106 Stat. 4237 (October 28, 1992), codified in 17 U.S.C. §§ 1001 *et seq.*

[24]*Annual Report of the Register of Copyrights, 1994*, (1995): 34, 36.

[25]Bill Holland, "Perf. Right Bill On Way to White House," *Billboard*, 28 October 1995: 6.

[26]H.R. 1506, P.L. 104–39, 109 Stat. 336, 104th Cong., 1st Sess. 1995.

[27]17 U.S.C. § 115 (a)(2).

[28]*Tempo Music, Inc. v. Famous Music Corp.* , 838 F.Supp. 162 (S.D.N.Y. 1993).

[29]*Woods v. Bourne Co.*, 841 F.Supp. 118, 121 (S.D.N.Y. 1994).

[30]17 U.S.C. § 115.

[31]37 C.F.R. § 201.19.

[32]29 Stat. 487 (1897).

[33]*Herbert v. Shanley,* 242 U.S. 591, 592 (1917).

[34]17 U.S.C. § 101.

[35]17 U.S.C. § 110.

[36]*Grand Upright Music Limited v. Warner Brothers Records, Inc.*, 780 F.Supp. 182 (S.D.N.Y. 1991).

[37]*Elsemere Music , Inc. v. National Broadcasting Co.*, 482 F.Supp. 741 (S.D.N.Y. 1980).

[38]*Selle v. Gibb*, 741 F.2d 896 (7th Cir. 1984).

[39]*Bright Tunes Music Corp. v. Harrisongs Music, Ltd.*, 420 F.Supp. 177 (S.D.N.Y. 1976).

[40]Susan Nunziata, "Harrison, ABKCO Suit 'Fine'ally Ending After 20 Years," *Billboard*, 1 December 1990: 80.

[41]Although there are claims that the Chinese invented movable type, with all due respect to Chinese inventiveness, there was no interest in the mass reproduction and distribution of works in China, and hence no development of copyright law. In fact, there was no copyright law in China until a desire to participate more broadly in international trade in the early 1990s motivated the Chinese to pass a copyright law so they could join the Berne Convention for the Protection of Literary Property. At any rate, it was Gutenberg's press that was imported into England and that gave rise to the copyright laws we inherited from England.

[42]Statute of Anne, 8 Anne C. 19 (1710), reprinted in, Robert A. Gorman and Jane C. Ginsburg, *Copyright for the Nineties* (4th ed.): 1.

[43]For an extended discussion of the history of copyright see Benjamin Kaplan, *An Unhurried View of Copyright* (1967).

[44]John V. Pavlik, *New Media and the Information Superhighway*, (1996): 125.

[45]Steve Traiman, "Publishers, Music Licensing Groups Seek Rights on Info Superhighway," *Billboard,* 10 June 1995: 39.

[46]Junda Woo, "Publisher Sues CompuServe over a Song," *Wall Street Journal*, 16 December 1993: B1, B16.

[47]Harrison Frahn, "CompuServe Settles Infringement Charges and Agrees to New Electronic Licensing," *The Exclusive Right*, 1:1, 1996:3.

[48]Edward Rosenthal and Jeanne Hamburg, "Are 'Net Providers Liable for Users' Infringement?" *National Law Journal*, 12 February 1996: C4.

⁴⁹Traiman, note 44.

⁵⁰David Nimmer, "The End of Copyright," 48 *Vanderbilt Law Review* 1385 (1995).

⁵¹"Intellectual Property and the National Information Infrastructure: A Preliminary Draft of the Report of the Working Group on Intellectual Property Rights, Executive Summary," 13 *Cardozo Arts & Entertainment Law Journal* 275 (1994).

⁵²*Report of the Register of Copyrights on the General Revision of the U.S. Copyright Law* (1961). As pointed out in the legislative history of the 1909 Copyright Act, U.S. copyright law is not based on any natural right of the authors in their works but is a means of benefiting the public. H.R. Rep. No. 2222, 60th Cong, 2d Sess. 1909.

11

Piracy and Other
Legal Problems

PIRACY OF PHONORECORDS

As used in the recording industry, the term *piracy* encompasses three types of unauthorized duplication and distribution of sound recordings. The Recording Industry Association of America (RIAA) defines *counterfeit* recording as "The unauthorized duplication of the prerecorded sounds, as well as the unauthorized duplication of original artwork, label, trademark and packaging of prerecorded music."[1] A *pirate* recording is defined as "the unauthorized duplication and distribution of only the sounds of one or more legitimate recordings."[2] A *bootleg* recording is "the unauthorized recording of a musical broadcast on radio, television, or of a live concert."[3] Piracy costs in the United States alone were estimated at $300–$325 million in displaced sales in 1995.[4] That represented a downward trend since the early 1990s when estimates of losses due to piracy ran from $400 million to $600 million. Table 11-1 indicates a ten-year trend in seizures of pirate recordings. The ease and low entry-level costs of cassette duplication made them the prime target for pirates during the late 1980s. During the mid 1990s the international growth of the CD market, accompanying dispersion of manufacturing facilities, and the decreased cost of building a CD replication facility began to make them the target of pirates, too. Cassette seizures through the RIAA and FBI went from about 300,000 in 1987 to a high of over 2.5 million in 1992 and had declined to 1.1 million by 1995. Pirate CD seizures, on the other hand, went from just 690 in 1992 to over 25,000 in 1995. In 1996 the RIAA announced a seizure of over 200,000 pirate, counterfeit, and bootleg CDs that had been manufactured in Taiwan and were being sold through a West Coast black market distribution system.[5]

TABLE 11-1   RIAA Piracy Data

Year	Cassettes Seized	LPs Seized	CDs Seized
1987	315,749	na	na
1988	912,099	na	na
1989	932,220	na	na
1990	1,056,900	na	na
1991	1,401,163	na	na
1992	2,548,030	na	690
1993	2,037,917	83,445	17,845
1994	1,212,110	13,675	14,845
1995	1,105,326	0	25,652

Source: Recording Industry Association of America.

Although piracy had been around since the early days of recordings, it was the advent of low cost tapes and low cost tape duplication in the late 1960s and early 1970s that made piracy grow by leaps and bounds. It began with 8-track tapes. In 1971 the FBI arrested twelve people for dealing in over 400,000 tapes.[6] In 1972 the major labels joined forces in a civil copyright infringement suit against tape pirate David Heilman. Heilman's firm, E. C. Tape Service, Inc., sold compilation 8-tracks, LPs, and cassettes, generally through advertisements in men's magazines. By 1974 an injunction had been issued against him, forbidding continued sale of his albums. Heilman protested that he had offered mechanical licenses to the publishers of the songs, and complained about what he called the "monopolistic" labels. The court was not impressed with his excuses and entered a $6.7 million judgment against him, including $1 million in punitive damages. The decision was upheld on appeal.[7]

Counterfeiting

While most pirate recordings are "plain brown wrapper" type with the cover or shell listing little more than the title of the album and artist, and perhaps the songs, the counterfeit recording seeks to duplicate the actual cover art in an effort to look more like the legitimate product. The artwork on some counterfeit recordings is so good that a casual observer would not notice the difference. Far from being the stuff of flea markets and street vendors, the counterfeit products often show up alongside legitimate product in record stores. The RIAA notes that most counterfeit products can be recognized by the following characteristics: blurred, smudgy printing of artwork or photos; insert cards of paper instead of card stock; low quality shrink wrap that is folded or loose; fake (or no) names of manufacturer or distributors; and compilations from artists on a number of different labels.

The biggest counterfeit case occurred in 1980 when investigators discovered $400,000 worth of counterfeit albums being returned from Pickwick International and the Sam Goody retail chain to PolyGram.[8] The ensuing trial of Sam Goody

President, George Levy, who was ultimately exonerated, and Vice President Samuel Stolon, who was ultimately convicted, revealed that the recordings had moved through a Canadian middleman into the Goody chain during the summer of 1978.[9] An RIAA survey in 1980 found that counterfeit merchandise was for sale in 90 percent of record stores sampled.[10] In 1996 the largest judgment in a counterfeit case was handed down when a court held that supplying the blank timed cassettes often used by counterfeiters was a crime. General Audio Video Cassettes and its owner, Mohammed Abdallah, were ordered to pay $7 million in damages.[11]

Bootlegging

Prior to 1995 there was no federal law that prohibited bootlegging. Most prosecutions were under a patchwork of state laws that prohibited falsely labeling the manufacturer or originator of recordings, or under copyright laws if the bootlegger did not pay a mechanical license to the music publishers of the songs recorded. Most recordings were of low quality, but they became collectors items because they included rare performances by many artists, particularly such acts as Bob Dylan and the Grateful Dead. In fact, the Dead allowed their fans to make recordings at concerts for their personal use. Many of these fan recordings later showed up in the back rooms and under the counters of record stores as bootleg merchandise. When the United States approved the 1994 version of the General Agreement on Tariffs and Trade (GATT) an amendment to the U.S. copyright law was passed to give performers the right to record and broadcast their performances.[12] By that time bootlegging CDs had become big business, by some counts a bigger problem than pirate and counterfeit CDs. Most bootleg merchandise was manufactured outside of the United States, often in China or Taiwan. The RIAA reported seizures of bootleg CDs for the first half of 1996 at nearly 900,000 copies.[13]

Remedies for Piracy

When sound recordings were first added as kinds of copyrightable works in 1972 they were put on the same footing regarding remedies for infringement as other kinds of works. Even in the 1976 Copyright Revision Act, criminal infringement, "willful infringement for commercial advantage or private financial gain," was punishable by only up to one year imprisonment and a fine of up to $10,000 dollars for a first offense—not even a felony. Some pirates simply took the fine and risk of imprisonment as a cost of doing business and kept right on with their illegal duplication, even after they had been prosecuted one time. By 1981 it became apparent that to stop record piracy effectively, harsher remedies, especially for criminal infringement, were needed. In 1982 the copyright statute was changed to make criminal infringement of sound recordings and motion pictures a felony (it had previously been only a misdemeanor), subject to a fine of $250,000 and five years imprisonment.[14] That same year the statute prohibiting trafficking in counterfeit labels for recordings and motion pictures was also strengthened. In passing the bill the Senate noted that counterfeiting had become, in the eyes of the Justice Department, "the third most troublesome area of white collar crime" and that "the indication [is] that organized crime is becoming increasingly involved in the manufacture and distribution of counterfeits."[15] In 1992 the copyright law was changed again to make any kind of criminal infringement a felony if at least ten copies of a retail value of more than $2,500 value were produced or distributed within a 180-day period. The punishment is up to five years in prison for a first offense and ten years for a second or subsequent offense. Fines may be as high as $250,000 for individuals and up to $500,000 for organizational defendants.[16] Even with increased penalties piracy continues to plague the record industry both domestically and internationally.

International Dimensions of Piracy

The International Federation of Phonogram Industries (IFPI) estimated that worldwide piracy totaled $2.1 billion in 1995. An estimated 866 million pirate cassettes and 84 million pirate CDs were sold in 1995, with Russia and China being the nations with the worst piracy rates. The IFPI estimated that 74 percent of the sales of cassettes and 51 percent of CD sales in Russia were pirate—about 221 million units. In China the percentages were about reversed, with 48 percent of cassette sales and 88 percent of CD sales being pirate—about 145 million units. Russia accounted for 23 percent of worldwide pirate sales and China about 15 percent.[17]

An interesting international trade dispute developed in the mid 1990s over the piracy situation in China and China's desire to join the World Trade Organization. The recording industry, the motion picture industry, and the computer software industry had been complaining loudly about "condoned" piracy in China. The situation in the home video industry had become so bad that major motion picture hits such as *Jurassic Park* and *The Lion King* were out on home video in China before they were on sale in the United States.[18] In the eleventh hour, before the United States was to impose trade sanctions, China decided to crack down on its own pirate facilities. The *Peoples' Daily* reported twenty-three raids on plants in China, seizing a reported 375,000 pirate recordings, including 75,000 bootleg compact discs. There were an estimated twenty-nine factories in China manufacturing pirate audio, computer, and video software.[19]

The piracy problems in China did not end with the 1995 agreements. By late 1995 the IFPI investigators in China were reportedly the subject of hired killers and death threats. The IFPI concluded that the threats were evidence that progress was being made.[20] By early 1996 it had become obvious that the piracy in China was still not under control and the United States again threatened trade sanctions. In April 1996 the RIAA reported that there were even more CD and video duplicating plants in operation than there had been in the previous year before the crackdown. Half of the pirate products were CDs and the other half a mix of CD-ROM, videos, and computer games.[21] Most of the pirate merchandise was being exported through Hong Kong. The RIAA and recording industry officials feared that the development of new CD replication equipment that did not require "clean room" technology and was small enough to fit in the back of a truck would make CD piracy in China (and elsewhere) even more difficult to police.[22]

Why, in addition to trade sanction threats from the United States, was China willing to close down pirate operations important to its own economy? China was a member of the original GATT that was signed in 1947 and entered into force in 1948. However, in 1950 China withdrew from the GATT following the Communist takeover in 1949. China was officially an "observer" of some parts, but not the main protocol, of the 1979 GATT Geneva Protocol.[23] By 1995 China wanted to join the World Trade Organization. China was the eleventh largest exporter, doing $91 billion in exports in 1993.[24] Because China was not a member of the 1979 GATT, it could not join the new World Trade Organization unless there was a consensus among existing members to let it do so. Unless China attended to its copyright enforcement, the United States was not willing to let China join. When China does join, it will contend that it is a "developing" country and entitled to a five-year phase-in of the Trade-Related Aspects of Intellectual Property (TRIPS) part of the GATT requirements.[25] China has a case as a developing nation when comparing its GDP per capita in 1993 of $2,100, to that of Taiwan at $14,000, and to that of the United States at $23,200. However, the sheer size of China's international trade is reason for the United States and other nations to maintain that China is not a developing nation in the usual sense of the phrase.[26]

Pirates in Cyberspace?

Internet audio broadcasts, and digitized photos and liner notes, zip around the world almost effortlessly. So do bootleg recordings of those broadcasts. "Moments" after a July 1996 Porno for Pyros "cyber" concert, a Web user posted that he had the whole thing on CD-ROM and through a deal with a duplicator in China would soon be making it available to record stores in the United States. Several Internet forums are available for swapping and selling bootleg or pirate recordings and CD-ROM.[27]

PAYOLA

"Here's three thousand, that ought to get it on."

"Thanks a lot man, I love your new song."
—NEIL YOUNG/BEN KEITH, "PAYOLA BLUES"
Used by permission

From the lay person's point of view, payola in the recording industry is paying a bribe to someone to perform or play a certain song or recording in order to increase exposure for that song or recording in the hope that the exposure will lead to increased sales. In that definition, it had been a common practice in the industry since the turn of the century.[28] Particularly, music publishers often made payments to performers or orchestra leaders to perform their compositions or to "plug" the song (see Chapter 3). Industry estimates in those days placed the cost of paying singers for plugs at $200,000 per year. When radio became a significant medium for the exposure of songs the publishers moved right over to paying orchestra leaders and directors for exposure on the radio. The practice picked up the label "payola" in 1938 from *Variety*. At that time some publishers had been paying orchestra leaders to influence not only exposure of the song but also ASCAP's logging of songs so they would receive more performance royalties.[29] By 1945 payola payments from publishers had risen to about $500,000 per year.[30] The practice crept into television broadcasting as well for the same reason. Eventually some television producers, not content to accept advance payments for songs used in their shows, began to form their own publishing companies to cash in on the lucrative performance royalties that the use of the songs in the shows generated.[31]

The payola and game show rigging scandals of the late 1950s caused Congress to pass legislation to clean up broadcasting. Since broadcasters exist because they sell air time for money, what had to be done was make the secret payment for air time, i.e., payola, illegal. The statute ultimately read:

> *All matter broadcast by any radio station for which any money, service or other valuable consideration is directly or indirectly paid, or promised to or charged or accepted by, the station so broadcasting, from any person, shall at the time the same is so broadcast, be announced as paid for or furnished, as the case may be, by such person.[32]*

The statute excepted such things as identification "reasonably related" to the broadcast, so a station could announce the title of a song and the artist, even if they had received the records for free in order to play them. In order to remove the disc jockeys from the end of the payola stream, the statute made station management responsible if employees failed to disclose payments. Penalties were set at fines up to $10,000 and jail terms up to one year.

The payola statute clearly has some limits. It requires an undisclosed payment to a broadcaster in exchange for airplay. If the payment is disclosed by the station then there is no wrongdoing. So, if a station announced that a "promotional consideration" had been paid for the play of a record, then there would be no violation. Similarly, if payments from independent promotion people, or even the labels directly, were simply "consulting fees" that program directors received without any specific directions or purpose of receiving play for a particular recording then that, too, would not be in violation of the statute. To avoid entanglement with the Racketeering Influenced Corrupt Organizations law (RICO) the labels went to paying independent promotion people.[33] There is some speculation that there might be Federal trade law violations if records were added to playlists and made to appear as though they had been added by some form of consumer demand.[34] This had the result of forcing programming decisions up to a higher level and giving the disk jockeys very little say in what music was played. The Top 40 format had already removed many programming decisions from the disk jockey, and the payola laws were the *coup de grace*. The lack of control over airplay apparently had damaging results on air personalities' creativity. While DJs continued to perceive themselves as creative in their announcements and humor, one 1990 study found them no more creative than the least creative college students.[35]

The payola hearings and scandals of the late 1950s are often characterized as a last ditch attack on rock and roll by the music business establishment of the time.[36] The attack clearly failed. The power of the new popular music to sell recordings and receive airplay convinced potential artists, songwriters, record producers, and label executives that the future lay in embracing new music and new artists. In his book, *Hit Men*, Fredric Dannen argues that the labels' expenditures of millions of dollars to independent promotion people was an attempt by the major labels to guarantee airplay of their recordings in a high stakes game that the smaller labels could not play. Estimates are that the labels paid out as much as $60 to $80 million for independent promotion in 1985.[37] Of course, even if the labels could guarantee airplay, the airplay could not guarantee sales of a recording unless the public liked it enough to buy it. Because the labels primarily made their money through the sale of recordings, argues Dannen, independent promotion had become too expensive.

There is no law that restricts retailers from selling advertising space in their stores, aside from some sign ordinances restricting outdoor advertising. The large chain superstores began by selling outdoor four-by-fours of album covers to the labels. Soon the practice moved inside the stores with the sale of display space on walls. While the labels had been giving the stores point-of-purchase display materials free, some stores began to limit display spaces and charge the labels for any use of the space. The stores soon found that not only would the labels pay for the space, they would send around their own personnel to set up the displays. By the mid 1990s retail record stores had taken cues from their other retail cousins and began charging for "positioning" of product in stores on special sale displays or end-caps. Since in-store airplay is not "broadcasting," it is not illegal to pay a store to play a recording in the store over the in-house system. All of these retail promotions are still no guarantee that the public will buy the recording.

Because word of mouth is an important factor in sales of recordings, the labels give away copies of entire albums or "sampler" albums to try to get people interested in purchasing the whole album, or in telling their friends that they had heard an interesting new album by such-and-such an artist. No payola there, either.

Independent Promotion and the Isgro Trial

The only person ever to go to jail for violation of the payola law was independent promotion person, Ralph Tashjian. As a result of the investigation begun in 1986, he pleaded guilty to one count of payola by distribution of cocaine in exchange for a promise of airplay, one tax evasion count, and one obstruction of justice count. His side of the plea bargain was the promise of his testimony against others involved, especially Joe Isgro.[38] On February 23, 1986, NBC's *Nightly News* broadcast a special report purporting to show that the record industry was making huge payments to independent record promoters and that one of them, Joe Isgro, allegedly had ties to organized crime figures in the New York area. The major record labels quickly moved to stop using independent promoters. Isgro filed suit against twelve labels, alleging antitrust violations. That dispute was ultimately settled by all of the twelve label defendants.[39] However, a three-year federal investigation ended in charging Isgro and others with fifty-seven counts of racketeering and other crimes.[40] During Isgro's trial the program directors testified that they had received payments ranging from $150 to $750 for an "add" to their playlists. Others testified that the payments totaled from $1,000 to as much as $5,000 per month.[41] The district court judge dismissed the trial for prosecutorial misconduct at failure to turn over contradictory statements that a prosecution witness had made at another trial either to the grand jury or to the defense. Even though that decision was overturned on appeal, the prosecution ultimately lost when the case was dismissed because the prosecution had violated Isgro's right to a speedy trial.

Organized Crime

The recording industry is high profile, high profit (at least potentially), and high rolling. That combination occasionally attracts the interests of organized crime. William Knoedelseder's book, *Stiffed*, details how some "deals" with cutouts at MCA Records got out of hand.[42] Ultimately the deal maker, Sal Pisello, not an official MCA employee, went to jail for tax evasion. Morris Levy, the founder of Roulette Records and the Strawberry's retail chain, went to prison for conspiracy to extort payment from the middleman-turned-informant, John LaMonte. Levy was sentenced to ten years in prison (he later died there of liver cancer) and "reputed organized crime figure Domenick Canterino" was sentenced to twelve years with Levy.[43]

ANTITRUST PROBLEMS

Like any businesses, the record labels also operate under the antitrust provisions of federal law. In Chapter 7 it was noted that the large labels and distributing corporations tend to operate like oligopolists in terms of pricing. There is no clear price leader, but they do tend to follow each other closely. In 1985 WEA, Capitol, Polygram, RCA, MCA, CBS, and ABC settled a decade-long price-fixing suit by independents and other distributors. A settlement fund of over $26 million was approved for distribution to distributors who purchased recordings for resale from January 1971 through December 1982.[44] In the mid 1990s the labels were again the target of suits contending that they had conspired to fix CD prices and a separate suit claiming that they conspired to keep some wholesalers out of the business of selling cutouts.[45] Finally, in 1996 the Justice Department began an investigation against Time

Warner, Sony, EMI, BMG, and Polygram for price-fixing of license fees for music videos. The altercation centered around an alleged attempt by the majors to keep "MuchMusic USA" from launching a music video channel.[46]

PERSPECTIVE

There are indeed some unsavory characters in and near the recording industry. Sometimes they do nothing illegal, but simply take advantage of would-be artists and songwriters. Sometimes they steal from the labels, publishers, artists, and songwriters through piracy. Success is highly rewarded and some people will stop at nothing to attain those high rewards. Still, most of the people in this highly competitive business, whether they work for one of the six transnationals or own their own "mom and pop" record store on the corner, work hard and honestly to earn their rewards, whether large or small.

NOTES

[1]Recording Industry Association of America, *1992 Annual Report* (1993): 22.

[2]Ibid.

[3]Ibid.

[4]Chris Morris, "Piracy Losses Shrink," *Billboard*, 1 April 1995: 1.

[5]Bill Holland, "RIAA Assists in Record Seizure of Bogus CDs," *Billboard*, 13 April 1996: 6.

[6]Joe Radcliffe, "3 Mill in Counterfeit Tape Grabbed in N.Y.: 12 Arrested," *Billboard*, 18 Sept. 1971: 1.

[7]"4 Mill Judgment Against David Heilman to Bring Appeal," *Billboard*, 5 Jan. 1980: 3; "Court Affirms Ruling on David Heilman," *Billboard*, 7 Nov. 1981: 3.

[8]John Sippel, "Huge Haul of Illicit LPs in Goody Return," *Billboard*, 9 Feb. 1980: 1.

[9]Leo Sacks, "Reporter's Notebook: Observations from Goody Trial," *Billboard*, 2 May 1981: 13.

[10]"RIAA Finds 90% Stores Sell Counterfeit!" *Variety*, 2 April 1980: 2.

[11]"Record $7 Million Judgment Made in Counterfeit Case," *Billboard*, 20 April 1996: 8.

[12]17 U.S.C. §1101; Uruguay Round Agreements Act, P.L. 103–465, 103d Cong., 2nd Sess. 1994, §512.

[13]Bill Holland, "Bootleg Seizures Up Under Piracy Act," *Billboard*, 31 Aug. 1996: 1.

[14]Bill Holland, "House Okays New Anti-Piracy Bill," *Billboard*, 22 May 1982: 3; Criminal Penalties for Copyright Infringement, P.L. 102–561, 106 Stat. 4233 (1992).

[15]S. Rep. No. 97-274, P.L. 97–180, (1992): 4, 5.

[16]18 U.S.C. § 2319.

[17]Jeff Clark–Meads, "IFPI: '95 Piracy Stable; Russia and China Cited," *Billboard*, 18 May 1996: 8.

[18]"Prospects of Trade Clash Between US and China Grows," *Times Newspapers Limited*, 2 Jan. 1995 (LEXIS).

[19]"China Raids Pirate Plants Ahead of U.S. Talks," *Reuter European Community Report*, 15 Feb. 1995 (LEXIS).

[20]Jeff Clark–Meads, "Piracy Fighters in China Fear Killings," *Billboard*, 23 Sept. 1995: 9.

[21]Bill Holland, "Chinese Piracy Still Rampant," *Billboard*, 27 April 1996: 6.

[22]Brett Atwood and Geoff Burpee, "War on Piracy Continues in China," *Billboard*, 20 July 1996: 1.

[23]Office of the U.S. Trade Representative, *MTN Agreements—Legal Status as 6 May 1994*, 7.

[24]"China and the GATT Reaching an Impasse," *The Economist*, 6 Aug. 1994: 52.

[25]The Agreement on Trade-Related Aspects of Intellectual Property Rights (TRIPS) Art. 65(2), General Agreement on Tariffs and Trade, 1994, Uruguay Round.

[26]*The Economist, supra* note 24.

[27]Ibid. at 75.

[28]For a detailed history of payola, see Kerry Segrave, *Payola in the Music Business: A History 1880–1991* (1994).

[29]Russell Sanjek and David Sanjek, *American Popular Music Business in the 20th Century* (1991): 74.

[30]Segrave, *supra* note 27: 16, 65.

[31]Ibid. at 173.

[32]47 U.S.C. §317(a)(1).

[33]Dave DiMartino, "Lawyers Mull 'Legal Payola,'" *Billboard*, 9 Jan. 1988: 5. See also, J. Gregory Sidak and David E. Kronemyer, "The New Payola and the American Record Industry," *Harvard Journal of Law and Public Policy*, Summer 1987: 521.

[34]Sidney Shemel and M. William Krasilovsky, *This Business of Music*, 6th ed. (1990): 125.

[35]Steven O. Shields, *"Creativity and Creative Control in the Work of American Radio Announcers,"* a paper presented to the Association for Education in Journalism and Mass Communication annual meeting, Minneapolis, Minn., August, 1990.

[36]For example, Philip H. Ennis, *The Seventh Stream, The Emergence of Rocknroll in American Popular* Music (1992): 261.

[37]Fredric Dannen, *Hit Men* (1990): 15.

[38]Dave DiMartino, "Tashjian Pleads Guilty to Payola," *Billboard*, 3 June 1989: 1.

[39]Dave DiMartino, "Lawyers Mull 'Legal Payola,'" *Billboard*, 9 Jan. 1988: 5.

[40]Chris Morris, "Federal Judge Dismisses Joe Isgro Case," *Billboard*, 13 April 1996: 96.

[41]Chris Morris, "Isgro Trial Testimony Bares Payoffs," *Billboard*, 8 Sept. 1990: 1.

[42]William Knoedelseder, *Stiffed: A True Story of MCA, the Music Business and the Mafia* (HarperCollins, 1993).

[43]Bruce Haring, "Levy Conviction Upheld by Court," *Billboard* 11 Nov. 1989: 105.

[44]*United National Records, Inc. v. MCA, Inc.*, No. 82 C 7589 (N.D. Ill. 1985). (Notice of hearing on proposed additional settlements, proposed plan of distribution, and allowance of expenses and attorneys' fees.)

[45]Don Jeffrey, "Embattled Majors Act to Protect Music Stores," *Billboard* 23 Dec. 1995: 67.

[46]Bill Holland, "Justice Dep't Investigating Music-Video Fee Collusion," *Billboard*, 2 March 1996: 1.

Appendix

The Recording Industry on the Internet

Listed below are some of the many Internet and World Wide Web sites that provide valuable information and insight into the recording industry—and some that are just plain fun. Anyone who tries to publish an Internet list on anything but the Internet and who updates it less than weekly is likely to be left in the silicon dust of this rapidly changing medium. Record labels, music publications, organizations, and others are adding web pages and sites at a feverish rate. I am sure that by the time this is published some of these sites will have disappeared, and others will form to take their places. Many of these sites contain listings and links to other good new sites. Surf's up!

LABELS

A & M Records and Almo Sounds
    http://www.geffen.com/almo/herbalpert/anm.html
American Recordings
    http://american.recordings.com/
Arista Records
    http://www.aristarec.com/
Bembe Records
    http://www.bembe.com/
BMG Records
    http://www.bmg.de

BMG Classics World
    http://classicalmus.com/
Columbia Records Radio hour
    http://www.sony.com/Music/ArtistInfo/CRRadioHour/
Curb Records
    http://www.curb.com/
Decca Records-Nashville
    http://www.decca-nashville.com/
Dedicated Records
    http://www.dedicated.co.uk/
Earache Records
    http://www.earache.com/
EMI-Online
    http://www.riv.nl/emi/default.htm
Thorn EMI
    http://www.demon.co.uk
Geffen Records
    http://www.geffen.com/
Hollywood Records
    http://www.hollywoodrec.com/
Imago Music
    http://www.tuna.net/imago/
I.R.S. Records
    http://www.rocktropolis.com/IRS/
Island Records, U.K.
    http://www.island.co.uk/
Jive Records and Zomba Records
    http://www.cyber.nl/bigbro/welcom.html
LaFace Records
    http://www.laface.com/
London Records
    http://www.polygram.com/london/
Mammoth Records
    http://www.mammoth.com/
Margaritaville Records
    http://www.margaritaville.com
MCA Records
    http://www.mca.com/mca_records/index.html
MCA Records-Nashville
    http://www.mca-nashville.com/
Metalblade Records
    http://www.iuma.com/Metal_Blade/
Polygram Online
    http://www.polygram.com/polygram/

Rhino Records
   http://pathfinder.com/Rhino/
Rowdy Records
   http://www.aristarec.com/rowdy/
Rudeboys Records
   http://www.rudeboysrecords.com/
Sony Music Online
   http://www.sony.com/
Sony Corp. (Japan)
   http://www.sony.co.jp
Sony-Australia
   http://www.sonymusic.at/
Squaredog Records
   http://www.comcept.ab.ca/squaredog/
Virgin Records U.S.A.
   http://www.virginusa.com/
Warner Brothers Online
   http://www.iuma.com/Warner
Windham Hill Records
   http://www.windham.com/

RECORD CLUBS

BMG Music Service
   http://www.bmgmusicservice.com
Columbia House
   http://www.columbiahouse.com

PERIODICALS

Access Online Magazine
   http://www.accessmag.com/main.html
Acoustic Guitar
   http://www.acguitar.com/
Acoustic Musician
   http://www.netshop.net/acoustic
B-Side Magazine
   http://www.ifnet.com/bside/index.html
Billboard Online
   http://www.billboard_online.com/
Blues Access
   http://www.he.net/~blues/ba_home.html

Blues Buyer's Guide
    http://www.vivanet.com/~blues/bbginc.html
Buzz Online
    http://www.buzzmag.com/
Cashbox Magazine
    http://www.silence.net/
Contempory Christian Music Magazine
    http://wwwmbb.cs.colorado.edu/~mcbryan/bb/27/3/summary.html
Creative Loafing Magazine
    http://www.cln.com/
Discorder Magazine
    http://www.ams.ubc.ca/services/citr/discord/discord.htm
Electronic Urban Report
    http://www.leebailey.com/EUR.html
Gavin
    http://www.gavin.com
Keyboard Central
    http://www.keyboardmag.com/
LCD or Lowest Common Denominator
    http://wfmu.org/LCD/
Leak CD Magazine
    http://www.daenet.com/leak/
Local Beat magazine
    http://ic.net/~fvincent/localBeat.html
Mix Magazine Online
    http://www.mixmag.com/
Music Business International (MBI)
    http://www.dotmusic.co.uk/MBIhome.html
Music City News
    http://www.hsv.tis.net/mcn/
Music Network U.S.A.
    http://www.mnusa.com/mnusa.html
Music Trades
    http://www.musictrades.com/
Music Universe
    http://www.musicuniverse.com/index.html
Musicweek Online
    http://www.ablex.co.uk/
Music Week
    http://www.dotmusic.co.uk/MWhome.html
Nashville Scene
    http://www.nashscene.com/
Pollstar
    http://www.pollstar.com

Record Mirror
    http://www.dotmusic.co.uk/RMhome.html
Rock and Roll Reporter
    http://www3.pgh.net/~rockreporter
Songplugger (newsletter)
    http://www.dotmusic.co.uk/newslettershome.html
Songtalk
    http://www.songtalk.com/
Spin website
    http://spinn.thoughtport.com/spinnwebe/
Strobe Magazine
    http://www.iuma.com/strobe/
United News & Media
    http://www.dotmusic.co.uk/UNMhomenew.html
Vibe magazine
    http://www.metaverse.com/vibe/index.html
Worldwide Free Press
    http://www.wwfreepress.com/

MUSIC PUBLISHERS

BMG Music Publishing
    http://www.emamulti.com/BMG/bmg.html
EMI Music Publishing
    http://emimusicpub.com/
McJames Music
    http://www.songnet.com/mcjames/
Music Publisher Agencies
    http://host.mpa.org/agency.html
Music Publishers Association (MPA)
    http://host.mpa.org/mpa/Welcome.html
Nashville Publishing Information
    http://www.telalink.net/~randy/list.html
Nashville Publishers Network
    http://www.songnet.com/npn/
Sony/ATV Music Publishing
    http://www.treepublishing.com/sonyopen.html

PERFORMING RIGHTS ORGANIZATIONS

ASCAP
http://www.ascap.com

BMI
   http://www.bmi.com
SESAC
   http://www.sesac.com
APRA Australia
   http://www.apra.com.au
BUMA Netherlands
   http://www.buma.nl/
GEMA Germany
   http://www.gema.de
PRS United Kingdom
   http://www.prs.co.uk/
SABAM Belgium
   http://www.sabam.be/

MISCELLANEOUS

Bluebird Cafe Regulars
   http://www.hidwater.com/bluebird/regulars.htm
CMT
   http://www.tvnet.com/tv/us/cable/cmt.html
Country Crossroads
   http://www.countrycrossroads.org/
Country Music Hall of Fame
   http://www.nashville-collection.com/deluxe/CMHOF.html
First Com, A Zomba Company
   htp://www.firstcom.com/aboutfc.htm
Great American Country
   http://www.countrystars.com
MTV Online
   http://www.mtv.com
MTV jobs
   http://www.mtv.com/jobs.html
Nashville Music Consultants
   http://www.infi.net/nmc/a1.html
Network Music
   http://www.networkmusic.com
Rock and Roll Hall of Fame
   http://www.rockhall.com
Roland Corporation International
   http://www.rolandcorp.com
RSP Technologies Circle Sound
   http://www.rocktron.com/rsp

Signature Sound
    http://www.signaturetech.com
Sweetwater
    http://www.sweetwater.com
Tascam
    http://www.zeus.snader.com/site/video/audio/tascam.html
VH-1
    http://vh1.com

THREE MUSIC LINKS ADDRESSES

http://soundwave.ipo.net/directories/major.html
http://axsamer.org/wcxs/musicdir/rcfull.html
http://www.musicsearch.com/commerce/labels.html#u

The addresses listed above are sites with links to many recording industry sites. Virtually every label can be accessed through at least one of these sites.

ORGANIZATIONS

Acoustical Society of America
    http://asa.aip.org
AMCOS (Australia)
    http://www.amcos.com.au
American Federation of Musicians
    http://www.afm.org
Audio Engineering Society
    http://www.aes.org
Austin Music Server
    http://www.txmusic.com
Australian Music Publishers Association
    http://www.amcos.com.au
Australian Recording Industry Association
    http://www.amcos.com.au/general/organis.html#aria
Backstage World
    http://www.stagelight.se/backstage/index.html
Black Gospel Experience
    http://www.yesonline.com/gospel
Canadian Country Music Awards
    http://www.nor.com/music/nwc/ccma.htm
Canadian Music Trade
    http://nor.com/music/nwc/cmt.htm

Christian Music Coalition
   http://www.cmcnet.org
Copyright Agency Limited (Australia)
   http://www.copyright.com.au
Copyright Office
   http://lcweb.loc.gov/copyright/copy1.html
Copyright Society of the U.S.A.
   http://www.csusa.org
Federal Communications Commission
   http://www.fcc.gov
Global Alliance of Performers
   http://www.gap.org
Grammy Awards
   http://www.grammy.apple.com
International Alliance for Women in Music
   http://music.acu.edu/iawm/home.html
International Bluegrass Music Association
   http://www.banjo.com/BG
Irish Music Rights Organization
   http://www.imro.ie
Mechanical Copyright and Protection Society
   http://www.mcps.co.uk
Music and Entertainment Industry Educators Association
   http://www.wiu.edu/users/mimusba/meiea
Music Network USA
   http://www.mnusa.com
Nashville Entertainment Association
   http://www.nea.net
National Association of Broadcasters
   http://www.nab.org/
National Association of Recording Merchandisers
   http://www.narm.com
National Music Foundation
   http://www.nmc.org
National Music Publishers' Association
   http://www.nmpa.org
National Online Music Alliance
   http://www.edge.net/noma
Nashville Publishers Network
   http://www.songnet.com/npn
Nashville Songwriter's Organization International
   http://songs.org/nsai
North by Northeast Conference
   http://www.nxne.com

Patent and Trademark Office
   http://uspto.gov/
Professional Lighting and Sound Association
   http://www.pavilion.co.uk/plasa
Radio and Records Online
   http://www.rronline.com
Society of Motion Picture and Television Engineers
   http://www/smpte.org/
Society of Professional Audio Recording Services (SPARS)
   http://www.spars.com/spars/
South by Southwest Conference
   http://www.sxsw.com/sxsw/directory.html
Texas Music Association
   http://www.geminet.com/TMA
Young Wonderful Aliens
   http://www.escape.com/~ywa

Glossary

A&R   Artist and Repertoire. In a record company this is the department in charge of finding new artists to record. "A&R person" refers to someone who fulfills A&R functions by scouting new talent or listening to demos of artists and songs to decide who and what to record. Traditionally A&R people also found songs for their artists to record and still do so if the artist does not record only their own compositions.

Add   A record added to the playlist at a radio station or video channel.

Adult Contemporary   A current radio format playing recordings by contemporary artists and primarily targeted at a listening audience that is over twenty-four years old. The overall sound tends to be softer than CHR or the various rock formats.

Advance   A prepayment of royalties or other earnings. For example, a recording artist may be paid a flat sum on delivery to the label of a finished master in advance of earning any royalties from the sale of copies of the recordings. Many items, such as recording costs or promotion expenses, may also be considered "advances" under the definitions in the agreement. Advances are used in many different agreements in the recording industry, including label–artist agreements, songwriter agreements, and master licensing agreements.

AES   The Audio Engineering Society. A trade and educational organization for audio engineers. Founded in the 1950s, its members include recording engineers, equipment designers, and other professionals involved in audio engineering. It helps set technical standards and publishes a technical journal for members.

AFM   The American Federation of Musicians of the United States and Canada, the musicians union.

AFTRA The American Federation of Television and Radio Artists, the singers and voice anouncers union.

AGVA The American Guild of Variety Artists, the union for live entertainers who are not AFM or AFRTA members.

Airplay Play of a recording on the radio, in a record store, or of a music video on a television or video channel or in a club.

Album A recording containing usually eight or more individual songs or "cuts," totaling thirty or more minutes of playing time. CDs can contain up to seventy-five minutes of playing time. Vinyl albums usually contained no more than forty-five minutes of playing time.

All-in royalty or deal A royalty rate paid to an artist designed to include any royalties paid to a producer. An all-in deal provides to the label the services of the recording artist and producer for a single royalty rate.

AMC American Music Conference, a non-profit organization which promotes music and music education.

Ancillary income In concert promotion, the term for revenues for the venue from parking or food sales that are not part of the gate and are not commissionable by the promoter or artist.

Artist concessions In concert promotion, artist revenues from the sale of merchandise at the concert such as T-shirts, hats, nightgowns, and so on that bears the artist's name and likeness. The venue may demand a percentage of artist concessions.

ASCAP The American Society of Composers, Authors and Publishers, an organization that licenses music performance rights for songwriters and music publishers. It was the first performing rights organization in the United States, started in 1914.

Audio engineer (See also *recording engineer*) A person who operates or designs equipment for recording and reproduction of sound. The term is broader than recording engineer.

Author In copyright law, the person who creates a work, whether a songwriter, recording artist, sculptor, poet, or novelist—all are called "authors."

Bar code Generally taken to mean the Universal Product Code appearing as a series of vertical black and white bars on a product that identifies the specific product and its manufacturer.

BDS (Broadcast Data Service) The company that monitors radio airplay with computers that identify what records are being played by comparing the broadcast to identifiable "signature" parts of the recording stored in the computer's memory. BDS can deliver the actual count of the number of times a particular record is played.

BET (Black Entertainment Television) As its name implies, cable television channel targeted primarily at African Americans, specializing in music videos and other entertainment programming.

Blacklist (see *Defaulters*)

Blanket license   A term used mainly in performance rights licensing where a performing rights organization gives a licensee such as a radio station of club the right to perform all of the songs in the PRO's repertoire as many times as the licensee wants. The "blanket" covers all of the songs as compared to a per-song or per-use license for one song at a time.

BMI (Broadcast Music, Inc.)   A performing rights organization started in 1940 and owned by broadcasters. It and ASCAP are the two largest performing rights organizations in the United States. It licenses radio and television stations, night clubs, retail outlets, and others to publicly perform musical compositions.

Boom box   A small portable stereo system with attached speakers.

Bootleg   A recording not authorized by the label of artist, usually of a live performance or studio outtakes, that is manufactured and sold to the public outside of the normal channels of distribution. Beginning in 1995, such recordings violated the performer's right in the copyright law to be the first to record or transmit their performances.

Boxed set   A special package containing usually three or more individual albums with special notes, photos, and other matter. The albums often contain previously unreleased cuts and alternative versions of recordings.

Branch distributor   A term still applied to a distributorship owned and maintained by one of the six conglomerates that operates on a regional basis.

Break   To "break" an artist or recording is to have sufficient airplay or other national exposure that is beginning to translate into significant sales and additional airplay.

Break-even point   In concert promotion, the point at which the promoter's gross revenues equal the fixed expenses, including artist guarantees, but not such things as any percentages for the artist or venue. In economics, the point at which total revenues have equalled total cost so the firm is showing neither a profit or a loss.

Breakage allowance   A deduction from a recording artist's royalties originally designed to account for the fact that lacquer and shellac recordings were brittle and easily broken. The label would deduct typically 10 percent of sales to account for broken records. The allowance still exists in some contracts even though cassettes and CDs rarely break.

Broad inventory   A selection of goods that crosses a number of different product lines, such as exists in department stores and mass merchandisers. Record stores typically have a narrow inventory.

Budget line   An album product line of a label that sells at a list price usually less than two-thirds of the current *front line* (new releases for established artists) album SRLP.

Burnout   As used in radio programming, a term indicating that the public is tired of hearing a particular recording.

Business manager   A person hired by an artist or the artist's personal manager to take care of managing the artist's money and business ventures.

Buy-back   In concert promotion, a deal between the promoter and the artist's agent to give the promoter the "right" to promote that artist the next time the artist plays in that promoter's area, city, or venue.

Call-out   Radio research initiated at the station (usually) in which someone calls random or selected listeners to ask their opinions on certain records or other programming that the station may be doing.

Cassingle   A cassette single, usually containing two or three cuts.

Catalog   Generally refers to all of the songs (actually the copyrights in those songs) owned by a music publisher, but may also refer to all of a label's master recordings, or to recordings that are not current hits, but are still available from the distributor.

Census   As used in performing rights, refers to a PRO's logging of every performance of every song by a certain broadcaster or other licensee. It is compared to a *sample,* whereby only some licensees or some performances of the licensee are logged.

Chain (retail)   A group of two or more stores that are owned by the same entity. Strictly speaking, even if "mom and pop" opened a second store it would be called a chain, but most people would still call it a "mom and pop store" with two locations.

CHR (Contemporary Hit Radio)   The successor to the Top 40 format, usually with fewer (20–25) current hits being played, instead of forty.

Clearance   In rights generally, permission to use a particular song, photo, or other work. In music publishing, the writer or publisher will "clear" a new song for licensing by listing it with the performing rights organization.

CMT (Country Music Television)   The cable channel devoted to programming country music videos and other programs featuring "country" artists and themes.

Coin-op   Early coin-operated "jukebox."

Commercially acceptable   A standard by which labels judge masters submitted to them by recording artists. It means the recording must be technically and artistically good enough in the opinion of the label executives to enjoy public sales and acceptance.

Collective work   A work (in copyright) formed by the assembly of a number of separate independent works into a collective whole, such as an anthology, periodical issue, or (perhaps) a record album.

Commission   The percentage of the artist's income taken by the agent for arranging the performance or by the personal manager for being the artist's manager.

Common-law copyright   Originally, the right of authors to be the first to publish their work as protected by common law, and not the federal copyright statute. Since 1978, common law copyright would only apply to works not fixed in a tangible medium of expression.

Compulsory license   Refers to a license to use a musical composition, sound recording, or other copyrighted work that is granted by the copyright act. It is "compulsory" because the copyright owner must permit the use if the user conforms to the requirements of the statute regarding payment of royalties, and so on. The term is often used in the music industry to refer to the compulsory mechanical license for phonorecords, but the term is really broader than that.

Concept video   A music video usually not much longer than a single song, which features visual images *other than* the artist performing the song. Usually these images tell a story or set a certain mood to accompany the song.

Configuration   The type of phonogram in which a recording is fixed, such as LP, cassette, or compact disc.

Conglomerate   A business corporation that is formed by the ownership of a number of other businesses or divisions operating in a wide variety of areas. For example, Sony Corp. owns record companies, music publishing companies, film production and distribution, and consumer electronics hardware manufacturing.

Container charge   A deduction from a recording artist's royalties to account for the fact that the label produces the package or container for the recording and claims they should not have to pay royalties on that part of the list price that covers the package. The reduction is usually from the list price of the recording and typically amounts to much more than the actual cost of manufacturing the recording and its container (15 percent to 20 percent for cassettes and 20 percent to 25 percent for CDs).

Contributory infringer   One whose actions make an infringement possible, who receives some benefit from the infringement.

Controlled compositions   Compositions (songs) written or owned, in whole or part, or controlled by the recording artist (or the producer in producers' agreements). The term usually appears in recording agreements between recording artists and record labels in a clause that attempts to get the artist to permit the label to use such compositions at a reduced rate.

Co-op advertising   Sometimes referred to as just "co-op money," this is advertising money given to retailers or distributors by the labels to advertise the label's records in local media. Usually this ad must feature the label product with mention of the retail location. More often than not the "co-op" is not really split between the label and retailer, but may be entirely paid for by the label.

Copublishing   Is an arrangement in which two or more music publishers own the copyrights in a given song.

Copyright   A property right in a creative work that allows the author, and those who receive rights from the author, to control reproduction and other uses of the work. Copyrights are intangible personal property.

Copyright administration   A music publishing function concerning the registration of songs for copyright, the recordation of other documents pertaining to those songs with the Copyright Office, and the licensing of those songs for various uses. The function is sometimes "farmed out" to another publisher in exchange for a percentage fee, especially when the copyright owning publisher is small and owned by a writer, artist, or producer.

Copyright Arbitration Royalty Panels (CARPs)   These are ad hoc panels designed to replace the Copyright Royalty Tribunal that was set up as part of the 1976 Copyright Revision Act. The CARPs can adjust or set compulsory royalty rates for compulsory mechanical, cable television secondary transmission, noncommercial broadcasts for nondramatic musical works, digital sound recording performances, and digital delivery of phonorecords. CARPs are only appointed when there is some dispute over a royalty distribution or a rate determination to be made.

Corporate   Often used as a derogatory term referring to recordings, those which "sound like" they were produced as products to fill a market niche instead of inspired performances by writers and recording artists, as in "corporate rock."

Counterfeit recordings   A form of record piracy whereby not only are the recordings duplicated, but also the packaging, so that the counterfeit not only sounds like, but looks like the original, legitimate recording. Counterfeit copies are sometimes so good that only someone working at the label can tell them from the legitimate copies. Sometimes they are so poorly done, with smudged ink, color registration errors, and things such as improperly printed or aligned UPC bar codes that anyone could recognize them.

Cover (band or versions)   Are recordings or performances of a song by artists and performers other than the artist who originally recorded the song. A "cover" band does mostly cover versions of songs originally recorded and performed by other artists.

Creative controls   Authority to exercise control over the creative aspects of a recording, such as selection of material to be recorded, studios to use, producer, and side musicians. Artists seek more creative controls.

Cross-collateralization   Is the practice (common in the recording industry) of using income from one source to recover advances made for a different source. For example, if an artist records an album that does not sell well, the recording advances for that album may be recovered out of royalties earned by a later album that sells well.

Deep inventory   A selection of goods covering a lot of different varieties of the same basic product. Record stores typically have fairly deep inventories of recordings.

Defaulters   Union term for people who do not pay musicians or vocalists for their performances in clubs or on recordings.

Demo   A demonstration recording made to promote an artist, songwriter, or song to an agent, manager, music publisher, or record company.

Derivative work   In copyright law, a work that is based substantially on a preexisting work or works that edit, recast, or change the form of the prior work into a new copyrightable work.

Development deal   Usually a recording contract in which a label gives an artist a small sum or perhaps an annual amount to remain obligated to sign a full recording agreement with the label. The label may want to keep the option of signing the artist while the artist works on songwriting, performance, or some other aspect that the label feels is not quite ready for master recording. Similar deals may also be offered to songwriters by music publishers.

Digital sampling   (See also *sampling*.) The electronic process whereby an audio signal is transformed into a numeric (digital) sequence that represents the level (amplitude) of the signal at various times during its duration. Those numbers are then stored in a digital form on some computer-readable device, such as a computer disc, audio tape, or compact disc. If the sampling device measures (samples) the level of the signal often enough it can then reproduce the level of the signal with the stored numbers that represent the amplitude at very close intervals of time. The closer the intervals of time, i.e., the higher the sampling frequency, the more accurate the picture of the complex audio signal can be. Compact discs, for example, have a sampling rate of 44.1 thousand times per second. The name *sample* comes from the fact that the digital representations are really only a sample of the entire signal. They are just so close together that when reproduced they sound so much like the original that the human ear cannot detect any difference.

Disc jockey   Person at a radio station who announces which recordings are being played. In the 1940s and 1950s these persons also tended to select which records were played but those decisions are usually now in the hands of a music director or program director.

Door   The revenues made from admission fees, usually at a club.

Dramatic performance   A performance of a work that tells a story. Usually associated with musical theater or opera and multiple songs, but a single song may be a dramatic performance if accompanied by other action or visuals.

Draw   Another term for an advance, more often heard in relation to exclusive songwriter agreements with music publishers, or in live entertainment where musicians performing in clubs may get a "draw" after performing for a portion of their contracted term, say three days out of a six-day engagement.

Dubbing   In copyright law, literal duplication of a prior recording. In audio engineering, taking a recorded sound and editing it into or with a preexisting recording.

Duopoly rule   The Federal Communications Rule that prohibited the same company from owning two radio stations in the same market. This rule was modified to allow ownership of AM and FM stations, then later abandoned completely.

Effective competition   A market situation in which it takes more than four firms to gain control of 60 percent of the market.

8-track tape   An audio tape with room to record eight separate "tracks" of information. Consumer 8-track tapes were endless loop tape cartridges, similar to those used in broadcasting, that contained four separate stereo programs. When the loop of tape had played all of two of the tracks (one program) a signal on the tape would cause the player to switch to playing back the next two tracks. On crudely recorded 8-tracks the program change would sometimes occur in the middle of a song.

Elasticity of demand   The percent change in quantity demanded (sold) that is brought about by a percent change in price. When the percent change in quantity demanded is greater than the change in price then the demand is said to be price elastic. When a given percentage change in price results in a smaller percentage change in quantity demanded it is said to be price *inelastic*.

End-caps The portions of record browsers (or other retail displays) located at the end of the aisles, facing the main aisles of the store.

Established artist A recording artist who has had at least one (labels would say two) successful album on a label of significant stature.

ET (Electrical transcription) A recording distributed to radio stations for the purpose of broadcast, and not for sale to the public. National advertisements, syndicated programs, and musical recordings (into the 1950s) were distributed to radio this way. The ET had higher quality audio than was available on consumer records.

Evergreen In music publishing, a song that is recorded by many artists and performed on a continuing basis for many years.

Exclusive artist A recording artist under agreement to make recordings only for one record company.

Exclusive contract Any arrangement whereby one party promises not to provide services or goods to any third party.

Exclusive license Permission to use a song or some other right that is given only to one user and may not be given to any competing user.

Exclusive songwriter A songwriter under agreement to write songs for only one publishing company.

Fair use A provision of the copyright law allowing some limited uses of works if the use is particularly beneficial to the public and does not do much harm to the copyright owner.

First sale doctrine Part of the copyright law that allows the lawful owner of a copy of a work to dispose of that copy in any way they wish. Copies may then be resold, rented, leased, or given away. There is an exception to the doctrine that allows the copyright owner to control rental of sound recordings and computer programs.

Flats Album sized (12" by 12") reproductions of the cover art of an album, usually just printed on a single sheet of cardboard or heavy paper stock used in creating record displays.

Flown Sound reinforcement, stage lighting, or other effects that are suspended from the rafters of a venue instead of being supported on the floor.

Folios Songbooks containing multiple songs usually either on a common theme or by the same artist or writer, as opposed to sheet music of single songs.

45 The 45 RPM single with one song recorded on each side.

Four walls In concert promotion a deal to rent a venue that includes only the right to use the facility with the venue providing nothing more than the "four walls," i.e., no box office, no ticket takers, no ushers, no clean up, and so on.

Free goods In recording artist contracts and record marketing, a term of art meaning recordings given away to a distributor or retailer as a method of discount. For example, the retailer may get one free copy for each nine copies that are ordered. These are to be distinguished from promotional copies, which are not meant for retail sale.

Free-standing store A record store whose walls are not attached to other stores, compared to a strip center or mall.

Front line   The label's most recent releases from their top artists. These are usually the highest priced "regular" releases.

Gate   The admission revenues from a concert. Same as *door* but the latter is usually a club term.

Gatekeeper   In communication theory, a person who decides which messages will be communicated from one channel to another. Thus, radio music directors are gatekeepers, deciding which recordings will be communicated through radio.

GATT (The General Agreement on Tariffs and Trade)   An international trade treaty that established the World Trade Organization and provides for trade sanctions for member nations that do not properly protect copyrights.

Gold   A standard of recording or music video sales set by the RIAA. Sales are certified by the RIAA at the wholesale level. A gold record must sell 500,000 units, a gold music video must sell 50,000 units. There are other "gold" standards for other kinds of video. See also *platinum*.

Good ears   A music industry term referring to the ability to tell which artists and recordings will be successful. When used by audio engineers, it refers to the ability to distinguish technical and performance nuances in the recording production process.

Grammy Awards   See *NARAS*.

Grand rights   Dramatic performance rights (see *dramatic performance*).

Guarantee   In concert promotion, the fixed amount that the artist will be paid, regardless of whether any tickets are sold.

Hard tickets   Admission tickets preprinted and distributed for sale, as compared to *soft tickets*, which are only printed at the time of sale.

Harry Fox Agency (HFA)   A collection and licensing agency created and run by the National Music Publishers Association. It was designed to serve as a clearing house for mechanical and other licensing. The agency issues on behalf of its member publishing companies mechanical, synchronization, electrical transcription, and other licenses, collects licensing fees from the record companies and other users, and distributes those collections to the appropriate publishers.

Hold   *In music publishing,* a verbal agreement between a publisher and producer not to pitch a song to other producers until the first producer decides whether to record the song. *In concert promotion,* a verbal agreement between a promoter and a venue to keep a certain date open for that promoter and not license the venue to another event for that date until the first promoter decides whether or not to use it.

Horizontal integration   An economic term describing the actions of a firm to buy out competing companies at the same level, such as one record store chain acquiring another record store chain.

Hype   Exaggerated claims as to the worth of a particular product or event. Short for *hyperbole*.

IATSE   The International Association of Theater and Stage Employees, a union for stagehands, lighting technicians, and other "behind the scenes" people who put on theatrical and concert events.

IMRA (Independent Music Retailers Association) An *ad hoc* group of record retailers who banded together to fight the labels' policies against stores selling used CDs.

In-house promotion A performance promoted by the venue itself, without any outside promoter.

Independent distributor A record wholesaler who distributes records from *independent labels.*

Independent label A record label not owned by one of the major six conglomerates or their subsidiaries. Independent labels may have their recordings distributed by one of the big six and still be referred to as "indies."

Independent producer (See also *staff producer.*) A record producer who is not on salary from a record label. Independent producers usually work on a royalty basis similar to recording artists and may also be paid fees for each recording completed.

Independent record store A record store that is not part of a chain; a "mom and pop" store.

Indie A term usually referring to an *independent label* or an *independent record store.*

Initiation fee A one-time fee to join a union, not to be confused with *dues,* which are paid on an ongoing basis.

Joint work In copyright law, a work created by two or more people with the intention that their contributions be merged into an integrated whole.

Jukebox The contemporary name for a coin-operated "record" player.

Librarian of Congress The appointed head of the Library of Congress, this person has important administrative duties for a number of the compulsory licenses in the copyright law. The Librarian is the ultimate overseer of the Copyright Office, which is part of the Library of Congress. The Librarian distributes the royalties collected through the Copyright Office and is also responsible for convening Copyright Arbitration Royalty Panels for the settlement of distribution disputes and for the establishment of certain royalty rates.

License Permission to use something, such as a song or a recording, for some particular purpose.

Lip-synch A performer pretends to be singing their song while a recording is being played, usually in motion pictures or television. This is sometimes done at concerts as well.

Liquidate reserves A recording contract term meaning that the label must pay out any *reserves for returns* that have not been accounted for with actual returns.

Listening station A kiosk or manned listening area where consumers can hear albums or singles or samples or selections.

Local (union) The organizational unit of a labor union that covers a particular city or geographic area.

Logging The practice of keeping track of individual songs or recordings played or performed, usually referring to the performing rights organizations.

Long-form video   Usually a video recording of a concert that includes a significant number of songs.

Loss leader   Any product sold below cost in order to attract customers into a store.

LP   The "long playing" 33 1/3 RPM disc phonograph recording, introduced in the 1950s, which usually contained eight to ten songs.

Megastore   A very large record store, typically over 20,000 square feet, that usually carries recordings, home video, computer software, and books.

Major label   A term, probably somewhat out of date, used to refer to a label owned by one of the big six that had its "own" distribution system. Now many small labels are owned by the big six and, therefore, technically have their own distribution because the distribution is owned by the same corporate parent.

Majors   The "majors" refers to the six recording/entertainment conglomerates.

Manufacturing clause   A part of the copyright law that requires that copies sold in the United States have specific permission of the U.S. copyright owner.

MAP (Minimum Advertised Price)   A price set by a label to discourage retailers from selling recordings below their cost. Most labels will cut off some advertising funds for a retailer that advertises that label's albums below the MAP.

Margin   The amount of revenue left from the sale of a product after deducting the cost of the item sold.

Marketing concept   The creation and delivery of a product or service that will satisfy consumer needs and allow a profit to be made.

Masters   The recordings from which other recordings are later going to be made or duplicated. May refer to a multitrack master, a stereo master, or a duplicating master.

Mechanical license   Permission from the copyright owner of a musical composition to manufacture and distribute copies of the composition embodied in sound recordings.

Mechanical royalties   Payments made from record labels to music publishers for the right to reproduce copies of songs (nondramatic musical compositions) in the recordings made by the labels. The term relates back to the 1909 copyright act, when Congress was creating a new right for music publishers that would give them the right to control recordings of their compositions in piano roll or recorded form. Player pianos and "talking machines" (phonographs/gramophones) were primarily regarded as mechanical devices on which the composition could be reproduced or performed. The term still applies to such rights, even though new devices may be less mechanical and more electronic in nature.

MEIEA (Music and Entertainment Industry Educators Association)   An organization of people who teach audio and music business courses, mostly at colleges and universities, but also some trade school teachers and related professionals.

Mid-line   A label's record albums that sell for about two-thirds to 75 percent of the SRLP of *front line* albums. (See also *budget line*.)

MIDI (Musical Instrument Digital Interface) A computer communications protocol designed to let synthesizers, controllers, and sequencers from different manufacturers communicate with each other. Now also used as a control language for lighting and other equipment as well.

Mom and Pop store A single store, usually a sole proprietorship, that is not part of a chain.

MOR (Middle-of-the-Road) Refers to pop music aimed at older audiences. May specifically refer to recording artists popular in the 1940s and 1950s who were not rock, R&B, or country, or a radio format playing recordings by those performers.

MSRP (Manufacturer's Suggested Retail Price) A term often used in contracts as a basis for computing a recording artist's royalties as a percentage of MSRP as opposed to wholesale price. (Same as SRLP.)

MTV (Music Television) The music video cable television channel launched in 1981 by Warner Communications.

NAIRD (The National Association of Independent Record Distributors) The trade association for indie distributors and labels.

NAMM (The National Association of Music Merchants) The trade organization for music store owners. Music instrument manufacturers are associate members.

NARAS (National Academy of Recording Arts and Sciences) Also known as the Recording Academy. Organization for creative people associated with the production of recordings, including performers, engineers, producers, graphic designers, and more. NARAS gives the annual *Grammy Awards* to recognize excellence in creative achievement in recordings.

NARM (The National Association of Recording Merchandisers) The trade association for all record retailers, and distributors. The labels are associate members.

Niche marketing Finding a small group of people who will purchase the product for sale rather than trying to sell to a mass market of a significant percentage of all consumers, for example, a record store selling only jazz recordings is niche marketing.

NMPA (The National Music Publishers' Association) Trade organization for music publishers. Formerly the Music Publishers Protective Association.

Nondramatic performance Performance of a single song in such a way that it does not tell any particular story; usually any performance of a single song that is not part of an opera or musical is nondramatic unless it tells a story accompanied by action or visuals. Nondramatic performances are the only kind licensed by the performing rights organizations (ASCAP, BMI, and SESAC).

Nonexclusive license Permission to use a work, such as a song or recording, where that same permission may also be given to other users. Performance licenses and mechanical licenses are nonexclusive.

Nonreturnable A term usually applied to an advance that does not have to be given back to the provider, even if no royalties are ever earned. The advance is therefore not a debt. Advances are usually recoupable, but nonreturnable.

Notice   In copyright law the copyright notice placed on published copies of works.

Oligopoly   A market situation in which there are only a few firms competing in the market. A "few" could be anywhere from two or three to twenty.

One-nighter   A performance engagement for only one night. Also known as a "one-night stand."

One-stop   A kind of distributor who sells all records from all labels to retailers.

Out-of-the-box   A radio term for adding a record to a playlist as soon as it is received, usually reserved for new releases by hot artists.

Overdub   An audio engineering term meaning to record an additional part along with a previously recorded part.

Packaging deduction (See *Container charge.*)

Parallel imports   Copies of works lawfully made outside of a country for distribution outside of that country but then imported back into the country of origin and sold alongside copies manufactured in the country of origin.

Pay-for-play   Refers to the practice of some popular clubs, particularly in Los Angeles, of having the performer pay to use the facility. The performer hopes to attract attention from label and other music industry professionals.

Payola   The practice of paying someone to perform a particular song or recording. Historically, music publishers paid performers to sing their songs. More recently it refers to attempts by labels to make undisclosed payments to radio stations or disk jockeys to play their recordings. The latter practice is illegal.

Per-program use (or license)   Permission to use a single recording or song on a one-time basis, as compared to a *blanket license.*

Perform publicly   A term of art in the copyright act meaning to perform a work at a place open to the public, or at a place where a substantial number of people outside the normal circle of a family and its circle of social acquanitences is gathered, or to broadcast a work for public reception.

Performance right   The right to perform a work publicly. Usually the right to perform a song, but the term can also apply to limited performance situations in which sound recordings are digitally transmitted by background music services.

Performance royalty   The royalty paid to songwriters and music publishers for public performance rights. The term can also apply in limited situations to royalties paid to record companies for the public performance of sound recordings by digital transmission on background music services.

Personal manager   An artist's representative who works closely with the artist at all stages and usually for all purposes to develop the artist's career.

Personality folio   A songbook featuring songs as recorded by a particular artist or writer.

Phonogram   The term most often used internationally for sound recordings, same as *phonorecords.*

Phonorecords   Tangible objects such as tapes, compact discs, or vinyl discs in/on which a sound recording is embodied.

Piracy   Unauthorized duplications of sound recordings in which the person or organization literally dubs a copy of the recording and sells a copy with identical sounds on it. Piracy is usually distinguished from *counterfeiting,* although the latter is a form of piracy.

Pitch   To promote a song to a music publisher or producer, or an artist to a label.

Platinum   A standard for measuring sales of recordings or music videos. The RIAA certifies sales at the wholesale level of 1,000,000 recordings or 100,000 music videos and for each equal amount after that. Thus an album selling more than two million copies is "multiplatinum."

Play-or-pay   *(See also pay or play.)* A clause in a recording artist's contract meaning the label can either have the artist *play* for a recording session, or simply *pay* them scale wages as if a session were held and fulfill their entire obligation to the artist.

Point-of-purchase materials (P-O-P materials)   Advertising and display materials intended to be used/displayed in a retail location that sells the merchandise advertised. A poster for a record album is P-O-P material distributed to record stores.

Point-of-sale   Literally the cash register or other device where the sale of an item is recorded and the payment made.

Power of attorney   A contractual right to act on someone's behalf in a way that legally binds that person to obligations entered into by the "attorney" on behalf of the person represented.

Prima facie evidence   A legal term meaning evidence that is sufficient on its face to make a case or prove a point. A copyright registration is *prima facie* evidence of the validity of the copyright and other information on the registration form. It would then have to be up to the other party to prove otherwise.

PRO   Performing Rights Organization. Not a formal term, but one used for convenience in discussing any or all such organizations that license performance rights and pay performance royalties to songwriters and music publishers.

Producer   In recording, the person in charge of all aspects of the recording process.

Professional manager   The person at a music publishing company who is in charge of finding new songs and songwriters, who may also negotiate special uses such as commercials or motion pictures.

Progressive   A radio format, initially rock, playing longer versions of records and other records and artists not usually heard on Top 40 formats.

Project studio   A recording studio, usually owned by an artist or producer, that is used mainly to make recordings for that particular artist or producer and is not rented out to outsiders.

Promotion man   Term applied to record label person whose job it is to get radio stations to play records released by the label.

Promotional copies   Copies of a recording given away to radio stations for the purpose of airplay or as giveaways to listeners, or given to album reviewers to expose the record to the public.

Public domain (P.D.)   A term of art regarding the status of works whose copyrights that have expired or that were not subject to copyright protection. Public domain works may be used by anyone without obtaining licenses or clearances because P.D. works have no copyrights.

Public performance (See *perform publicly.*)

Publishing administration A deal in which one music publisher, usually a small artist or producer-owned company, has a larger music publisher issue licenses and collect royalties in exchange for a percentage of the money collected.

Rack jobber A distributor who buys records from branches or independent distributors and services the record departments in mass merchandiser stores or other nonrecord stores.

Rack locations Those stores that have rack jobber-serviced record departments.

Rating A radio station's percentage of the total available listeners at any given time or over a given time span (cf. *share*).

Recording Trust Fund Also called the Music Performance Trust Fund, this fund is established by the labels, which pay a small percentage of the list price of recordings sold into an AFM fund. That fund is then used to pay musicians who perform for free concerts for the general public. The idea of the fund is to make more live music available to more people.

Recording artist A person who makes phonograph recordings under a contractual arrangement with a record label whereby the label pays the performer a percentage royalty based on sales of the recordings, distinguished from a side musician or background vocalist who does not receive a royalty.

Recording engineer A type of *audio engineer* whose job it is to operate equipment in a recording studio to capture and reproduce sounds being made for a recording.

Recording fund A kind of advance whereby the record label designates a fixed amount of money available to produce a master recording. Usually the artist and producer are allowed to keep any money that has not been used to create the finished master.

Recoupable Recoverable out of royalties actually earned or otherwise due. Advances are usually recoupable but nonreturnable, meaning that they are *not a debt* which would have to be repaid whether or not any royalties were earned.

Recurrent Radio programming term for a recent current hit. A recurrent is not a hit at the present time, but is still popular enough to play fairly regularly, compared to a current hit or an "oldie."

Release A recording made available to the public, or to make a recording available to the public.

Release date The day designated by the record label when a recording is available to the public.

Renegotiate A term used in the recording industry to refer to the practice of artists who are under a recording agreement and use their substantial success as an opportunity to redefine the terms of the agreement.

Reserve for returns An amount of royalties or the royalties that would be paid for a certain amount of sales that are not paid to a recording artist because records are shipped to retailers and wholesalers subject to being returned at a later date. Artists are not paid for recordings that are returned. (See also *liquidate reserves.*)

Returns   Records sent back to the distributor or label because they have not been sold at the retail level. Returns may include defective merchandise as well as simple overstock.

Reversion   A term usually seen in songwriter–publisher agreements referring to the writer's right to recapture the copyrights in the songs. There is a statutory reversion right called the *Termination Right (q.v.)* in the Copyright Act. The reversion may also be strictly contractual.

RIAA (The Recording Industry Association of America)   The trade association for record labels and manufacturers.

Rider   An attachment to an agreement. In concert promotion, the artist spells out specific requirements for the performance in a rider, such as sound, lights, size of stage, power requirements, kind and amount of food, and other considerations. There may be a technical rider and a separate food rider with requirements that the promoter is expected to meet.

Right to work   A provision of the laws of some states, particularly in the South, that prohibits unions from requiring that all employees of a particular firm belong to that union.

Rotation   Radio programming term referring to a group of records that is played through in a certain period of time. A station may have several rotations, such as a "power rotation" that is played through entirely every couple of hours and an oldies rotation that is played through every few days.

Royalties   Payments to writers or performers due from the sale of copies, performance, or other individual uses of their works.

Sampling   Commonly understood as the process of capturing a portion of a recording via some digital recorder so that the sound in a previous recording can be used to create part of a new recording. The sampled signal is manipulated through signal processing or computer sequencing to form an integral part of the rhythm, melody, lyrics, or overall production of the new recording. The process of sampling is important because the sounds can be manipulated much more than an analog recording. (See also *digital sampling.*)

Scale wages   Payments to musicians or vocalists at the amount (scale) required by the union.

Self-contained   Usually refers to performing artists who write their own material, it can also refer to a band that does not require any additional musicians for their performances.

78   The 78 RPM record, usually with one song recorded on each side, that was the standard record from its introduction until the 1950s, when the 45 and LP formats were introduced.

SESAC   The smallest of the three main performing rights organizations in the United States. SESAC used to stand for Society of European Stage Authors and Composers, but now does not have any particular meaning beyond its letters as the name of the organization.

Share   The percentage of people actually listening to any radio station that are listening to a particular station. Thus, if a station has a 15 percent share, 15 percent of the people listening to radio at that time are listening to that station. The other 85 percent are listening to other radio stations.

Shed   Another term for an outdoor amphitheater.

Shelf price   The usual price at which comparable albums are sold in a given store. This is usually not the SRLP but is often below that. To be distinguished from a sale price.

Short-form video   A music video, usually just containing one song.

Shortfall   A kind of *tour support* with the label making up any difference between an agreed-on amount per performance and the amount the artist actually makes per performance.

Showcase   A performance, usually in a small club, designed to promote a performer to radio programmers, label A&R people, music publishing people, or some other industry audience, as opposed to the general public.

Shrinkage   Loss of inventory due to factors not accounted for, such as theft, damage, or accounting errors.

Side   In recording contracts, a recording of a single song, but it can also be used in a nonlegal sense to refer to all of the songs on one side of an LP or cassette or single.

Single   A single composition released by itself on a recording, or with only one other composition. CD-5 or maxi singles usually have four or five cuts on them.

Small rights   Nondramatic public performance rights, i.e., the kind licensed by ASCAP, BMI, and SESAC.

SMPTE (The Society of Motion Picture and Television Engineers)   An organization for the technical people associated with the production of television programs and motion pictures. It includes people in multimedia productions. Audio engineers often belong to this and *AES*.

Soft tickets   Tickets for an event that are not printed in advance of sale, but are printed by a computer at the time of sale.

Song plugger   Person who works for a music publishing company whose job it is to get the song recorded, performed, and used in other ways.

Sound-alike   A recording made to sound as much like the one by the original artists as possible. It is a new recording, but the musicians and singers imitate the sounds on the previous recording.

Sound recording   A kind of copyrightable work in which sounds created by various sources are captured, or "fixed" in some tangible medium such as tape or disk. These works are to be distinguished from the underlying works, such as musical compositions or dramatic works that are recorded, and the material objects, or "phonorecords" in/on which the recordings are fixed. Sound recordings do not include sound accompanying motion pictures; those recordings are part of the motion picture copyright.

SoundScan   The company that collects point-of-sale information from the UPC bar code scanners at a variety of record retail outlets to sell sales pattern information to the labels or other parties.

Soundtrack The audio, usually musical, accompaniment to a motion picture or television program.

SPARS (The Society of Professional Recording Services) A trade organization for recording studio owners and tape and CD replicators.

Special payments fund A fund administered by the AFM composed of payments from record labels based on a small percentage of the price of recordings sold. The fund is distributed to musicians on an annual basis based on the amount of master recording sessions on which the musician had played over the previous year.

Sponsored tour A live appearance tour where part of the costs and probably some advertising is underwritten by a third party who uses the appearances of the artist to promote and sell nonartist-related merchandise, such as soft drinks or clothing.

SRDS (Standard Rate and Data Service) A series of publications that lists media outlets, their facilities, policies, and advertising rates.

SRLP (See *MSRP*.)

Staff writer A songwriter who works under an exclusive agreement with a music publisher, usually on a weekly or monthly advance.

Statutory rate A term usually applied to the compulsory mechanical royalty rate. Originally, the rate was set by Congress in the 1909 Copyright Act and later the 1976 Copyright Act, hence the term "statutory." Later, when changes of the rate were left up to the Copyright Royalty Tribunal, and later still the Librarian of Congress and Copyright Arbitration Royalty Panels, it was still referred to as a "statutory" rate.

Stiff A record that does not sell well at all or gets hardly any radio airplay.

Strip center A shopping center with stores spread out in a row, usually along a main road, with common walls, and no enclosed pedestrian area.

Superstore A very large record store, typically 12,000 to 20,000 square feet.

Synchronization right The right of the owner of a musical composition copyright to use the composition in time relation to visual images, such as in movies or television shows, or perhaps in multimedia.

Take A recorded attempt by the recording artists or musicians at a complete performance of a song.

Technically acceptable In recording contracts, this means that a master is of high enough quality to be suitable for release to the public. This is distinguished from *commercially acceptable*, which implies a higher standard, and the label's judgment as to whether a particular recording will be successful commercially as opposed to artistically.

Termination rights Statutory rights of authors (or certain of their heirs) to end transfers of copyrights and nonexclusive licenses during a five-year period beginning after thirty-five years from the date of transfer and running through the fortieth year. (If the transfer includes the right to publish, then the five-year period starts after forty years after the date of transfer or thirty-five years after the date of first publication, whichever is earlier.) Thus, the author can "recapture" the transferred copyrights.

Tight oligopoly An *oligopoly* where four firms control 60 percent or more of the market.

TNN (The Nashville Network) A cable television channel devoted to country music and other "country" lifestyle programming.

Top 40 The radio format that plays the forty most popular recordings in the broadcaster's market. Used generically to refer to any format that plays the most popular recordings, including *CHR*.

Tour support Usually monetary support for new recording artists to help them make personal appearance performances. Tour support is often given when the label believes that live appearances will help sell recordings. It is usually a *recoupable advance*.

Track A recording of one particular instrument or vocalist that is separate from the other performances on the session for that song. A segment of the recording medium that can be recorded and played back separately from the others for that song or can be used to keep track of radio airplay.

Trades The magazines devoted to a particular business. In the recording industry, *Billboard, CashBox, Radio & Records*, the *Gavin Report, Performance, Pollstar*, and *Variety* are among the important trade publications.

Transcription license Permission to make a recording of a song when copies of the recording are not intended for distribution to the public. Radio stations frequently receive transcription recordings for broadcast purposes of advertisements or programs.

Turntable hit A recording that receives lots of radio airplay, but does not generate many sales.

UPC (See *Bar code*.)

Venue The place where a live appearance happens. It could be a club, a theater, an auditorium, a stadium, or an open field.

Vertical integration A market situation in which a firm owns more than one portion of the total distribution chain from manufacturer to consumer. A record label that owned a pressing plant is an example of vertical integration, as is a distributor that owns record stores.

VH-1 The cable television channel programmed to viewers who prefer a wider range of music and softer music than programmed by the rock/urban oriented MTV.

Videogram A video recording of a motion picture, music video, or other visual work. Usually the term refers to videograms that are manufactured and distributed for consumer purchase.

Work dues Dues paid to the union by performers based on their earnings from live appearances.

Work made for hire   In copyright law, a work made by an employee within the scope of employment, or a commissioned work of certain kinds if the parties agree in writing that the work is to be considered for hire. The employer or commissioning party owns the copyrights in works made for hire.

World Trade Organization (WTO)   The international trade organization created in 1995 by the General Agreement on Tariffs and Trade treaty of 1994. WTO members promise to provide "Berne Level" protection to copyrights and may be subject to trade sanctions from the organization and other members for failure to do so. Major disputes between the United States and China over China's lack of protection for recordings, motion pictures, and computer software has excluded China from the organization.

Bibliography

"4 Mill Judgment Against David Heilman to Bring Appeal," *Billboard*, 5 January 1980: 3.

29 Stat. 487 (1897).

"57th Statistical Issue and Marketing Report," *Merchandising*, March 1979: 31.

"73rd Annual Statistical Surveys and Report," *Dealerscope Merchandising,* July 1995: 35.

"96 Tour Slate Is Heavy on Festivals, Classic Acts." *Billboard,* 13 April 1996: 97.

1909 Copyright Act, Title 17 U.S. Code §1(e).

"1995 Studio Business Operations Survey," *Pro Sound News*, September 1995: 18–20.

"1994 Pro Sound News Recording Studio Operations Survey," *Pro Sound News*, September 1994: 28.

"A & R—A Week in the Life," *Musician*, August 1994: 31.

"ABC Radio, SoundScan to Feed Sales Info to Affiliates," *Billboard*, 16 April 1994: 85.

Ackerman, Paul. "New Income Studies Face Publishers as Sheet Music Income Drops," *Billboard*, 15 January 1955: 1.

The Agreement on Trade-Related Aspects of Intellectual Property Rights (TRIPS), Art. 14, 65(2), General Greement on Tariffs and Trade, 1994 Uruguay Round.

Alexander, Peter J. "Entropy and Popular Culture: Product Diversity in the Popular Music Recording Industry," 61 *American Sociological Review* (1996): 171.

"American Radio Merging with Henry Broadcasting," *Broadcasting and Cable*, 25 March 1996: 14.

American Society of Composers, Authors and Publishers. "Music for Money" (pamphlet). New York: ASCAP, 1996.

Annual Report of the Register of Copyrights, 1994, (1995): 34, 36.

Atwood, Brett. "Multimedia in Stores," *Billboard*, 30 March 1996: 59.

_____. "Indie Film Soundtracks Help Expose Modern Rock Acts," *Billboard*, 8 October 1994: 8.

Atwood, Brett and Geoff Burpee, "War on Piracy Continues in China," *Billboard*, 20 July 1996: 1.

Audio Home Recording Act of 1992, P.L. 102–563, 106 Stat. 4237 (October 28, 1992), codified in 17 U.S.C. §§ 1001 *et seq.*

285

Ayre, Rick. "Five Virtual Record Stores," *PC Magazine*, 28 May 1996: 56.

"Band Is Held Not Liable in Suicides of Two Fans," *New York Times*, The Arts section, 25 August 1990.

"BDS, CMR to Merge Services," *Mediaweek*, 23 January 1995: 41.

Belinfante, Alexander and Reuben R. Davis, Jr., "Estimating the Demand for Record Albums," *Review of Business and Economic Research*, (Winter 1978–1979): 47, 51.

Bessman, Jim. "At the Heart of Cajun Country, Floyd's Record Shop has Finger on Region's Pulse," *Billboard*, 20 January 1996: 61.

_____. "Indie Distributor Changes More Than Name," *Billboard*, 20 May 1995: 47.

"Billboard Debuts Piece Counts on Two Music Charts," *Billboard*, 25 May 1991: 1.

"Billboard Examining Hot 100 Revamp," *Billboard*, 31 August 1996: 133.

"The Bionic Radio," *Billboard*, 21 May 1977: RS-71 (Century of Recorded Sound Special Issue).

BMG Music v. Perez, 952 F.2d 318 (9th Cir. 1991).

Boehlert, Eric. "Pay to Play," *Rolling Stone*, 22 August 1996: 34.

_____. "Is Moshing Murder?" *Rolling Stone,* 11 July 1996: 19.

_____. "Play-by-Play Account of Pearl Jam Saga," *Billboard*, 8 July 1995: 85.

_____. "Labels Put New Spin on Indie Promo; Many Eye BDS Data for Payment Plans," *Billboard*, 22 January 1994: 1.

Boehm, Eric. "For Those with Cash EMI Has the Flash," *Variety,* 12 August 1996: 7.

_____. "Rap Braces for Big Chill," *Variety*, 6 January 1992: 89.

Boswell, William R. *Life on the Road*. Needham Heights, MA: Ginn Press, 1991.

Borzillo, Carrie. "Unable to Compete with Chains, Indies Offer Alternatives," *Billboard*, 30 March 1996: 66.

"Both Retailer, Label Claims Backed by Used-CD Survey," *Billboard*, 2 October 1993: 4, 112.

Brabec, Jeffrey and Todd Brabec. *Music, Money and Success*. New York: Schirmer Books, 1994.

Braheny, John. *The Craft and Business of Song Writing*. Cincinnati, OH: Writer's Digest Books, 1988.

Bright Tunes Music Corp. v. Harrisongs Music, Ltd., 420 F.Supp. 177 (S.D.N.Y. 1976).

Broadcasting & Cable Yearbook, 1986 and 1995.

Broadcast Music, Inc. v. Columbia Broadcasting System, Inc., 99 S.Ct. 1551, at 1562–1563 (1979).

"Brooks Delivers Used-CD Ultimatum," *Billboard*, 10 July 1993: 6.

Burnett, Robert, *The Global Jukebox*. New York: Routledge, 1996.

_____. "The Implications of Ownership Changes on Concentration and Diversity in the Phonogram Industry," *Communication Research*, December 1992: 749.

"Cake, Candles Not Included," *Time*, 31 October 1988: 59.

Campbell v. Acuff-Rose Music, Inc., 114 S.Ct. 1164 (1994).

"Can Retail's Shaky Health Be Cured?" *Billboard*, 23 December 1995:1.

Capitol Records, Inc. v. Mercury Record Corp., 221 F.2d 657 (2nd Cir. 1955).

Carter, T. Barton, et al., *The First Amendment and The Fourth Estate* (6th ed.). Westbury, NY: Foundation Press, 1994.

Caves, Richard. *American Industry: Structure, Conduct and Performance* (6th ed., 1987).

CBS Records. "Today's Singles Buyer," distributed at the NARM Convention.

"CD Prices Start to Tumble," *Billboard*, 7 July 1984: 1.

"CD Prices: Why so High?" *Consumer Reports*, February 1996: 17.

"Chancellor Agrees to Buy 8 Radio Stations," *New York Times*, 16 May 1996: C4-national.

"Chart Histories," *Billboard 100th Anniversary Issue 1984–1994*, 1 November 1994: 262–273.

"China and the GATT Reaching an Impasse," *The Economist*, 6 August 1994: 52.

"China Raids Pirate Plants Ahead of U.S. Talks," *Renter European Community Report*, 15 Feb. 1995 (LEXIS).

Christman, Ed. "2 Deals Alter Rackjobbing Landscape," *Billboard*, 12 February 1994: 5.

_____. "3 Big Chains Test Used-CD Waters," *Billboard*, 5 December 1992: 1.

_____. "Alliance Breathing Easy after Failed Metromedia Merger," *Billboard*, 18 May 1996: 52.

_____. "Alliance Shifts Distrib Gears: Trans World Fills No. 2 Slot," *Billboard*, 5 February 1994: 64.

_____. "Alliance to Acquire Red Ant Entertainment," *Billboard*, 24 August 1996: 3.

_____. "Blockbuster to Add Super Club to Expanding Retail Portfolio," *Billboard*, 16 October 1993: 5.

_____. "The Brass Tacks of Camelot Music's Financial Restructuring," *Billboard*, 3 February 1996: 62.

_____. "Closings Reveal Chinks in Chains' Long-Term Strategies," *Billboard*, 28 October 1995: 66.

_____. "D.C.-Area Indie-Intensive Record Shop is Ready to GO!" *Billboard*, 5 June 1993: 73.

_____. "Disney Records Pulls Out of Record Clubs," *Billboard*, 3 February 1996: 59.

_____. "EMI–Capitol Creates Marketing Arm," *Billboard*, 13 April 1996: 5.

_____. "MAP Policies Bring Price War Cease-fire," *Billboard*, 1 June 1996: 3.

_____. "MAPing the Route to Consistent Pricing," *Billboard*, 30 March 1996: 59.

_____. "Million-Dollar Times Square Gamble by Virgin Megastore," *Billboard*, 4 May 1996: 54.

_____. "More Downsizing at Camelot," *Billboard*, 13 April 1996: 68.

_____. "Musicland to Shutter More Stores," *Billboard*, 20 April 1996: 72.

_____. "PGD Reduces Boxlot Prices, Boosting Retain Profit Margins," *Billboard*, 23 December 1995: 5.

_____. "The Positive Sounds of Hear Music's Expansion," *Billboard*, 4 March 1995: 64.

_____. "WEA Remains Top U.S. Music Distributor in '95," *Billboard*, 20 January 1996: 55.

_____. "WEA's '94 Market Share Dips Slightly, But Still Top U.S. Distributor with 21.1%," *Billboard*, 21 January 1995: 54.

Christman, Ed and Don Jeffrey. "Record Clubs Focus of Closed-Door Meeting," *Billboard*, 23 March 1996: 1.

Christman, Ed, et al. "Discount Singles Spark U.S. Cost/Benefit Debate," *Billboard*, 31 August 1996: 1, 133.

_____. "WEA Reduces Wholesale Prices on CDs," *Billboard*, 13 March 1993: 9.

Clark-Meads, Jeff, et al. "Thorn EMI Demerger Proceeding Smoothly," *Billboard*, 31 August 1996: 1.

_____. "10-year Dispute Over Japanese Record Rental Business Settled," *Billboard*, 29 April 1995: 5.

_____. "HMV's 75th Year Marked by Celebration, Expansion," *Billboard*, 16 March 1996: 1, 116.

_____. "IFPI: '95 Piracy Stable; Russia and China Cited," *Billboard*, 18 May 1996: 8.

_____. "No longer banned, parallel imports cause woes for EU," *Billboard*, 5 August 1995: 1.

_____. "Piracy Fighters in China Fear Killings," *Billboard*, 23 September 1995: 9.

_____. "PolyGram Takes Globe via London," *Billboard*, 22 July 1995: 36.

Code of Federal Regulations, Title 37, § 201.19.

Cohen, Jane and Bob Grossweiner. "1995 Year End Analysis," *Performance*, 29 December 1995: 8.

"Columbia and WEA Top Charts for 3rd Straight Year," *Billboard*, 17 February 1993: 1.

Columbia Broadcasting System, Inc. v. Scorpio Music Distributors, Inc., 569 F.Supp. 47 (D.C. Pa. 1983).

Community for Creative Non-Violence v. Reid, 490 U.S. 730 (1989).

Cooper, Jay L. "Current Trends in Recording Contract Negotiations," *NARAS Institute Journal*, 2, (1978): 14.

Copyright Act of 1909, § 10.

"Copyright Term Extension Act of 1995," H989 and S483, 104th Cong., 1st Sess. (1995).

Cosola, Mary. "Going Global," *Electronic Musician*, December 1996: 52.

"Court Affirms Ruling on David Heilman," *Billboard*, 7 November 1981: 3.

Criminal Penalties for Copyright Infringement, P.L. 102–561, 106 Stat. 4233 (1992).

Cronin, Peter. "Country Labels, Radio Adjust to Reality of Boom," *Billboard*, 29 April 1995: 1.

Cusic, Don. *Music in the Market*. Bowling Green, OH: Popular Press, 1996.

_____. *The Sound of Light: A History of Gospel Music*. Bowling Green, OH: Popular Press, 1990.

Daft, Richard L. *Management*. New York: Dryden Press, 1988.

Daley, Charles P., Patrick Henry, and Ellen Ryder. *The Magazine Publishing Industry*. Boston: Allyn & Bacon, 1997.

Daley, Dan. "Music Studios Face Challenges of the '90s," *Pro Sound News*, April 1996: 1.

_____. "The Big Shift: When Personal Studios Go Public," *Mix*, February, 1996: 98.

_____. "Studios Develop Coping Skills as Margins Shrink," *Pro Sound News*, February 1996: 14.

Dannen, Fredric. *Hit Men*. New York: Vintage Books, 1990.

Davis, Clive. *Clive: Inside the Record Business*. New York: Ballantine Books, 1994.

Davis, Sheila. *Successful Lyric Writing*. Cincinnati, OH: Writer's Digest Books, 1988.

"The Day Radio Died," *Music Retailer*, April 1975: 29.

DeCurtis, Anthony. "Concert Insurance Crisis," *Rolling Stone*, 11 September 1986: 15.

DeFleur, Melvin L. and Everette E. Dennis. *Understanding Mass Communication* (4th ed.). Boston, MA: Houghton Mifflin, 1991.

Denisoff, R. Serge. *Tarnished Gold*. New Brunswick, NJ: Transaction Books, 1986.

_____. *Solid Gold*. New Brunswick, NJ: Transaction Books, 1975.

Derr, Joshua. "Year End Charts," *Performance*, 29 December 1995: 9.

Dezzani, Mark. "BMG Buys Europe's Last 'Major' Indie," *Billboard*, 20 August 1994: 38.

Diamond, Michael. "Music Companies Try to Crack Down on Sales of Used CDs," *Gannett News Service*, June 17, 1993 (LEXIS).

DiConstanzo, Frank. "Print Music Strikes Profitable Chord," *Billboard*, 24 September 1994: 64.

DiMartino, Dave. "Tashjian Pleads Guilty to Payola," *Billboard*, 3 June 1989: 1.

_____. "Lawyers Mull 'Legal Payola,'" *Billboard*, 9 January 1988: 5.

"Dispute between Music Companies and Record Store Owners Over Sale of Used CDs Is Settled," 15 *Entertainment Law Reporter*, April 1994: 26 (LEXIS).

Dranov, Paula. *Inside the Music Publishing Industry*. White Plains, NY: Knowledge Industry Publications, 1980.

Drucker, Peter F. *Managing for the Future*. New York: Truman Talley Books, 1992.

Duffy, Thom. "N.Y. Says Concert Ads Deceived Public on Tix Pricing," *Billboard*, 8 August 1992: 10.

"Dutch Conglomerate VNU to Purchase BPI Communications," *Billboard*, 22 January 1994: 3.

Elsemere Music, Inc. v. National Broadcasting Co., 482 F.Supp. 741 (S.D.N.Y. 1980).

Ennis, Philip H. *The Seventh Stream: The Emergence of Rocknroll in American Popular Music*. Hanover, NH: Wesleyan University Press, 1992.

Farber, Donald S. (ed.). *Entertainment Industry Contracts: Negotiating and Drafting Guide*. New York: Matthew Bender, 1989.

Flanigan, Bill. "We Three Kings," *Musician,* April 1991: 52, 59.

Fleming, Charles, and Kevin Zimmerman, "Charts Off Course," *Daily Variety*, 31 December 1990: 1.

Flick, Larry. "A&R Role Expanding for Publishers," *Billboard*, 5 November 1994: 18.

"The Folio 500," *Folio*, 1 July 1996: 52.

Frahn, Harrison. "CompuServe Settles Infringement Charges and Agrees to New Electronic Licensing," *The Exclusive Right*, 1, 1 (1996): 3.

Frascogna, Xavier M., Jr. and H. Lee Hetherington. *Successful Artist Management*. New York: Billboard Books, 1990.

Frith, Simon. "The Industrialization of Popular Music," in *Popular Music and Communication, Second Edition*, (James Lull, ed.). Newbury Park, CA: Sage Publications, 1992.

_____. "Critical Response," in Deanna Campbell Robinson, et al., *Music at the Margins*. Newbury Park, CA: Sage Publications (1991): 287.

Garofalo, Reebee. "How Autonomous Is Relative: Popular Music, the Social Formation and Cultural Struggle," *Popular Music*, January 1987: 77.

Gehman, Nev. "The Year's Music Roundup," *Billboard*, 2 January 1954: 11.

_____. "Poll Clocks 35 Also-Rans for Every Solid-Selling Disk Hit," *Billboard*, 3 January 1953: 1.

Gett, Steve. "Promoters Balk at Flat Fees," *Billboard*, 4 October 1986: 1.

Goldstein, Seth. "Managing Ever-Changing Sell-Thru," *Billboard*, 6 January 1996: 43.

_____. "Direct Moves Pinch Levy Home Ent.," *Billboard*, 18 July 1992: 6.

Gore, Tipper. *Raising PG Children in an X-Rated Society*. Nashville, TN: Abingdon Press, 1987.

Grand Upright Music Limited v. Warner Brothers Records, Inc., 780 F.Supp. 182 (S.D.N.Y. 1991).

Gray, Herman. *Producing Jazz*. Philadelphia, PA: Temple University Press, 1988.

Greene, Kelly. "Local Retailers Win Settlement in Battle Over Used CDs," *Business Journal-Charlotte*, 11 July 1994: section 1, p. 1 (LEXIS).

Greenfield, Robert and Bill Graham. *Bill Graham Presents* (1992).

Grunwald, Edgar A. "Program Production History 1927 and 1937," in *Variety's 1937–1938 Radio Directory*. New York: Variety (1937).

Gubernick, Lisa. "We Are a Society of Collectors," *Forbes*, 24 July 1989: 80.

"A Guide to Profitability, " *Music Retailer*, July 1975: 34, 50.

Hadler, Pat. "Rap, Vinyl Fans Boogie to Columbus' Groove Shack," *Billboard*, 7 January 1995: 78.

Halloran, Mark. *The Musician's Business and Legal Guide*. Englewood Cliffs, NJ: Prentice-Hall, 1991.

Hamlin, Jesse. "Big Labels Declare War on Used CDs," *San Francisco Chronicle*, 16 June 1993, Daily Datebook Section, D1 (LEXIS).

Haring, Bruce. "Levy Conviction Upheld by Court," *Billboard,* 11 November 1989: 105.

Henn, Harry G. "The Compulsory License Provision of the U.S. Copyright Law," *Study No. 5 for the Senate Committee on the Judiciary, Copyright Law Revision, Studies Prepared for the Subcommittee on Patents, Trademarks, and Copyrights*, 86th Cong., 2d Sess. (1960).

Herbert v. Shanley, 242 U.S. 591 (1917).

Heuton, Cheryl. "The Large Get Larger: SFX Purchase of Liberty Continues Run on Stations in Big Markets," *Mediaweek*, 4 December 1995.

Hinkley, David. "Suit Calls CD Prices a Steal—for Companies," *New York Daily News*, 11 July 1966, New York Now section: 2 (LEXIS).

Hirsch, Paul. *The Structure of the Popular Music Industry*. Ann Arbor, MI: Institute for Social Research, University of Michigan, 1969.

Holland, Bill. "Bootleg Seizures Up Under Piracy Act," *Billboard*, 31 August 1996: 1.

_____. "Chinese Piracy Still Rampant," *Billboard*, 27 April 1996: 6.

_____. "RIAA Assists in Record Seizure of Bogus CDs," *Billboard*, 13 April 1996: 6.

_____. "Justice Dep't Investigating Music-Video Fee Collusion," *Billboard*, 2 March 1996: 1.

_____. "Perf. Right Bill On Way to White House," *Billboard*, 28 October 1995: 6.

_____. "Labels Lose Legal Ground Over Lax Library of Congress Filings," *Billboard*, 27 February 1993: 1.

_____. "House Okays New Anti-Piracy Bill," *Billboard*, 22 May 1982: 3.

H.R. 1506, P.L. 104–39, 109 Stat. 336, 104th Cong., 1st Sess., 1995.

H.R. Rep. No. 102–873(I), 102nd Cong., 2d Sess., 1992.

H.R. Rep. No. 98–987, 98th Cong., 2d Sess., 2, 1984.

H.R. Rep. No. 94–1476, 94th Cong., 1st Sess., 1976.

H.R. Rep. No. 92–487, 92nd Cong., 1st Sess., 1971.

H.R. Rep. No. 2222, 60th Cong., 2d Sess., 1909.

Hull, Geoffrey. "The GATT and the Media: How the Uruguay Round of the General Agreement on Tariffs and Trade Affects Media in the United States," paper presented at the Southeast Colloquium, AEJMC, Law Division, March, 1996.

_____. "The Aging of America: The Recording and Broadcasting Industries' Awareness of Shifting Demographic Patterns," *NARAS Institute Journal*, 1, 1 (1977): 3.

_____. *Atlanta Record Buyers Survey*. Atlanta: Georgia State University, 1977.

Hutchison, Thomas W. and James A. Progris. "Study Shows Music Biz Graduates are Given Top Priority," *NARM Sounding Board*, November 1996: 8.

"Indies' Surprise Survival," *Billboard*, 3 December 1949:1.

"In Other On-line News," *Billboard*, 7 October 1995: 91.

"Intellectual Property and the National Information Infrastructure: A Preliminary Draft of the Report of the Working Group on Intellectual Property Rights, Executive Summary," 13 *Cardozo Arts & Entertainment Law Journal* 275 (1994).

The International Convention for the Protection of Performers, Producers of Phonograms and Broadcasting Organizations, adopted at Rome on 26 October, 1961.

Jackson, Joe. "Video Clips: A Personal View," *Billboard,* 16 June 1984: 10.

Jeffrey, Don. "Acquired by BMG, Private Music Begins a New Age," *Billboard*, 5 February 1994: 6.

_____. "ASCAP Revamps Live Show System," *Billboard*, 30 September 1995: 10.

_____. "Atlanta's Wax 'n' Facts is Hip—and Hot," *Billboard*, 17 July 1993: 93.

_____. "CD Singles, Music Vids Lead Modest Growth," *Billboard*, 31 August 1996: 1.

_____. "Embattled Majors Act to Protect Music Stores," *Billboard,* 23 December 1995: 67.

_____. "Holidays Bring Retail Optimism," *Billboard*, 9 December 1995: 3, 93.

_____. "Musicland Reports Double-Digit Profit Hike in '93," *Billboard*, 12 February 1994: 85.

_____. "Shrinkage Ebbs at Music/Vid Stores," *Billboard*, 26 November 1994: 63.

_____. "Survey, Listening Posts 'Important' to Customers," *Billboard*, 8 June 1996: 1.

Jepsen, Cara. "Mainstream Rock Updates Itself," *Billboard*, 20 April 1996: 91.

Jolson–Colburn, Jeffrey. "Merchandisers Call for Study on Used CDs," *Dallas Morning News*, 17 June 1993: Today section, 14C.

Jones, Steve. *Rock Formation*. Newbury Park, CA: Sage Publications, 1992.

Joseph, Jai. *Writing Music for Hit Songs*. Cincinnati, OH: Writer's Digest Books, 1989.

Kaberline, Brian. "Used CDs are Good and Cheap—Unless You Manufacture New Ones," *Kansas City Business Journal*, 18 June 1993: Sec. 1, 1 (LEXIS).

Kalogerakis, George. "Keeping Score," *Vogue*, May 1996: 170.

Kaplan, Benjamin. *An Unhurried View of Copyright*. New York: Columbia University Press, 1967.

Keat, Paul and Philip K.Y. Young. *Managerial Economics: Economic Tools for Today's Decision Makers*. New York: Macmillan, 1992.

Knoedelseder, William. *Stiffed: A True Story of MCA, the Music Business and the Mafia*. New York: HarperCollins, 1993.

Kohn, Al and Bob Kohn, *Kohn on Music Licensing* (2nd ed.). Englewood Cliffs, NJ: Aspen Law & Business, 1996.

Kosser, Michael. "Big Hits Mean Big Money," *American Songwriter*, January/February 1995: 34.

Kozak, Roman. "Court Ruling Hits U.S. Importers," *Billboard*, 7 August 1982: 1.

Kramer, Gary. "Record Firm Rule of Thumb Slips from Fickle Public Pulse," *Billboard*, 22 December 1956: 1.

La Cienega Music Co. v Z. Z. Top, 44 F. 3d 813 (9th Cir. 1995).

Lacy, Stephen, et al. *Media Management*. Hillsdale, NJ: Lawrence Erlbaum, 1993.

Lashinsky, Philip. Speaking in a concert promotion class at Middle Tennessee State University, 20 September 1994.

Levenson, Jeff. "BET to Bow Jazz Network," *Billboard,* 2 October 1993: 8;

Levin, Mike. "PolyGram NV Buys 50% of MTV Asia," *Billboard*, 29 April 1995: 5.

Lewis, Lisa A. *Gender Politics and MTV*. Phidelphia, PA: Temple University Press, 1990.

Lichtman, Irv. "1995 Receipts, Distributions Break ASCAP Records," *Billboard*, 24 February 1996: 6.

_____. "1995 a Year of Deals, Court Action, and Legislation," *Billboard*, 23 December 1995: 57.

_____. "Famous to BMG in Global Shift," *Billboard*, 28 October 1995: 1.

_____. "Firth Says BMG Publishing Can Double Biz in 5 Years," *Billboard*, 10 July 1993: 6.

_____. "Japan Hops to 2nd in NMPA Survey," *Billboard*, 20 July 1996: 34.

_____. "King Karol Tests Disk Rental Idea," *Billboard*, 16 May 1981: 1.

_____. "MCA Music Eyes 'Mid-size' Power," *Billboard*, 4 May 1996: 39.

_____. "Publishing Legend Lou Levy Dies at 84," *Billboard*, 11 November 1995: 8.

_____. "SESAC Boosts Profile With Dylan, Diamond Signings," *Billboard*, 4 February 1995: 1.

_____. "Sony Establishes New Vigor in Market Share," *Billboard*, 17 April 1993: 1.

_____. "Sony Pub Adds Nile Rogers, Fisher Catalogs," *Billboard*, 17 June 1995: 14.

_____. "Strong NMPA Stats in Past Indicate Happy Times Now," *Billboard*, 25 December 1993: 24.

_____. "War Waged on Words: Pubs Expand A&R Role," *Billboard*, 26 December 1992: 22.

_____. "WB Publications Agrees to Buy C.P.P./Belwin," *Billboard*, 7 May 1994: 6.

Lindey, Alexander. *Lindey on Entertainment, Publishing and the Arts*. New York: Clark Boardman, 1988.

"LP Crown to Columbia, Victor Tops in Singles," *Billboard*, 5 January 1963: 4.

Lull, James. "Popular Music and Communication," in *Popular Music and Communication* (2nd Ed.). James Lull, ed. Newbury, CA: Sage Publications, 1992: 1.

MacDougall, John. "Small Record Stores Feud with Big Distributors Over Used CDs," *Houston Business Journal*, 21 June 1993: Sec. 1, 1 (LEXIS).

Malueg, David A. and Marius Schwartz, "Parallel imports, demand dispersion, and international price discrimination," 37 *Journal of International Economics*, 167 (1994).

Mandrell, Jim. *The Studio Business Book* (2nd ed.). Los Angeles, CA: First House Press, 1995.

Marco, Guy A. *Encyclopedia of Recorded Sound in the United States*. New York: Garland Publishing, 1993.

Marty, Daniel *The Illustrated History of Talking Machines*. Lausanne, Switzerland: Edita, 1981: 146.

Matzer, Marla. "Ticket to Ride," *Brandweek*, 8 July 1996: 20.

Mayfield, Geoff. "Between the Bullets," *Billboard*, 23 December 1996: 106.

_____. "Camelot Pulls Live Crew," *Billboard*, 2 May 1987: 87.

McClure, Steve. "Tower Records to Open in Seoul," *Billboard*, 9 July 1994: 39.

_____. "Sam Goody Joins Japan's Retail Wars," *Billboard*, 2 July 1994: 80.

McCormick, Moira. "SoundScan: Boon or Bane for Indies," *Billboard*, 21 March 1992: 14.

McQuail, Dennis. *Mass Communication Theory* (3rd Ed.). Thousand Oaks, CA: Sage Publications, 1994.

Middle Tennessee State University. *Music Videos and Record Store Customers* (a 1995 study for the Music Video Association).

Mills Music, Inc. v. Snyder, 496 U.S. 153, (1985).

Mix Magazine, *The Mix 1996 Master Directory* (1996).

Mondy, R. Wayne and Shane R. Premeaux. *Management Concepts, Practices, and Skills* (6th Ed.). Boston: Allyn & Bacon, 1993.

Moody's Handbook of Common Stocks Winter 95–96. New York: Moody's Investors Service, 1996.

Morning Edition, *National Public Radio*, 14 July 1993 (Transcript, LEXIS).

Morris, Chris. "April Sets Mark Milestones for Alanis, Beatles," *Billboard*, 18 May 1996: 12.

_____. "Federal Judge Dismisses Joe Isgro Case," *Billboard*, 13 April 1996: 96.

_____. "Fla. Clerk Faces Obscenity Charge for Cassette Sale," *Billboard,* 2 May 1987: 1.

_____. "Garth Takes Solo Sales Record," *Billboard,* 16 March 1996: 13.

_____. "George Harrison Wins $11.6 Mill. in Suit vs. Ex-partner," *Billboard,* 3 February 1996: 13.

_____. "Isgro Trial Testimony Bares Payoffs," *Billboard,* 8 September 1990: 1.

_____. "MCA Purchases 50% of Interscope," *Billboard,* 2 March 1996: 13.

_____. "Piracy Losses Shrink," *Billboard,* 1 April 1995: 1.

Morris, Edward. "Hilley Named President/CEO at Sony Tree," *Billboard,* 5 February 1994: 9.

_____. "NCN Cites $1.1 Mil Paid for Use of Music Videos," *Billboard,* 29 May 1995: 26.

_____. "NSAI Blasts Controlled Composition Clause," *Billboard,* 15 January 1994: 8.

_____. "SESAC Puts Out Its Welcome Mat," *Billboard,* 26 February 1994: 13.

"Music Video Sales Chart Moves to SoundScan Data," *Billboard,* 24 April 1993: 6.

National Association of Music Merchants. *1996 Music USA.* Pub.: NARM, 1996.

National Association of Recording Merchandisers. *Annual Survey Results 1995.* Pub.: NARM, 1996.

_____. "Parental Advisory Program Bolstered," press release on NARM's Internet site, 12 September 1996.

_____. *Consumer Research Study: The Growing Adult Market,* March 1976.

_____. "Industry to Enhance Awareness of Parental Advisory Logo," *NARM Sounding Board* (on-line version), November 1995.

_____. "Soundata Consumer Panel," *NARM Sounding Board,* September 1996 (on-line version).

_____. "Soundata Consumer Panel," *NARM Sounding Board,* August 1996 (on-line version).

_____. "Soundata Consumer Panel," *NARM Sounding Board,* June 1996 (on-line version).

_____. "Soundata Consumer Panel," *NARM Sounding Board* (on-line version), March 1996.

_____. "Soundata Consumer Panel," *NARM Sounding Board* (on-line version), February 1996.

_____. "Soundata Consumer Panel," *NARM Sounding Board,* (on-line version) January 1996.

_____. "Soundata Consumer Panel," *NARM Sounding Board,* (on-line version) December 1995.

_____. "Soundata Consumer Panel," *NARM Sounding Board,* December 1994: 10.

_____. "Censorship Is Back . . . But So Are We!" *NARM Sounding Board* (on-line version), August 1995.

_____. NARM Survey, 1981.

_____. *What UPC Means to the Recording Industry* (1979): 20.

National Music Publishers' Association. *International Survey of Music Publishing Revenues.* Pub.: NMPA, 1996.

_____. *International Survey of Music Publishing Revenues* (1991).

"The New Empire of the Air," *U.S. News and World Report,* 1 July 1996: 10.

"New Technology Will Strengthen Accuracy of BDS," *Billboard,* 1 July 1994: 1.

Newman, Melinda. "Consumer Music Mags Win Clout," *Billboard,* 23 December 1995: 1.

_____. "The A&R Angle," *Billboard,* 3 June 1995: 53.

_____. "Colleagues Recall Hulett's Cutting-Edge Tour Biz Work," *Billboard,* 14 August 1993: 10.

_____. "Joel Wins Another Round in Suit vs. Ex-manager," *Billboard*, 20 March 1993: 12.

_____ , and Thom Duffy. "PolyGram Enters Concert Biz With Scher," *Billboard*, 6 October 1990: 1.

Nimmer, David and Melville Nimmer, *Nimmer on Copyright*. New York: Matthew Bender, 1996.

Nimmer, David. "The End of Copyright." 48 *Vanderbilt Law Review* 1385 (1995).

Novia, Tony. "Is CHR an Endangered Species?" *R&R*, 10 May 1996: 28.

Nunziata, Susan. "Bodyguard Album, Single Soar at Sales Counters," *Billboard*, 16 January 1993: 10;

_____. "CD Plants Expand in Anticipation of Business Boom," *Billboard*, 25 July 1992: 6.

_____. "Harrison, ABKCO Suit 'Fine'ally Ending after 20 Years," *Billboard*, 1 December 1990: 80.

Office of the U.S. Trade Representative, *MTN Agreements—Legal Status as of 6 May 1994*.

Oland, Pamela Phillips. *You Can Write Great Lyrics*. Cincinnati, OH: Writer's Digest Books, 1989.

Olson, Catherine Applefield. "Camelot Music Unveils Ambitious Web Site," *Billboard*, 11 January 1997: 68.

"Ontario Place Corp.," *Billboard*, 4 June 1994: 77.

Passman, Donald S. *All You Need to Know About the Music Business*. New York: Simon & Schuster, 1994.

Pavlik, John V. *New Media and the Information Superhighway*. Boston: Allyn and Bacon, 1996.

Peter, J. Paul and James H. Donnelly, Jr. *Marketing Management: Knowledge and Skills*. Plano, TX: Business Publications, 1986.

Peterson, Richard A. and David G. Berger. "Measuring Industry Concentration, Diversity, and Innovation in Popular Music," 61 *American Sociological Review* (1996): 175.

Petrozzello, Donna. "Alternative Rock in the Mainstream," *Broadcasting & Cable*, 20 May 1996: 51.

_____. "Radio Group Heads Foresee Consolidation, Format Diversity," *Broadcasting & Cable*, 24 October 1994: 3.

Phalen, Tom. "Easy Street Stores A Family Affair," *Billboard*, 20 November 1993: 93.

Philips, Chuck. "Wherehouse ups ante in Used CDs," *Los Angeles Times*, 29 June 1993: Calendar: Part F; p. 3, Col. 1. (LEXIS).

Pollstar. *Summer 1996 Agency Rosters*. Fresno, CA: Pollstar, 1996.

Pollstar. "1995 Top 50 Tours," *Pollstar*, 31 December 1995: 7.

Practising Law Institute. *Counseling Clients in the Entertainment Industry*. New York: PLI, 1994.

Price, Deborah Evans. "Benson, Z Music's Retail Team-Up," *Billboard*, 20 May 1995.

_____. "Christian Music Searches for Sales Strength for Its Journey," *Billboard*, 13 January 1996: 1.

_____. "Sony Adds to Country Music," *Billboard*, 7 October 1995: 74.

_____. "Writer–Producers Churn Out Hits in Music City," *Billboard*, 20 April 1996: 38.

"Price List Reflects Firmer Structure in Cost of Disks," *Billboard*, 15 June 1955: 5.

Pride, Dominic and Melinda Newman. "MTV Deal Marks Strategy Shift for Sony," *Billboard*, 12 Nov. 1944: 5.

_____. "W. H. Smith Plans to Add More Bricks to the Wall," *Billboard*, 4 September 1993: 12.

"Prospects of Trade Clash Between US and China Grows," *Times Newspapers Limited*, 2 Jan. 1995, (LEXIS).

Radcliffe, Joe. "3 Mill in Counterfeit Tape Grabbed in N.Y.: 12 Arrested," *Billboard*, 18 September 1971: 1.

"Radio Billings 1935–1974," *Broadcasting Yearbook* (1976): C-298.

"Radio Meets the TV Challenge and Re-invents Itself," *Media Week, Radio 75th Anniversary Supplement*, 4 September 1995: 20.

"Radio, Promo People Said to Sell CDs," *Billboard*, 7 December 1995: 79.

Rathburn, Elizabeth H. "The Reordering of Radio," *Broadcasting & Cable*, 1 July 1996: 6.

RCA Mfg. Co., Inc. v. Whiteman, 144 F.2d 86 (2d Cir. 1940).

"Record $7 Million Judgment Made in Counterfeit Case," *Billboard*, 20 April 1996: 8.

"Record Clubs: An Inside Look at an Evolving Enterprise," *Billboard*, 30 March 1996: 1.

"Record of Radio Station Growth Since Television Began," *Broadcasting & Cable Yearbook* (1995): B-655.

Record Rental Amendment of 1984. P.L. 98–450, 98 Stat. 1727, 98th Cong., 2nd Sess. (1984).

Recording Industry Association of America, *1992 Annual Report* (1993): 22.

_____. 1995 Year End Statistics (Press Release).

_____. *Gold and Platinum Record Awards* (1984).

_____. *Inside the Recording Industry: A Statistical Overview 1987*.

_____. "Recording Industry Releases 1995 Consumer Profile," (press release) 5 April 1996: 2.

_____. *Rewind/Fast Forward: 45 years and Beyond @ the Recording Industry Association of America.* (1996).

Reibman, Greg. "Boston's Don Law Launches Ticketing Firm," *Billboard*, 3 February 1996: 6.

Report of the Register of Copyrights on the General Revision of the U.S. Copyright Law (1961).

Ressner, Jeffrey. "You Can't Always Get What You Want," *Rolling Stone*, 3 September 1992: 13, 80.

Restatement (Second) of Agency (1957).

"RIAA Finds 90% Stores Sell Counterfeit!" *Variety*, 2 April 1980: 2.

Ringer, Barbara. "The Unauthorized Duplication of Sound Recordings" (1957), *Study No. 26 for the Senate Committee on the Judiciary, Copyright Law Revision, Studies Prepared for the Subcommittee on Patents, Trademarks, and Copyrights*, 86th Cong., 2d Sess. (1960).

Robinson, Deanna Campbell, et al. *Music at the Margins*. Newbury Park, CA: Sage Publications, 1991.

Rogers, Robert P. and John R. Woodbury, "Market Structure, Program Diversity, and Radio Audience Size," *Contemporary Economic Policy,* January 1996: 81.

Roland, Tom. "Not an Easy Way to Make a Buck," *The Tennessean*, 5 January 1995: E1.

_____. "Record Labels Debate Research," *The Tennessean*, Business Section, 5 June 1995: 1.

Rolontz, Bob. "72 Labels Landed on Charts in '58—a Feverish Year," *Billboard,* 5 January 1959: 3.

_____. "Artist Pressure Liberalizing Standard Record Contracts," *Billboard*, 19 December 1960: 2.

_____. "Disk Clubs Zoom to 2 Mil Subscribers," *Billboard*, 5 October 1959: 1.

Rosen, Craig. "CD Singles Spurred by Addition of Non-Album Cuts," Billboard, 30 March 1996: 5.

_____. "MCA Publishing Lands New Talent," *Billboard*, 28 October 1995: 46.

_____. "Used CD Rivals Near Truce," *Billboard*, 11 September 1993: 1.

_____. "Wherehouse Suit Hits Used CD Policies," *Billboard*, 31 July 1993: 8.

_____, and Ed Christman, "Retailers Sound Used CD Alarm," *Billboard*, 7 December 1991: 1.

Rosenblum, Trudi Miller. "Audiobooks Aimed at Record Stores," *Billboard*, 15 July 1995: 61.

Rosenthal, Edward and Jeanne Hamburg, "Are 'Net Providers Liable for Users' Infringement?" *National Law Journal*, 12 February 1996: C4.

Rosette v. Rainbo Record Manufacturing Corp., 345 F. Supp. 1183 (S.D.N.Y. 1973).

Russell, Deborah. "Video Kills the Radio Star," *Billboard 100th Anniversary Issue 1894-1994*, 1 November 1994: 196.

_____. "No Art to Making Vid a Class Act," *Billboard*, 11 June 1994: 56;

_____. "Austin Scene Spawns Vid Network," *Billboard*, 7 May 1994: 44.

Sacks, Leo. "Reporter's Notebook: Observations from Goody Trial," *Billboard*, 2 May 1981: 13.

"Sage Acquires Stations," *New York Times*, 26 June 1996: C3-national.

"Sales of Beatles Set Give Retailers Hope," *Billboard,* 2 December 1995: 5, 106.

Sanjek, Russell and David Sanjek. *American Popular Music Business in the 20th Century*. New York: Oxford University Press, 1991.

Sandler, Adam. "FTC Subpoenas Record Distribs in Used CD Case," *Daily Variety*, 3 May 1994: 1.

Schlager, Ken. "On The Boards, 1894–1920," *Billboard 100th Anniversary Issue* (1994): 18.

Schoepe, Zenon. "Management Maven." *1996 Performance Guide: Talent/PM*. Carlsbad, CA: Performance, 1996.

Schwichtenberg, Cathy. "Music Video, The Popular Pleasures of Visual Music," in James Lull, (Ed.), *Popular Music and Communication*, 2nd Ed. Newbury Park, California: Sage Publications, 1992: 116.

Seay, David. "The Sound of Movie Music," *Billboard*, 3 April 1993: S3.

"SESAC, BDS to Monitor More Genres," *Billboard*, 24 February 1996: 12.

Segrave, Kerry. *Payola in the Music Business: a History 1880–1991*. Jefferson, NC: McFarland, 1994.

Seideman, Tony. "Four Labels Ink Vidclip Deals With MTV," *Billboard*, 23 June 1984: 1.

Selle v. Gibb, 741 F.2d 896 (7th Cir. 1984).

Severin, Werner J. and James W. Tankard, Jr. *Communication Theories: Origins, Methods and Uses in the Mass Media*, 3rd Ed. White Plains, NY: Longman, 1988.

Shemel, Sidney and M. Willliam Krasilovsky. *This Business of Music*, 6th Ed. New York: Billboard Publications, 1990.

Shields, Steven O. "Creativity and Creative Control in the Work of American Radio Announcers," a paper presented to the Association for Education in Journalism and Mass Communication annual meeting, Minneapolis, Minn., August, 1990.

Sidak, J. Gregory and David E. Kronemyer, "The New Payola and the American Record Industry," *Harvard Journal of Law and Public Policy*, Summer 1987: 521.

Silverman, Tom. "Preserving Diversity in the Music Biz," *Billboard*, 18 May 1996: 6.

Sippel, John. "Huge Haul of Illicit LPs in Goody Return," *Billboard*, 9 Feb. 1980: 1.

Sobel, Lionel S. "Regulation of Talent Agents and Managers: Registration and Licensing Requirements for Those Who Seek Employment for Entertainment Industry Talent." *American Bar Association Forum on the Entertainment and Sports Industries 1996 Annual Meeting, Vol. II.* American Bar Association: Chicago, Illinois (1996).

Sony Corporation and Consolidated Subsidiaries Annual Report 1995, on-line edition (http://www.sony.co.jp/Corporate Cruise/).

Sony Corp. v. Universal City Studios, Inc., 464 U.S. 417 (1984).

"SoundScan Releases 1996 Music Industry Figures," Reuters Financial Service, 6 January 1996 (Lexis).

Spahr, Wolfgang. "Movie Soundtracks Start Moving Units in Germany," *Billboard*, 17 September 1994: 50.

Spethmann, Betsy. "Sponsors Sing a Profitable Tune with Event Promos," *Brandweek*, 24 August 1994: 20.

S. Rep. No. 97–274, P.L. 97–180, (1992): 4, 5.

Standard and Poor's Corporation. *Standard and Poor's Stock Reports.* New York: Standard and Poor's, 1996.

Standard and Poor's Corporation. *Standard and Poor's Industry Surveys.* New York: Standard and Poor's, 1996.

Standard Rate and Data Service's (SRDS) *Business Publication Advertising Source*, July 1996.

_____. *Consumer Magazine Advertising Source*, July 1996.

Stander, Kevin. "Used CDs Integral to Industry," *Billboard*, 14 August 1993: 4.

Stark, Phyllis. "Interep Studies Country Listeners," *Billboard*, 2 April 1994: 69.

"State of the Industry," *NARM Sounding Board*, May 1995 (on-line version).

Statistical Abstract of the United States, U.S. Department of Commerce (1995).

Statute of Anne, 8 Anne C. 19 (1710), reprinted in, Robert A. Gorman and Jane C. Ginsburg, *Copyright for the Nineties* (4th ed.). Charlottesville, VA: Michie, 1993: 1.

Stein, Howard and Ronald Zalkind. *Promoting Rock Concerts.* New York: Schirmer Books, 1979.

Stern, Kevin E. "The High Cost of Convenience: Antitrust Law Violations in the Computerized Ticketing Services Industry," 16 *Hastings Comm/Ent Law Journal* 349 (1994).

Stewart, Al. "Suppliers Weigh $14.95 Vid Prices," *Billboard*, 1 April 1989: 1.

Stratton, Jon. "Capitalism and Romantic Ideology in the Record Business," *Popular Music*, 3 (1993): 183.

Strauss, Neil. "Pennies That Add Up to $16.98: Why CDs Cost So Much," *New York Times*, 5 July 1995, final edition, C-11 (LEXIS).

"Study Reveals Top Advertisers," *Billboard*, 13 April 1996: 85.

Sutherland, Sam. "Taping Losses Near $3 Billion," *Billboard*, 3 April 1982: 1.

Szabo v. Errisson, 68 F.3d 940 (5th Cir. 1995).

Taylor, Chuck. "Format Issues Tackled at Gavin Seminar, " *Billboard*, 24 February 1996: 90.

TB Harms Co. v. JEM Records, Inc., 655 F.Supp. 1575 (D.N.J. 1987).

Tempo Music, Inc. v. Famous Music Corp., 838 F.Supp. 162 (S.D.N.Y. 1993).

Terry, Ken. "Labels to Billboard: Balance New POS Charting System," *Billboard*, 1 June 1991: 1.

"There's 'Nothin' Like the Reel Thing,'" *Billboard*, 18 May 1996: 4.

Thigpen, David. "Are They Worth All That Cash?" *Time*, 29 January 1996: 54.

"Top Pop Catalog Albums", *Billboard*, 12 October 1996: 83.

"Top Pop Records, 1949" *Billboard*, 12 January 1950: 14.

Traiman, Steve. "Finally, Retailers Get Smitten by 'CD ROMance,'" *Billboard*, 25 February 1995: 76.

_____. "Off-Price Millions: The Secret in the Vault," *Billboard*, 13 April 1996: 50.

_____. "Publishers, Music Licensing Groups Seek Rights on Info Superhighway," *Billboard*, 10 June 1995: 39.

"U.K.'s Niche Stations Willing Battle Against Homogenization," *Billboard*, 13 April 1996: 85.

United National Records, Inc. v. MCA, Inc., No. 82 C 7589 (N.D. Ill. 1985).

United States Code, Title 17 § 101, *et seq.* (Copyright).

United States Code, Title 18 § 2319.

United States Code, Title 47 §317(a)(1).

United States Department of Commerce, *Census of Retail Trade*. 1977, 1987, 1992.

Uruguay Round Agreements Act, Statement of Administrative Action, P.L. 103–465, 103d Cong., 2nd Sess. 1994, §512. Codified in 17 U.S.C. §1101, *et seq.* Reprinted in 6 U.S. Code Congressional and Administrative News (108 Stat.) 4040, at 4281.

"U.S. and Canada Radio Programming Formats," *Broadcasting and Cable Yearbook* (1995): B-592.

U.S. Dept. of Labor, Bureau of Labor Statistics, *Monthly Labor Review,* November 1995.

Statistical Abstract of the United States, 1995. Washington, DC: U.S. Department of Commerce, Bureau of the Census, 1995: 568.

Verna, Paul. "RIAA Report Shows Stagnant '95 Shipments for Music, Video," *Billboard*, 2 March 1996: 3.

_____. "Ogden Acquires 50% of Metropolitan," *Billboard*, 16 September 1995: 5.

"Victor's LP Offer Sets Trade Buzzing," *Billboard*, 30 December 1957: 11.

Vogel, Harold L. *Entertainment Industry Economics*. New York: Cambridge University Press, 1986.

Warner Communications, Inc. "The Prerecorded Music Market: An Industry Survey," *NARAS Institute Journal* 2, 1, (1978): 78.

"Warner Cos. Restructured as WEA Inc.," *Billboard*, 11 November 1995: 60.

"WEA Raises LP & Single Basic Prices," *Billboard*, 30 June 1979: 3.

Webb–Pressler, Margaret. "The Unsound of Music," *Washington Post*, 29 April 1995: C1:

Whitburn, Joel. *Top Country Singles 1944–1988*. Menomee Falls, WI: Record Research, Inc., 1989.

_____. *Joel Whitburn's Pop Singles Annual 1955–1986*. Menomee Falls, WI: Record Research, Inc., 1987.

White, Adam. "Villain: Home Taping," *Billboard*, 5 January 1980: 3.

White-Smith Music Publishing Co. v. Apollo Co., 209 U.S. 1 (1908).

Willis, Jim and Diane B. Willis, *New Directions in Media Management*. Boston: Allyn & Bacon, 1993.

Woo, Junda. "Publisher Sues CompuServe Over a Song," *Wall Street Journal*, 16 December 1993: B1, B16.

Woods v. Bourne Co., 841 F.Supp. 118, 121 (S.D.N.Y. 1994).

Wyatt, Robert O. and Geoffrey P. Hull. "The Music Critic in the American Press: A Nationwide Survey of Newspapers and Magazines," *Mass Comm Review,* 17, 3 (1990): 38.

Zimmerman, Kevin. "Rap Braces for the Big Chill," *Variety,* 6 January 1992: 89.

_____. "Security in the Eye of Summer Storms," *Variety*, 5 August 1991: 56.

Index

A & R
  administration, 40
  budgets, 126
  development deal, 126
  function, 13, 39,123
  good ears, 125
  signing artists, 124–126
Accountants, 92
Accounting department, label, 37
Adult Contemporary listeners, 105
Advances. *See under* Artist agreements,
    Producers, record, and Exclusive
    songwriter agreements
Advertising department, label, 38
Aeolian Organ Company, 221
"After the Ball," 47
Agents and agencies. *See* Talent agencies and
    agents
Alabama (musical group), 174
Albums, prices, 157–159
Albums, sales
  best selling, **6, 7, 8, 9, 10**
  distributing labels market share, **35**
  labels, market share, **34**
  live events, at, 89
  seasonal, **169**
"Alone Again, Naturally," 234
American Bandstand, 106
American Federation of Musicians (AFM), 82,
    90–91, 134
American Federation of Television and Radio
    Artists (AFTRA), 82, 134,
American Guild of Variety Artists, 91

A & M Records, 29, 32
Antitrust, 15, 88, 252–253
Arista Records, 29
Artist agreements
  advances, 130, 133
  basics, 127
  commitment, 127
  controlled compositions, 132–133
  creative controls, 139
  marketing guarantees, 128
  master delivery, 139
  stature of artist, and, 125
  publishing rights, 131
  re-negotiation, 129
  risk, 127–128
  royalties, 129–131
  video rights, 133
Ariola Records, 29
Artist relations, label, 39
American Society of Composers, Authors and
    Publishers (ASCAP), 61. *See also*
    Performing rights organizations
Attorneys, 92
Audio engineers, 141, 144, **145**
Audio Engineering Society (AES), 145
Audio playback hardware, sales 4
Beatles, The, 214
Berman, Jay, 5
Big six
  corporate structure, 35–36
  defined, 30
  horizontal and vertical integration, 16, 35
  market shares, 34, **166, 167**

Boldface indicates reference to table or figure.

Billboard Magazine, **103**, 104, 114
Black Entertainment Television network (BET), 108
Block, Martin, 98
BMG, 32, 112, 193. See also Big six
BMG Music Publishing, 49
"Boogie, Chillen'," 206
Bootleg recordings, 245, 247
Branch distribution, 165
Broadcast Data Systems (BDS), 18, 65–66, 104, 172–173
Broadcasters, 22, 223. *See also* Radio
Broadcast Music, Inc. (BMI), 62. *See also* Performing rights organizations
Brooks, Garth, 3, 194
Business affairs, label, 36
Campbell v. Acuff-Rose Music, Inc., 210
Capitol Records, 28, 29, 33
Caruso, Enrico, 129, 140
Cassettes, 17. *See also* Albums
CBS Records, 29
CDs. *See* Albums, and Singles
CD-ROM, 190, 248
Cellar Door Productions, 85
Chain record stores. *See* Retail
Charts, popularity, 29, 102, 104
Cherry Lane Music, 68
China, 248
Chrysalis Records, 29
Circuit City, 8
Clubs, record. *See* Record clubs
Columbia Records, 28, 29, 31
Community for Creative Non-Violence v. Reid, 213
Compulsory mechanical licenses, 222, 230–232, **231**
Concert promoters
  artist agreements, 85–86
  function, 22
  liability, 84
  role, 82–83
  top 10, **84**
  venue agreements, 86
Concert promotion
  basics, 75–76
  industry structure, 83, 84
  in-house, 87–88
  label role, 89
  players, **75**
  revenues/expenses example, 86–87
  risks, 83
  sponsored tours, 90
  tickets, 84, 88
  vertical integration, 89–90
Concerts, top artists, **73**
Concerts West, 83
Consumers, media and 4, **5**
Consumers, recordings 10–12, **11**

Controlled compositions, 133
Counterfeit recordings, 245, 246–247
Copyright
  common law, 217, 229
  duration, 204
  history, 221, 237–238
  fair use, 209–210
  infringement, 234–237
  Internet, 240–241
  joint authorship, 211
  musical arrangements, 229
  musical groups, and, 211–212
  notice, 205–207
  parody, 210
  poor man's copyright, 217
  public domain, 205
  recording industry, and, 15, 203–204, 214–215, **238**
  registration, 207, 208–209, **208**, 217
  songs, 207, 229, 235–236
  sound recordings, 205, 207, **208**, 234
  termination rights, 213–215
  works made for hire, 212
  World Trade Organization, 206
Country Music Television (CMT), 108
Cover versions, 51
CPI USA, 85
Davis, Clive, 125, 195
Decca Records, 28, 33
Digital performances, 228
Digital sampling, 234–235
Distribution
  history, 165–166
  system, 16, **164**, 165
Distributors, 22, **166**
Diversity and
  big six, 43
  entropy, 13
  label sales, 34
  place of sale, 9
  radio, 99–102
  trends, 43
Economy, influence of, 15, 16
Edison, Thomas, 28
Edmonds, Kenneth "Baby Face," 54
Education, audio and music business, 145–146
Effective competition, 29
8-track tapes, 222
Electrical recordings, 140
Electrical transcriptions (ETs), 98
EMI, Ltd., 30, 32–33, 193, *see also* Big six
EMI Music, 49
Engineers, recording, 141, 144, **145**
European Union, 216
Film, recording industry and, 110–112
Free goods, 155
Gatekeeper theory, 19
Gavin Report, 16, **103**

Geffen Records, 33
General Agreement on Tariffs and Trade
    (GATT), 14
Gold and platinum status, 8, 110
Gore, Tipper, 14
Graham, Bill, 90
Grand rights, 62
Green Day, 8
Hal Leonard Publishing, 68
Handleman Co., 180, 181
"Happy Birthday," 51
Harrison, George, 78, 236
Harry Fox Agency (HFA), 66–67, 241
Herbert, Victor, 232
Hirsch, Paul, 96
Hit Men, 251
HMV Group, 33, 186
Home recording, 18, 223, 226
Home Recording Act of 1992, 227, **228**
Hootie and the Blowfish, 8
"How Deep Is Your Love," 236
"I Love New York," 236
Independent distribution, 42, 164, 165
Independent labels
    album sales, 34
    defined, 41
    distribution,164
    history, 29, 30
    profits, 42
    role, 41
    size, 42
Independent promotion, 251
Independent Music Retailers Association
    (IMRA), 194
Independent stores, 179, 187, 188, **188,** 189
Infringement. *See* Copyright, infringement
International Association of Theatrical and Stage
    Employees (IATSE), 91
International division, label, 37
International Federation of Phonographic
    Industries (IFPI), 226, 248
Internet, 241, 249
Isgro, Joe, 252
Island Records, 32
"I Will Always Love You," 51
Jackson, Michael, 3
Jagged Little Pill, 55
Jazz Singer, The, 110
Joel, Billy, 3, 78
Jukeboxes, 179
Kenny G, 7
K-Mart sales, 8
Labels, record. *See also* Independent labels
    concert promotion, 89
    functions, 20, 27
    presidents, 36
    structure, 36–40, **37**
La Cienega Music Co. v. ZZ Top, 206

Law, Don, 89
Listening stations, 163
Live entertainment and unions, 90–91
Live entertainment income stream, 73, 93
Lull, James, 18
Lyrics, song, 14
Manager, personal. *See* Personal managers
Manager, professional, 52
Manufacturers, record, 21
Manufacturing Clause, 215–216
Marketing recordings, 150
    boxed sets, 153
    Broadway cast albums, 151
    catalog product, 153
    Christian/Gospel music, 152
    Christmas buying, 168–169
    configuration changes, 153–154
    country music, 151
    four Ps of marketing, 149
    functions, 149
    greatest hits albums, 153
    jazz music, 151
    marketing concept, 149
    product availability, 167–168
    product placement, 168
    release dates, 168
    repackaging, 153
    research, 173
    risk reduction, 174
    specialty genres, sales, **152**
    singles, 154
    soundtrack albums, 151
    styles of music, 151
Marketing division, label, 38
Masters, 139
MCA, 30, 33, 89, 112, *see also* Big six
MCA Music Publishing, 49
McQuail, Dennis, 18
Mechanical licenses, 66–68, **67**
    compulsory, 222, 230, **231**, 232
    royalties, 59, 204
Media consumption, 4
Media expenditures, **5**
Mercury Records, 29, 32
Metropolitan Entertainment, 85
MGM Records, 32
Miami Vice, 109
Minimum advertised prices (MAP), 161
Mom & pop stores. *See* Independent stores
Morissette, Alanis, 55
Motown Records, 32
Musical Heritage Society, 139
Musical Instrument Digital Interface (MIDI), 18
Musical instrument sales, 4
Music and Entertainment Industry Educators
    Association (MEIEA), 146
Music books 190
Musicians, 4, 22

Music publishing. *See also* Songwriter
    agreements
  administration aspects, 52–53
  big six, and 49–50
  chart shares, 49, **50, 51**
  company structure, 52
  copyrights, and, 51–52
  copyright acquisition, 53, 55
  co-publishing, 60, 61
  cover versions, 51
  creative aspects, 52
  functions, 22, 52
  Harry Fox Agency, 66
  history, 47–48
  income sources, 46–47, **47, 48, 61, 62, 69**
  market structure, 48
  print music, 68
  relation to recordings, 46–47
  rock and roll influence, 54
  synchronization licenses, 67, 69
  tape piracy, and, 224
Music Sales Group, 68
Music Television (MTV), 107–108
Music video
  charts, 110
  costs, 107
  development of, 107
  effects on TV music use, 109
  licenses, 230
  networks, 107–108
  pay for play, 108
  profitability, 110
  record buying, and 108
  recordings, as, 133
  sales, 109–110, **109**
"My Sweet Lord," 236–237
Nashville Network, The (TNN), 108
National Academy of Recording Arts and
    Sciences (NARAS), 146
National Music Publishers' Association
    (NMPA), 15, 66
New artist releases, 131
North American Free Trade Agreement
    (NAFTA), 14
"Oh, Pretty Woman," 210
Oligopoly, generally, 27–28
Oligopoly, in recording industry, 28–30
One-stops, 129, 165
Organized crime, 252

Parallel imports, 215–216
Parental advisory label, 14
Payola, 15, 250, 251
Performance royalties, 59
Performance royalties, digital, 228
Performing rights, 62, 243–233
Performing rights organizations
  ASCAP, BMI, SESAC comparison, 65–66
  function, 22, 61, **64**

Internet licenses, 241
  licensing, 62–64
  royalty distribution, 64
  sampling (methodology), 66
Personal managers
  agreements, terms, 78–79
  as talent agents, 77
  conflicts of interest, 92
  functions, 22, 76–78
  industry structure, 76
  labels, and, 77
  management team, 92
Pearl Jam, 88
Petty, Tom, 7
Philips Electronics, 32
Piracy
  compulsory mechanical license, 222
  criminal penalties, 247–248
  cyberspace, 249
  defined, 245
  8-track tapes, 246
  international, 248
  sales, 222
  seizures, 245, **246**
Politics and the recording industry, 14
PolyGram, 30, 32, 89,112, 193. *See also* Big six
PolyGram Music Publishing, 49
Popular music as communication, 14, 18, 19
Popular music listening habits, 14
Presley, Elvis, 3, 78
Print media, recording industry
  consumer publications, 115–116
  cultural effects, 113
  effects on record sales, 113
  influence, 112–113
  relative size of, 116
  revenues of, **114**
  trade publications, 113–115
Prices
  album, 157–159
  demand, and, 158–159
  antitrust actions, 252
  average CD prices, **160**
  minimum advertised (MAP), 161
  profits, and, 160, **161**
  singles, 155
Producers, record
  A & R, 136
  advances, 137
  artists as, 136–137
  function, 21, 40, 135, **135**
  independent, 136–137
  royalties, 137
Product, recordings as, 150
Production, record, 137–138, 14
Professional managers, 52
Profits, label, 40–41, **41**
Promoters, concert. *See* Concert promoters
Promotion, record, 162–163

Promotion division, label, 38
Public, in three income streams, 22, 23
Publicity, label department, 39
Public performance rights, exemptions, 232–233
Rack jobbers, 9, 179–181
Radio
  disk jockeys, 98
  FM, 101
  formats
    changes, 16
    CHR, 104
    country, 106
    diversity, 17, 102
    music, growth of , **96**
    Top 40, 98–99
    trends, **105**
  45s influence, 98
  listeners, 105
  market for recordings, as, 179
  numbers of stations, **100**
  ownership and diversity, 100, 101–102, **101**
  programming history, 97–98
  record sales, and, 96
  revenues, 99
  rock and roll, influence of, 99
Radio and Records (R&R), 16, **103**, 104, 173
RCA Victor, 28, 29, 125
Record companies, 27. *See also* Labels, record
Record clubs
  antitrust suit, 195
  BMG Music Service, 195
  Columbia House, 31, 194, 195
  function, 194
  label pull-out, 196
  profits, 195–196
Recording artists, 20. *See also* Artist agreements
Recording contracts. *See* Artist agreements, and
    Producers, record
Recording engineers, 21, 144–145
Recording industry, generally, 18, 28–30
Record rental, 223, 225
Record Rental Amendment, 191, 225
Recordings, income stream, 20
Recordings, sales, **5**, **6**, 7, **8**, **169**, 220
Record labels. *See* Labels, record
Record producers. *See* Producers, record
Recoupment, artist advances, 130
Retail. *See also* rack jobbers
  chain record stores, 181
    closings, 184
    growth, 182, **182**
    decline, 185–186
    distribution to, 165, 166
    largest, 184
    mall stores, 186
    market concentration, **182**
    one-stops, and 166
    price competition, 184
    weaknesses, 183

digital delivery, 196
function, 22, 177
future, 196
history, 9, 178–179
growth, **181**
independent stores, 179, 187, 188, **188,** 189
international, 186
Internet sales, 196
inventory, 190
market share of stores, **185**
multiple configurations, 189
number of locations, 177
packaging concerns, 189–190
rock and roll, impact of, 179
shrinkage, 190
store image, 178
sales per store, **183, 189**
sizes of stores, **197**
Returns limits, 168
Rhino Records, 139
Rolling Stone, 115
Royalties. *See* Artist agreements, Producers,
    record, Songwriter agreements, and Music
    publishing
Sam Goody chain, 186, 246–247
Samplers, 163
Sampling, 234–235
Sales division, label, 38
Sales of recordings, 8, **9**, 10, **154**, **156**
"Satin Doll," 229
Saturday Night Fever, 111–112
Seagrams Co., 33
SESAC, 62. *See also* Performing rights
    organizations
Shalett, Mike, 176
Sgt. Peppers Lonely Hearts Club Band (movie
    strk.), 180
Shoplifting, 190
Showcase, 126
Shortfall, 89
Side musicians and vocalists, 21
Singles
  CD, 156–157
  demand, 156
  prices, 155
  sales, **154**, **156**
Small rights, 62
Society, recording industry influences, 13
Society of Motion Picture and Television
    Engineers (SMPTE), 145
Society of Professional Audio Recording
    Services (SPARS), 145
Song pluggers, 53–54
Songs, 14, 53
Songwriters:
  artists as, 54
  producers as, 54
Songwriter agreements
  development deals, 55

Songwriter agreements *(continued)*
 exclusive, 58–59
 single song, 56–58
 trends, 56
 royalties example, 59–60
Songwriting, 54–55, **55**, 69–70
Sony Corp. v. Universal City Studios, Inc., 226
Sony Music, 30, 31, 193. See also Big six
Sony Music Publishing, 49
Sound-alike recordings, 224–225
Sound recording copyrights
 history, 220–223
 performance rights, 223
 public domain status, 205
 rights, 224
SoundScan
 charts, and 104, 171
 history, 170–172
 influence, 18
 marketing information, 172
 music video sales, 110
Soundtracks, film, 110–112
Statutory license. *See* Compulsory mechanical
  licenses
Stiffed, 252
Storz, Todd, 98–99, 105
Studios, recording, 140–143
Suicide, popular music and, 15
"Sweethearts," 232
Synchronization licenses, 67, 69
Systems theory, 12–13, **13**
Talent agencies and agents
 agreements, 82
 earnings, 80, **81**
 function, 22, 79
 kinds, 80
 licensing of, 81–82
 management team, 92
 market structure, 81
 number of, 80
 size, 80
 structure, 80
Tashjian, Ralph, 251–252
Technology, and
  CD prices, 160
 concert ticket sales, 88
 copyright, 238–242
 diversity, 147
 kiosks, 173
 production process, 141
 recording studios, 170–171
 SoundScan, 172
Technology, influence of, 17
Television, 106. *See also* Music Television

Three income streams model, 19–21, **21**, 23–25
 cash flows, **23**
 complexities, **24**, 25
 law and, 201
 players, 20–23
TicketMaster, 88
Ticket sales. *See* Concert promotion
Time Warner, 30, 112, *see also* Warner Bros.
  Publications and Big six
Top 40 listeners, 105
Touring income, 73, 74, **74**
Tours. See Concerts
Tour support, 89
Tower Records, 186
Travis, Randy, 132
2-Live Crew, 15, 210
"Unchained Melody," 240
Universal Product Code (UPC), 18, 170
Universal Studios, 33
Used CDs
 club recordings, 196
 copyright law and, 191
 independent stores, 188
 label policies, 192–193
 market for, 191–193, **193**
 prices, 192
 promotional copies, 192
 retailers selling, 191
 suits against labels, 194
Variety (Daily Variety), 114
VH-1 network, 108
Victor Talking Machine Company, 28
Violence in popular music, 14
Virgin Retail, 187
Venue-promoter agreements, 86
Venues, 86–88
 function, 22
 number of, 74
 sizes, 74, **74**
"Walk This Way," 51
Wal-Mart, 8
Warner Bros. Publications, 68
Warner/Chappell Music, 49
Warner Music Group, 30–31, 193. *See also* Big
  six
"When the Red, Red Robin . . . . ," 229–230
White-Smith Music Publishing Co. v. Apollo Co.,
  206
W. H. Smith stores, 186–187
William Morris Agency, 80
Works made for hire, 213
World Trade Organization, 204, 225, 249
World Wide Web, *see* Internet and Appendix A
"Your Hit Parade," 106